MADNESS in Buenos Aires

Ohio University Research in International Studies

This series of publications on Africa, Latin America, Southeast Asia, and Global and Comparative Studies is designed to present significant research, translation, and opinion to area specialists and to a wide community of persons interested in world affairs. The editor seeks manuscripts of quality on any subject and can usually make a decision regarding publication within three months of receipt of the original work. Production methods generally permit a work to appear within one year of acceptance. The editor works closely with authors to produce a high-quality book. The series appears in a paperback format and is distributed worldwide. For more information, contact the executive editor at Ohio University Press, 19 Circle Drive, The Ridges, Athens, Ohio 45701.

The Ohio University Research in International Studies series is published for the Center for International Studies by Ohio University Press. The views expressed in individual volumes are those of the authors and should not be considered to represent the policies or beliefs of the Center for International Studies, Ohio University Press, or Ohio University.

University of Calgary Press Latin American and Caribbean Series

Christon I. Archer, General Editor

ISSN 1498-2366

This series sheds light on historical and cultural topics in Latin America and the Caribbean by publishing works that challenge the canon in history, literature, and postcolonial studies. It seeks to print cutting-edge studies and research that redefine our understanding of historical and current issues in Latin America and the Caribbean.

- No. 1 · **Waking the Dictator: Veracruz, the Struggle for Federalism and the Mexican Revolution** Karl B. Koth
- No. 2 · **The Spirit of Hidalgo: The Mexican Revolution in Coahuila** Suzanne B. Pasztor · Copublished with Michigan State University Press
- No. 3 · **Clerical Ideology in a Revolutionary Age: The Guadalajara Church and the Idea of the Mexican Nation, 1788–1853** Brian F. Connaughton, translated by Mark Allan Healey · Copublished with University Press of Colorado
- No. 4 · **Monuments of Progress: Modernization and Public Health in Mexico City, 1876–1910** Claudia Agostoni · Copublished with University Press of Colorado
- No. 5 · **Madness in Buenos Aires: Patients, Psychiatrists and the Argentine State, 1880–1983** Jonathan Ablard · Copublished with Ohio University Press

Jonathan D. Ablard

MADNESS in Buenos Aires

Patients, Psychiatrists, and the Argentine State, 1880–1983

OHIO UNIVERSITY RESEARCH
IN INTERNATIONAL STUDIES

Latin America Series No. 47
OHIO UNIVERSITY PRESS
Athens

UNIVERSITY OF
CALGARY
PRESS

University of Calgary Press
2500 University Drive NW
Calgary, Alberta
Canada T2N 1N4
www.uofcpress.com

Published in the United States of America for the Ohio University Center for International Studies by Ohio University Press, Athens, Ohio 45701
www.ohioswallow.com

18 17 16 15 14 13 12 11 10 09 08   5 4 3 2 1

LIBRARY AND ARCHIVES CANADA CATALOGUING IN PUBLICATION

Ablard, Jonathan
Madness in Buenos Aires : patients, psychiatrists, and the Argentine state, 1880-1983 / Jonathan D. Ablard.

Copublished by Ohio University Press

(Latin American and Caribbean series, ISSN 1498-2366 ; 5)
Includes bibliographical references and index.
ISBN 978-1-55238-233-2 (University of Calgary Press).–
ISBN 978-0-89680-259-9 (Ohio University Press)

1. Mental health policy–Argentina–History. 2. Mental illness–Argentina–History. 3. Mental health services–Argentina–History. 4. Psychiatry–Argentina–History. 5. Argentina–Politics and government. 6. Argentina–Social conditions. I. Title. II. Series.

RA790.7.A7A35 2008   362.20982   C2008-901049-3

The University of Calgary Press acknowledges the support of the Alberta Foundation for the Arts for our publications. We acknowledge the financial support of the Government of Canada through the Book Publishing Industry Development Program (BPIDP) for our publishing activities. We acknowledge the financial support of the Canada Council for the Arts for our publishing program.

Alberta Foundation for the Arts   Canada   Canada Council for the Arts   Conseil des Arts du Canada

Cover design, page design and typesetting by Melina Cusano

To Delia and Lisa

Table of Contents

Acknowledgments

The first time that I visited an Argentine psychiatric hospital was in the mid-1990s while conducting my dissertation research. I had made an appointment with the chief librarian at the men's hospital in Buenos Aires. (A few weeks later I visited the women's hospital which is across the street.) As I neared the entrance to the hospital, I realized that the guards were not there to keep anyone out, but to keep the patients in. I joined a steady stream of doctors, hospital staff, family members, and community volunteers who were entering the hospital. The guards at the security gate asked no one for identification. Before I realized it, I was inside one of the oldest and largest psychiatric hospitals in South America.

Many of the patients were unshaven and unwashed. Some walked around bumming cigarettes from visitors or staff. The physical grounds of the hospital were in terrible condition as well. Smashed windows, broken concrete, canine and human feces, and garbage were everywhere. Over the next weeks, I shared these experiences with *porteños*, who expressed deep regret but not surprise. Reports on the conditions in the asylums have been a familiar topic of newspaper exposés for decades.

My initial shock was slowly replaced by a deep affection for the place and for the people who lived and worked there. In part thanks to the volunteer-run *Radio Colifata*, which broadcasts from the hospital every Saturday, I was able to meet with patients in a relaxed and informal atmosphere. I also owe a debt to the staff of the hospital, most of whom were as helpful as time and resources could permit. The one person that I could always count on was Hector Andreoli, who worked in the hospital's library and lived in a small room above it. Aside from helping me to find materials, he kept me loaded up with coffee, oranges, and whatever else was at hand. I owe much to Hector, who died before this book could be finished.

Before I started the dissertation, I was lucky to have as teachers Steve Volk at Oberlin College and then Herbert Braun and William Taylor at the University of Virginia. At the University of New Mexico, my dissertation committee, Linda Hall, M. Jane Slaughter, Judy Bieber, and David Bennahum provided the perfect mix of insight, patience, and advice. Fellow graduate students Michael Ann Sullivan, John Herron, Catherine Kleiner, and Jeff Roche, were a constant source of moral support and read much of this work in its early phase. A huge debt is also owed to Dr. Betsy Jameson, who later, as a member of the faculty at the University of Calgary, kindly mentioned my work to Christon Archer. I also benefited from working with Melissa Bokovoy, Robert Kern (who passed away in 2000), Karen Remmer, and Ken Roberts.

To the extent that I used patient records effectively, it was because Braulio Montalvo generously served as an unofficial mentor. He has been a constant source of moral and intellectual support. Over many cups of coffee, he shared his own clinical experience, and in the process allowed me some insight into what my documents might reveal.

In Argentina, special recognition is owed to Mariano Plotkin, Hugo Klappenbach, Sergio Visacovsky, Pedro Herscovici, Cecile Herscovici, Ricardo Grimson, Raul Camino, Fernando Pagés Larraya, Guillermo Vidal, Alfredo Moffatt, Dalia Szulik, Daniel Matusevich, Alfredo Kohn Loncarica, Ricardo Salvatore, Ana María Shúa, Eduardo José Cárdenas, Nélida Aguero, Eduardo Saguier, and Evelyn Kohli. Thanks to Peter Bardaglio, I made contact with Tamara Chichilnisky de di Tella, Graciela Chichilnisky, and Alberto Ramón Chichilnisky. They kindly sent me their father's unpublished memoir. The staff of the Archivo del Poder Judicial de la Nación, the Archivo General de la Nación, and the Instituto Histórico provided invaluable assistance and advice. The Archivo General de la Nación generously gave permission to publish many of the photographs that are in this book. Staff and patients at the Hospital "José T. Borda" and the Hospital "Braulio Moyano" provided hospitality and support. Juan Carlos and the other participants of Radio Colifata provided insight into life in these hospitals. I was fortunate to meet the director of the Hospital Interzonal "Domingo Cabred," Carlos Wertheimer, whose fight to make psychiatric care more humane has been an inspiration. Special recognition is also due to the staff, cooks, and patients of the "Domingo Cabred," for their hospitality. Finally, Mother Superior Ofelia Rausch and the other Hermanas de Caridad-Maria del Huerto shared their small archive.

In the United States, Julia Rodriguez, Kris Ruggiero, and Donna J. Guy gave advice on writing and sources. Jonathan Sadowsky and Mariano Plotkin read the finished dissertation and provided useful advice on how to improve it.

I also benefited from invitations to present portions of what eventually became the book in Buenos Aires, Toyko, and Toronto. For the wonderful exchanges that came out of those workshops and conferences, I am indebted to Alfredo Kohn-Loncarica, Akihito Suzuki, and David Wright.

Aran MacKinnon, Ron Love and the staff of Ingram Library at the University of West Georgia were essential in helping me to keep this project moving forward. I will also never forget the great moral and material support of Adela Sampson of Carrollton, Georgia, who cared for my daughter during her first year. Since moving to Ithaca, I have received invaluable help from the following individuals at Ithaca College: Jason Freitag, the Interlibrary Loan staff, Fred Estabrook, Erin Tustin, and Priyam Banerjee. Also in Ithaca, Ray Craib and Aaron Tieger read portions of the manuscript and offered useful insights. Thanks are also due to the staff of Corner of the Sky preschool, and especially its director Valerie Akers.

I have been fortunate to have some incredibly loyal friends. Michael Martin, Amy Groom, Olga Nazario, and Thomas von Huene gave encouragement, especially when I was (slowly) finishing the dissertation.

The comments from the anonymous readers (two from Calgary and one from Ohio) were both encouraging and helpful. Peter Enman, Melina Cusano, John King, and Christon Archer of the University of Calgary Press and Gillian Berchowitz of Ohio University Press have demonstrated incredible forbearance, especially when I kept postponing delivery of the final manuscript. Of course, none of the above-mentioned people bear any responsibility for this book's defects. Those are mine.

My parents, Doris and Charles Ablard, my sisters Katie and Jennifer Ablard and their families, and the Nicholas family in New Hampshire and California all cheered me on as I slowly finished this book. The biggest debt is owed, many times over, to Lisa and to Delia, whose love and humour kept me going.

1

1: INTRODUCTION

> There is something fundamentally tragic in madness. It attracts. This phenomenon has already been observed. The most interesting doctors of the insane enjoy the reputation of being slightly off. Madness is contagious. Like lead for typographers, or mercury or arsenic, it ends up soaking into your marrow, slowly, imperceptibly.[1]
>
> – Roberto Arlt

In the 1987 Argentine film *Man Facing Southeast*, a nurse in a cavernous and decrepit *porteño* (Buenos Aires) mental hospital informs the supervising psychiatrist, Dr. Denis, that a new patient has mysteriously appeared in the ward. When finally located, the new patient tells the doctor that he came to earth in a space ship from another planet. During a series of conversations, the doctor comes to believe alternately that the patient, who calls himself Rantés, is a criminal hiding from the law; a lunatic; and, finally, perhaps a saint. Meanwhile, Rantés inverts the roles of patient and doctor and tries to cure the psychiatrist of his deep loneliness and alienation while also ministering to the physical and spiritual needs of his fellow patients. Soon the patients are in awe of Rantés, whom they hold in higher esteem than the doctors. Concerned about the new patient's threat to their authority, hospital administrators order Dr. Denis to pacify Rantés through medications. The well-intentioned doctor reluctantly obeys but the injections prove fatal to the gentle Rantés.[2]

The film, which was made inside the Borda psychiatric hospital in Buenos Aires, reflects the decades-long popular critique of the relationship of the psychiatric profession and its institutions to broader social and political issues.[3] Since the 1960s, activists inside and outside of the mental health professions have argued that the neglect and abuse of involuntary psychiatric patients is symptomatic of a political system that violates human rights

Madness 1 Borda Hospital: An unfinished ward, 1998. Source: Author's photograph

and neglects social welfare. Such attitudes became only more prevalent following attacks on progressive psychiatrists and psychologists during the military dictatorship of 1976–83.[4] A recent study on human rights abuses in two of Argentina's rural facilities for the mentally handicapped located the root of abuses in the late nineteenth century when the fields of criminology, penology, and psychiatry converged. A logical outcome of that tradition, the report argued, was that many psychiatrists tended to view their patients as potential criminals who, for the good of society at large, should be confined against their will. The abuses, then, were not so much an aberration but integral to the historical development of Argentine psychiatry.[5]

The popular critique of psychiatry finds its parallel in the historical literature on social control in Argentina. (By *social control* we mean "the successful subordination of people's own inclinations of social behavior or behavior sought by other social organizations in favor of the behavior prescribed by state rules," and it is measured by "the capacities to *penetrate* society, *regulate* social relationships, *extract* resources, and *appropriate* or use resources in determined ways.")[6] A number of historians of Argentina have clearly demonstrated that the project to contain deviance, whether of a criminal, psychiatric, political, or social nature, was tightly connected to nation building and modernization, but eventually also to the elaboration of ever-more-violent state-sponsored repression of political dissent in the second half of the twentieth century.[7]

The Borda, site of the film, and the Moyano, a women's hospital located across the street, offer an apt setting to reconsider the Argentine state's relationship to both modernity and social change and to civil society during the twentieth century. The institutions are also a logical place to reconsider the contentious place of psychiatry in modern Argentina. The history of psychiatric hospitals suggests that there were profound discrepancies between the agenda of Argentina's state builders and the final product. The experience of psychiatric patients serves as a useful case study of how the Argentine state developed and functioned over the last century and of how Argentines interacted with it. Briefly, this study argues that the capacity of the state to provide social services and also in different ways to control the populace was often circumscribed to an extent hitherto not recognized in the scholarly literature. By extension, these same conditions limited the opportunities in the public sector for professionals.[8] In turn, these limitations, which had their origin in factors both internal and external to Argentina, shaped the experiences of patients, their families, and doctors, and also influenced medical and lay ideas about the nature and significance of mental illness.[9] These experiences, and the institutional framework in which they were imbedded, had a profound impact on how Argentine psychiatrists discussed not only mental illness, but also a host of related themes including immigration, poverty, and the role of the state in mitigating social problems.[10]

Elite social reformers created the two asylums in the mid-nineteenth century just as Argentina was emerging from decades of civil war and dictatorship. By the 1880s, following years of neglect by the state, both hospitals had caught the attention of a new generation of liberal reformers who were inspired by western European advances in public health. As with social reformers throughout the Atlantic world, Argentina's urban elite envisaged the renovated asylums as places to cure mental illness and as humane instruments of social control. Yet Argentine doctors also took the hospitals' symbolic importance quite seriously and saw them as emblems of the republic's entrance into the family of modern nations. From the 1880s through 1914, the federal government oversaw renovation of existing hospitals and the construction of several new provincial hospitals. That prominent European travellers to Argentina held up the hospitals as a sign of the republic's coming of age only encouraged reformers' optimism.[11]

Behind the façade of international accolades, however, lay a web of structural problems, including chronic overcrowding and understaffing, that perennially undermined the effectiveness and reputation of the hospitals. Renovation of existing buildings or the construction of new ones was usually so delayed that, when inaugurated, they were already considered out of date. The hospitals also had difficulty in maintaining the medical and legal records of patients and often failed to adequately comply with the legal stipulations that governed hospitalization. A number of factors explain this tangle of problems. First, the long delay between independence and the establishment of a viable national state in 1880 laid a weak foundation for public health reform. As Argentina began to integrate into global commodity markets, the state adopted a policy of limiting outlays for public health and welfare. The state's parsimony in public welfare was in large part fuelled by suspicion towards the growing population of foreign-born people whose arrival was seen as an engine of economic development but also a source of political unrest and social decay and the primary cause of the overcrowding of the country's hospitals.

By the 1920s, doctors began to express optimism that new medical and social interventions, mostly developed in Europe, would facilitate the wholesale renovation of Argentina's decrepit asylums. Mental hygiene, with its emphasis on the social reintegration of the mentally ill, and new biochemical and surgical procedures, gave hope to many doctors that they could transform the large urban asylums into therapeutic hospitals where those suffering from mental disorders would voluntarily seek help. For those without hope of recovery, or who were a threat to themselves or to others, doctors envisioned the development of a network of rural colonies where patients would stay busy with outdoor work and recreation. After the coup of 1930, which ended Argentina's two-decade-long experiment with representative democracy, the country began to experience almost constant political instability. This, in tandem with declining terms of trade for export goods, limited the hospitals' ability to make long-range plans or to implement reforms.[12]

Despite challenges posed to the health system by Argentina's political and economic conditions, there were nonetheless periods of optimism. In 1943, a clique of nationalist military officers seized power and took the first steps towards reorganizing Argentina's public health. The trend picked up momentum when Colonel Juan Perón was elected president in 1946. Yet, despite a spate of official reform initiatives, Perón's government failed to create long-lasting or deep solutions to many of the underlying defects in Argentina's public health system. Following Perón's violent fall from power in 1955, community-based care of the mentally ill began to flourish, with support from both military and civilian governments. The doctors who advocated for and operated therapeutic communities, psychiatric clinics in general hospitals, and community mental health centres were often, however, in a precarious position. Military coups deposed civilian regimes with startling regularity, whilst the overall political climate was characterized by unprecedented levels of polarization and violence.

This fragile period of innovation came to a brutal end with the military coup of March 1976. Military officers took over hospital administration; many progressive doctors were tortured, killed, or exiled. In the vacuum created by their absence, more conservative psychiatrists regained their positions of prominence. Since the fall of the military in 1983 and the return from exile of many of Argentina's ablest mental health professionals, some strides have been made in protecting and caring for the mentally ill. Nonetheless, Argentina's large psychiatric institutions remain plagued by horrific conditions. The renewed decay of these hospitals is a product not just of the military's political legacy, but also of more recent neo-liberal reforms, which have compelled the state to reduce outlays in social services and public health.[13]

Patients, Families, and Doctors

Argentine hospital administrators wanted the public to utilize their services in ways consistent with the medical professions' goals and standards.[14] But in Argentina, hospital conditions created a huge gap between doctors' stated desire to confine and treat all "deviants" and their ability to meet that objective. Furthermore, the gulf between the ideal and the possible exercised a profound influence upon how doctors viewed their profession and its relationship to the state and civil society, as well as to the insane, and especially those who were not confined to hospitals.

Psychiatrists argued that the asylum's population reflected many of the social ills wrought by modernization.[15] Their proposed solutions to these threats to national well-being included modernization of the network of hospitals, establishment of less coercive modes of treatment, but also better medical inspections of immigrants, and even more drastic measures such as preventative confinement and forced sterilization. Yet while these proposals echoed those of their European and North American counterparts, Argentina's political and economic instability prevented most reforms from coming to fruition.[16] For many doctors, nothing better represented their failure to garner support of the state than statistics that demonstrated that Argentina had lower rates of psychiatric confinement than most of Europe. (In keeping with the Argentine elite's European orientation, they rarely discussed the fact that Argentina's rates of confinement were higher than those of most of the rest of South America.)

The danger of the mentally ill, therefore, was not simply an inherent "fact" of their condition, but was, in the minds of many doctors, a product of the very indifference of the state and society. Frustration over resistance by both the state and society encouraged doctors to maintain the belief that the mentally ill posed an inherent threat to Argentine society. Doctors frequently argued that problems such as immigration, racial degeneration, changing social mores about gender and sexuality, and other "destructive" forces of modernization were not simply dangers in and of themselves. Rather, the state's neglect of these problems, which was evidenced in the country's low rates of confinement, aggravated the dangers and made their work all the more difficult.

If there were not enough hospitals, existing ones were frequently in deplorable condition. Doctors believed that the decay of the hospitals and the resulting medical and legal neglect of patients had the effect of discouraging public acceptance of their work. Popular distrust of the profession was supposedly most clearly demonstrated by families' hesitation to confine ill relatives, and worse, their willingness to withdraw relatives from hospital care against medical advice. According to medical doctrine, such autonomous actions by families only aggravated the mental illness of patients whose recovery required both prompt hospitalization and well-considered release. Yet if doctors worried that conditions would repel families and patients alike, the very conditions in the hospitals undoubtedly affected the legal and medical interpretations of persons suspected of having a mental illness.[17] Medical students, hospital doctors, and court-appointed examiners interviewed and treated dirty and sleep-deprived patients. Until the 1940s, most were foreign-born. The idea of degeneration, with its emphasis on the physical markers of psychic disturbance, no doubt exacerbated the tendency of doctors to view their patients as social and biological dangers to society.

Considering the condition of the hospitals, it is hardly surprising that, although doctors wanted to exercise vigilance and control over their wards, patients often became lost, forgotten, and invisible to the outside world.[18] Indeed, the violence, communicable diseases, bureaucratic confusion, and discomfort – the common lot of patients – were the result of decades of neglect of the hospitals and their inhabitants. In contrast to theoretical notions of the medical "gaze" (or the penal "panopticon"), doctors often made important decisions based on brief and superficial examinations of their subjects.[19] And often, important legal and medical decisions, including the decision to confine an individual, were not made by doctors but by staff. Moreover, medical examinations were highly routinized. Doctors and staff were prone to accept family testimony at face value, ignore statements by those confined that might have made comprehensible their strange behaviour, and accept outdated medical evaluations of a patient as valid and relevant.[20] Contributing to the chaos of hospitals was an anachronistic civil code (which regulated hospitalizations) and an overburdened court system. During most periods under consideration in this book, a majority of patients were admitted to hospitals without the legal oversight mandated by law.

Despite the relative weakness of the psychiatric project to fortify the health of the nation, psychiatric ideas about work, family, and gender nonetheless did have a profound influence on the experiences of patients.[21] After all, as many historians of psychiatry have observed, the authority to describe, diagnose, and label bestows a certain degree of social prestige and power.[22] Of the social ideas of psychiatrists, perhaps the most central was the view of the traditional family as a bulwark against insanity. Yet psychiatrists also consistently argued that mentally ill persons should not be cared for in the home, lest their mania or delusion spread to other family members. Lastly, psychiatrists worked to clearly delineate gendered norms of behaviour for men and women. Women were supposed to care about housework, possess maternal instincts, and behave in a sexually correct manner. Men were expected to work, support their families and abstain from excessive drinking to the extent that it encroached on their familial duties.

But doctors were not the only ones to employ this rhetoric. Patients and their families also developed an awareness of the medical rhetoric of work, family, and gender and used it in an array of ways that often subverted the goals of the psychiatrists themselves.[23] The emergence of a common lexicon between doctors and the lay public, along with the weak legal and medical regimen of the hospitals, produced paradoxical results.[24] Heads of households, for example, frequently employed aspects of this rhetoric to explain to doctors why "unruly" or "defiant" women, including both relatives and domestic servants, should be confined. At the same time, however, battered and abused wives learned to use the legal and medical system to contain and control violent or irresponsible husbands and fathers.

Yet not all uses of the hospital were the product of cynical manipulation. As many doctors had begun to observe in the 1920s, many families saw the hospitals as a valuable resource. Although the care was often inadequate, poor families often saw the hospital as a legitimate resource for help in the care and cure of very ill family members. Ultimately, Argentine psychiatric hospitals balanced precariously between their functions as institutions of social control and normative coercion and as hospitals treating and sheltering persons who very often were suffering not only from psychiatric or psychological distress, but also from serious physical ailments.

Methodology of the History of Psychiatry

The history of psychiatry, particularly when scholars enter into the clinical realm, is an intellectual minefield. Reviewing case histories, many scholars inevitably begin to wonder whether subjects were actually 'mentally ill' – a concept which itself is fraught with controversy. Key to my thinking on this problem has been the work of Jonathan Sadowsky on colonial Nigeria.

> We must work from what we know – that these people were *considered* mad – rather than speculating about the validity of these considerations. Since my subject matter will in part be the historical meaning of psychiatric labels, it would be ahistorical to encumber the analysis with reference to "real" mental conditions. On this point, Foucault's *The Archaeology of Knowledge* may be more apposite than his works on madness and incarceration: "We are not trying to find out ... whether his disturbances were identical with those known to us today.... We are not trying to constitute what madness itself might be."[25]

Thus, my main interest is in the social, legal, medical, and ideological pathways that persons *deemed* insane followed in and out of the hospitals. Again, Sadowsky, following the earlier work of sociologist Allan Horwitz, is instructive when he argues that one should look for the kinds of behaviours, social conditions, and circumstances that will lead most often to psychiatric hospitalization.[26]

Not only is it difficult for historians to adequately assess the accuracy of clinicians' notes, but doctors at the time were often uncertain about the diagnoses and prognoses that they made.[27] In medical files, it is not uncommon to see doctors change a patient's diagnosis in a short period of time. Even in articles published in the major psychiatric and medical journals of the day, doctors sometimes doubted their ability to effectively diagnose and treat the insane. As new medical interventions were developed in the 1920s, for example, doctors often tempered their enthusiasm with an acknowledgment that if the treatments did indeed work, it was not altogether clear how or why.[28]

Moreover, psychiatric diagnoses or labels are not value neutral. Rather, the social distance between practitioner and subject (defined by socioeconomic status, race, gender, ethnicity, behaviour, political ideology, and so on) is a major determinant of whether a person is "insane." These social determinants also shape the kind of treatment that patients receive and how and when a patient will be released.[29]

From a methodological perspective, research on the social history of psychiatry in Argentina has presented a series of vexing challenges. Information on the experiences of patients is relatively thin, especially in comparison with the wealth of data available in western Europe and North America. Political instability and cycles of deepening economic crisis since the 1930s in large part explain the often poor condition of Argentine archives. During the course of my own research, I often discovered that documents had been destroyed or lost. The records of the Advisory Commission for Regional Hospitals and Asylums, for example, appear to have been destroyed by the Perón government. Much of my information on their work comes from an index of documents that was compiled in the 1940s during the creation of the Ministry of Public Health. The records of the National Institute of Mental Health seem to have met with a similar fate. In both cases, of course, future researchers may uncover these materials.

It also was impossible to acquire access to all but a few patients' clinical files at either the men's or the women's hospitals. During the 1990s, a very kind nurse brought me to a room in one of the Borda hospital's last remaining nineteenth-century buildings where the *historias clinicas* of thousands of men had been dumped. There were holes in the roof and the files were filthy. I calculated that at least a year would be required to organize the files. When I returned to the hospital in March of 2004, I was pleased to discover that a team of volunteers from the University of Buenos Aires were trying to order and preserve the files. They were doing so with no financial support and with little coordination from the hospital's administration.

Piecing together the lives of patients, then, required working through alternate sources, including insanity proceedings, official hospital reports, medical publications, newspaper and magazine stories, and even fictional literature. The insanity proceedings, which involved a medical examination on behalf of the court, were conducted on a minority of the total patients during this period; most people admitted to an Argentine psychiatric hospital did not have a judicial review. I nevertheless found that these sources contained a wealth of information about how mental illness was described, and also how patients, families, and other social forces participated in the process of hospitalization. I have changed all of the names in order to respect the privacy of these individuals and their families. Where a patient's name was published in newspapers or other public material, I use the actual name.[30]

Paradoxically, the period that was most difficult to research was the recent past. The political instability that marks Argentine history since 1946 has wreaked havoc on the country's institutional memory. Not only do archives generally have little to offer on this period, but many institutions, including hospitals, often ceased to regularly publish annual reports. I chose to not examine insanity proceedings dating from the period after 1955, out of a desire to respect the privacy of individuals who may still be alive. However, I was fortunate to make contact with a number of senior psychiatrists who provided me with interviews and unpublished papers. Because of these limitations, this book may seem at times like the report of an archaeologist who must take the available evidence and piece together a likely story.

For the sake of simplicity, I use the common language of the day to describe the individuals who were treated in hospitals or who were suspected of having mental illness. My use of terms like "mentally ill," "insane," and "mentally retarded" in no way implies that these diagnoses were accurate or fair. I decided not to use the term "patient," however, since many of the individuals herein discussed were not necessarily confined to a hospital.[31] Finally, I recognize, as I show in this book, that these very terms had a powerful influence on the individuals whose experiences I describe in this book. Likewise, my decision to use photographs of patients was guided by a desire to allow readers to see images that were widely circulated in Argentina. There are few photographs of women in this book because the women's asylum forbade the press to photograph its patients.

Jujuy
Salta
Formosa
Tucumán
Chaco
Misiones
Santiago del Estero
Catamarca
Corrientes
La Rioja
Santa Fe
Córdoba
San Juan
Córdoba
Santa Fe
Entre Ríos
San Luis
Mendoza
Buenos Aires
Buenos Aires
La Pampa
Neuquén
Río Negro
Chubut
Santa Cruz
Malvinas
(Falkland Islands)
Tierra del Fuego
0 100 200 300 500 km
0 100 200 300 miles

2: FOUNDATIONS, MYTHS, AND INSTITUTIONS

In *Madness in Argentina*, which was first published in 1920, the internationally renowned Argentine psychiatrist José Ingenieros argued that the Spanish conquerors of the Americas brought with them an unsophisticated and theocratic understanding of madness. As a multi-racial colonial society emerged, the Catholic delusions of the Spaniards melded with the primitive belief systems of both African slaves and the conquered indigenous people so that, as Ingenieros observed "[i]t is difficult to know who was more superstitious, the Indians or the Spaniards."[1] With superstition came cruelty. During the colonial period, the mad spent their days chained to the walls of prison cells, hidden away in secret rooms in the family home, or wandering the streets and byways. Treatments were limited to the useless, if not harmful, counsels of traditional healers and Catholic priests. The situation for Argentina's mentally ill did not improve with independence, when constant civil strife, foreign invasions, and dictatorship impaired the development of adequate and humane treatments. Ingenieros believed that the chaos and despotism of the post-independence era had disrupted social hierarchies and encouraged an increase in madness. In Ingenieros' narrative, national consolidation and the establishment of constitutional government in 1880 was a decisive turning point for the treatment of the mentally ill. In the following three decades, the Argentine state reformed existing asylums and developed a network of modern institutions designed for the humane confinement and treatment of the mad.

By 1920, Ingenieros had earned a global reputation for his work in the medico-legal dimensions of psychiatry, and for creating institutions and journals to advance the position of the profession inside Argentina's growing national state. It is not surprising, therefore, that he saw in the history of madness and its treatment a reflection of a wider narrative of Argentina's transformation from a "typical" Latin American nation to a far-flung outpost of European civilization.[2] For reformers like Ingenieros, publicly funded scientific and medical institutions, including psychiatric hospitals, universities, penitentiaries, and research centres had been instrumental in civilizing and pacifying the nation and had reinforced Argentina's international reputation as a prosperous and progressive nation.[3]

Such optimism was not unfounded. To celebrate the 1810 centennial of independence, the two principal mental hospitals of Buenos Aires, the Hospicio de las Mercedes and the Hospital Nacional de Alienadas (hereafter Hospicio and HNA, respectively), published commemorative albums. The pictures show orderly and clean wards, carefully tended grounds that resembled city parks, and patients busy at a range of work and leisure activities.[4] Foreign visitors to Argentina, whose opinions were highly prized by the country's modernizing elite, frequently commented on the republic's remarkable social progress. During his 1908 tour of South America, Georges Clemenceau, future president of France, visited the Hospicio's recently opened rural satellite facility. In his oft-cited memoir of the trip, Clemenceau reported that the ten-year-old National Colony for the Insane was a "model for the older peoples" of Europe to emulate. Forcible restraints and isolation cells were absent, and patients lived in modern, spacious, and comfortable cottage-style dormitories when they were not engaged in work and recreational therapies.[5]

Yet for all of the celebration, the outward appearance of Argentina's public institutions masked a host of chronic problems. The Italian writer Cesarina Lupati Guelfi, in her otherwise glowing account of Buenos Aires (including mention of the men's asylum), observed that "the truth is that the good Argentines, just like other peoples, show the good side of things; but they hide the bad, and it is impolite for a guest to insist."[6] Although she was impressed with a number of the republic's institutions in the urban centres, she was dismayed to discover that public health was virtually non-existent in most rural areas. And even Buenos Aires, which by now had been dubbed the "Paris of the South," lacked the range of specialized institutions commonly found in major urban centres of western Europe.[7]

The tension between Ingenieros' celebratory mood and Lupati Guelfi's brief aside about the downside of Argentina's progress provides two perspectives from which to consider care of the insane from the colonial period through the early twentieth century. By the early twentieth century, progress made since the colonial and the early independence era served as the central motif through which to celebrate Argentina's future prospects. The public image of progress, however, was difficult to reconcile with the continuities between the twentieth century and earlier periods. Despite major medical advances, the hospitals continued to serve as poorhouses for the dying, the abandoned, and those incapable of caring for themselves.

This chapter also addresses the relationship of psychiatry to Argentine state formation. Since the 1980s, scholars have debated the central role played by public health and welfare to state building in Argentina. With Argentina's rapid integration into global commodity markets after the 1870s and the resulting influx of European immigration, the elite established institutions that were designed to civilize, domesticate, and control citizens through work and the creation of normative codes of behaviour.[8] The impetus for many of these reforms was the conviction that the immigrant masses, whom many considered more difficult to control than the native poor, posed moral, biological, and political dangers to the health and well-being of the republic.[9] Although these scholars have approached the subject with a much more critical eye, they share with Ingenieros an emphasis on the growing power of the national state in late-nineteenth-century Argentina. Moreover, they have shared with Ingenieros the tendency to use the case of Buenos Aires to explain national trends. This chapter argues, by contrast, that the agenda of psychiatric reform was quite different from the final product and that this simple fact has been ignored not only by early-twentieth-century boosters of Argentine psychiatry but also, ironically, by contemporary scholars.

Remembering the Mad: From Colonial Times to National Consolidation

The historical reconstruction of madness, and of the asylums and doctors charged with its cure, was crucial to giving form and purpose to the late-nineteenth-century reform of Argentina's public health system. Influenced by medical interest in degeneration, suggestibility, and scientific racism, writers like Ingenieros saw the anarchy, superstition, and moral decay of the period before the 1880s as having exercised a pernicious influence on the mental equilibrium of the average Argentine. Worse still, without proper asylums it was impossible to humanely defend the healthy portion of the populace from the moral and physical threats posed by the mad through their segregation and treatment.

As elsewhere in the Atlantic world before the nineteenth century, hospitals were for the poor, and especially people of colour, who were generally only confined if perceived to be a threat to public well-being.[10] These patients were expected to render service for the upkeep of the hospital. The better-off classes cared for sick relatives at home, in a local convent, or in private homes that offered care and/or vigilance for a price.[11] In some cases, families built cells to confine a relative; some were so well hidden that their existence only came to be known after a death in the family led to the division of family assets.[12] Afro-Argentines and Indians reportedly, and perhaps with good reason, eschewed European medicine. And just as whites sought the counsel or attention of a favoured priest, Africans patronized faith healers (*hechiceros*) affiliated with their own nations. It was common knowledge, however, that some whites made secret visits to the traditional healers of their slaves and servants.[13] Like his Brazilian and Cuban counterparts, Ingenieros argued that religious approaches to mental illness were sure signs of atavism and that African rituals and dances provoked delusions in blacks and whites alike, but especially in women.[14]

Prior to the mid-1700s, Buenos Aires' hospitals were modest establishments when compared with those of larger Spanish colonial urban centres. Buenos Aires' first general hospital, the Hermita del Señor San Martín, founded sometime between 1605 and 1608 (it was renamed Hospital San Martín in 1611), was little more than a miserable shack attached to an adjacent chapel.[15] Ingenieros caustically noted that the hospital's chief was a Spaniard with no medical experience and that the hospital's sole purpose was to "burn candles in the chapel."[16] Only in 1670 did the hospital begin to provide patients with beds, though access to medical attention was further impeded by the city's poverty, which offered no incentives for doctors (or priests) to settle there permanently.[17] Specialized care for women was delayed by several more decades, however, largely out of the fears by officials that such an institution might be converted into a convent, thereby further impeding the natural increase of white colonists.[18]

The major reforms of the hospital system occurred in the decades following the ascension of the Bourbons to the Spanish throne in 1700. Naming Buenos Aires the capital of the new viceroyalty of Rio de la Plata (which stretched from Buenos Aires to Upper Peru and Paraguay) in 1776, and the opening of Buenos Aires to direct trade with Spain in 1778, spurred both population growth and increases in municipal revenue. It was in that context that the town council, or *cabildo*, of Buenos Aires began to see the development of hospitals (as well as other public institutions) as necessary and economically feasible.[19] By the 1740s, a number of religious orders, including first the Bethlemites and later the Jesuits, established hospitals and other charitable institutions throughout the city. The early hospitals were designed exclusively for the care of men, and each had a special ward for the containment of the mentally ill, whose presence in public threatened public order and "morals."[20] By 1800, the Jesuit hospital, its order having been expelled several decades earlier, had been remodelled and renamed the Men's General Hospital. The new institution boasted four new wards, of which the Cuadro de Dementes (Ward for the Insane) was reserved exclusively for the mentally ill.[21] By 1759, construction had begun on the Women's General Hospital, which was administered by the Hermandad de Caridad (Sisters of Charity) a female religious order. Renovations during the 1790s included construction of a ward for the insane.[22] Royal officials also established an orphanage and a women's jail, institutions that were frequently used to house the female insane.[23]

From the perspective of writers like Ingenieros, however, the great achievement of the Bourbon period was in the realm of forensic medicine. In 1780, the viceroy established the office of Medical Inspector (*Protomedicato*) to regulate medical practice, oversee public health projects, facilitate the diffusion of the latest in medical ideas, and perform forensic inspections of subjects thought to be mad. The inspector also attempted, without success, to round up and confine the city's vagrant and insane population, whose presence on the streets was seen as an affront to public morality.[24] Most likely, however, these orders remained unenforced because of both popular resistance and a lack of hospital space.[25]

Modernization of health care proved short-lived, however, as Argentina began to feel the ideological and military effects of the French Revolution and the Napoleonic Wars. Following the defeat of the two British invasions of Buenos Aires in 1806 and 1807, and the collapse of the Spanish monarchy to Napoleon's army in 1808, the local militia began to occupy a central position in the politics of the city. When in May of 1810 news arrived of the fall of the Seville junta that had been ruling in the name of the deposed king, Buenos Aires declared itself capital of all the territories within the viceroyalty, which quickly led to war with royalists throughout South America.

In keeping with their revolutionary agenda, the radical government, which ruled from 1811 to 1813, seized all assets of the Bethlemite fathers in 1812.[26] By the end of 1813, however, a more conservative junta had taken power, which in turn was replaced by the so-called Supreme Directorship. In 1816, representatives of the newly created United Provinces of the Rio de la Plata voted for independence and named Juan Martín Pueyrredón as Supreme Director. Pueyrredón, who held this position until he was overthrown in 1819, returned the assets to the Bethlemites in December of 1816.[27] By February 1820, Buenos Aires' aspiration to lead the new country had been quashed, and from that point until mid-century, the United Provinces was to be no more than a loose-knit federation of provinces, each ruled by a *caudillo.*

During the 1820s, the province and city of Buenos Aires, with its strong cultural and trade ties to Europe, maintained a fairly independent course of action. The key leader in this period was Bernardino Rivadavia, who as Minister of Government and Foreign Affairs, and, briefly, as president of the United Provinces, tried to purge Buenos Aires of its colonial legacies, especially the influence of the Church, in the administration of education and social welfare.[28] Soon after coming to office, Rivadavia founded the University of Buenos Aires, which during its first incarnation would produce significant works on the nature of mental illness.[29] In May 1822, Rivadavia established a commission to study the state of the hospitals and to take over the responsibilities previously held by the Protomedicato.[30] The commission noted the particularly sad state of the city's insane – who had become the majority of the hospitals' population – and recommended both the construction of asylums and the confinement of the city's insane and vagrant populations.[31] Following the commission's suggestion, the president ordered the sale of monastic orders' properties and their removal from the hospitals.[32] He also nationalized and remodelled the General Hospitals. In January 1823, Rivadavia established the publicly funded and semi-autonomous Society of Beneficence to take care of needy women and children. The Society, which was run by the city's elite women, was modelled on similar lay welfare organizations in France. Other health and welfare projects were placed in the hands of the men's Philanthropic Society in 1827.[33]

Although Rivadavia's ambitious plans became an important historical model for late-nineteenth-century reformers, they evaporated in the wake of his violent fall from power in 1827. After several more years of civil strife, the caudillo Juan Manuel de Rosas was named as ruler of Buenos Aires in 1829.[34] Seen as a restorer of order, Rosas ruled the United Provinces, but according to the Federal Pact of 1831, the national government's primary purpose was to negotiate with foreign states.[35] Constant warfare with interior provinces and Uruguay and embargos by France and Britain provided a rationale for Rosas to cut the hospitals' already small subsidies. At the same time, ideological differences with the Society of Beneficence, the Philanthropic Society, and the nascent University of Buenos Aires, which represented the liberal and "Europeanizing" ideals of the previous government, moved him to shutter their doors.[36] With these acts, Rosas also effectively put an end to the first wave of public health and welfare reform in Argentina.[37]

While for later historians Rivadavia embodied the promise of secular liberal reform, the Rosas era presented its antithesis.[38] Ingenieros, for example, noted that "public welfare returned to its old state during the tyranny, whose conservative and clerical spirit erased with a ruthless hand the most beautiful creations of the Rivadavian era."[39] Paradoxically, while Rosas' political rhetoric extolled the virtues of authority, morality, and order, his later critics accused him of exerting a pathological influence upon Argentine society by inverting the social hierarchy as an instrument of political terror.[40] Most galling was the dictator's reputed use of poor non-whites, including many supposed "lunatics," as henchmen and propagandists to humiliate his elite opponents. Roving gangs on his payroll were sent out into the streets to announce victories, harass the opposition, and sow fear in the populace.[41] From the fall of Rosas in 1852 through the early 1920s, then, historians and doctors also argued that this period had witnessed an upswing in the incidence of mental illness, and especially a condition known as "moral insanity."[42] Influenced more by the new revolutionary threat of the post-1917 world than by archival evidence, Ingenieros commented that

> [n]o one denies that in periods of political terror mental disturbances often increase. In general, it involves emotional trauma, represented by phobias in men and by hysterical episodes in women, aside from the manic agitations that in the terrorists themselves often provoke the abuse of alcohol and criminal cruelty.[43]

With the defeat of Rosas by provincial caudillos in 1852, and his exile to London, Juan María González, the new first minister of the province of Buenos Aires, quickly reinstated the Beneficent Society and the Philanthropic Commission, and also reopened the nation's faculty of medicine.[44] For liberal elite Argentines, now restored to power, the Rosas interlude represented a period of barbarism in which racial, class, and gender boundaries had been destroyed.[45] The continued presence of the insane in public spaces was a particularly stark reminder of that savagery.[46] The construction of asylums that were both secure and humane would therefore serve to reclaim Argentina from its difficult past while simultaneously returning the young nation to the European orbit.[47] After initial attempts to round up the city's vagrant insane proved ineffective, city leaders began to discuss building proper asylums. The president of the newly reconstituted Beneficent Society, Tomasa Velez Marshfield (1797–1876), and the Philanthropic Commission's director, Dr. Ventura Bosch (1814–1871) led these efforts. Their first concern was the city's female insane population, whose public presence may have been seen as especially scandalous to public morals.[48] Bosch directed public authorities in June 1852 to collect all known female insane in the city, whether living on the street or in jail cells, and to bring them to the Women's General Hospital from which, in March 1854, the Society had them transferred to a new building, the Convalecencia.[49] It would be almost another decade before a similar effort would be directed to the male insane.[50] Thanks to the efforts of Dr. Bosch, who had already served as the women's hospital's first director, the men's Casa de Dementes was inaugurated in 1863 with Bosch as its director.[51]

Support for building the asylums was stronger than the desire to maintain them. Henceforward, the pitiful budget allocated to the hospitals shaped the life of staff, doctors, and patients. Faced with the challenge of finding inexpensive labour to operate hospitals and schools, the new liberal government began to recruit foreign religious orders. (Despite Rosas' supposed clericalism, he had allowed the church to wither during his rule.) Within a decade or so, female religious orders had become instrumental to the daily operation of both hospitals.[52] The sisters earned the praise of administrators for providing reliable service for a fraction of the wages spent on regular staff. In later decades, however, the sisters became the object of scorn by doctors who wished to "modernize" public health care.[53] The early medical directors, by contrast, who also worked for little or no pay, were praised for their selflessness. Both Dr. Osvaldo Eguía (1826–1897), who served as medical director of the women's asylum from 1871 to 1890, and Dr. José María de Uriarte of the men's asylum, were praised for their charity, hard work, and heroic but futile efforts to increase the hospitals' funding.[54] The fabled beneficence of these doctors was further confirmed when newspapers reported that at Uriarte's funeral in 1876, his patients, out of love for the doctor, followed his casket through the streets of Buenos Aires to the cemetery.[55]

The severe budgetary constraints also influenced the adoption of a moral therapeutic approach to patient treatment and hospital management.[56] Moral therapy, which remained a mainstay of hospital directors well into the 1940s, was premised on the paternalistic authority of the asylum director, who was to guide his patients back to mental well-being by fostering a safe and home-like environment, isolating patients from harmful influences, and developing activities that would redirect patients back to mental health.[57] Aside from its emphasis on the authority of the medical director, considered all the more important because of the lack of trained staff, moral therapy provided a medical veneer to what became the financial lifeblood of the institutions: work therapy. Although the hospitals' workshops kept patients busy, and – it was believed – fostered recuperation by diverting patients towards calm and rewarding activities, patient labour was also critical to the hospitals' paltry budgets.[58] Women sewed uniforms for the army and produced a range of products such as brooms for sale to the city. Men performed similar tasks but also provided the bulk of the labour for periodic renovations to the hospital. At both institutions, patients also served as unpaid orderlies and servants.[59]

Structural factors also shaped the decisions about where to build the asylums. Although medical thinking of the day called for placing institutions outside of cities, as was being done in North America and Britain, Argentina's limited transportation network dictated their placement in the Barracas barrio at the edge of the city.[60] Its location in this insalubrious slaughterhouse district clearly defied the precepts of nineteenth-century medicine.[61] Most likely the reformers accepted the location because the land was affordable while its relatively remote location rendered unnecessary, at least in theory, the excessive confinement of patients in cells.[62]

Considering the poverty of the national state, it is hardly surprising that life in the overcrowded hospitals was miserable. A report from 1879 recounted the men's asylum's early years.

> During 1863 and 1864, the insane lived in overcrowded conditions, many without any bed but the hard cold floor, in humid, dark and pest-ridden cells. Chains were the most common method of calming and containing the patients. [In addition to scarce food], treatment was so insufficient and empirical, as is easy to imagine, that one might have thought our doctors were completely in the dark as to modern scientific progress that had occurred since Pinel came to Bicêtre in 1792.... The only therapeutic agents used were bleeding, sedatives, revulsives, and opium.[63]

Overcrowding was the most serious and recurrent problem at both hospitals and reflected the city's rapidly growing population, which had grown from 40,000 at the end of the eighteenth century to almost 180,000 by 1869.[64] At the women's hospital, for example, the number of patients grew from 60 in 1853 to 265 a decade later. In December 1881, with 377 patients, but room for only 200, the women's hospital closed its doors to new admissions. This measure produced a scandalous situation in which public authorities were forced to resort to the colonial-era practice of confining insane women to jails and the Asilo de Mendigos.[65] Overcrowding also hampered efforts to administer sedatives and other therapies. In the late 1870s, for example, the women's hospital inaugurated a hydrotherapy ward but staff shortages prevented its effective use.[66] Perhaps more importantly, these conditions impaired efforts to humanely segregate violent patients who continued to be confined to cell blocks.[67]

Overcrowding was itself a product of the shortage of medical or welfare institutions not only in Buenos Aires, but also in the provinces. With the expansion of railroad linkages during the 1880s, local charities, the police, the army, and individual families in the territories and provinces increasingly sent anyone deemed in need of institutionalization to the asylums of the capital.[68] Not because of the absence of a medical model of insanity, but because the hospitals lacked the staff and resources to perform medical evaluation of incoming patients, they often had difficulty weeding out medically unnecessary admissions. Inadequate screening at the hospitals was aggravated by the absence of legal guidelines to regulate hospitalization as well as pressure from the police and other public officials to admit a wide range of incapacitated individuals, including elderly paupers, who were deemed in need of shelter.[69]

Many doctors understood overcrowding as a symptom of increasing rates of insanity among Argentina's populace.[70] In explaining this apparent rise, attention shifted from the country's non-white populace toward a new menace: immigrants.[71] Long considered fundamental to Argentina's political and economic evolution, and to overcoming the supposedly insidious Spanish, African, and indigenous colonial inheritance, by the late nineteenth century, immigration was at the centre of almost all discussions of the country's social ills.[72] The perceived relationship between immigration and insanity, which was confirmed by their numerical over-representation in the asylums, became one of the principal social themes of Argentine psychiatric discourse well into the 1940s.[73] (Spain and Italy were the primary countries of origin.) While most accepted that a disproportionately high percentage of immigrants lost their minds soon after arriving in Argentina, the exact reasons were subject to some debate.[74] If, as some suggested, immigration attracted those people least able to care for themselves or to prosper, the problem might be explained by the failure of the national state to control who entered the country. According to historian Eduardo Zimmerman, Argentina's 1876 *Ley de Inmigración*

> ... prohibited the admission of anyone suffering from contagious disease, those unable to work, the demented, beggars, criminals, and those over 60 years of age unaccompanied by their families. Enforcement of the law appears to have been lenient. Between November 1907 and June 1910, for instance, of 662,170 immigrants arriving in Argentina only 65 were excluded in accordance with the law.[75]

Fears about who was entering Argentina were accentuated by stories of corrupt immigration agents in Europe who made deals with criminal organizations to provide passage to persons whose visas Argentine consuls had not approved.[76]

For many writers, unregulated immigration was tightly woven into the wider problem of modernity. Its symptoms, including urbanization, the intensification of the market economy, and changes in women's roles, explained the increasing incidence not only of insanity, but also of mental retardation, alcohol abuse, crime, prostitution, and sexual deviance for men and women alike.[77] Doctors also began to argue that factors inherent to the immigration process, especially greed, isolation, and alcohol, encouraged the development of mental illness.[78]

Of the three, alcohol occupied the centre stage in psychiatric discussions about male immigrants, who comprised three quarters of the alcoholics admitted to the men's asylum.[79] Many saw alcoholism as the product of industrialization: work conditions drove men to drink more, and modern distilleries made drink cheaper and stronger. Doctors were also convinced that for some national groups, including Spaniards and Italians, excessive drinking was socially acceptable.[80] In scientific terms, alcoholism was understood less as a disease *sui generis* than as a causative agent of other, usually degenerative, disorders such as dementia, *delirium tremens*, and congenital defects.[81]

While for decades, male immigrant insanity was easily explained – a classic example of prejudice being confirmed by science – psychiatrists paid much less attention to the question of immigrant women. In part this may be explained by the fact that the proportion of foreigners to native-born in the women's hospital remained well below their ratio in the city's population.[82] Moreover, women's diagnoses were more varied, and therefore less attractive to any kind of totalizing explanation, but also more closely associated to biological and emotional factors that were considered common to women across cultures.[83] (In 1880, thirty-two patients were admitted to the women's asylum for "moral reasons" and nineteen with diagnoses related to their reproductive organs, including hysteria.) While no specific diagnosis was attached to immigrant women, doctors did appreciate that sociological factors, including the stress the migration and the non-traditional roles that immigrant women took on when they came to Buenos Aires, predisposed them to madness.[84]

The over-representation of male immigrants in asylums (and also jails) was probably the result of a combination of social, demographic, and economic factors. Most important was the behaviour and social composition of the overwhelmingly native-born *porteño* police, whose professional mission included the control not only of crime and political unrest, but also any and all disruptive public behaviours.[85] The composition and mission of the police no doubt collided with the social and economic precariousness of many immigrants who lacked even a stable address, much less familial or other personal support networks.[86] Many immigrants' alien customs, including drinking habits, language, and dress, as well as the association of immigrants with political and social disorder, may have attracted additional attention from the constabulary.[87] The heavy immigrant presence in asylums was also a product of the demographic reality of immigration. As Ingenieros had astutely observed – though few paid attention – immigrants were over-represented in asylums and jails because of that population's higher ratio of adults to children when compared with the native-born.[88]

REFORM, 1880s–1910

Growing concern about new forms of social unrest and moral decay coincided with the emergence in 1880 of a truly national state. With the last of the regional caudillos subdued, the federalization of Buenos Aires as the national capital, and increasing revenues produced from Argentina's successful integration into global commodities markets, a coherent national state began to emerge intent on modernization and bureaucratization.[89] The objective was to replace informal modes of governance and social control that had been established after 1852 with more bureaucratized, scientific, secular, and efficient systems and institutions.[90] There was also a growing imperative to eradicate infectious diseases such as plague, yellow fever, and cholera, which, in addition to threatening urban health, were believed to reduce Argentina's appeal to "desirable" immigrants.[91] Reforms were therefore designed to contain the emerging social, political, and biological dangers of modernity. To that end, a generation of doctors, scientists, and jurists forged alliances with various sectors of the state.[92]

A critical scientific foundation of much of these reforms was the idea of degenerative heredity.[93] Degeneration theory, which in reality was a patchwork quilt of medical theories and social prejudice, was a key instrument in the formation and justification of social policy as it provided a comprehensive system for understanding social ills.[94]

> According to this theory certain families suffered a steady though not necessarily irreversible hereditary deterioration over the course of four generations. These families customarily displayed symptoms such as moral depravity, mania, mental retardation, and sterility.[95]

Doctors and jurists saw evidence of degeneration, which was understood to be a product of both acquired and inherited traits, in abstract phenomena like weakness of spirit, absence of a moral compass, marital conflicts, and sexually immorality, and in more concrete manifestations such as criminal behaviour, extreme mental disturbance, tuberculosis, syphilis, and even adherence to radical political ideologies.[96] It was the duty of the state, therefore, to contain the threat of degeneration not only through progressive policies to foster the health of the population, but also to contain people who, because of inherent biological traits or of dangerous behaviours or ideas, threatened the national well-being. Reflecting broader demographic changes, the target of elite anxiety, and repression, shifted from people of colour to the new immigrant, and especially anarchists.[97] Following Italian criminological thinking, forensic psychiatrist Francisco de Veyga went so far as to argue in 1906 that there were three kinds of anarchists: the criminal, the passional, and the insane.[98]

Medical practitioners laid claim to expertise on an array of social and political ills, and argued that science and technology would not only solve the problems of disease and other social ills, but could be employed to create an obedient, civilized, and educated citizenry. At the same time, doctors began to articulate an understanding of mental illness that situated it in the middle of the dense web of crime, immigration, social disorder, and revolution. Emblematic of this approach was the 1894 speech of national deputy Eliseo Cantón, a doctor and native of Tucumán province. In his presentation of legislation to regulate psychiatric hospitals, he reminded his colleagues that there was no such thing as an "inoffensive madman." He went on to note several cases where mentally ill persons who were thought to be peaceful suddenly turned violent, killing or maiming those unfortunate enough to cross their paths. Cantón argued that psychiatrists possessed the expertise to identify and classify the mentally ill, if only the state would provide them with the necessary resources.[99]

Cantón's speech occurred at a time when popular and medical attitudes towards the mentally ill were beginning to converge.[100] Notwithstanding the erection of two asylums in Buenos Aires, and periodic attempts to confine the city's insane, late-nineteenth-century *porteños* still maintained traditional attitudes towards the mentally ill, or so many doctors believed. This was characterized most vividly by the tolerance, and sometimes celebration, of *locos lindos* (it literally translates as "beautiful madmen"). Each barrio lay claim to one or several eccentrics, who were the butt of jokes but probably also enjoyed the fruits of an informal neighbourhood welfare network.[101] A variety of factors, including perhaps changing notions about public decorum, were forcing a change.[102] In a magazine article from 1899, reporter

Fabrio Carrezo provided his readers with a number of forensic case studies. Although Carrezo betrayed a continued loyalty to the memory of the *loco lindo*, he concluded that the "vagabond is neither needy nor licentious, but rather ill."[103] For Carrezo, the *loco lindo* had been transformed into a social deviant in need of the care and tutelage of medical expertise.[104]

The case studies that Carrezo referred to came from Francisco de Veyga's Servicio de Observación de Alienados (Police Psychiatric Observation Unit), which had opened in 1899 to examine criminal suspects for signs of mental illness. José Ingenieros, named chief clinician by de Veyga, and who later became its director, explained the background to the Service's creation. The foundation of asylums at mid-century, as well as other measures, had not visibly reduced the number of vagabonds or street lunatics.

> The vagrancy of the insane continued, nevertheless, until 1900 [*sic*] when professor Francisco de Veyga founded the 'Police Psychiatric Observation Unit,' that in its first two years collected and interned in the asylums around 100 vagabonds, signifying the disappearance of these types who are neither beggars nor delinquents.[105]

The goals of the Service were both scientific and pragmatic and fit into the broader psychiatric imperative to identify and classify the mentally ill. Most obviously, the Service was designed as a processing centre for persons picked up by the police for strange or dangerous behaviour. After determining the mental condition of detainees, the Service sent them to an appropriate destination – a city asylum, jail to await trial, or released them back into the public.[106]

The creation of the service was itself the product of an important convergence of medical studies, especially psychiatry, with law, penology, and criminology.[107] An important step had been the passage of Argentina's first Criminal Code in October 1888.[108] The Code mandated that all accused criminals be given a medical examination that would include a psychiatric evaluation. (Although this represented a potential expansion of psychiatric influence, the judge was at liberty to select a general practitioner to make a psychiatric evaluation.)[109] The founding of the journal *Archives of Psychiatry and Criminology* in 1902 and the creation of the Society of Psychiatry and Legal Medicine in 1912 further institutionalized the place of psychiatrists, and most notably Ingenieros himself, at the centre of all debate over the relationship of crime, deviance, and revolution to insanity.[110]

Important changes were also underway in the management of public health. When the city of Buenos Aires created the Public Assistance office in 1883 to oversee the city's hospitals, it was understood that this was the first step towards the creation of a national health system along the lines of what was developing in France.[111] Under the leadership of Dr. José María Ramos Mejía (1842–1902), the author of a number of works on the social and political threat of the masses, Public Assistance gained a solid reputation for the operation of all municipal hospitals.[112] But although effective in administering a great number of existing health facilities and coordinating disease eradication, many doctors felt that the new health bureaucracy failed to overcome the deeply decentralized nature of health care delivery and the continued power of women in health and education. Nowhere was this better illustrated than in what was described by doctors as the "wasteful and anachronistic" power of the Society of Beneficence.[113] According to some critics, even the nationalization of the Society, and its placement, first under the Ministry of the Interior in 1880 and then under the Ministry of Foreign Relations and Religion in 1898, failed to contain its tremendous autonomy.[114] Public health authorities repeatedly expressed frustration that the women's insane asylum, renamed the Hospital Nacional de Alienadas (hereafter the HNA), often refused to admit female lunatics, either because of overcrowding or because the prospective patient was deemed a threat to the moral order of the institution.[115] Failure of the Society to cooperate with the municipality was attributed to the supposed lack of authority of the male medical director over the Society. There were also widespread complaints that the Society prevented researchers from studying their female patients and resisted efforts by public authorities to create a single psychiatric hospital for both men and women.[116]

In contrast to its sister institution, the men's asylum had been integrated into the network of Public Assistance institutions and enjoyed cordial relationships with the scientific and academic communities, as well as with state functionaries. This growing relationship began in earnest following the death of the director Dr. Uriarte in 1876. The Municipality decided to allow the Faculty of Medicine of the University of Buenos Aires and the city's Hygiene Council to select a new director. The final choice was Dr. Lucio Meléndez (1844–1901). Born to modest means in the impoverished province of La Rioja, Meléndez graduated from medical school in 1872 and thereafter spent several years teaching medicine.[117] As director, Meléndez was instrumental in forging strong ties between the Hospicio and the University of Buenos Aires. Named as chair of the department of mental pathology in 1886, Meléndez began to use the Hospicio as a teaching hospital.[118]

As director from 1876 until 1892 he faced the daunting task of renovating what was considered the most deteriorated and overcrowded of all city hospitals.[119] In May 1887 the city government inaugurated renovations that Meléndez had requested and also changed the hospital's name to the Hospicio de las Mercedes, in honour of the Virgin of Mercy, patron of convicts and the insane.[120] Patients' labour was essential to the timely and economical completion of the renovation, which included expansion of the hospital's patient capacity and the creation of specialized wards for patients deemed a threat to self or others.[121] Despite these developments, the municipal government of Buenos Aires viewed support of the Hospicio as a burden since the hospital served the entire nation.[122] (During the 1880s, the province of Buenos Aires opened its own psychiatric hospital, raising hopes that it would alleviate overcrowding in the city's asylums.)[123] By the early 1890s, the Hospicio's newer wards for tranquil and paying patients, known as *pensionistas* (created by Meléndez), were in good shape, but the overall condition of the hospital was poor, and agitated and violent patients were still housed in a primitive cellblock.[124]

By the 1890s, at the height of the push to reform and renovate Argentine society, the city's two asylums appointed new directors. Domingo Cabred (director from 1892 to 1916) and Antonio Piñero (director from 1890 to 1905), of the men's and women's asylums respectively, received their medical training in Buenos Aires. Inspired by visits to psychiatric institutions and training facilities in western Europe, the directors sought to transform their asylums into modern urban institutions for the short-term care of patients. Smaller urban institutions would also serve as teaching hospitals and centres of medical research. Piñero and Cabred strongly argued, however, that urban short-term facilities could only thrive if there were rural institutions for the care of chronically mentally ill patients. The hope was that rates of recovery at the urban institutions would improve for acute patients who would benefit by being segregated from chronic patients.[125] The ideal hospital could not be developed, however, without improving the legal and medical admissions procedures, which at the time were in a state of confusion.[126]

Soon after becoming director in 1890, Dr. Piñero (1859–1921) caused a public scandal by reporting to the press that the HNA was a national disgrace.[127] By his account, non-paying patients slept jammed together on the floor in poorly heated and overcrowded cells or dormitories. Accommodations for paying patients were not much better and the quality and quantity of the food was inferior to that provided to prisoners of the national penitentiary. (Safe and clean living conditions, particularly abundant and nutritious food, after all, were considered critical to the curing of mental illness.) Piñero placed much of the blame upon the Society of Beneficence, who he claimed focused a disproportionate amount of resources on construction of new wards for paying patients. Their approach to the growing number of indigent patients was to simply construct new but cheap buildings with little planning. As a result the hospital had become a warren of wooden houses, covered passageways, and patios in which there was little space designated for any of the growing number of therapies. Further, it was difficult to segregate the violent patients and to maintain cleanliness.[128] Piñero also found the hospital's staff to be entirely inadequate, as it was comprised of what he considered a motley crew of semi-literate Catholic female religious, ex-convicts, recent arrivals from Europe, and even patients.[129]

These deficiencies led to the neglect and abuse of patients by an overworked and under-trained staff. The poor condition of the room used for hydrotherapy, for example, had converted water therapy at the hospital into an inadvertent but insidious form of torture. Work therapy had never been fully developed at the hospital. Instead, those who were able engaged in sewing, work that provided the hospital with some income but deprived the patients of healthy outdoor activities. Many patients, however, were not physically or mentally capable of sewing, and had little to do all day.[130]

"Hospicio de las Mercedes, 1899." Source: "El Asilo de las Mercedes y la Colonia de Alienados," *Caras y Caretas* (May 20, 1899).

Piñero's publicity campaign proved successful in attracting financial support. In 1894, Congress approved plans for the renovation of the Hospital under the direction of Carlos Nystromer, a Swedish engineer who had had a hand in the redesign of the famous Parisian asylum of Salpêtrière.[131] The new plan called for the destruction of the old tottering physical plant and the construction of twenty-eight new buildings, with a projected capacity for eight hundred beds, a central kitchen, general dormitory wards, a section for agitated and violent patients, a recreation room, workshops, and a special ward for paying patients. On July 31, 1898, the first sections opened their doors to great fanfare and publicity.[132] The buildings, which have survived to the present, are monumental structures and give the hospital the feel of a well-planned city in miniature with tree-lined walkways that crisscross the grounds.[133]

Piñero believed, however, that without a rural colony asylum to house chronic patients, there was no hope of effecting a true modernization of the hospital. The admission of the chronically mentally ill, as well as the many women who had been placed at the hospital for social rather than medical reasons, was unhygienic, costly, and, Piñero reasoned, delayed the admission of those who might receive immediate benefit from treatments.[134] For the director, the first step was to remove to the city's outskirts those deemed incurable.[135] In 1904 the Society obtained the necessary funds to begin construction on a satellite facility in the province of Buenos Aires. The Asilo-Quinta de Lomas de Zamora opened its doors in September of 1908 – three years after Piñero had resigned – in the suburban municipality of Temperley, just over the border from the capital.[136]

For the new director, there were also significant problems with hospital staff. First, although Piñero relied on the sisters' diligence and hard work, he nonetheless viewed their central role as antithetical to a modern and scientific institution.[137] Piñero focused his attention, however, on the various assistants and attendants who served in subordinate positions to the sisters and began to require that these women be literate and of "good morals." A major accomplishment in this area was the inauguration in March 1899 of a school of psychiatric nursing on the grounds of the hospital.[138]

Reforms at the men's hospital followed a similar pattern, except that the earlier connections to medical training and university research intensified. (In 1904, the Hospicio, which had been a municipal hospital, was nationalized and, like the HNA, was placed under the Ministry of Foreign Relations and Religion.) The new director, Domingo Cabred, had spent his entire medical career at the Hospicio. He started at the Hospicio in 1884 as a ward doctor. Two years later, Director Lucio Meléndez named Cabred as associate director. By November 1892 he had been named director.[139] Before becoming director of the Hospicio and during a later leave of absence, Cabred travelled to Europe in order to gather information on the latest methods of psychiatric care and training.[140]

In 1893 Cabred reported to the mayor of Buenos Aires that the new sections of the Hospicio for paying patients and tranquil indigent patients were in good shape. However, the delinquent and agitated insane were still housed in a building that was so overcrowded that it was impossible to segregate patients with violent behaviours or infectious diseases from the rest of the hospital population.[141] Cabred also complained that the Hospicio continued to operate without an encircling wall. As a result, escapes were commonplace and many patients were obliged to remain indoors. A properly built wall would permit, ironically, greater freedom for patients to enjoy the therapeutic benefits of outdoor activities.[142]

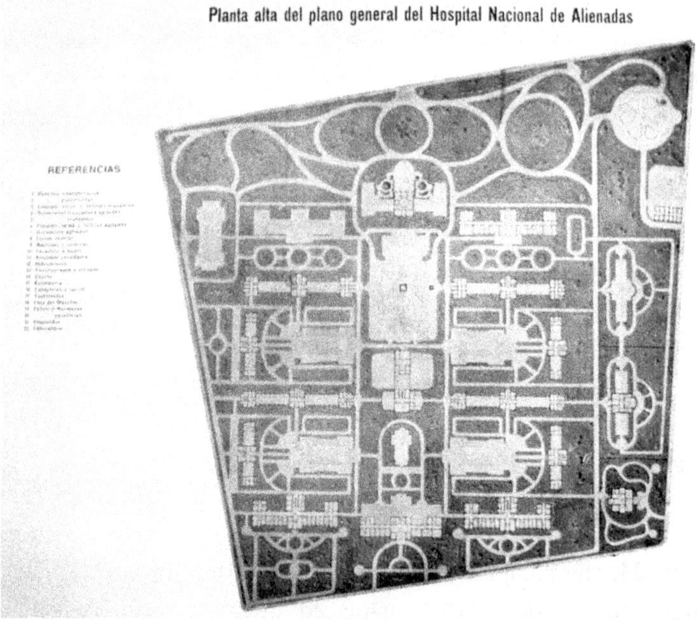

Plan for the women's asylum. Source: *Sociedad de Beneficencia de la Capital, 1823–1936.* (Buenos Aires, 1936).

One of Cabred's major goals was to provide a better administrative and physical atmosphere for the application of moral therapy.[143] From the beginning of the asylum's existence, patients had laboured at the Hospicio, yet Cabred had become convinced that the system was poorly managed and exploitative of patients, who were rarely paid.[144] Under his plan, work was to be used as both a distraction and a therapy, and patients were to receive a stipend payable upon their release – the full amount if they were released permanently, or a partial amount if their release was provisional.[145]

Cabred recognized that a well-paid and well-trained staff, that was also closely supervised, was the mainstay of any psychiatric hospital.[146] One of his first requests to the city government was the purchase of a time clock to allow tighter control of the work of employees. He also wrote and distributed an employee rulebook outlining the considerable responsibilities of nurses, guards, and orderlies. Under the new rules, staff lived under a regimen similar to that of the patients. Staff were expected to live on the grounds of the hospital, where doctors could better monitor and supervise not just their work behaviour, but also their more general comportment. The Hospicio could fine staff for both mistreatment of patients and negligence. Thus, if a patient escaped, the on-duty personnel at the time of the escape were responsible for the cost of the patient's recapture. The daily routine for the hospital staff was divided into a fourteen-hour day shift and a ten-hour night shift. During their work, staff members were expected to maintain the personal hygiene of patients and prevent or dissuade patients from sitting on the floor. Likewise, nurses were to oblige depressed patients to spend the better part of the day outside of their rooms.[147]

Cabred provided explicit instructions on how to treat agitated patients and what to do in case of various emergencies.

> When a patient becomes violent or excited, under no pretext may the assistants place a knee upon any part of the patient's body. As such a practice can easily result in serious injury; any employee who violates this prohibition will be fired.[148]

Although Cabred attempted to elevate the dignity and rights of the patients, he also sought to control their personal lives. For example, the administration maintained the right to censor all outgoing mail from patients, a policy that stands in stark contrast with his vision of giving patients maximum freedom. Visitation privileges, however, were much more liberal at the Hospicio than at the HNA. Patients could receive visitors on Thursdays and Sundays. A special room was designed for these visits, but it is not clear if it was ever built.[149]

Like the HNA, the therapeutic regime of the Hospicio was based on methods that would have been familiar to European and North American alienists and psychiatrists. Cabred considered isolation as the primary therapy of the hospital.

> One of the most important resources for the treatment of certain classes of patients is seclusion that is the complete isolation from the exterior world and from natural excitants of the nervous

Patients at Lomas de Zamora. Source: *Sociedad de Beneficencia de la Capital, 1823–1936.* (Buenos Aires, 1936).

> system. Often other therapeutic agents fail, or are slowed down, if when applied, the patient is not in an appropriate environment.[150]

The hospital also used a variety of sedative drugs and baths. [151]

Cabred was also an advocate for the so-called criminally insane.[152] As an official representative to a conference on criminal anthropology in Geneva in 1896, Cabred made a motion that the criminally insane should be treated in special sections of asylums rather than in prisons. Three years later, he established Latin America's first ward for the criminally insane. The ward was based on the principles of hygiene, observation, security, and therapy, and, at least in theory, it attempted to balance the need to protect society with the provision of a degree of humanitarian care. As in the rest of the Hospicio, the criminally insane were expected to work but, unlike jail inmates, patients in the criminal ward were not to be coerced into working.[153]

All of Cabred's ambitious reforms hinged upon the establishment of a rural satellite hospital to alleviate recurrent overcrowding. He was particularly interested in developing a rural colony asylum based on the Scottish cottage system, which provided patients with the illusion of liberty by placing the asylum far from population centres so that walls and cells were not necessary.[154] In October of 1897, Congress authorized the construction of such a hospital, largely thanks to the support of President Julio Roca.[155] In August 1901, the Hospicio transferred the first eleven patients to the Colonia Nacional de Alienados (National Colony for the Insane), which was situated sixty-seven kilometres outside of Buenos Aires near the religious centre of Luján, province of Buenos Aires. The colony, which was also known as the Open Door, operated as a satellite facility of the Hospicio until the 1940s.

Idealistically, Cabred hoped that the Colonia would be the first step in the reorganization of Argentina's treatment of the mentally ill. In his inaugural speech, Cabred observed, "at least 80 percent of the asylum population can receive psychological and physical benefits from real liberty, and without posing a threat to those around him."[156] Furthermore, confinement in closed asylums was prejudicial to both the human rights of patients and to the scientific progress of psychiatry.[157] The Colonia's therapeutic program was based on "liberty, work and physical and moral well-being, in an open door facility, with no mechanical restraints."[158] According to the Colonia's report from 1908 to 1909, 90 per cent of the patients were engaged in some sort of productive work.[159] A recent Argentine scholar argues, however, that the selection of patients to be transferred to the Open Door was based less on clinical criteria than on their construction and farming skills, desperately needed both to finish the asylum and to make it economically self-sufficient.[160]

Cabred was also determined to modernize psychiatric training through the creation of a Faculty of Psychiatry on the grounds of the Hospicio.[161] In November of 1910, the Institute of Psychiatry was inaugurated.[162] Cabred hoped that the new Institute would help to incorporate the new fields of neurology and chemistry into psychiatric practice.[163] In 1910, Cabred inaugurated a modernized bed-rest ward, and integrated it into the Institute.[164] The ward fulfilled numerous pedagogical and therapeutic goals. First, the Hospicio could provide acute cases with supervised bed rest, which at the

Work therapy at the Hospicio de las Mercedes, ca. 1910. Source: Archivo General de la Nación.

time was considered a major advance in psychiatric healing. While guaranteeing proper medical attention, bed rest also helped staff to exercise greater vigilance over patients, avoiding what Cabred referred to obliquely as "accidents." This new method, of course, was premised on a close ratio of patients to staff, as well as doctors' careful oversight of the underpaid staff. Bed-rest therapy also facilitated the clinical study of mental illness as medical students and their professors were now afforded the possibility of walking from patient to patient to study and compare conditions and treatments. Finally, bed rest represented the mentally ill person's "reconquest of their rights as ill people." It was a noble sentiment: if the physically sick patient should rest in bed, why should the mental patient not enjoy the same treatment?[165]

Conclusion

By the time that Ingenieros published *Madness in Argentina*, the country's system of psychiatric hospitals was large by the standards of Latin America; aside from Brazil, no other country possessed more than one psychiatric hospital.[166] Equally significant, Argentina's psychiatrists had developed a reputation on both sides of the Atlantic for their advanced research and clinical practices. A significant contributing factor to that reputation was the creation of a national office to coordinate the delivery of health care in the many underserved provinces. After years of campaigning by Cabred, who had been inspired by a series of French laws that mandated the construction of asylums in each department, the Argentine federal government created the Advisory Commission on Regional Asylums and Hospitals (Comisión Asesora de Asilos y Hospitales Regionales) in July 1906.[167] The Commission's official purpose was to design, construct, and supervise a national network of hospitals and asylums. Aside from proposing new hospitals, the Commission was charged with inspection of all dependent facilities.[168] Furthermore, the recently nationalized Hospicio and its Colonia were placed under the Commission. By 1914, the Commission had constructed two major institutions for the mentally handicapped, the Olivia Regional Coed Colony Asylum for the Insane in Córdoba province and the Torres Regional Coed Colony Asylum for the Retarded in Buenos Aires province.[169] At a time when most of Europe's institutions were at least fifty years old, those of Argentina were considered model institutions of global stature.

If the Commission came to symbolize the impending marriage of a modernizing state to a highly trained scientific elite, many public health advocates were disappointed by the continued influence of the Society of Beneficence. After all, the Society had managed to avoid incorporation into the Commission. Following his dismissal in 1905, Piñero published a letter in *La Nación* where he argued that the Society's control over the hospital was an anachronism that both imperilled public health and stymied the development of a modern state.[170] Piñero resurrected a now-familiar, if exaggerated, litany of charges, including that the Society of Beneficence spent too much time and money on frivolous activities that only raised the envy of the poor. A modern state's health policy should not rely on charity but rather should be a cornerstone of government; health care was a right, not a privilege.[171] Piñero continued his attack on the Society in the following year, after his election to the Chamber of Deputies. During debate on his proposed law concerning the rights and treatment of the mentally ill, Piñero charged that the Society opposed reform of the laws governing the insane because it would undermine their monopoly of health and welfare services for women and children. Piñero called for the centralization of mental health care under the Ministry of the Interior, as well as the creation of a national standard for commitment and an inspection commission for all hospitals. As matters stood, the Society inspected its own facilities, and only in times of crisis did they grudgingly allow outside observers onto the grounds.[172]

If on one hand the Society managed to hold its ground against change, Cabred's commission proved ineffectual in transforming the national landscape of mental health care. As early as 1915, several well-established doctors and politicians were commenting that the commission was ineffectual, in part because of poor funding. By the 1940s, when it was finally closed, the commission had built no other major institutions since the first decade of its existence, and some high-placed officials were even suggesting that the Society of Beneficence take over its operations. (See Chapter 3.)

The Argentine government's fiscal restraint is a critical piece in explaining the slow pace of change in the system of mental health care.[173] While public health bureaucracies had made crucial strides in the eradication of

Patients at the Colonia Nacional de Alienados, 1910.Source: Archivo General de la Nación.

infectious disease (a key to attracting immigrants), the traditional elites maintained an ambivalent view of social welfare projects.[174] As Ernest Crider has pointed out:

> [b]y implication, ... such assistance was limited to that necessary to preserve the social structure and the prominent role of the oligarchy; therefore it could not lead to fundamental changes in the living standards and quality of health care extended to the poor.[175]

Thus, while Argentina experienced massive social transformations, and especially a startling population explosion, its political and bureaucratic structures remained stagnant.[176] The most striking symptom of this anomaly was the placement of all of Argentina's national hospitals, as well as the Advisory Commission, under the authority of the Ministry of Foreign Relations and Religion. This administrative arrangement no doubt proved economical to the national state, but it is unlikely that the ministry was suited for, or interested in, overseeing the operation of psychiatric hospitals. Available evidence, as seen in the following chapters, suggests that the ministry was rarely attentive in its duty to oversee and manage the hospitals.

While it is abundantly clear that the relative weakness of formal state-building explains the continued survival of the oft-maligned Society of Beneficence, the results were paradoxical. As Karen Mead has elegantly argued, the success of the Society was in large part a reflection of the weakness not just of the Argentine state, but of the Catholic church as well.

> The history of the organization between 1880 and 1920 suggests how Argentine women attempted to take advantage of structural opportunities to participate in the state-building efforts that characterized the era, as well as how they used available notions of gender to enhance their maternalist prerogatives.[177]

Of course, the influence of female religious orders was also enhanced by fiscal and political constraints to state-building.

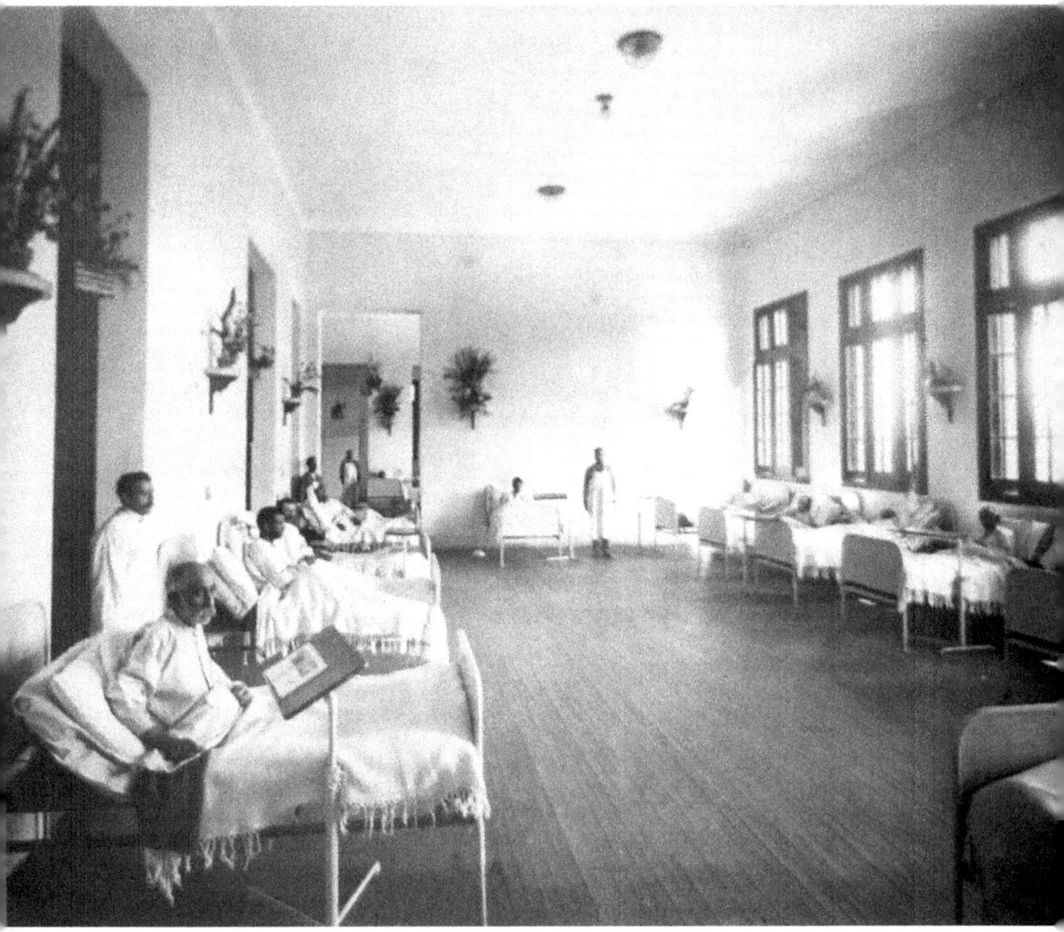

Bed Rest Ward, Hospicio de las Mercedes, ca. 1910. Source: Archivo General de la Nación.

Ironically, the work of the Society at the HNA provided a number of benefits to the women's hospital that were conspicuously absent from the Hospicio. Most importantly, authority was divided between the Society and an appointed medical director. The medical director, whose two-year appointment could be renewed and usually was, had the authority in all scientific, educational, and medical decisions. The Society, however, was

Faculty of Clinical Psychiatry, Hospicio de las Mercedes, ca. 1910. Source: Archivo General de la Nación.

in charge of all administrative and budgetary matters and appointed from within its own ranks a group known as *Señoras Inspectoras*, who made weekly inspections of the hospital and reported back to the president of the Society. Direction of the men's asylum, by contrast, was vested almost entirely in the medical director. Although in theory he answered to the municipal government, and after 1904, the federal government, the available evidence suggests a relative absence of oversight. Such a state of affairs may have played a significant role in the Hospicio's problems in the following decades.

3

3: INNOVATION AND CRISIS

While in 1910, Argentines could celebrate with ease the accomplishments of Piñero and Cabred, two decades later, it had become impossible to ignore that the institutions were in a state of serious decay. The newly appointed director of the HNA, Julio Nogues (1879–1956), captured the pessimism of many of his colleagues when he asked in 1925:

> What would we say of a surgeon who operated in the old chambers of the Hospital de Hombres – or of a service for sick children where patients with pneumonia, whooping cough, and measles were all mixed together? In both cases we would say that the responsible party had committed a crime of *lesa medicina.* The same should be said of a psychiatric hospital in which 700 patients are treated in a ward built for 250, where the excited, depressed, persecuted and anxious are all mixed together.[1]

In addition to the humanitarian problem – there tended to be more sympathy for female patients – there was the problem of the hospitals' role in maintaining the public order. In January of 1928, a group of patients' failed attempt to escape from the ward for the criminally insane at the Hospicio turned into a riot in which five guards were injured and one patient died. Newspapers concurred with the asylum's director, Dr. Alfredo Scárano, that the criminal ward, and by extension the entire hospital, possessed neither adequate staff nor an appropriate physical plant to fulfill its important mission to contain and cure the mentally ill.[2] One paper wondered how there were not more of these sorts of incidents in such a decrepit and overcrowded ward.[3]

The Hospicio's troubles were far from over. In early February, a Spanish-born psychiatric patient named Antonio Rojo approached a group of doctors and staff who were standing in front of the Hospicio's administrative offices.

"Prisoner Argüellos is forced by firefighters to jump from an ombú tree where he had been hiding." From "Uprising of prisoners at the Hospicio de las Mercedes," *Caras y Caretas* (January 1928). Source: Archivo General de la Nación.

Suddenly Rojo pulled out a knife that he had fashioned from a wooden spoon handle and cut Dr. Lucio López Lecube's throat. The doctor died instantly. A daily newspaper reported that the perpetrator was fifty-three years old, and because of his "proverbial calm, [Rojo] had been included into a group of non-dangerous patients."[4] At the doctor's funeral Helvio Fernández (1873–1951) eulogized López Lecube as "yet another victim to be registered in the prolonged medico-psychiatric martyrdom, a symbol of the professional risk, a routine of service in mental asylums."[5] Fernández reminded the assembled psychiatrists that their patients were "swords of Damocles, perennially hanging over our heads." The work of psychiatrists and their broader mission, then, was distinct from that of doctors who dealt in physical illness.

> Thus the psychiatrist, without hope of support, suffers in the august mission of the doctor who treats and cures but with a difference from doctors in general hospitals: the psychiatrist serves as a shield to protect society; to monopolize the ill will, the hatred, the strange and unusual demands that easily become pathways to violence; he is the center of all reactive reprisals; he is the target of all the insults, target of all the violence, and most painful, the receptor of all the ingratitude.[6]

The daily *La Nación* echoed Fernández's sentiments about the danger that the mentally ill posed but added that hospital mismanagement represented a

> ... permanent danger for those who live and work near the insane and for the general public, as there is little to prevent one lunatic, or a group of them, from overpowering the asylum's guard and running out into the street to commit other violent acts.[7]

The Hospicio administrators responded by noting the problems of managing a large number of mentally ill persons in an institution that was antiquated in design, lacked sufficient state funding, and was chronically overcrowded. "The only way to relieve the danger of future similar incidents to which we are exposed to daily," they observed, "is to construct new wards in which we can practice better vigilance of the patients."[8]

These incidents and the ensuing critiques were symptomatic of what many in the medical profession recognized as a crisis in public health, and especially in the psychiatric hospitals. The most obvious symptom of the crisis was overcrowding, which had grown worse since the early twentieth century as hospital construction had failed to keep pace with the overall population growth. Moreover, the nature of the patient population, from a medical and socio-economic perspective, was presenting new challenges to the hospitals as more poor patients with chronic conditions began to fill the wards. Argentina also began to experience increasingly frequent cycles of economic downturn that produced, in addition to rising unemployment, growing pressures on the country's public institutions. At the same time, immigration rates recovered from their decline during World War I. The new waves of immigrants were different from earlier arrivals, however, with many more coming from eastern Europe and the Middle East. At the same time, the process of rural-to-urban migration accelerated. As a result, Buenos Aires' population more than doubled from just under 1 million in 1904 to almost 2.5 million thirty years later.[9]

The period from the late 1910s through 1946 was also a time of convulsive political and social transformation in Argentina. The passage of universal obligatory male suffrage in 1912 inaugurated a brief experiment with formal democracy spearheaded by the Radical Civic Union party. But with democratization came growing political tensions that often spilled over into the operation of public institutions, including asylums, as accusations of malfeasance and corruption became more common.[10] Argentina's limited democratic experiment (women could not vote and the Radicals displayed certain anti-democratic tendencies, including frequent use of interventions) came to crashing halt with the coup of September 1930. From the coup until 1946, with the election of Juan Perón, the influence of the military on politics grew as that of the traditional parties declined.

Despite the growing and increasingly visible crisis in the hospitals, the inter-war period was a time of tremendous innovations in both medicine and administration. Employing the methods of mental hygiene, psychiatrists began to encourage greater cooperation from the families of the mentally ill, as well as school teachers, employers, general medical practitioners, and the courts. The social approach to mental illness coincided with, and was encouraged by, the growth of biochemical interventions. The promise of these treatments led many doctors to believe that the era of curing mental illness was not far off. Progress, however, came with costs. First, many of the new social and medical approaches involved more intrusive interventions into the bodies and social space of the mentally ill. Moreover, many of the more ambitious projects depended upon emptying the urban hospitals of their so-called "chronic" (or incurable) cases to rural asylums where, it was argued, their presence would not burden the work of providing efficient short-term care to individuals who could benefit from intervention. By vacating the chronically ill from urban hospitals, doctors hoped to diminish the stigma attached to seeking treatment in a psychiatric hospital.

By the mid-1930s, however, rising expectations about these new interventions clashed with conditions in the hospitals. The tension between the institutions' therapeutic goals and their custodial functions became impossible to ignore as doctors' training and vision surpassed the capacity of the state to support their work. As these contradictions became blatant, some doctors began to articulate a systematic analysis of public health. They argued that the problems of an individual hospital were the product of inadequate national and provincial health budgets and policies (or the lack thereof), rural-to-urban migration patterns, changes in the nature of immigration, the shortage of provincial psychiatric facilities, and the effects of global economic conditions. For these reasons, no matter how sophisticated the administrative or medical techniques of the hospitals became, they could not overcome their role as human warehouses.[11] It was bitter irony for the medical profession, however, that even as overcrowding became worse, Argentina's rate of psychiatric confinement nonetheless remained considerably lower than in much of Europe and North America; doctors rarely mentioned the fact that Argentina's numbers were higher than those of the neighbouring Latin American countries.[12] Like their compatriots in other professions, then, the tension between the ideal of modernity, on the one hand, and their growing understanding of the limitations of Argentine economic and social development on the other, became paramount in their understanding of the national reality.[13]

SCANDAL

When Dr. Daniel Pombo, who was about to retire from the HNA, publicly denounced the Society of Beneficence in 1918, his allegations were hardly surprising. According to Pombo, the doctor–patient ratio was upwards of one to three hundred and there had been an outbreak of skin and eye infections. In many wards, patients were obliged to sleep on the floors of bathrooms and dining halls. Worse still, patients with widely divergent diagnoses were improperly housed together, thereby endangering the physical and psychological well-being patients and staff alike. There was also a notorious absence of legal oversight for persons committed to the hospital.[14]

Pombo's well-publicized attack drew the attention of Buenos Aires' celebrated muckracking journalist Juan José Soiza Reilly (1879/1880–1959) who reported the death of an HNA patient named María Baldessari de Russo. Such was the poor administration of the hospital that her husband received the news of his wife's death not from the hospital but from the neighbourhood funeral home. An official inquest reported that her corpse was covered with bruises, bite-marks, and parasites. Soiza Reilly suggested that the strange circumstances around her death were part of a broader pattern of incompetence, corruption, and indifference at the hospital.[15] The vice-director's private clinic was a case in point.[16]

> [w]hen they bring a crazy woman from a good family [*loca de buena familia*], they always say that there are no beds available, and they indicate the convenience of bringing her to the Sanatorium of Váldez [the doctor in question]. [HNA director] Esteves authorizes these transfers.[17]

Soiza Reilly seemed bent on laying much of the blame for these problems on the Society, of whose six hospitals none had a spare bed.

> Yet the Society has luxurious salons for parties for the ladies. Once, the Society was in charge of the schools. But Sarmiento [Liberal president of Argentina, 1868–74] ended that. Why can't a new "Sarmiento" take the Hospitals away from them?

The only solution to what he saw as deeply entrenched corruption was for all hospitals to be placed under the management of the national Public Assistance.[18]

If the accusations were revealing so too was the response of HNA director José A. Esteves (1863–1927). He readily acknowledged the charges; HNA overcrowding (there were 1,659 patients but only 800 designated beds) was the result of the willingness of the Society and his administration to admit all who required care. Esteves also pointed out that the vice-director who ran a private clinic had offered to resign his public post. Esteves had refused the offer.[19] In a pattern that was quite typical in cases of public scandal, after a flurry of calls to investigate the HNA, attention on the hospital quickly abated.[20]

By March 1923, however, the question of the Society's role in public health care returned to the front pages when Radical deputy Leopoldo Bard urged Congress to thoroughly investigate the Society. For Radicals, whose short-lived ascendancy had begun with the election of Hipólito Yrigoyen in 1916, the privileged position of the Society served as a political target from which to promote a more modern administration of public office and to attack elite *porteño* society.[21] Bard's attack was also a reflection of both the democratization of politics in Argentina and the changing image of once sacrosanct public institutions.[22] Concern about the HNA was based on information from the hospital's own annual reports and, as in 1918, was readily acknowledged by the administration. Overcrowding gave nurses little time for training sessions and classes. And because they were also the worst paid in their profession for the whole city, the HNA had a difficult time hiring and retaining quality staff.[23] By the summer of 1922, water and sewage service had become so irregular that many wards reeked of feces. Infectious diseases, including tuberculosis, were posing a renewed threat to patients and staff alike.[24] Bard's analysis was coloured by partisan animus against the Society.

> The ladies of the Society worry about other things. They take on the work of the hospital out of vanity, a desire for fun, sometimes as a form of medical treatment against too much 'spleen.' Naturally, between the opinion of the hospital director and some

of women – at least the inspector – the opinion of the ladies always wins out.[25]

The official response was predictable and reasonable.[26] The Minister of Foreign Relations and Religion, Ángel Gallardo, made a public statement on conditions in public psychiatric institutions. The issue of overcrowding – in March of 1923, there were 2,175 patients in a hospital designed for approximately 800 – was less the result of mismanagement than the lack of space for women in other hospitals and a nation-wide shortage of psychiatric hospitals. These conditions were seen as sufficient to explain the apparent decline in cure rates from about 18 per cent in 1908 to below 10 per cent in 1923.[27] Gallardo claimed that the Hospicio was free of irregularities, but the rural Colonia had become the site of very public and scandalous violence. At present, the Advisory Commission on Regional Hospitals and Asylums was planning to conduct a thorough investigation of the disturbances.[28]

Deputy Bard's response to the minister was restricted entirely to the question of the HNA and did not depart from the now-familiar list of problems, including the absence of a proper rural colony, habitual wasting of public monies, the inability to separate patients with communicable diseases, and the failure to create specialized wards for distinct psychiatric diagnoses. He also claimed that the hospital made it a regular practice to leave beds empty in the pensioner ward rather than to give them to indigent patients when there were no beds available in the regular wards. The HNA was a national disgrace with a staff comprised of illiterate immigrant women who, often directly hired at the port of arrival, stayed but briefly before moving on in search of better pay and working conditions.[29]

Bard ignored the issue of the Hospicio, but Radicalism's opponents on the left and the right did not. Socialist deputy Enrique Dickmann charged that medical director Alfredo Scárano had transformed the Hospicio into a tool of the Radical party for the dispensation of jobs, votes, and even food. Another deputy raised the issue of the questionable partisan activities of the Advisory Commission on Regional Hospitals and Asylums.[30] For the Socialists, the blame could be squarely laid at the feet of the Radical party, and particularly its perennial chief, Hipólito Yrigoyen. "The scandal at the Hospicio de las Mercedes is a *residue* [*colaso*] of the scandal of the last administration [Yrigoyen's] that in its last years has become unbearable, upsetting and [disruptive of] all public services." Dickmann opined that he knew not a single public institution of any kind that had not suffered at the hands of the Yrigoyen administration.[31] Radical deputy Rodeyro rebutted Dickmann's charges against the Hospicio, by arguing that the problems at the Hospicio were not the product of Scárano's administration; rather, they were the inheritance of his predecessor, Domingo Cabred, who, like Scárano, struggled against a shortage of hospitals in the provinces and an inadequate social security network.[32]

Socialist deputy Matías González Iramain, however, shifted the discussion towards the growing list of allegations of financial and political misconduct at the Hospicio's rural Colonia. "Can an election-obsessed [*electorero*] government stand to lose the political capital of institutions that pay out huge amounts of national money to employees?"[33] As with the Hospicio, the Colonia had become integrated into the Radical patronage network, providing jobs to supporters and funds for the purchase of votes. The allegations of both mistreatment of patients and corrupt accounting and provisioning practices that had resulted in both the theft of patients' wages and the deterioration of the quality and quantity of food merited a full scale investigation.[34]

Of the three hospitals that fell under the scrutiny of congress, the Colonia was the only institution that saw any concrete action. In July 1923, the General Accounting Office (Contaduría General de la Nación) took over operation of the asylum that had already been under investigation since 1922 and named Dr. Alejandro Raitztin (1889–1973) as interim director.[35] A July 1924 report later confirmed a wide range of irregularities at the hospital and suggested that the asylum should be administratively separated from the Hospicio.[36]

No more serious actions were taken until after the September 1930 coup, when the newly installed military government of General José F. Uriburu purged most state-run institutions of administrators with Radical party affiliation.[37] Significantly, the institutions of the Society remained untouched (perhaps due as much to their good management as to political connections) while the Hospicio and its satellite facility were placed under intervention and Scárano was removed.[38] According to a later newspaper article, the Ministry of Interior's report found irregularities at the Hospicio so outrageous that

> [an] establishment designed for the unfortunates, who deserve mercy and the help of society, has been converted, through the acts of a guilty administration, into a place of torture, characterized by some truly Dante-esque traits.

Such was the degree of disorder that orderlies and nurses had been signing off on paperwork, including certificates of insanity, in violation of the civil code and hospital regulations.[39] There were also suggestions that Scárano had neglected his duties as director, in order to focus on his private practice and fundraising for the Radical party and that he used employment at the Hospicio and the Colonia to reward political supporters and their clients.[40]

Mental Hygiene and Medical Innovations

Such scandals only confirmed psychiatrists' conviction that the chronic overcrowding and deterioration of the urban asylums necessitated their transformation into smaller, more specialized institutions. By the 1920s, a variety of factors encouraged a renewed push to simultaneously release patient and doctor from the narrow confines of the asylum whilst integrating psychiatry into the mainstream of medicine.[41] Mental hygiene practices and a range of biomedical interventions, the former based on social medicine and the latter on the most modern of scientific innovations, raised the hope that the profession could move its work beyond the asylum to both general hospitals and the community at large.[42]

Although historians of Argentine mental hygiene have focused on the movement's obsession with race, heredity, and deviance, many of the movement's advocates were also strongly influenced by their professionally frustrating experiences inside state institutions.[43] Its advocates urged the creation of a broad-based network of social and medical services for the mentally ill and their families outside of the country's overcrowded and decrepit institutions. Such steps brought benefits to psychiatrists as well by offering them opportunities outside of the institutions and the possibility of improving their public image by weakening popular association between psychiatric hospitals and forcible confinement, while early treatment would lead to shorter stays in hospitals and faster recovery.[44] Of equal importance was the emphasis placed on the use of psychotherapies, including psychoanalysis, for the treatment of mild mental disorders and neuroses. In the process, therefore, advocates of these new approaches not only laid claim to treatment modalities that departed from the somatic model, but also were staking out new areas of expertise for the profession.[45]

These innovations would facilitate the development of a network of smaller more specialized institutions. External clinics would allow psychiatric assistance to a broader segment of the population, and even offer a degree of preventative treatment, while also affording prompt medical attention for the mentally ill. Transformation of urban institutions was seen as impossible, however, without the establishment of a sufficient number of rural colony asylums for the large number of so-called chronic cases.[46] As psychiatric hospitals began to focus on acute and curable cases, doctors would begin to have the time and prestige to extend their reach into schools, the military, and the private sector through vocational and aptitude testing. Such efforts would prove to be of service to the public and private sector and would also secure a measure of social prophylaxis.[47] Interestingly, mental hygiene advocates also hoped that the deinstitutionalization of psychiatric practice would transfer some of the authority of hospital directors to individual practitioners.[48]

None of these advanced techniques were possible, however, without the development of more advanced statistical methods and clinical record-keeping. These administrative innovations were seen as crucial to determining how and when to apply the new interventions and to ascertain their success. Statistics were also critical for campaigns to improve the quality and quantity of psychiatric facilities, as doctors would be able to show the true extent and character of mental illness.[49] Better record-keeping would also facilitate monitoring of former patients, as was already being done with tuberculosis sufferers and former convicts.[50] The aspirations of mental hygiene were ultimately quite ambitious. The dream was that as Argentina began to develop a mental hygiene system that included preventative treatments and post-hospital care, psychiatry would begin to integrate into general medicine, and, more importantly, mental illness and its sufferers would finally begin to shake off the centuries of stigma and opprobrium.[51]

The first experiments with extramural treatment were not conducted under the direction of the large psychiatric institutions, but in a variety of mutual aid clinics that were operated by ethnic or political organizations.[52] Following their lead, Juan Obarrio opened a psychiatric external clinic at the HNA in 1924 or 1925 for the treatment of women who came in for voluntary consultations. It was hoped that the clinic would attract women suffering from relatively minor conditions such as neurasthenia, phobias, emotional distress, etc.[53] By the early 1940s, the clinic was receiving more day patients than were admitted to the hospital.

Hospital Nacional de Alienadas: Patients Treated at Clinic and Hospitalized[54]

Year	*Clinic*	*Hospitalized*
1935	243	826
1936	442	793
1937	811	1,278
1939	1,390	1,173
1940	807	935
1941	1,506	1,287
1942	1,085	960
1943	closed	613

Doctors at the HNA, however, felt that its location within the hospital hampered its effectiveness. In an internal memorandum, a participating doctor, Dr. Luis Esteves Balado (1887–1968), noted:

> It is certain that attendance is low. The reason for poor attendance is obvious. It is only with great trepidation that patients will go to a clinic located in an insane asylum. If friends, neighbors, or acquaintances find out that they are visiting such

> an establishment, they will stop coming. Nobody wants to be labeled crazy, ... and for this reason clinics in psychiatric hospitals suffer from low attendance.[55]

Inspired by a recent sabbatical trip to clinics in western Europe, including Italy, Esteves Balado, who later served as director from 1934 to 1947, argued that the HNA needed to become an urban psychiatric facility dedicated to short-term care of acute cases where psychiatrists could have constant contact with doctors in other specialties. By contrast, rural asylums tended to isolate psychiatrists from mainstream medicine.[56] Urban hospitals could also more easily be used as teaching hospitals. There were also important therapeutic advantages to urban hospitals.

> The hospital being close, families will send an ill relative more quickly to the hospital. The families will have the hospital close at hand, know that they will be able to visit their loved one, and also receive frequent reports from the doctors.[57]

Proximity of families would also allow doctors to collect more up-to-date information on patients' social and medical backgrounds while also reducing the likelihood of social abandonment.[58] Ironically, the modernization of urban hospitals could only occur when its so-called chronic patients had been sent to rural colonies. Such actions had an ambivalent character to them, however, since the implication was that neither family nor the patient should have any voice in the medical decision.[59]

In the following year, Esteves Balado and fellow staff doctor Julio d'Oliveira Esteves offered a more precise analysis of the relationship of the hospitals to the country's "current and future resources, our idiosyncrasies and our needs."[60] The direct causes of overcrowding were incongruence between budget and patient population, incomplete social welfare programs (*asistencia*), the absence of both national health policy and accurate statistical data from the provinces, and antiquated hospital regulations. The construction of new wards or services needed to be based on careful consideration of therapeutic goals in order to reverse the hospitals' decided bias towards custodialism. In the HNA, the external clinic should serve as a gatekeeper to determine which patients truly required hospitalization. They noted that too often persons were hospitalized who could be treated in an outpatient setting. None of these changes would be permanent, however, without the development of an effective national mental hygiene program and of a network of institutions for persons whose conditions were too severe to benefit from short-term care or attention.[61] (In 1927, the two doctors, in collaboration with Dr. Arturo Ameghino, established the short-lived Argentine Social League for Mental Hygiene.)[62]

Like his counterparts at the HNA, Hospicio director Alfredo Scárano questioned the validity of the closed asylum model and aspired to convert the Hospicio into an urban clinic with an open psychiatric service. The need to expand the work of the Hospicio out into the broader community was in part a response to frequent letters from families of released patients asking how to best care for their loved ones.[63] Optimistically, Scárano envisioned the creation of a city-wide network of mental hygiene clinics that would provide early diagnosis and intervention for a wide range of illnesses. Such a program would serve to shrink the asylums' populations while also allowing psychiatrists to branch out into a wide range of public- and private-sector endeavours. (Ideally, psychiatrists could be employed by business, schools, the military, and immigration offices to weed out potential troublemakers and pathological individuals.)[64] It is testament to either his poor stature in the medical community, his disinterest, or, less likely, the absence of political connections, that none of his projects came to fruition.

Despite the centrality of Buenos Aires to the psychiatric profession, it was not there but in a provincial city that the first truly modern psychiatric hospital was built. In October 1927, the city of Rosario, in the province of Santa Fe, opened its Hospital Psiquiátrico with an external clinic that was to serve persons of the community.[65] (By this point, some of the smaller provincial general hospitals had also been experimenting with providing limited psychiatric care, in large part out of necessity.)[66] The hospital was founded with the hope of not only fostering a more humane treatment of the mentally ill – the hospital was limited to a relatively small number of patients – but also of encouraging important psychiatric and neurological research. The latter was possible because the hospital was directly connected to the medical school of the local university, whose dean was the prominent psychiatrist

Gonzalo Bosch (1885–1965). As a provincial hospital, it was hoped that it would provide direct care to its citizens – provinces, one doctor observed, are best suited for dealing with local health issues for "reasons of affection but also for social and economic reasons."[67] In keeping with the thinking of time, it was widely recognized that the modern and well-organized hospital would ultimately fail without the development of a rural colony asylum for those deemed incurable.[68] Within a year of the hospital's inauguration, administrators were already complaining, however, that demand for their services was outstripping the hospital's limited capacity.[69]

The Rosario hospital had an influence on Buenos Aires; after the coup of 1930, the new government named Bosch as director of the Hospicio.[70] Already well established in his clinical and teaching career at the Rosario hospital, Bosch was also a founding member of the Argentine Mental Hygiene League in 1929. (This was a different organization than the short-lived Argentine Social League for Mental Hygiene.)[71] Facing an understaffed and decaying hospital with almost 2,300 patients but with a capacity for only 1,000, Bosch quickly began to apply the mental hygiene approach to solve the most immediate of problems.[72]

During the next decade and a half, the Hospicio began to engage in a tremendously innovative and ambitious program that in many respects dwarfed the work of its sister institution. In September 1931, the Hospicio opened an outpatient clinic, through the patronage of the women's auxiliary of the Argentine Mental Hygiene League.[73] The number of persons treated grew three-fold, from 5,081 in 1938 to 15,228 in 1942. These figures were considerably higher than those from the HNA's clinic.[74] In October 1934, the League established the School for Mental Hygiene *visitadoras*, or female social workers, on the grounds of the Hospicio. The school trained young women, and later men, in mental hygiene social work, including some training in psychotherapeutic techniques.[75] Principal responsibilities, however, did not encompass clinical work, but rather focused on "home visits to collect psychiatric background, which the hospital often lacks, studies of the patient's home life, counseling the families of patients, and preparing the family to help reintegrate the returning patient."[76] In September of 1938, the Hospicio inaugurated a social service unit within the clinic to better coordinate the work of the *visitadoras* with that of hospital staff and doctors.[77]

The social workers, most of whom were single young women, collected information from patients and their families either at the clinic or at the home of the patient. In 1938, the *visitadora* Raquel Margot de la Rosa, for example, visited a patient at home in order to collect what was believed to be important hereditary data. In another case, Juana Winitzky visited a former patient to check up on how he was progressing since his release from the Hospicio.[78] Although the press focused excessively on the fact that these middle-class women visited the homes of poor people, it represented an important first step in the incorporation of women into the professional ranks of mental health.[79]

In his capacity as director of the Hospicio, Bosch also resurrected Cabred's emphasis on "moral therapy" by encouraging physical exercise and participation in group activities, such as musical choruses and bands. Motivated as much by therapeutic as fiscal concerns, Bosch also began to reinstitute work therapy on the hospital premises.[80] In an effort to reduce patients' isolation, Bosch set up a temporary radio station at the Hospicio in 1931, and patients periodically broadcast messages and music to the outside world.[81] Bosch also sought to re-establish his authority as director, a key precept of moral therapy since the mid-nineteenth century. Echoing Cabred's work, he acquired a time clock to better regulate the schedules of the nurse staff and attempted to prohibit staff from selling food and tobacco to patients. Bosch removed several doctors and nurses who, for no medical purpose, had been living on the grounds of the Hospicio and managed to hire 188 new nurses and 18 interns (*practicantes*). That he took such steps is suggestive of the degree of decay at the institution during the tenure of its previous director.[82]

The growing interest in mental hygiene coincided with, and was informed by, the introduction of new medical procedures.[83] Doctors viewed the social and somatic interventions as mutually beneficial, and many, including Esteves Balado and Bosch, published widely on both approaches. Without effective medical treatments, ambitious plans to convert asylums into vibrant hospitals for a reduced number of patients who would stay for a short term would inevitably fail. Furthermore, more sophisticated and frequent medical interventions necessitated the development of the very same kinds of record-keeping systems and statistical methods advocated by mental hygiene. Just as such information was critical in determining the number and kind of hospitals to build, so too was it relevant for tracking the effectiveness of medical interventions.[84] Throughout the world, many doctors also argued that safe and effective medical therapies which could cure the underlying physical dimensions of psychiatric illnesses would allow psychotherapeutics and even psychoanalysis to become widely effective.[85]

The emergence of new therapies also represented a significant shift in how doctors related to their patients' bodies. While doctors had been fascinated with the bodies of the mad in the nineteenth century, especially because of the influence of the theory of degeneration, there was little to do with, or to, those bodies from a medical perspective. Most nineteenth-century somatic interventions did little more than pacify and/or punish the patient in order oblige changes in behaviours. By contrast, the medical interventions, which had filtered into Argentina from Europe after World War I, promised to target not just symptoms, including behaviour, but the actual underlying illness.[86] As doctors became increasingly optimistic about developing cures for a range of psychiatric conditions, no aspect of patients' biochemistry was beyond the scrutiny of the doctors, including their diets.[87] As in the rest of the world, innovations in somatic treatments in Argentina were usually the result of psychiatric patients in public hospitals being subjected to medical experimentations against their will (or without their consent). Doctors justified these measures as essential to finding cures for hitherto incurable conditions, including epilepsy, schizophrenia, and progressive general paralysis. They often justified the coercion by claiming that for patients who had spent decades in hospital, a radical treatment was justified as a heroic last-ditch effort.[88] From the perspective of patients, these treatments were often painful, and the prospect of undergoing them filled many with dread and fear.[89] Their fear was not unfounded. As one historian has noted, "treatment for psychotic illnesses before the 1950s were, for the most part, useless and often, very dangerous."[90] Yet, some treatments seemed to be effective and were even sought out by patients who were desperate for a cure. As outpatient clinics developed, more and more people were willing to try certain interventions, especially for the treatment of syphilis.[91]

The most common set of medical procedures were various forms of shock. One of the earliest was lactotherapy – the intramuscular injection of milk, or other lactose-based substances, for the purpose of calming agitated patients. Agitation was considered to be a critical symptom of mental illness, and one that endangered everyone. The calming of the patient occurred, it was believed, because of the intense pain of the injection.[92] This procedure, which had been discovered in 1916, was being used in public hospitals in Argentina by the late 1920s. Doctors also employed chemically induced shocks with injections of insulin, cardiozol, and various fever-inducing substances.[93] By the early 1940s, electroshock therapy, which had first been used in Italy a decade earlier, was introduced into Argentina hospitals.[94] Malaria-therapy, which scored some success for the treatment of progressive general paralysis, was also used in Argentina as a convulsive therapy.[95] Argentina's psychiatric hospitals proved to be as up-to-date in the application of these innovative treatments as their counterparts in western Europe and North America.[96]

By 1943, the HNA reported that six hundred patients had received shock treatments with cardiazol, insulin, and electricity and that the effects were generally positive.

> The percentage of patients who are cured or improved and received a release, thanks to these new modalities of treatment is much higher than in previous periods.[97]

Shock therapy was also credited with facilitating the integration of patients into work therapy programs at the hospital.[98] There was also an increased use of neurosurgeries, especially after 1931 when the Hospicio opened up a neurology department.[99] For 1932, Bosch reported the use of several new neurosurgical procedures for epilepsy and dementia praecox (schizophrenia), including lobotomy.[100]

Argentine medical journals reveal an initial optimism that these new techniques were inaugurating an era of medical discovery. As patients became more manageable, hospitals would be able to start granting more releases. Effective treatment modalities would also facilitate the transformation of the asylums into modern short-term hospitals, more akin to their counterparts in the mainstream of medicine. Writing in an Argentine medical journal, Brazilian psychiatrist Enrique Roxo argued:

> The matter of mental illness' curability must come as a surprise to non-specialists who have asserted that they are incurable and that the mentally ill have no other option but to remain in the asylum, where they should spend their remaining days, caged up. For this reason, it could seem an extravagance to speak of modern therapeutics for those for whom there was no cure. Yet those who make this claim make a huge mistake for certain mental illnesses are as curable as physical illnesses. And if some physical illnesses, including cancer, leprosy, tuberculosis etc., still do not have cures, so too are there still some mental illnesses without cures.[101]

Yet even practitioners like Roxo expressed unease with the empiricism of these new therapeutic regimens. He remained unconvinced, for example, of the usefulness of malaria-therapy as a shock treatment for schizophrenia, an illness that many considered the "black hole" of psychiatry.[102] Likewise, Luis Esteves Balado praised its effectiveness for certain conditions but noted that "if it is true that we can observe cases of improvement or cure, we do not observe these improvements in a high enough percentage to feel terribly optimistic."[103]

Probably because of the development of more effective somatic treatments, the Hospicio began to report significant numbers of voluntary admissions. In 1936, for example, thirty-two men voluntarily entered the Hospicio and thirty-four did so in the following year.[104] Although these were a small fraction of the total admissions, the numbers stand in marked contrast to a decade earlier when no voluntary admissions were reported.[105] There is even some evidence that patients may have requested certain treatments, especially malaria-therapy for tertiary syphilis.[106] One such patient had a self-assessment that must have pleased the doctors:

> Logical judgement, stands up for self, protesting against the prolongation of his internment, as he believes that he can care for himself effectively "as well as tuberculosis sufferers, who are

> much more contagious and dangerous," while also recognizing the effectiveness of his treatment, which he wishes to continue.[107]

While the advent of both social and somatic approaches to psychiatry inspired a growing confidence in medical practitioners, the precise impact of these treatments remains unclear.[108] It is likely, however, that with massive overcrowding and funding shortages, a lower percentage of Argentina's patients received these therapies than doctors had hoped. Many of these treatments, including insulin and cardiozol therapy, required an ample and well-trained staff to monitor patients as they came out of the shock phase.[109] Despite structural limitations, however, doctors viewed these innovations as the instruments through which they might transform their asylums into true hospitals.

Collapse

Medical directors' cautious optimism about the transformative potential of the new therapies was quickly dampened as overcrowding in public institutions began to reach critical proportions. While the number of patients had always exceeded the official number of available beds, the imbalance grew much worse during the 1930s and 1940s.[110] (See Appendices: General Movement of Patients.)

Overcrowding at Psychiatric Institutions, 1934[111]

Hospital	*Capacity*	*Population*
HNA	1,600	3,054
Hospicio	1,100	1,990
Colonia	1,200	3,239
Oliva	1,975	4,016
Torres	902	1,271

By 1939, the Advisory Commission on Regional Hospitals and Asylums reported that "we have 4,475 beds for the mentally ill but the three institutions' [Hospicio, the Colonia Nacional de Alienados, and the Oliva Asylum] total population is 10,564, leaving us with an excess population of 6,089 people."[112] A report from six years later said that overcrowding at the Hospicio, the Colonia, and Torres had only grown worse. Rural hospitals were under the added burden of even more extreme staff and doctors shortages.[113] It was also growing difficult to maintain order. Even the HNA, renowned for its orderly administration, had become the scene of notorious public disturbances by the early 1930s.[114]

Extreme overcrowding at the HNA – over three thousand patients in a hospital designed for 1,900 – compelled the Ministry of Foreign Relations and Religion in late December 1933 to authorize the hospital to refuse new admissions. To some degree the Ministry's decision was shaped by the recent decision by the Oliva Asylum to admit no new patients.[115] In the same resolution, the ministry released funds for renovations that had been promised in the budget of 1929 but never delivered.[116]

The practice of closing the HNA to new admissions became fairly common through the 1930s and 1940s. Although it served the interest of the hospital, it had a damaging effect on many patients in need of shelter and services, and also their families. Refusing to accept new patients also prevented the kind of cooperation between psychiatrists and their families that was seen as so valuable. In May 1934, for example, a mother wrote to the president of the Society, pleading for the readmission of her daughter. Despite the young woman's good care, her condition had begun to deteriorate on her return home, and she now posed a "constant danger to both her three sisters and to self." Although the family could not afford a private clinic, the Society responded that because of the temporary closure of the HNA, they were unable to accept her daughter.[117]

Since the women's hospital's policy was to admit only those sent by the police, families began to abandon mentally ill female relatives at the doors of police stations throughout the city. Soon there were reports about women being confined to police stations and jails where they were placed under the supervision of male police officers. Despite a lack of viable alternatives – the city's considerable number of private clinics offered few spaces – the new admission policy gave rise to renewed criticisms of the Society's admission practices.[118] There were even accusations that the Society was refusing patients out of convenience. In February 1934, for example, *La Nación* reported that the police had picked up a "dangerous female lunatic," whose admission the hospital had denied even with the proper legal paperwork.[119]

Despite the controversy that it engendered, the closure gave the administration time to begin serious renovations, while the patient population slowly fell to a more manageable 1,760 patients. Several outbuildings were demolished and in July 1934 the cornerstone was laid for a future clinical and admissions ward with four hundred beds, and sewer and water lines were repaired to prevent the return of typhoid.[120] Such a service would ideally serve to treat acute cases and to provide the hospital with a more efficient gatekeeper that could exclude inappropriate admissions. Other services, such as X-rays, diathermy treatment of syphilis, and physiotherapy were improved.[121] Perhaps in keeping with the growing social orientation of psychiatry, visiting hours were also finally expanded to include the weekends.[122]

By the end of 1935, better funding, improvements in the physical plant, and reduction in the patient population offered the ever-elusive hope of the hospital becoming a "true psychiatric hospital."[123] The administration's optimism proved short-lived. Early in 1937, with seven hundred patients over capacity and most provincial asylums shut, the Society received permission from President Agustín P. Justo to close the hospital again. By executive decree, which remained in force until the end of 1941, the hospital could refuse to treat all but the most acute cases and those who were a danger to self or others. The hospital also closed its external clinic, which families had come to see as an easier way to hospitalize relatives.[124] The rules were further amended following the inauguration of new dormitories at Lomas de Zamora in July of 1940. All national, provincial, and municipal authorities, including the police, were required to obtain permission to admit a patient prior to bringing them to the hospital. All persons deemed mentally retarded were to be categorically denied admission.[125] The issuance of new regulations appeared to have little effect and the practice of "dumping" the mentally ill continued unabated.[126] By the time that an executive order was issued in July 1942 to close the HNA, in order to give them time to complete an expansion project into an adjoining property, some wards were so crowded that there was no room to walk at night.[127] A new admission policy required families to request hospitalization through public authorities, and especially the police. [128] Because the police were only authorized to hospitalize extreme and dangerous cases, the hospital was probably admitting a higher percentage of individuals with serious conditions. Ironically, those so confined also tended to experience more delays in gaining their release because of backlogs with paperwork. Observing that the closure was itself perhaps causing a whole new set of problems, the medical director finally recommended in December 1943 that the order be revoked.[129]

The Hospicio faced similar problems. By 1932, overcrowding was making it "impossible to establish the necessary separations [between agitated and tranquil patients]."[130] The problem of space remained intractable, and by 1935 the Hospicio housed 2,580 patients, more than double its capacity. Bosch's despair at the lack of progress is reflected in the fact that in his annual reports he began simply to quote reports from prior years. (Surprisingly, general hygiene remained satisfactory and mortality rates dropped from 18 per cent in 1918 to 8.6 per cent in 1935.)[131] By the end of 1936, the Hospicio's population had risen to 2,750 patients. Bosch concluded that all the efforts at minor repairs of the physical plant were futile and that the Hospicio required the construction of "open and modern constructions, more so if one considers that for many years, nothing has be built on the hospital grounds, a fact that makes our continued struggle all the more useless and unsuccessful."[132]

The crisis of the *porteño* hospitals, and especially the periodic closure of the HNA, had a pernicious influence on the rural asylums. By the end of 1934, the Oliva Asylum in Córdoba province housed over 4,000 patients but was designed for only 1,200. This was largely a product of the slow progress in expanding the number of hospitals in the other provinces. By 1941, other than the small hospital in Rosario (which was by now also overcrowded), there were only small psychiatric annexes in three general hospitals in Tucumán, Mendoza, and Entre Ríos provinces.[133] Worse, with the temporary closure of the Melchor Romero Hospital in the province of Buenos Aires, Oliva became the only major psychiatric hospital that would accept female patients. This only contributed to the continued deterioration of Oliva, where shortages of food, medicine, and staff became critical.[134]

Overcrowding at the Hospicio, from "Forty thousand lunatics on the loose: a visit to the Hospicio de las Mercedes," *Caras y Caretas* 37 (June 23, 1934). Source: AGN.

By 1939, the Oliva Asylum director observed that his institution served not only as an escape valve for the asylums of Buenos Aires but also for the northwestern and northeastern provinces.[135]

The ripple effect of nationwide overcrowding finally led the Oliva Asylum to declare its own severely restrictive admissions policy.[136] At the time of the decision to restrict admissions, which was in effect from September 1939 until September of 1942, Oliva held 4,500 patients.[137] The hospital managed to reduce its patient population to 3,600 by April 1941.[138] As had happened during the period of restrictive admissions at the HNA, public concern grew about the number of unconfined "lunatics." According to an Oliva doctor, during the two years of its closure, the province of Córdoba alone had approximately four hundred 'psychopaths' living "in their homes, at police stations or jails, thus constituting in each case a social plague."[139] As at the HNA, however, the Oliva Asylum was unable to refuse all requests for admission.

> We cannot hermetically seal the institution, as we immediately realized that we could not apply the closure with absolute inflexibility, that we could not ignore the pleas of families or policemen who had often brought ill persons from great distances, in such a state that it made it impossible to send them back without great risk to the health of the patient and the safety of their attendants.[140]

If the crisis of the 1930s and 1940s damaged the morale of the urban staff and doctors, it was even worse at rural institutions like Oliva where low pay and an anemic budget gave the impression that they were all but forgotten by the national government.[141]

Explaining the Crisis

Despite the often sharp partisan barbs at the two institutions (the Hospicio for its supposed connection to Radicalism, and the HNA for its ties to the elite Society), the hospitals shared a common set of challenges that were a product of both the nature of mental institutions and the national context of public health.[142] Even Socialist deputy Ángel Giménez, who had issued a stinging attack on the Society in 1915, two decades later, could acknowledge that the Society ran good hospitals and that their officers rarely interfered with decisions made by medical professionals. In his proposal to create a national health office that would oversee the diverse health establishments, he proposed that the Society of Beneficence should not be dissolved as he had suggested in 1915, but be better incorporated into a national health project.[143] Still, Argentina desperately needed an efficient, modern, and preventative health system. On the last point, Giménez was adamant, and he noted that "we make [natural] selection in reverse, with the best intentions we bastardize the race. Medical help always arrives too late, when the condition is irreversible."[144] Conservative editorialist Eduardo Crespo shared Giménez's concern about the chaos of public health but placed some blame for the crisis on the shortage of private hospitals[145]

The clearest symptom in the asylums of the national crisis was that overcrowding was growing worse. A prominent doctor at the Hospicio observed in 1927 that over the previous decade Argentina's population had increased by 40 per cent but not a single new asylum had been constructed. In the same period, the rate of psychiatric confinement had grown from between 0.82 and 0.97 per thousand inhabitants in 1915 to 1.21 per thousand in 1922. While everyone recognized that overcrowding delayed the recovery of many patients, there was also growing concern about the large number of mentally ill and mentally retarded individuals who were not confined to an institution. Argentina's low rate of confinement, compared to "more advanced" industrial nations suggested a national defect that merited attention.[146]

Of course, the federal government had already, in theory, attempted to simultaneously increase rates of hospitalization and relieve overcrowding when it created the Advisory Commission on Regional Asylums and Hospitals in 1906. The inauguration of the Advisory Commission's Oliva Asylum in July 1914 led to hope that the crisis of overcrowding would soon pass. Tellingly, within weeks of its opening, the President of the Society of Beneficence announced that they already had 600 female patients ready to be transferred from Buenos Aires to the new hospital.[147] The first group of patients departed from Retiro train station at the end of October, followed by three more groups in the next month.[148] Between 1914 and 1928, a total of 1,680 female patients from the HNA, under escort by nurses, assistants, and sometimes a doctor, made the long train trip to Oliva.[149] Patients who came from outside of Gran Buenos Aires or who received no visitors were usually the first chosen for transfer.[150] By September of 1914, a large number of male patients had also been transferred – 100 patients from the Open Door and 477 from the Hospicio.

Yet the usefulness of the Oliva to relieve overcrowding in Buenos Aires was short-lived. Of the total admissions to Oliva in 1914, 93 per cent were transfers from the HNA, the Colonia, and the Hospicio, but, by the next year, only 33 per cent came from these hospitals. By 1919, only 3 per cent of Oliva's admissions were coming from other institutions. The shift was largely a response of provincial governments in the northwest of the country who took advantage of the relatively close federally funded institution.[151] For this reason, Oliva itself quickly became overcrowded. Within five months of opening in 1914, and with a staff of only 55, the colony's population stood at 1,177 men and women.[152] Through the rest of the decade, HNA administrators would be repeatedly frustrated in their efforts to send patients to Oliva.[153]

Because Oliva became so severely overcrowded in a short period of time, the practice of sending patients to the *porteño* hospitals from the provinces continued.[154] At the Hospicio, for example, the percentage of *porteño* patients grew only from 51 per cent in 1902 to 61 in 1936; in the latter year, over 12 per cent of the patients still came from outside of Gran Buenos Aires.[155] The HNA appeared to have more success in curtailing the admission of provincial patients, most likely due to their stricter admissions policies. In 1900, of the 626 admissions, 423 were from the capital, 95 from the province of Buenos Aires, and 108 from interior provinces.[156] In 1920, 18 percent of newly admitted patients came from interior provinces.[157] By 1943, less than 1 per cent of all patients came from outside of Gran Buenos Aires. Yet, many of those who were categorized as *porteño* or *bonarense* may have been rural migrants who had come to the city in search of work but had ended up in the asylum. In some cases, the police of the province of Buenos Aires may have "dumped" such individuals inside city lines.[158] (See Appendix A: "Domestic Origin of Patients.")

Much of the blame for the absence of asylums in the provinces was directed toward the Advisory Commission on Regional Hospitals and Asylums. Some, like Arturo Ameghino, criticized the Advisory Commission for its failure to build enough new hospitals.[159] Others, like Socialist deputy Ángel Giménez, criticized the Advisory Commission for having deviated far from its original purpose of proposing and funding the construction of hospitals, and in the last decade, it had become a "sui generis office of national public assistance."[160] Giménez further noted that the Commission tended to construct identical institutions – a one-size-fits-all policy that ignored the specialized needs of distinct institutions and their clientele and one that failed completely in its promise to offer national coordination of health care. The Advisory Commission was held in such low regard that in 1931, and again in 1942, the Ministry of the Interior proposed that the Society of Beneficence take over the operation of the commission's institutions. On both occasions the Society declined the offer.[161]

By the 1930s, doctors were beginning to understand the crisis as part of a systemic failure of the country's regionally imbalanced public health system. Bosch, amongst others, was especially struck by how in North America and Europe, each city, state, or province had its own mental health facility. The absence of a sufficient number of institutions, he argued, had very deleterious effects on the mental and physical well-being of patients.

> Evidently, the insane from the entire Republic come to these hospitals; this is prejudicial to the material and moral condition of the patient. Distance obliges in the majority of the cases, that the patient undergoes the primary evolution of his disease in the heart of the family, and in general is poorly observed and lacks correct treatment; in the best of cases this leads to the individual being brought to the local police station, where the saber replaces the bromide, or the local jail where they are placed in cells, where they await transfer to a psychiatric hospital, when the number of insane grows to the point that it is economical. The prejudicial effects of this system are obvious ... including the separation of the patient from his family. The proximity of the family is not only helpful for the patient, but also for the doctor for whom this

is often the only way to acquire full knowledge of the patient's personal and family antecedents.[162]

The shortage of specialized institutions for individuals with chronic or permanent conditions also remained a very serious problem. In 1915, the Advisory Commission opened the Asilo Regional Mixto de Retardados in Luján, Estación Torres for the care of the mentally retarded.[163] As with the Oliva, the Torres facility quickly filled to over-capacity and was unable to serve the needs of the HNA and the Hospicio. In 1923, for example, the HNA complained that in the prior nine years, they had only successfully transferred seventy-two *idiotas* to the new facility.[164] And even with the stringent admissions policies of the 1930s and 1940s, the HNA was rarely able to overcome pressure from family or the police to admit mentally retarded women.[165]

More intense overcrowding coincided with, and may have contributed to, a growing concentration of patients with more chronic conditions. (The available evidence does not allow a firm conclusion about the relationship of the two phenomena.) Perhaps the most striking area where this is seen is in the drop in diagnoses of alcoholism, a condition that in most cases resulted only in a brief stay in hospital, at the Hospicio. Whereas in 1901, 57.8 per cent of all patients admitted were diagnosed alcoholics, by 1939, the figure was down to 16.87 per cent.[166] The drop in alcoholism diagnoses coincided with a decline in the percentage of immigrant patients. By 1939, for the first time, native-born Argentines outnumbered immigrants in the total number of admissions to the Hospicio. Considering the long-held obsession with linking madness and immigration, it is curious that the 1939 annual report made no attempt to explain the rising percentage of native-born men.[167] (Appendix B: Alcoholic Patients in the Hospicio.)

As the Hospicio's native-born population grew, some doctors began to observe that this group was actually more prone to serious and chronic psychiatric disorders. (Even before the shift began, José Ingenieros, had observed that mental retardation was an almost exclusively native-born phenomenon, and especially in certain regions of the interior *sierra*.)[168] The Hospicio's limited statistical analysis of its own patients reveals a similar trend. In 1937, of the 385 schizophrenics admitted to the Hospicio, 232 were Argentine. So, while immigrants continued to be over-represented in the hospital, native-born were over-represented in this one rather significant diagnostic category.[169] It is possible that immigration served as a process of self-selection, wherein persons with serious organically based diseases (such as schizophrenia or mental retardation) were less likely to be able to make the trip to Argentina. Ironically, anti-immigrant writers often made the opposite argument – that immigration tended to attract the least adaptable.[170] The evidence for the HNA is less clear. The 1910 annual report listed mania, melancholy, and systematized insanity as the most common illnesses.[171] By 1920, periodic, systemic, and puerperal insanities (a range of mental disorders relating to menstruation and child birth) and dementia praecox (an early term for schizophrenia) were the most prevalent diagnoses.[172] Various forms of schizophrenia, however, were the most common diagnoses by 1943.[173]

The hospitals' population was also growing poorer, especially during the Depression of the 1930s. One piece of evidence is that fewer patients were willing or able to pay for the privilege of being housed in the paying wards. Since the late nineteenth century, administrators had tried to attract paying patients, known as *pensionistas*.[174] As funding for hospitals was highly dependent on lotteries and the vagaries of budgets, the pension system brought in a fairly reliable stream of revenue to pay for the care of indigent patients.[175] *Pensionistas*, who did not have to wear a uniform, were divided into four categories depending on how much they paid.[176] Between 1900 and the early 1920s, however, there was a perceptible decline in the percentage of paying patients. Thereafter, HNA annual reports ceased to even report this figure.

Paying and Non-paying Patients: HNA[177]

Year	Pensioners	Indigents	% Pensioners
1903	118	574	20
1915	118	950	12
1920	87	1,140	7

Evidence from the Hospicio is more ambiguous; of the 801 patients in 1893, 13 percent were listed as pensioners.[178] By 1917, the Hospicio's annual report would only say that the percentage of pensioners was dropping because of competition with private asylums that often offered better care.[179] By the mid-1920s, however, director Scárano claimed that demand for pensioner service was at a reasonably high level (roughly 10 per cent of all patients in 1925–27) and demonstrated popular confidence in the hospital.[180] But even the optimistic Scárano acknowledged that the failure to continue to construct new wards for paying patients would ultimately undermine the revenue generating potential of this population.[181] And as with the HNA, by the 1930s, the Hospicio's annual reports did not list the number of paying patients.

As the number of paying patients dropped, those who entered paying wards were more likely to be unable to render payment.[182] In part the difficulty derived from the fact that because care was significantly better in the pension wards, both hospitals faced a constant flood of petitions from families and state agencies requesting that people with few resources be admitted to the pension wards but that the fees be waived or reduced.[183] This problem became especially acute during the worldwide Depression of the 1930s.[184] Typical was the tragic case of a thirty-year-old single maid who in 1933 requested that her hospitalized sister not be removed from fourth level pensioner ward (the cheapest for paying patients) into the indigent class ward. In her plea, the sister noted that she believed that life in indigent care would only serve to stall or reverse her sister's cure. Citing growing requests for reduction in fees, the president of the Society of Beneficence rejected the request.[185] Women, unless attached to men employed in the formal sector economy, were the least likely to have access to social insurance programs.[186] Public assistance programs were only beginning to be developed during the 1930s and their reach remained fairly limited; programs were either directed out of specific hospitals or tended to focus on those employed in the formal sector of the urban economy.[187]

There is also occupational data on patients that further suggests a pauperization of the hospital population. At the Hospicio, the percentage of patients whose listed profession was either day labour, unknown, or without occupation grew steadily throughout the first half of the century. Evidence for the HNA is more ambiguous; the increasing percentage of women in low-paying work sectors like domestic service and factory work may simply reflect women's growing participation in the formal economy.[188] As social critics across the political spectrum were observing by the 1930s, those in marginal sectors of the labor force were less likely to be connected to any sort of social insurance program.[189]

As the number of pauper patients increased, so too did the number of families who actively engaged in sending their relatives to the hospitals. The trend was especially pronounced at the Hospicio. In 1893, patients' families initiated only 2 per cent of confinements to the Hospicio. But during the first half of the twentieth century, the figure grew steadily. By 1913, that figure was up to 33 per cent, and by 1918 it was up to 64 per cent. In 1939 a full 70 per cent of patients had been confined by their families.[190] The evidence of family pressure on the women's asylum, however, is more ambiguous. From 1900 until 1934, family members and friends affected the vast majority of commitments to the HNA, but police confinements increased thereafter as a result of restrictive admissions policies. Initially, doctors saw this as a positive sign and ignored the possibility that increasing urban poverty forced or enticed families to see the asylums as a component of family survival strategy.[191] When Director Esteves explained HNA overcrowding in 1923, he emphasized the importance of growing public demand for psychiatric services, especially from families.[192] In the 1930s, the director of the Hospicio reported: "the increasing percentage of hospitalizations made by family members ... clearly demonstrates the degree of confidence that the public has for our system of medical care in this establishment."[193] Considering the condition of the hospitals, it is far from clear whether this trend reflected public acceptance of psychiatry or the plight of families desperate to find somewhere to put an ill relative. Anecdotal evidence suggests that families actively sought admission for loved ones but also recognized that the hospitals' general wards were often unsanitary and deficient in the delivery of medical care. Whatever the motives of families, increasing demand for the services of the hospitals no doubt contributed to increasing overcrowding.

Subtle but significant shifts in the national origins of patients may have also posed new challenges for hospital administrators.[194] As World War I drew to a close, Argentina began to receive more non-Catholic immigrants

Pensioner ward, Hospicio de las Mercedes. Source: Archivo General de la Nación

from Eastern Europe, Russia, and the Middle East. In some sectors of society, the response was explicitly anti-Semitic and racist, or expressed fear that the migrants were psychically traumatized by the war or "infected" with the ideas of the Russian Revolution.[195] Increased poverty and growing numbers of women in the work force further aggravated xenophobic attitudes among the middle class in later decades.[196]

The hospital populations reflected these changes. At the HNA, for example, only 10 out of 626 patients admitted in 1900 came from Eastern Europe or the Middle East. By 1943, 41 of 613 were coming from those areas. At the Hospicio, there were no reported immigrants from these areas in 1893, but by 1917, they constituted over 5 per cent of the patient population, and by 1936 they counted for over 10 per cent of the patients admitted.[197] Another sign of the changing demographics was that at the HNA, between 1905 and 1943, the percentage of Jewish patients rose from 1 to 6 per cent.[198]

For hospital staff, the major challenge of the demographic changes was how to communicate with patients. With a more variegated patient population, language and cultural misunderstandings may have increased. The daughter of a Syrian-born day labourer, for example, complained that her father had been found insane because of a communication gap.

> [U]pon examining my father the court doctors had observed that he does not speak Spanish and that it was not possible to understand him adding that his nervous state also prevented him from expressing himself clearly.[199]

A similar problem may have contributed to the plight of Ivan G., a Ukrainian sailor who, in late November of 1911, arrived to the Hospicio with two doctors' certificates from the Police Service for the Observation of the Insane. The doctors reported him as suffering from "dementia praecox." Ivan had arrived in Buenos Aires only two months earlier as a crewman of a ship. When the hospital finally interviewed him through a translator, in January of 1912, the sailor claimed good mental health prior to a recent drinking bout, and the Hospicio doctors changed his diagnosis to "an acute alcoholic episode," and noted that he was ready to be discharged.[200]

In addition to these various demographic shifts, the toll of years of neglect of the hospitals was mounting. Chronic funding shortages stymied efforts at renovating the physical plants and often rendered projects obsolete before being completed. At the Hospicio, for example, delays in completion of a 1905 renovation project were so protracted that, by 1913, the incomplete project was already considered out of date.[201] Likewise, the HNA complained in 1911 that the 1895 plans for the hospital were not only unfinished but, ironically, now considered anachronistic as they called for too many dormitories, which would only encourage accepting more patients.[202] In his May 1924 letter of resignation, José Esteves lamented that the original plan of 1895 was still not put into place.[203]

The deterioration of the hospitals made them unappealing places to work. In 1925, Director Scárano complained that the hospital had the same number of staff as it had in 1914, but with five hundred additional patients.[204] After a celebrated case in which a patient was murdered by two nurses at the Hospicio in 1926, one newspaper complained that the hospital's staff mostly possessed but a "rudimentary social background."[205] At the HNA, the problem of retaining good staff was aggravated by the hospital's notoriously low pay, which until the 1940s, was well below the average rate for other hospitals in the city.[206]

> All the best ones leave, and those that replace them are increasingly worse. Often they are women just off the boat, who have never cared for an ill person. Worse still, our desire not to hire illiterates is made impossible by the slim choices available.[207]

But the hospitals were caught in a bind. Those who received literacy and professional training at the hospital became the employees most likely to have success in finding better employment elsewhere.[208] Of course, an untrained or indifferent staff posed dangers. In the tuberculosis ward, for example, failure to follow established protocols put everyone in the hospital in danger of infection.[209]

Even doctors and medical directors appear to have suffered from low salaries, leading many to moonlight at private clinics, many of which were owned by high level public hospital employees. As late as 1935, a proposal was made to reform hospital career opportunities so that more doctors could enjoy a salary. Aside from the problem of pay, the HNA's lower scientific profile made it difficult to find doctors and medical students willing to work there.[210]

Conclusions

By the 1930s, doctors had become acutely aware of the ever-widening chasm between their medical expertise, and knowledge of the latest medical advances, and their capacity to put that knowledge into use. In 1940 Esteves Balado, director of the HNA since 1934, glumly reported that "[p]sychiatry is an unappreciated specialty, and for that reason our hospitals do not have the same number of doctors as go to other types of hospitals."[211] And when Bosch, the Hospicio director, was asked in a 1945 interview about the status of his hospital, he assured the reporter that the institution was up-to-date in all the latest medical approaches; the only thing missing, he quipped, was money.[212] Even with the growth of confinements by families, as well as the development of mental hygiene clinics and a range of medical interventions (some of which patients submitted to voluntarily) doctors were becoming more acutely aware of the negative popular opinion towards their institutions.[213]

While the state of existing hospitals was cause for great concern, both for the sake of the patients and the safety of everyone, worse still for many doctors was the fact that only a fraction of the country's mentally and morally "defective" were confined.[214] By the late 1920s, this was a source of both professional anxiety and national shame. In 1927 Hospicio psychiatrist and neurologist Arturo Ameghino (1869–1949) noted that the construction of new psychiatric hospitals had not kept pace with national population growth and that the rate of hospitalization was inferior to "all the civilized nations of the world."[215] As will be discussed in the next chapter, that population was increasingly viewed as a moral, biological, and physical threat to all Argentines.

Despite success in some areas of reform, including the amazing ability of such overcrowded institutions to actually lower patient mortality rates to those of comparable institutions in wealthier nations and to attract some voluntary patients, the hospitals' reputations had become permanently tarnished. Because of weak state support, and the failure to expand the health system as the population grew and changed, the hospitals had become ambiguous institutions. Patients could experience, for good or ill, the latest in medical interventions, but were forced to sleep at night in bathrooms or in garrets. And while a medical rhetoric claimed the necessity of confining all of Argentina's mentally ill, the institutional reality made that goal impossible to achieve.

4

4: AMBIGUOUS SPACES: LAW, MEDICINE, PSYCHIATRY, AND THE HOSPITALS, 1900–1946[1]

The historian Roy Porter has commented that the main difference between general and psychiatric medicine is the degree of coercion that patients face.

> Over the past two or three hundred years, those people suffering from serious mental disturbance have been subjected to compulsory and coercive medical treatment, usually under conditions of confinement and forfeiture of civil rights. Sick people in general (i.e. those suffering from somatic diseases such as measles or gout) have typically had the right to seek, or the right to refuse, medical treatment; have typically enjoyed their own choice of practitioner; and, insofar as they have been cared for in institutions such as hospitals, they have been legally free to come and go as they please.[2]

While coercion is a universal reality of psychiatric hospitalization, what is particularly striking in the case of Argentina is the degree to which national, provincial, and municipal governments failed to provide legal oversight with respect to that coercion. Their failure to adequately regulate hospitalization is a clear expression of the weakness of the Argentine state's ability to regulate civil society. And just as with the deterioration and overcrowding of hospitals, the absence of proper legal oversight had a profound impact on patients and doctors.

In the absence of effective oversight from outside authorities, administrators served as the de facto mediators between patients and the outside world. Poor oversight of the hospitals meant that patients had few protections from physical abuse and neglect, unwanted treatments or involuntary transfer to other, often distant, hospitals. In the event that a patient was either the victim or perpetrator of a crime, hospital administrators, not independent bodies, decided whether to call in outside authorities. At a more mundane level, administrators controlled patients' access to information and contact with family through restrictive visiting hours and the censorship of mail. In some cases, patients also lost control over their property, which often fell into the hands of their own family or neighbours.

Patients' legal status was profoundly shaped by the material conditions of the hospitals. Despite a spate of promising reforms between 1890 and 1900, all of Argentina's psychiatric hospitals continued to suffer from extreme overcrowding, a problem which reached its apex in the 1930s and 1940s. These conditions adversely affected both the medical treatment of patients and the ability of hospital staff to keep up with the paperwork concerning the confinement and release of patients. For different reasons many private psychiatric clinics in Buenos Aires also negelcted their patients' rights.

Since the end of the nineteenth century, jurists and doctors had bemoaned the absence of a proper legal regimen to oversee the various facets of hospitalization. The issue of patients' legal status mirrored a wider discussion about how to transform the execution of justice in Argentina, where case backlogs, a shortage of judges in rural areas, and a shortage of penal institutions were a constant source of concern. The problem also revealed a pragmatic concern: the absence of judicial oversight exposed doctors and administrators to potential lawsuits by disgruntled patients and their families.

While few doctors denied that legal reform was needed to make confinement legally transparent, many also argued that the essential problem was that the loose legal regimen allowed far too many mentally ill, and especially those who seemed "normal" in the eyes of lay people, to evade hospitalization and treatment. Inspired by measures that had been enacted to control political dissent, immigration, and other social ills, these doctors and reformers advocated a range of measures to insure the speedy confinement and monitoring of all mentally ill persons. (The convergence of approach and rhetoric is hardly surprising, given the long-standing institutional connections between psychiatry, criminology, penology, and the legal system itself.) Advocates of this model viewed the families of the mentally ill as potential adversaries who, perhaps because of the same hereditary pathology that afflicted their mentally disturbed relations, were often pleading for the medically ill-advised release of a patient. Argentina's very low rates of institutionalization for the mentally ill and mentally retarded, compared with those of North America and northern Europe, provided additional ammunition for those who advocated confining more of the nation's infirm. After all, they argued, how could the problem of mental patients' legal rights be a serious consideration when so few were actually confined?

Law and Hospitalization

Despite widespread acknowledgement of the importance of distinguishing the mad from the criminal, Argentine psychiatry had developed in near lockstep with the allied fields of penology, criminology, and criminal law, and there was a high degree of collaboration between the fields.[3] After doctors' testimony in legal proceedings became a requirement in the mid-1880s, the ability to identify and classify the insane became fundamental to the psychiatric reform project, if for no other reason than to protect society and the individual patient.[4] Psychiatrists wished to identify and classify individuals according to two basic criteria: mental status and dangerousness.[5] The former was germane to culpability in the criminal context and hospitalization in the medical context. The latter, to varying degrees, was attributed to all mentally ill and determined whether they would be placed in an asylum or a prison. Only the trained professional, psychiatrists argued, could evaluate their mental state and dangerousness. Doctors took the matter quite seriously, for it had professional, ethical, and medical ramifications for both patient and practitioner. In 1907, for example, José Ingenieros noted that qualified medical examinations guaranteed that the mentally ill would receive adequate medical treatment. He rejected the notion that it was irrelevant whether a delinquent was confined to a jail or an asylum, arguing that social defence needed to be applied in a scientific and rational manner. A madman in a jail or a common criminal in an asylum represented threats to the internal working of either institution and, by extension, threatened the broader social welfare.[6]

Prior to 1871, there were no legal guidelines for hospitalization. From 1871, with the passage of the Argentine Civil Code, until 1983, the Code, in conjunction with rules developed in each hospital, theoretically regulated insanity proceedings, hospitalization, and guardianship.[7] The Civil Code mandated that judges base rulings on mental competence on the findings of two medical doctors' examination of the subject.[8] Professional medical evaluations of suspected lunatics could take place in private homes, jails, general hospitals, and even the police's Psychiatric Observation Service.[9]

The Civil Code defined insane persons as "individuals of either sex who are in a habitual state of mania, dementia or imbecility, although they may have periods of lucidity, or the mania may be only partial."[10] (This criterion would change in 1968. See Chapter 6.) A spouse, another relative, the courts charged with the care of legal minors, or, in the case of foreign nationals, the respective foreign consul could request a declaration of insanity. Any other citizen could also make a request for a finding of insanity but only "when the insane person is furious, or inconveniences his or her neighbors."[11] (The question of whether non-citizen residents could make requests was ignored.) The code called for the naming of a temporary guardian upon the initiation of insanity proceedings. Should a person be found insane, his or her personal property became the responsibility of the appointed guardian. Incapacity could only be rescinded after the patient was re-examined by doctors and a judge declared the interdiction lifted.[12]

The civil code also regulated hospitalization, stating that "the insane person will not be deprived of liberty except in cases where it is feared that exercising it, he will injure himself or others. Nor can he be sent to a psychiatric hospital without judicial authorization."[13] As strict and comprehensive as these procedures were on paper, often they had little effect on the actual practices of courts, hospitals, or the police in the hospitalization of the mentally ill. For although the civil code demanded judicial authorization prior to psychiatric hospitalization, in the vast majority of the insanity proceedings reviewed here, patients had already been in the hospital for lengthy periods of time before their case came before a judge.[14] In emergencies, hospital doctors, the police, and other officials, often with the tacit support of patients' families, deliberately circumvented the law, since the civil code lacked a provision for immediate hospitalization. Because staff was overwhelmed by the excessive patient population and could not keep up with the medical and legal paperwork, it was not uncommon for patients to find themselves in a bureaucratic vacuum between the courts and the hospitals.[15]

One of the most common legal irregularities was the delay between hospitalization and its approval by the courts. By law, patients were to be examined prior to hospitalization. Archival material indicates, however, that not only did the hospitals admit patients without examination, there were often delays of months and even years before a court approved the hospitalization. Aside from their technical illegality, delays meant that no public authority outside of the hospitals was aware of the patients' physical confinement.

Some time during 1920 or 1921 an Italian immigrant named Francisco had his sister María, also an immigrant, confined to a private psychiatric clinic in the city of Buenos Aires. By March of 1921, the family decided that her continued treatment at the hospital was too expensive so they transferred María to the HNA. It is not clear whether María consented to the initial transfer, nor whether it was done according to the strictures of the civil code. Approximately six months after her admission, in November 1921, administrators finally requested from the presiding court that the internment of María be "regularized." They noted that the certificates of two medical doctors who attested to her insanity had accompanied her admission. It was another three weeks before medical examiners of the court finally examined María at the HNA.[16]

In some cases, patients' legal status remained unclear for many years. Josefina D., a twenty-three-year-old native of Argentina who asphyxiated her five-week-old baby in August 1924, remained at the HNA for over a decade without court-appointed examination. Upon her arrest for the murder, the police remanded her to their psychiatric observation facility, from whence, on the order of two staff doctors, she was placed in the women's hospital in October 1924. Little is known of her life in the hospital, save a brief mention that the isolation felt by all patients was perhaps worse for Josefina as she was deaf and her speech was difficult for doctors to understand. It appears, nonetheless, that Josefina adapted to hospital life and was considered obedient and helpful with chores. In 1937, the city's Office of Minors informed the hospital that proceedings to establish the subject's insanity had never been carried out. Only in October of 1937, did court-appointed doctors examine her and find her insane.[17] Josefina's experience was not an isolated case; Silvia O. was confined in 1932, but her case did not go before a judge until 1937.[18] Carolina M., who accused her father of sexual abuse, waited four years before her 1943 confinement was approved by a court.[19] (These cases are discussed in great detail in Chapter 5.)

Patients also frequently experienced protracted delays between the moment when a hospital determined that they were fit to be released and when a court verified that decision and ordered the release. José P., suffering from "mental confusion caused by alcoholism," was sent to the Hospicio in July 1925. By September the same year, hospital authorities communicated to the court that he was fit to leave. Yet the following month, the Hospicio sent an identical communication to the court.[20] Thus, the patient, whose ultimate fate is not mentioned in the document, remained hospitalized at least for an additional month due only to delays by the court. A Russian sailor, whom the police sent to the Hospicio after a bout of heavy drinking, faced a similar dilemma. Hospicio director Domingo Cabred was obliged to request that the courts lift the sailor's interdiction not once but twice.[21] In a similar case, the federal police sent Samuel J., a thirty-four-year-old Czech, to the Police Psychiatric Observation Unit after he was arrested for disrobing in public. From there, the police sent Samuel to the Hospicio. In March 1935, forensic psychiatrists communicated to the court that they had judged the subject mentally competent and recommended his release. However, his judicial record shows that he was not released until three months later.[22] Another Czech, Carlos Luis endured similar complications. The federal police brought the thirty-eight-year-old day labourer to the Hospicio in March 1932 for reasons not made clear in his file. Five months later, in August, the Hospicio communicated to the court that Carlos Luis "was in condition to be released." In October of the same year, however, the Hospicio notified the court that the patient was still in its care. In their letter to the judge, Hospicio administrators reported "[s]ince as of this date we have received no resolution in favor of Carlos Luis' release and because his medical improvement persists, I reiterate to your honor, the request that was made in the cited note."[23] Finally, in May 1933, after the Hospicio had requested three times to have Carlos Luis' case resolved, the court approved

"'Oh father Adam ...!' And this man who wanted, like the first man, to go naked, is subjugated and covered by hospital orderlies," from "Not everyone who should be is there...an hour in the Hospicio de las Mercedes," *Caras y Caretas* 26:1300 (September 1, 1923). Source: Archivo General de la Nación.

his release. For Paulina C., an Argentine-born maid committed by her employers in 1933, there was a six-week delay between the HNA's declaration that she was cured and her release from the hospital.[24] Delays seem to have been even more protracted for patients in rural hospitals because of the greater difficulty of bringing outside inspectors and patients together.[25]

Since the hospitals were overcrowded and unsanitary, prolonged stays, whether medically necessary or not, jeopardized the health and safety of the inmates. After a two-week delay following a finding by the medical examiners that he was mentally competent, Francisco N. addressed himself to the court:

> On December 28 [1946] medical examiners determined that I was cured, and ready to be released. As is public knowledge, we [hospital patients] are crammed together and poorly fed. I request my speedy release. Remaining in the hospicio during this past month has caused me irreparable damage.[26]

Francisco's complaint about the situation of the hospital is consistent with official reports of deterioration in all national mental health facilities.

The weak legal oversight also made it difficult for patients to maintain control over property and personal finances. The absence of full civil rights for women and the tradition of depositing female relatives may have made women more susceptible to these sorts of abuses.[27] Although María, who had been confined to the HNA by a brother in 1921, had hired an attorney, she reported to the court that she had been unable to protect either her assets or her dependents from this same brother, with whom she had lived after the death of her husband. In a 1925 correspondence to a judge, María, who was now out of the hospital complained that her brother had only visited her once during her time at the HNA and that he had tried to hide his place of residence from her. She was now living with the godparents of her son Carlos and not, as her brother claimed, with people of "questionable morality." During her confinement

> ... [m]y furniture, clothes, etc., although modest, in the period when I was interned were worth that sum that I have indicated; but as my brother failed to take proper inventory of them, my brother can say and claim whatever he wishes.

The brother's possible theft of her property was made worse by his behaviour towards her children. She was thankful that her brother had sent three of the children to a children's home,

> ... but I would have appreciated it more if he had done the same with my eldest daughter Juana, whom he preferred to keep at his side for reasons unknown to me, first as a servant of a lawyer, and then and now in his own house. I do not know in what conditions or with what design she remains there.

She requested that the daughter be returned to her care.[28]

One of the most commonly acknowledged explanations for the legal complications was the inherent flaw in the civil code. The civil code only covered the institutionalization of persons already under the supervision of a judge; there was no legal procedure for emergency short-term hospitalizations.[29] Legal delays may have also resulted from hospitals' policies that only the authority requesting hospitalization had the power to terminate it. For example, Article 67 of the regulations of the Hospicio stated that a person who had been sent to the hospital by public authorities could only be released on order of those same authorities.[30] This often produced situations where patients were essentially lost in an ambiguous space between the courts and the hospitals.[31]

Many doctors also expressed concern that even when the civil code and hospital regulations were followed, insanity and commitment proceedings, as with most legal proceedings, were conducted through written documents and not with oral presentations.[32] As a result, the person in question rarely came before a judge. Worse still, in some cases the public defender never met the person whose interests they were supposed to be protecting. The system of dealing with determinations of insanity entirely through paper tended to encourage the courts to simply rubber stamp the findings of medical examiners.[33] In the late 1940s, the minister of the newly created Ministry of Public Health noted that the problem persisted:

> Under the actual system, the mentally ill person, represented totally by the guardian, cannot speak before the judge. As it is,

> if the ill person does not have a well-intentioned guardian who brings him or her before the judge, the latter will not have the opportunity to hear from the patient.[34]

The matter was also of concern to patients. Celia B., confined to a private hospital by her parents in 1949, pleaded in vain with the presiding judge that she be allowed to present herself before the court to demonstrate her sanity.[35]

The technical problems of the civil code were aggravated by the material condition of the hospitals. Overcrowding made it difficult for public hospitals to keep up with the paperwork necessary to follow the letter of the law, even by the late nineteenth century, when overcrowding was relatively less extreme.[36] In a case that was probably quite typical, the director of the HNA complained to a presiding judge in 1946 that, while he was able to serve as guardian of a patient's physical well-being, he could not assume similar responsibilities for her property due to his institution's enormous caseload.[37] And even when hospital administrators expended a sizeable amount of time communicating the status of patients to the courts, they seem to have always been falling behind because of shortages of nursing, administrative, and medical staff.[38] By the 1930s, it was not uncommon for the urban hospitals to have only one doctor for every three hundred patients, and in rural institutions, there were often five hundred patients for a single doctor. (See Chapter 3.) Left on their own, orderlies and nurses signed off on medical and legal documents.[39] The Argentine legal system was also so notoriously overburdened that following the strictures of the civil code may have been impossible, especially in cases where immediate hospitalization was deemed urgent. In rural areas, there was an even greater shortage of both judges and doctors with psychiatric training.[40]

The legal and administrative vacuum, however, meant that hospitals exercised tremendous de facto authority over their patients, especially in cases where hospitalization had occurred "outside" of the law (that is, where the courts' involvement was minimal or nonexistent). Most importantly, because of the absence of independent oversight, the hospitals could and did make decisions about what the outside world learned about the internal workings of the institution. In cases of violence, for example, administrators often had the discretion as to whether or not to contact outside authorities. Available evidence suggests that the *Señoras Inspectoras* were probably more diligent in serving as outside monitors of the HNA than the oft-disparaged Advisory Commission on Regional Hospitals and Asylums. If the latter body had inspectors, they were never mentioned in any of the available documentation.[41] Obviously, in many cases, the hospitals dutifully reported incidents such as suicides or attempted suicides.[42] Similarly, the HNA duly reported the case of Angela L. de D., who was erroneously sent to the morgue while still alive, only to die a few hours later.[43]

In some cases, however, the hospitals jealously guarded their prerogative to investigate and take action as they saw appropriate. Such was the case in the infamous 1902 murder of Hospicio patient Saverio Tallarico. Initially, the police had been under suspicion for the murder, since the Italian immigrant had been in their custody prior to his transfer to the Hospicio. Eventually, however, three Hospicio employees were fingered in the crime. It was not just the murder itself that aroused public consternation, but the Hospicio's refusal to provide a prompt and accurate account of the events. There was also a great deal of dismay as to how there could have been confusion about where the man received his fatal blows. After all, patients admitted to the hospital were supposed to receive a thorough physical and mental evaluation upon admission.[44] For the working class press, the murder of Tallarico confirmed that asylums and prisons, and the men who worked in them, were all cut from the same cloth. Echoing criticisms of the hospitals in the 1890s, the Rosario-based paper *Solidaridad* observed in the month before the true culprits had been fingered:

> Tallarico was killed by the legendary brutality of the police or of the *loqueros* [asylum workers], or by both at the same time.
>
> The spirit of class solidarity obliges doctors, *loqueros*, and the police to cover for each other.
>
> Asylums, hospitals, and similar institutions, serve to eliminate society's castaways through hunger, mistreatment, etc. and to experience in living flesh all of the exaltations of the doctors minds that suffer from the monomania of Glory.[45]

Almost four decades after the Tallarico case, an even deadlier tragedy occurred at the Hospicio. In August 1939, two nurse orderlies poisoned four recently admitted patients, three of whom died the next day. Although the police were brought in to investigate, the director, Gonzalo Bosch, stymied efforts by the press to learn more about the nature of the case and what it might reveal about conditions in the hospital.[46]

The physical and financial well-being of patients was also compromised by practices designed to restrict patients' contact with the outside world.[47] Visitation rules, created in the early twentieth century to help the hospitals maintain order and to assist in the recuperation of the patient, limited patients' ability to communicate to the outside world. At the HNA, for example, before 1935, families could only visit relatives during the work week.[48] And even with the advent of mental hygiene, with its emphasis on the family, visitation remained highly restrictive.[49] Perhaps more telling was that the hospitals reserved the right to censor patient mail. Although it was often done in the interest of sheltering patients from disturbing images or family problems, there was no outside authority regulating the practice.[50]

Patients also seemed to have little or no way to resist being transferred to distant hospitals. At the HNA, those who received neither visits from family nor letters were generally the first to be forcibly sent to the Oliva Asylum.[51] Patients who came from outside Gran Buenos Aires, and especially those deemed "tranquil" in comportment, were also likely candidates for transfer.[52]

As with confinement, legal norms for transporting patients did exist – a court had to finalize judgments of insanity on patients before they could be sent to Oliva – but compliance was weak.[53] As a result, many patients experienced often protracted delays in their release once they had been sent to Oliva. These bureaucratic tangles were often the product of confusion about what entity maintained responsibility for the patients. In many cases, for example, authority over the patient remained in the hands of either the HNA or a *porteño* court, whereas the patient herself was residing in Córdoba. The confusion was magnified when families were far from their hospitalized relatives. Many families no doubt lost contact with relatives who had been transferred to the Oliva from the HNA.[54]

Clearly the hospitals were unprepared for the administrative logistics that transfers entailed. The HNA had not even formulated a policy when it first began sending women to Oliva. (What the policy of the Hospicio was is not clear.) It was only in April 1915, that the president of the Society of Beneficence, Elena Napp de Green communicated to a *señora inspectora* that "in the future, patients of the HNA who have family in the capital *not* be sent to the asylum at Oliva."[55] The policy was spurred by the complaint of Rosa F. regarding the involuntary transport of her relative, María F.[56] José Esteves, medical director of the HNA observed that, in the case of María F., she

> ... [h]as been in this hospital for 7 consecutive years and in this long period, her family has visited her but once, just once and has sent her only two letters. Do the *Señoras Inspectoras* believe it fair, that after caring for their relative in this way, that the family should complain that she is sent to Córdoba? I believe that it would be proper to take some means so that she cannot return to this hospital.[57]

Significantly, there is no mention in these communications of whether the patient had an opinion about her transfer to Oliva.

There were also massive legal and administrative tangles involved in releasing transferred patients. In April 1915, President Elena Napp de Green received a communication from the Advisory Commission advising her that María del Socorro L., a transferee from HNA was ready to be released from Oliva.

> I must also state that the referred to patient, entered the Asylum at Oliva [only] as María del Socorro. Once her condition improved, she was able to tell us her last name.[58]

Two issues are particularly striking in this case. First, that the HNA transferred a patient to a provincial hospital without first knowing her last name. Second, although María del Socorro L. had been placed at the Oliva, it appears that responsibility for her release remained in the hands of the HNA administration.[59]

Prisoners and psychiatric patients being transported together in a train in the late 1930s or early 1940s. Source: Archivo General de la Nación.

Patients who came from underserved rural areas to Oliva faced even greater legal neglect. In 1935, Dr. Máximo Agustín Cubas, a staff doctor at the Oliva Asylum, argued that certification of the insane (the formal process of establishing insanity prior to confinement) was plagued by bureaucratic and professional routine and carelessness.[60] Frequently the rural doctors who provided certificates of insanity to the hospitals either did not directly examine the patient prior to signing the papers or had absolutely no training in psychiatric medicine. Moreover, it was not uncommon for family members to deposit someone at the colony and send medical certificates to the director well after the fact, which raised questions about whether a doctor had ever met with the patient.[61]

Poor transportation networks in the countryside also had ramifications for the legal status of patients. In small towns it was common practice to house suspected lunatics in local jails until there was a sufficient number to warrant their collective transport to an asylum. In these cases, police medical inspectors often would simply extend the certificates of insanity to all detainees, regardless of whether their condition remained serious. Cubas went on to note that, as a consequence,

> ... many times individuals arrive [to Oliva] in a state of perfect mental lucidity who may have suffered temporary mental confusion brought on by mere intoxication or similar causes. During their time in jail, which often lasted months, they get better. Yet, because the individual arrived [at the hospital] with a medical certificate of insanity, the hospital is obliged to maintain them for a period of time to make sure the episode is over.[62]

When finally released, the ex-patient would likely face social marginalization and also be a target of police scrutiny, which increased the likelihood of their return to the institution.[63]

Cubas' concern was not, however, solely for the well-being of patients, for, as he observed, without proper legal outlines for hospitalization, doctors and administrators were exposing themselves to legal action by patients or former patients.[64] Conrado O. Ferrer, also a doctor at Oliva, shared this concern about doctors' liability. In a 1938 article he observed that

> ... [b]ecause of the lack of a law of the insane, interned mentally ill persons find themselves deprived of liberty by virtue of guidelines which have been established by practice, but which lack legal force. Thus our current incarceration would be considered a criminal act of arbitrary kidnapping and the directors of hospitals would be sanctioned by the Penal Code.[65]

Ferrer's concern with arbitrary hospitalization reflected both a concern for professional legitimization and patients' rights. Argentine psychiatrists' work was tainted, according to Ferrer, by unscrupulous families, irresponsible police forces, and a shortage of qualified specialists. To save the hospitals and medical practitioners, reform legislation was required.[66]

"Deprived of their liberty without the knowledge of any civil judge": Debates and Proposals

From the 1870s onward, doctors and parliamentarians decried the lack of legal protection for these wards of the state.[67] Many argued that the situation weakened Argentina's claim as a civilized and advanced nation, and pointed out that the republic lagged behind western Europe, the United States, Great Britain, and even some neighbouring republics in providing legal safeguards for psychiatric patients.[68] The absence of proper legal controls over hospitalization was also a matter of professional concern, and many psychiatrists argued that a more workable law would protect them from accusations of wrongful confinements. Despite these concerns, however, Congress did not pass legislation on this matter until the 1980s.

The first attempt to craft legislation for the treatment of the mentally ill came from Emilio R. Coni. One of the founders of the Asistencia Pública for the city of Buenos Aires, Coni's legislative proposal is found in his 1879 Argentine Medical Code. Although the section devoted to psychiatric legislation was never put before congress, it served as the basis for many future proposals. Coni called for regulation of all private and public psychiatric facilities through the offices of the municipal Asistencia Pública. He also developed guidelines for admission and release of patients in order to prevent potential abuses by public authorities or families of patients. Each admission, for example, was to be accompanied by medical certificates, and hospitals were required by law to keep close track of admissions and releases.[69]

As part of their effort to reform the treatment of psychiatric patients, Dr. Antonio Piñero, director of the HNA, and Domingo Cabred, director of the Hospicio, each presented legislation on psychiatric hospitals before Congress in 1894. Piñero called for the creation of a commission to inspect hospitals to better ensure prompt reporting of admissions and releases, since in many emergency hospitalizations, doctors and other public authorities ignored the civil code because there was no time to obtain court sanction. His proposal therefore allowed for persons to be confined prior to a judge's approval, provided that the proper authorities were notified within three days.[70] (When, in 1906, Piñero, now working in private practice, reintroduced the 1894 legislation, he noted the paradox that in Argentina, criminals' due process protections were more secure than that of the mentally ill who were confined to hospitals.[71]) Piñero's 1894 congressional sponsor, deputy Félix M. Gómez, argued that the lack of adequate legislation with regard to the mentally ill might be excused by the relatively late formation of the Argentine state. Nevertheless, Argentina was clearly behind most of the world in terms of the development of comprehensive legislation. Gómez continued:

> We face a problem of our sociability, which is that as many as 98 percent of the insane locked away in our asylums are there illegally. The dispositions contained in Titles X, XI and XIII of the civil code, which pertain to insanity, are dead letter in the majority of cases with regard to the treatment, confinement and the exercise of guardianship of the insane.[72]

For Gómez, the question of national pride was a central concern because in its lack of such legislation Argentina had fallen behind, not only the nations of western Europe, but also the neighbouring republics of Chile and Brazil, as well as the United States.[73] Similarly, deputy Eliseo Cantón, who presented Cabred's proposal argued that Argentina was in the ranks of the more backward nations of eastern Europe, including tsarist Russia.[74]

By the 1920s, overcrowding and decay of public psychiatric hospitals led to heightened scrutiny of patients' rights by both the print media and members of congress.[75] (Critics now recognized that overcrowding contributed to delays in the legal proceedings of patients.) Responding to such concerns, Radical party deputy Leopoldo Bard offered legislation in 1922 to regulate confinement and treatment in psychiatric institutions. His proposal allowed for a variety of confinements, including emergencies, while it also sought to guarantee the physical safety and civil rights of patients. Influenced by a broader eugenic discourse, however, Bard argued that the national government was obliged not only to protect the property, reputation, and civil rights of the presumed insane, but also to safeguard citizens from the mentally ill who, because of family resistance or loopholes in the laws, evaded psychiatric confinement.[76]

Hospital conditions also motivated national deputy Guillermo R. Fonrouge to request in September 1926 that the government investigate the legal status of patients held in national psychiatric facilities. Fonrouge pointed to the lack of regulatory statutes or procedures for the hospitals, as well as to rumours of husbands using hospitalization to punish their wives. Rather cryptically, Fonrouge cited a "semi-official" report that calculated that of the "3,700 patients at the Hospicio de las Mercedes, 80 percent, that is, around 3,000 have been deprived of their liberty without the knowledge of any civil judge."[77]

Ironically, many doctors and critics argued that it was the vast network of unregulated private hospitals which had the least legal oversight of their patients. The issue came to the public's attention when a wealthy businessman was confined to a private clinic by his son in 1928. The confinement did not proceed quietly and the father's employees and other businessmen started a boisterous campaign to free the man.[78] The following September, national deputy Aníbal Mohando cited the case when he proposed a bill to regulate the practice of medicine in private psychiatric clinics. Mohando observed that while the probity of these doctors was beyond question, nevertheless, "these clinics operate with complete liberty of action, without any efficient control by the National Department of Hygiene."[79] Many of these private institutions were staffed by, and often under the directorship of, doctors who also worked in state-run hospitals. In later years, critics would claim that the private clinics' guarantee of absolute discretion was critical to their financial success.

Defending the Nation and the Profession: Psychiatry and Social Defence

Despite frequent indictments of the hospitals' legal practices, psychiatrists were far from united on the issue of how to protect the rights of their patients. For some, the question of professional privilege and the tension between institutional transparency and medical confidentiality complicated the issue of court involvement in hospitalizations. In a December 1926 newspaper editorial, Adolfo M. Sierra, a well-regarded psychiatrist, criticized the various legislative proposals of Bard, Fonrouge, and Mohando. One of his principal arguments was that obliging doctors to communicate hospitalizations violated the penal code's rule of medical confidentiality. Anyone claiming wrongful confinement could have legal recourse to the penal code's kidnapping statute. Optimistically, Sierra concluded that psychiatric patients already enjoyed adequate legal protection under existing statutes.[80]

In a later essay, Sierra observed that the major problem was the absence of regulations guiding admissions to private clinics. By contrast, Sierra noted that confinement to public facilities was characterized, in fact, not by lawlessness, but by excessive legal formalism.[81] At the Hospicio and its Colony, for example, "there is a lawyer, on salary, who exercises *a priori* the function of guardian of the hospitals' patients; said lawyer must give notice of all confinements to the corresponding judge." At the state-run HNA, in contrast, there was no lawyer; instead the director of the establishment served as the patients' guardian and had to report their confinement within twenty-four hours to the judge.[82]

Many in the legal and medical professions concurred with his underlying assumption that the essential legal question of the mentally ill was how to protect society from their potential threat. Such a view may have been encouraged both by psychiatry's close professional and institutional links to criminology and penology and their shared interest in how to confront the threats of anarchism, immigration, and degeneration. By the early twentieth century, major legal and medical journals advocated a sort of "medicalization" of crime and of the criminal. Emblematic of this approach was the revision of the 1921 criminal code, which stipulated that "offenders should be subjected to psychological and medico-legal evaluation of their degree of dangerousness."[83]

The reform of the criminal code to encompass notions of dangerousness was part of a broader effort to infuse the legal system with notions of "social defence," a medico-legal concept that envisioned that jurisprudence would shift from a focus on "free will" to one that centred on "degrees of responsibility, linked to dangerousness." Implicit in this movement was a desire to essentially medicalize criminal law and to allow courts to "quarantine" socially and politically threatening individuals who may or may not have been found guilty of a specific crime.[84] It was the responsibility of the state, therefore, to protect its populace from persons who posed a biological, criminal, or moral threat to society. Confinement or other punishment was not, however, based on guilt, sin, or intent but on the individual's inherent threat to society.[85] The trajectory of this line of thinking ran back as far as the late 1890s but was revived by growing anxiety over immigration and other social changes.[86] While the rhetoric of social defence encouraged fairly extreme proposals, there was an underlying misplaced optimism by its advocates that the national state would take up their cause and support their work, something which for the most part did not occur.

The theoretical link between medical and social pathology was clearly established in the medico-legal study of anarchists, especially following the 1909 assassination of the Buenos Aires chief of police by a Russian-born anarchist.[87] However, even before the 1902 Residency Law, anarchism had been targeted by police and the courts. Doctors had participated in these efforts by attempting to demonstrate the medico-legal dimensions of anarchism. While some, including the Italian-born doctor Pietro Gori, had argued that anarchism was a product of social conditions, others, including José Ingenieros, considered anarchism as a product of individual and collective suggestibility. Although no one ever presumed to connect the ideology to specific mental pathologies, psychiatrists did contemplate its relationship to race, ethnicity, heredity, and even climate.[88]

Emblematic of the intractable link between madness and anarchism was the curious and bloody case of Esteban Lucich. In November 1924,

Lucich, a Yugoslav-born anarchist who had recently been transferred from the Ushuaia Penitentiary, murdered a police officer who was a patient at the Hospicio. (The police officer had been confined to the Hospicio after murdering another anarchist activist.)[89] For his part, Lucich's criminal career had commenced when he murdered a Hospital Rivadavia doctor in 1919. (Lucich murdered another Hospicio doctor in October of 1932.)[90] Not surprisingly, Alberto Bonhour's 1941 thesis on the murder of doctors by patients devotes a great deal of attention to the Lucich case. For Bonhour, the case provided clear confirmation of José Ingenieros' admonition that "the mad can be divided into two groups, by their reactions, into less dangerous madmen and more dangerous madmen. Therefore, none are 'inoffensive,' and all require vigilance."[91] Such attitudes survived well into the twentieth century, although they grew less prevalent. (See Chapter 6.)[92] While these ideas were common in Argentine psychiatric journals, most of which dedicated a large portion of their pages to criminal matters, it is not entirely clear how such influences shaped day-to-day medical practices.

Of course, in some cases, persons who were later deemed insane had engaged in dangerous behaviour that attracted the attention of law enforcement. In 1917, the Buenos Aires police sent Pedro O. to the Hospicio for disorderly conduct after they found him on the street screaming "they are going to kill me."[93] Catalina F., a twenty-year-old single Spanish maid, was picked up by the police and sent to the HNA after she was found "screaming and dancing in the street."[94] Samuel J., a thirty-four-year-old Czech, found himself in the Hospicio after disrobing in public. He claimed that spirits were chasing him, giving him cocaine and trying to poison his food.[95] Gustavo N., a fifty-year-old Argentine, was arrested and hospitalized after firing a pistol in public. The examination reported that he claimed that he had fired the pistol out of fear that someone was going to murder him and that he had heard conversations in which people had expressed the desire to eliminate him.[96] Russian-born Rodolfo G. was likewise confined to the Hospicio in 1932 after screaming in public with a pistol in his hand and a knife in his belt.[97] No doubt such cases fuelled both public and professional attitudes about the correlation between criminality and madness.

Yet perhaps the single most important factor that reinforced the conceptual link between danger and madness was the shortage of psychiatric facilities. As a result, public authorities, especially in rural areas, were often obliged to temporarily confine the mentally ill in common jails. Some individuals spent long periods of time in such places before being transferred to a hospital. [98] As such, the pathways that led many persons to confinement in the asylum often involved the participation of the police. Saverio Tallarico, who was murdered by Hospicio staff in 1902, had initially been arrested for a minor infraction. Prior to arriving at the Hospicio, Tallarico already had passed through three different jails.[99]

The conceptual criminalization of the insane was also encouraged by doctors' anxiety about the complete absence of specialized institutions to confine people with so-called borderline conditions, such as the "feebleminded." Doctors' awareness of the problem was itself a product of the close attention that they paid to developments in North America and Europe, where elaborate networks of institutions for such populations had proliferated.[100] From a scientific standpoint, the feebleminded were the clearest example of a diagnostic category encompassing criminality and madness.[101] Dr. José Belbey, a forensic doctor in the province of Buenos Aires, offered clear proof of the connection in a 1937 essay.[102] Despite admitting to uncertainty as to its precise definition and aetiology, Belbey described the feebleminded thus:

> It is his mode of conduct that announces the existence of a problem. The environment acts strongly upon them; they oscillate in accord with the spiritual and moral climate that surrounds them. They are suggestible to a high degree, like weather vanes moved by the wind. They do not think much or deeply about that which comes before them and as a result make foolish decisions.[103]

As with the morally insane, the feebleminded were predisposed towards criminal behaviour. Belbey cited a study from the capital of Buenos Aires that had examined a thousand arrestees. Thirty per cent were characterized as feebleminded, degenerate, or otherwise mentally deficient.[104]

The problem for the criminologically minded psychiatrist was not so much the existence of this population as the absence of specialized institutions for their containment. Indeed, by the 1930s doctors had started to express pronounced anxiety about the dangers of Argentina's large population of non-institutionalized insane. This vague and amorphous population, whose location and numbers were unknown, emerged as a consistent theme in both psychiatric and popular literature, spurred on in part by doctors' newfound fascination with statistics. In 1931 Gonzalo Bosch complained in a small book about the widely acknowledged problem of the lack of precise statistical information on the number of mentally ill.[105] What was known was that in 1930 there were fourteen thousand persons in Argentine institutions, or 1.26 of every thousand Argentines. Taking into account both a rise in the general population and an increase in the incidence of insanity, Bosch allowed that there theoretically *could* be between forty-three and fifty-four thousand insane and mentally retarded in Argentina.[106] But a conservative estimate of two "defectives" per thousand persons translated into a total population of twenty-four thousand. Therefore, Bosch concluded

> ... at least 10,000 insane receive absolutely no psychiatric care and if we take into account the fact that all the public hospitals hold a number of patients that surpass their capacity, the problem of care for the insane takes on tragic proportions that are a disgrace to our national culture.[107]

Bosch pointed to the low rate of confinement as a symbol of the country's disgraceful lack of regard for the welfare of its citizens.[108]

Ironically, while Bosch had sought to elicit sympathy for the mentally ill, his pamphlet took on a life of its own, and journalists, politicians, and medical practitioners selectively used his calculations to raise the alarm about the number and threat of the non-institutionalized mad.[109] Three years after the publication of his book, for example, the popular weekly magazine *Caras y Caretas* featured Bosch in an article and photographic essay on the Hospicio entitled "Forty Thousand Lunatics on the Loose: A visit to the Hospicio de las Mercedes."[110] It reported as fact that "[a]ccording to statistics, we have 40,000 lunatics wandering about the streets. The majority of delinquents are not criminals. They are ill. They are the 40,000 lunatics that walk about free."[111] While paying lip service to Bosch's humanitarian concerns, the reporter claimed that each one of those forty thousand represented a potential bomb that could explode at any moment.[112]

Others in the medical community shared this more pessimistic interpretation. In his suggestively titled "Mental Hygiene-State Action for the Improvement of the Race" of 1935, Arturo Ameghino, a Hospicio doctor, argued that, while Europe could eliminate the degenerate through the natural selection of war, the strain of subsistence, overpopulation and misery, and emigration, Argentina "has open doors, and it is enough to recall that the simple mix of races can produce degeneration, to understand the danger posed by these regenerative wastes."[113] Worse still, Ameghino saw the decision to emigrate as determined largely by the lack of social adaptability of the emigrant.[114] Whereas the nations of Europe enjoyed hospitalization rates of between three and seven per thousand, in Argentina it was a lowly 1.3 per thousand – a figure that had risen slightly since Bosch's essay was published.[115] Argentina's large number of *alienados libres* (non-institutionalized insane), made it urgent to build more hospitals as a means of social policing. At the same time, existing hospitals were overcrowded.[116] For Ameghino, the country's lax immigration control was at the centre of a problem that had reached the level of absurdity.

> I myself was involved in such a case several years ago. A Rumanian was detained for suspicious activity in the secretariat of the presidency of the Nation. They learned that he had gone there to demand several million pesos from the government. He was then sent to my hospital service where I learned the following troubling fact: during a trip to his country of origin, he attacked the Argentine consul in Bucharest; thus the police knew that the incident involved a naturalized Argentine citizen and they "repatriated" him.[117]

Clearly the national state needed to subsidize the work of the Mental Hygiene League, as it had with other social welfare organizations, if there was to be any hope of effective mental prophylaxis. Yet Ameghino was also skeptical of mental hygiene's decided bias in favour of the rights of the insane. He urged updating earlier social control measures, including those against foreign-born pimps and the expulsion law of 1902, to facilitate the systematic weeding out of Argentina's insane population. Key to its success was the implementation of stricter immigration controls such as those that had been issued in the United States between 1921 and 1927.[118]

Such general anxiety about the non-institutionalized insane motivated national deputy Carlos Pita, who cited Bosch's book in 1941 to argue in favour of the construction of more hospitals, and also noted that since the book's publication, World War II had broken out.[119] As during World War I, the global conflict raised concerns about the numbers of mentally imbalanced who would come to Argentina at the conflict's conclusion.[120]

For many concerned doctors and politicians, the solution to the multiple challenges posed by the mentally ill was the passage of a national social defence law that would facilitate the confinement of persons predisposed to crime because of medical or psychiatric conditions. Such proposals had occasionally been made since the early twentieth century but became more comprehensive, and scientific, by the 1920s.[121] The neurologist Manuel Obarrio, who helped run the external clinic at the HNA, called for the detention of persons who, because of behaviour or past psychiatric problems, were considered to pose a potential threat to society.[122] In the presentation of the law, the bill's sponsor expressed interest both in protecting individuals from wrongful confinement and closing loopholes that allowed the insane to remain in society. The proposal, which never passed into law, included preventive detention of the insane, drug-addicted, and feebleminded and the obligatory denunciation by doctors and public officials of such individuals. The bill also contemplated the creation of a National Registry of the Insane, the Disabled and the Drug-addicted.[123]

Such efforts were undoubtedly encouraged by laws and practices in Europe and North America that had facilitated the confinement of the feebleminded. Soon after the passage of such a law in Republican Spain in 1933, Madrid law professor Luís Jiménez de Asúa argued in an Argentine journal that such laws in fact supported the rule of law and stable liberal governments. By his logic, since local police routinely pushed vagrants from city streets, laws were needed to give sanction to what de Asúa saw as necessary. Furthermore, de Asúa noted that every society had a right to defend itself through legal channels against potentially dangerous persons, even if they had not committed a crime.[124]

While the mental hygiene model sought to solidify ties between family and patients, social defence advocates saw the family as a potential impediment to the orderly confinement and treatment of persons deemed mentally ill. Leopoldo Bard's 1922 bill on the mentally ill cited the case of a mentally ill man who assaulted a doctor on several occasions. "The police intervened, but could do nothing as the family of the lunatic refused to hospitalize him."[125] José M.L. Vega, in his 1946 study on crime and mental illness, shared a similar negative view of families. "[C]onfinement to sanatoriums and asylums of non-delinquent insane is done by family members who have the power to withdraw the subject at any given moment, even when it goes against the opinion of doctors and may pose a danger to the patient." After all, he argued "[i]t is very human that the relatives let their affective impulses guide them ... oblivious that they are allowing back into their home and into the core of society an individual who poses a latent threat."[126] Vega encouraged the reform of the Penal Code to allow the obligatory confinement of anyone with a strong "probability of having antisocial behavior" and to reduce the power of families in such cases.[127]

There was also serious discussion about the merits of developing a system to identify, register, enumerate, and monitor all of Argentina's suspected lunatics, and especially those who had recently immigrated.[128] These proposals were not mere fantasy any more, since by 1933 the National Office of Identification issued identification cards, to all citizens.[129] A 1942 proposal advocated obligatory denunciation to public authorities by doctors of anyone thought to be suffering from a mental illness.[130] Other proposals were explicit in drawing a clear line between unregulated immigration as the source of Argentina's social problems.[131] In 1942, Dr. Raúl Ocampo Oromi wrote an essay calling for better inspections at ports of entry. He argued that Argentina was

> ... [a] vain country that received 200,000 to 300,000 immigrants annually, with hospitality without measure, without racial prejudice or xenophobic caution. Argentina received, at the cost of her interior peace, the exalted anarchist, the *mafiosa*,

> the vagabond, the mentally imbalanced, the potential lunatic, the psychopath, the psychoneurotic, the epileptic, etc.[132]

Even during the war, Ocampo Oromi claimed, the Argentine government was attempting to give asylum to European immigrants, in blatant disregard to the precepts of social prophylaxis.[133] Clearly then, Argentina required neuro-psychiatric inspection at ports to "avoid, in our opinion, the overrunning of the Republic with people who cannot adapt, vagabonds, lazy people, bums incapable of the least effort, much less work of any sort."[134]

Calls for immigration control inevitably turned on the question of identifying defective newcomers. Psychiatrist Bringas Núñez noted that, although the law prohibited the admission of the insane into Argentina, "they enter anyway, many in *flor de locura* [a state of imminent madness]." In sum, it was easy for borderline cases, or those whose outward symptoms were in remission, to enter the country undetected. Although many of these individuals would find their way to a state-run facility, many would not. Therein lay another danger.

> By contrast, the predisposed, the incipient lunatic, the silent carriers of constitutional and infectious traits [*taras*], those with drug addictions, etcetera, as they are capable of exercising their civil rights, will incorporate into national life. And in that life, in the midst of the favorable conditions that this society offers, they will transmit to their descendents the germ plasm of their madness or delinquency.[135]

Since the end of World War I, psychiatrists had grown concerned about war's impact on recent immigrants to Argentina. Bringas Núñez, for example, suggested that the damage done to these individuals probably explained why the ratio of immigrants in hospitals did not drop faster during lulls in immigration.[136]

Conclusion

In spite of the mountain of evidence to the contrary, much of it supplied by psychiatrists themselves, psychiatrist Nerio Rojas asserted in his classic medical-legal textbook from 1959:

> The practice of confinement, inspection of establishments, the situation of the psychiatric patient, hospitalized or not, but not the interdicted, are not legislated here. It is a sad state of affairs, which is usually overcome for good or bad, thanks to regulations or the good faith or honesty or experience of doctors and family.[137]

While expressing faith that those with the power to confine would exercise it responsibly, the book's author dismissed as hyperbolic the notion that wrongful confinement frequently occurred:

> I will not bother discussing the supposed 'abduction' of sane people, another of the popular prejudices favored particularly by lucid insane persons whose psychosis is unknown or denied by him and by his friends or family who often work from their own interests.[138]

Had a patient read these words, he or she would have wondered what hospitals Rojas had visited to come to such optimistic conclusions.

Despite protestations to the contrary, involuntary psychiatric hospitalization in Argentina was governed more by the whims and vagaries of a poorly funded medico-legal bureaucracy than by an efficient state apparatus.[139] The legal status of patients, therefore, provides an important perspective into the day-to-day operations of the Argentine state and compels us to reconsider both the capacity of state functionaries to exercise diligence over citizens and the relationship of social reform rhetoric to everyday practices. For several generations of scholars, Michel Foucault's description of the Panopticon – a prison design that allows the guards to carefully monitor each prisoner – has been an attractive metaphor to explain the historical experience of psychiatric patients.[140] The Argentine patient, however, suffered not only from the burden of psychiatric scrutiny but also from invisibility and abandonment. The Hospicio and the HNA, as well as rural institutions, were places where patients' lives were controlled, not through a bureaucratically efficient system, but by the application of very particular, and often isolated, expressions of power.

The failure of successive governments to pass comprehensive legislation or to enforce existing laws to protect the mentally ill was consistent with the overall history of social legislation during the twentieth century.[141] But the failure to regulate hospitalization was probably not born out of some nefarious plan to deny immigrants their rights, or to exercise fiscal constraint. First and foremost, it was widely acknowledged that private hospitals were even more negligent in legal matters than were public institutions. The directors and clinicians of these private clinics were quite often the very same men who ran the public hospitals or served as court-appointed medical examiners. The financial success of these clinics was heavily premised on guarantees that strict medical confidentiality would be maintained, something that a court proceeding necessarily negated. Doctors' multiple professional loyalties, therefore, gave further incentive for them to resist interference from the state.[142]

Yet economic self-interest was surely not the sole source of the medical community's ambivalence about overhauling the system (and we should note that bureaucratic and judicial systems are never easy to change!). The Mexican case, as discussed by María Cristina Sacristán, is suggestive. Like Argentina, Mexico did not have a comprehensive law to monitor hospitalization, but only civil interdiction. In Mexico, however, doctors argued that excessive legalism would impede the free flow of patients into, and out of, hospitals. If the scrutiny of the courts was automatically brought to bear in each hospitalization, well-intentioned families might balk out of fear that they would never see their relative again; if psychiatry was to win the confidence of the Mexican public, hospitalization needed to be completely divorced from the legal system.[143] Lax legal oversight therefore may have afforded some benefit to patients in countries like Argentina and Mexico, where the legal regimen was relatively weak. Certainly the complaints of Argentine doctors would suggest that many families did indeed exercise their de facto right to withdraw relatives from the asylums. Sometimes they did it within days of confining a family member.

If legal protections for the presumed insane were weak, so too was support for passage of laws mandating the forcible monitoring and confinement of those deemed mentally ill. One might conclude, considering what has been written about the huge network of asylums in North America and Europe, that Argentina's population who were labelled as insane derived *some* benefit from living under a negligent state. By contrast, countries with reputations for rule of law and democracy rounded up and confined those deemed insane or otherwise defective with startling efficiency. In the United States, for example, almost twice as many people as in Argentina were confined to hospitals in 1933 – about 2.5 per thousand. And some states, such as New York, had rates of confinement as high as 4.3 per thousand.[144] What is even more striking is the significantly greater expansion of categories of human "defect," including the so-called feebleminded, who were deemed to require institutionalization in places like the United States, and the widespread popular support that it enjoyed.[145]

Ironically, negative public opinion about psychiatrists, a topic about which doctors wrote about often, was probably a product of both their arbitrary, but very real, power to confine and their eugenicist-tinged, but often fanciful, rhetoric about the need confine all of the country's insane. That questions about the undue power of psychiatrists in Argentine society continue to be raised to this day by both laymen and professionals is in some way a product of that curious combination.[146]

5

5: PATHWAYS TO THE ASYLUM, 1900–1946

Hospitalization entailed complex negotiations, involving not just doctors and patients, but also lawyers, judges, families, hospital staff, the police, and neighbours. These interactions ultimately shaped life inside the hospitals. Indeed, as historian Constance McGovern observed more generally, psychiatric hospitals are the site of a "complex vortex of institutional politics, medical theory and practice, career exigencies, doctor-patient interactions, and the perceptions of the public."[1] Of course, in Argentina the influence of families in the confinement process was highly controversial and laid bare doctors ambivalent position toward the family as an institution. No doubt some of that ambivalence was itself a product of the absence of what they considered adequate state support, not only to build and manage institutions for the insane, but to control the influence of outside groups in medical decision making.[2]

Ironically, despite their suspicion of families, as elsewhere in the world, "[a]sylum doctors ... merely confirmed a diagnosis of insanity already made by families, by neighbors, or by non-medical authorities."[3] Part of the reason that doctors listened to the explanations of petitioners, and especially family members, was because psychiatric discourse was never isolated from the social context. Indeed, oftentimes psychiatric diagnoses were produced out of an amalgam of scientific observation and pre-existing social values.[4] Whether motivated by professional duty, familial affection, or some dishonest goal, petitioners needed to know the language of psychiatry and be able to call attention to the "boundaries of incarcerable behaviors" which would justify an internment.[5] Those boundaries were primarily defined around psychiatric and lay notions of familial duty and responsibility. Patients, families, and other petitioners and doctors all negotiated hospitalization through these terms and frequently invoked domestic strife, neglect of housework and family well-being, and immorality to argue for or against a confinement. Patients also displayed a remarkable awareness of the intersections between familial and psychiatric discourse and deployed the appropriate language when trying to gain their release from confinement.

Although the family was the most common site of these conflicts, psychiatrists and their supporters, including the Society of Beneficence, frequently extolled the traditional domestic sphere as the foundation of both individual health and national well-being.[6] A 1905 medical journal article on suicide, for example, warned readers not to dismiss too quickly the notion that "marriage is the foundation of all civilized societies."[7] Likewise, a national deputy, in expressing support for a piece of legislation regarding psychiatric hospitals, argued that the family was the "fundamental base" of Argentine society.[8] Belief that marriage and family were the bedrock of social harmony and individual well-being was confirmed by studies that demonstrated that married persons were less likely to commit suicide. For men, family life provided diversions from toxic influences such as prostitution and drinking. For women, by contrast, marriage, but especially motherhood, provided a biological shield against mental illness. The national census of 1914 even predicted that mental illness for women would increase as they "emancipated themselves from the domestic traditions of yesteryear."[9] This belief that the family was a source of moral support and biological protection, and, paradoxically, a toxic influence that had to be contained, shaped how psychiatrists viewed patients and the decision to confine, treat, and release them.

Since the family was the source of moral well-being, however, it needed to be protected from mentally ill relatives whose presence was supposedly a psychic and physical danger. As a 1909 medical thesis on the transmission of madness argued:

> The insane in general, no matter the form of their delirium, should not remain with their families. The probabilities of the transmission of a delirium are much reduced, as much as the patient receives the necessary care from a non-relative.[10]

Similar arguments were made concerning the mentally retarded. At the inauguration of the Torres Asylum, Domingo Cabred reminded the assembled that the mentally retarded were not only incapable of benefiting from regular schools, but that "they also constitute an element of disorder and even of danger for the normal scholastic population."[11] He suggested that such individuals might need lifetime confinement. Similar cautionary notes against allowing the insane to live with the sane continued to appear in professional and popular literature well into the 1940s.[12] The notion of mental illness's "contagiousness" also existed in popular culture. A short story appearing in *Caras y Caretas* in 1925, for example, suggested that contact with "abnormal children" would cause normal people to suffer from depression and anxiety.[13]

Although the mental hygiene movement encouraged psychiatrists to develop good relationships with the families of patients, in their daily practices doctors often viewed families as potentially meddlesome and quarrelsome forces. This attitude was all the more prevalent during periods of acute overcrowding, when doctors became especially sensitive to the possibility that sick individuals were being "dumped" into their care.[14] Curiously, of equal concern was the problem of families who refused to confine their mentally ill relatives.[15] In 1914, the director of the HNA complained that "daily we face numerous persons who refuse to resign themselves to hospitalizing a loved one in the indigent wards and who also lack sufficient resources to place the relative in a private institution."[16] And ironically, even though doctors depended on the collaboration of families, both to bring in patients and to provide information, these same doctors viewed the families of their patients as the hereditary and/or social cause of patients' disorders.[17]

Just as doctors had a wide range of often contradictory attitudes towards families, so too is it difficult to characterize the influence of families in one-dimensional terms. Families sometimes challenged psychiatric competence and sought to extract loved ones from the care of the hospitals or, in many cases, refused to send relatives to the asylums.[18] In other cases, however, they manipulated doctors in order to effect the confinement of someone for whom the hospital was seen as the best resource for their basic care. What is not clear, however, is whether families saw the medical care offered by the hospitals as useful or valid, or whether they saw the hospitals' function as purely custodial. Moreover, it is difficult to discern when hospitalization was being abused by families or neighbors to rid themselves of a troublesome individual.

"Trivialities that lack the consistency of soap": Diagnosing the Mad

The ideas of degenerative heredity provided doctors with a powerful diagnostic framework that was at once ideologically consistent with their attitude toward the family and accessible to the lay public.[19] Faced with essentially "invisible" illnesses, for which there were no objective criterion, degenerative heredity, then, allowed doctors to communicate their expertise to other professionals and state functionaries and to the lay public. Unlike physical illnesses, mental illness was and is diagnosed through subjective interviews. In the period under consideration, doctors were especially keen to acquire their patients' "hereditarian antecedents." These included the medical and moral background of their subjects and their families and could be used to explain past behaviour as well as to predict future behaviour. Doctors were especially interested in tuberculosis, syphilis, alcoholism, mental retardation, loose morals, and of course insanity.[20] And although there was no way to connect the inner workings of the body to behaviour or mental outlook (except in the case of testing for syphilis), doctors did examine the body for "evidence" of a deformed hereditary legacy. Malformed teeth, oddly shaped ears, obesity, and other "markings" were all potential signs to explain "bizarre" behaviours. Degeneration provided a powerful way to confirm a diagnosis, to raise questions about the peril posed by an individual and to suggest their incurability. The term "degenerate" had also entered into the popular lexicon as a way to describe a person who was profoundly, and permanently, ill in either mind or body, or who lacked moral fibre.

If degeneration was discerned through observation of appearance, horrific hospital conditions and the degraded physical state of mostly foreign-born and poor patients no doubt further prejudiced the examining doctors to view them as insane.[21] Such conditions may in part help to explain why doctors were often quick to find evidence of degeneration. In both published case histories and archival sources from hospitals, it is rare *not* to find some mention of a "physical or psychic degenerative stigma" even when doctors could find no familial or physical explanations for the patient's problems.[22] Doctors inspecting a Spanish-born construction worker in 1917, for example, wrote that "morbid antecedents of hereditary or familial origin are not known. Degenerative and neuropathic inheritance are presumed."[23]

If the worldview of degenerative heredity prejudiced doctors toward certain attitudes, its appeal to doctors is understandable. First, there was convincing evidence that certain physical illnesses and traumas, including syphilis, long bouts of fever, and even surgeries could render individuals susceptible to mental imbalance. Second, because of the transient nature of the *porteño* society, doctors often did not have access to the families and friends of patients who might have, in theory, provided them with relevant information about the subjects' earlier medical and social history. In such cases, the physical examination was one of the few resources available for doctors.

When medical examiners met with HNA patient María in December 1921, her brother provided the doctors with her medical background. (Her case is also discussed in Chapter 4.)[24] Paraphrasing the brother, the doctors noted that "this woman has always been strange, dissatisfied and disaffected with family, violent and aggressive since childhood, but that which was normal and bearable while living in matrimony, later became unbearable [upon the death of her husband]." (The doctors incorrectly recorded María as a twenty-two-year-old Spaniard.) Typical of insanity files of the day, the doctors noted that the patient "presents a variety of physical degenerative stigma, including craneo-facial asymmetry, small body and head." Psychically, "she presents herself as indifferent, is tranquil, and stares at the floor." Although she was distracted, doctors conceded that she spoke "easily and with good articulation." María was reticent to speak of her brother or father, whom she accused of theft and plotting to murder her. The doctors concluded that she suffered from "systematized delirium" and was judicially incompetent. In practical terms, the ruling meant that María was not allowed to leave the hospital unless a competent adult, named as her guardian, wished to supervise and care for her.

In February 1922, the HNA reported to the presiding judge that, although "feebleminded," María was fit to leave the hospital. The next month,

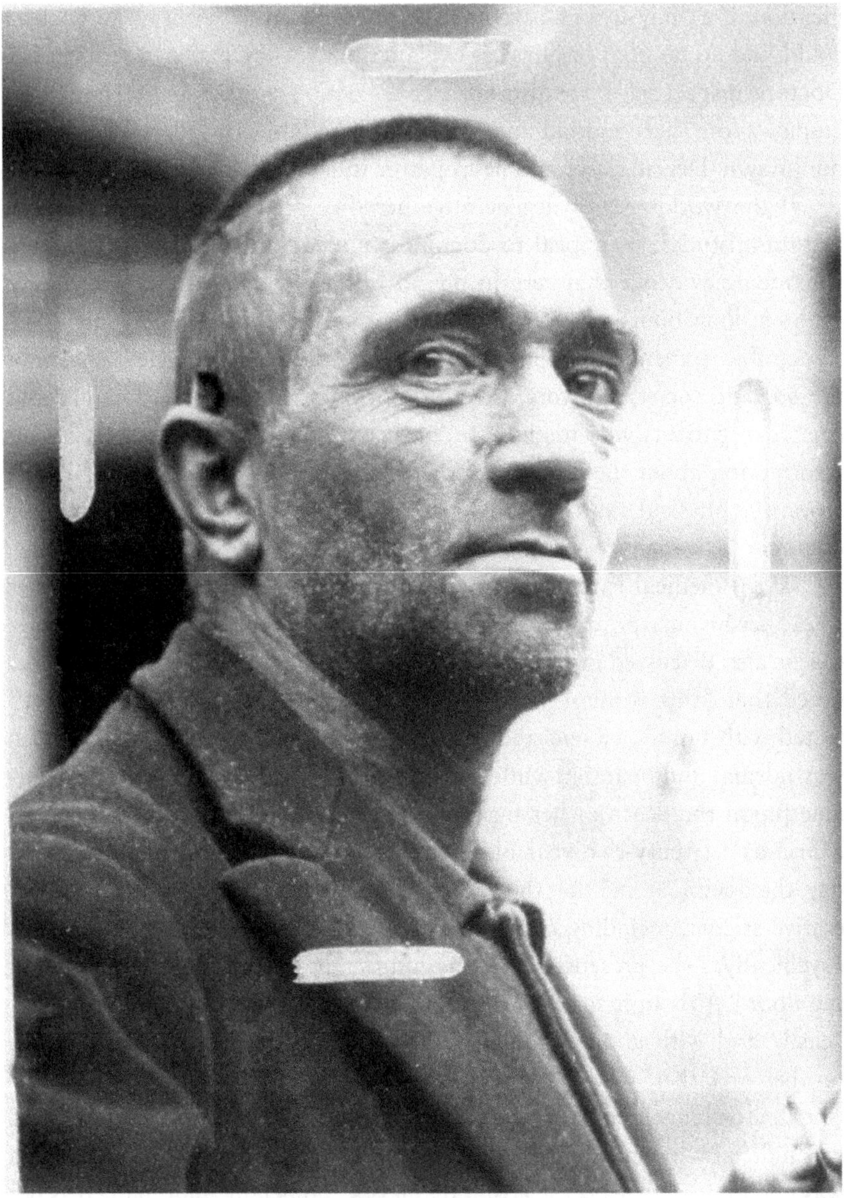

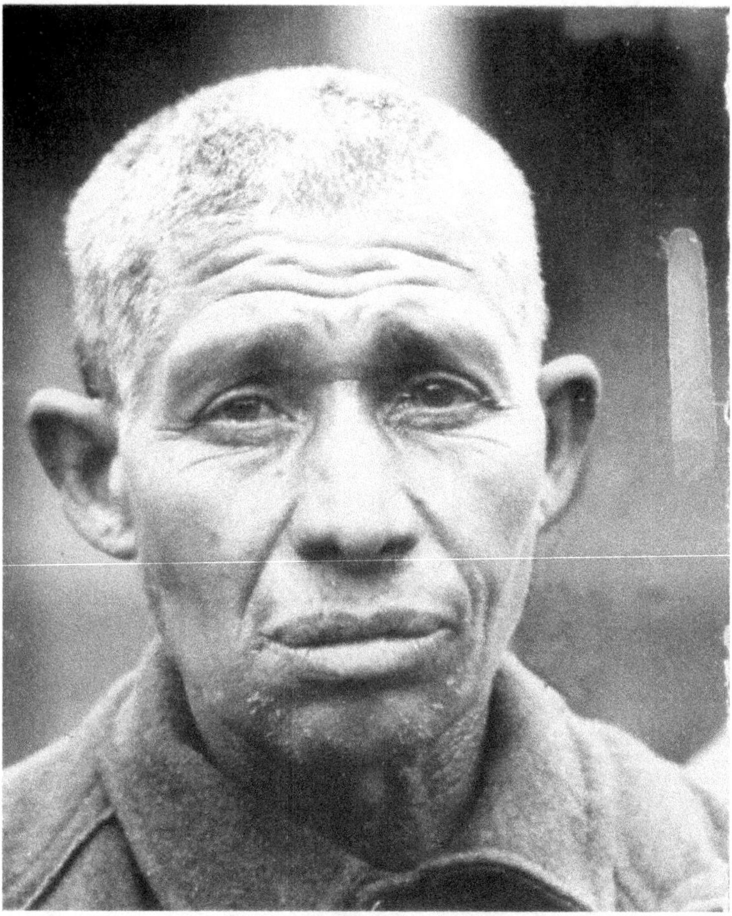

Pictures of Hospicio patients from the article "Forty thousand lunatics on the loose: a visit to the Hospicio de las Mercedes." *Caras y Caretas* 37 (June 23, 1934). Source: Archivo General de la Nación.

court medical examiners visited with María to determine the wisdom of releasing her. In their March 27 report to the judge, Doctors Carro Campo and Gorostiaga referred back to the earlier December 1921 report for any background on her diagnosis. Although her condition had improved, the doctors noted without irony that since María continued to make complaints against her family, she could only return "to the family milieu" if monitored by family members. However, they also determined that she was not well enough to have civil interdiction lifted; she thus remained a legal minor. Despite her obvious conflict with her immediate family, in September 1923 medical director Esteves approved granting guardianship of María's person, family, and possessions to her brother (following the father's death).

Some time during early 1922, María hired a lawyer to help gain her release from the hospital and to have her minority status lifted. In an undated letter to the judge, attorney Eduardo Isla attacked the medico-legal reports that had found his client insane. Isla noted four major areas of contradiction in the reports. First, the report had noted that María was a "violent and aggressive woman since childhood." Yet María "was born in Italy and lived there until adulthood. By virtue of what extraordinary phenomenon could the doctors learn about such incidents in her childhood?" Isla observed that the doctors could not possess such information except as provided by some third party. Isla derided the doctors' mention of the subject's asymmetrical face: "trivialities that lack scientific value in modern psychiatry." With irony, Isla suggested that if everyone with a crooked face were considered mad, "almost all of humanity would be in a state of dementia." With regard to María's disputes with her family, Isla asked who did not have such problems. Finally, Isla noted that the report listed "psychic and physical stigmata" without bothering to specify what they were, or how they related to her condition. Worse, the doctors admitted that the patient had "clear and articulate speech and that her "affective sensibility is normal." "Where, then, is the delirium?" wondered the lawyer. "It seems to be based entirely on the fact that she has crooked ears."

Isla then went on to attack the report in general terms. "It lacked the consistency of soap bubbles." María was not ill, and never had been, and the director of the HNA himself had acknowledged that she was "in condition to be released." The only question that remained was when María's full rights should be restored. Isla concluded that María had suffered from a "delirious episode." According to the law, an episode, by definition brief in duration, did not require guardianship. (Paradoxically, Isla terminated his defence of María by suggesting that "a delirious episode may be either epiletoid or hysteriform and occur most frequently in women.")

Isla's apparent familiarity with, and disdain for, notions of degenerative heredity, suggests the widespread diffusion of the language of heredity. When Alberto C. made a complaint against a fellow tenant for her disturbing behaviour in 1922, he wrote to the judge that "I suffer the annoyances of the mentioned woman who searches me out, and tries to make me look like a degenerate to all the neighbors, accusing me of fantastic crimes...."[25] In 1916, Lorenzo A., a thirty-one-year-old Argentine petty merchant, was interned at the Hospicio at the request of his mother. In November, a medical examination was given to determine whether the mother should gain guardianship. Doctors noted that Lorenzo had an alcoholic father of Italian birth and "a brother who is a 'classic idiot' and has been 'interned' in the same hospital since childhood, serving yearly as a case study for clinical psychiatry courses. All of his other brothers are *inquietos* [restless], and some suffer nightmares."[26] The doctors then quoted the patient, who blamed his own disturbed psyche on a defective inheritance and stated "both of my parents are cancerous."[27]

In many cases, the term "degenerate" seems to have been applied simply to medicalize socially distasteful behaviour. The police sent Ricardo L., a twenty-year-old baker's assistant, to the Hospicio in November of 1921. Doctors diagnosed him with "manic excitation in a degenerate." Medical examiners confirmed and elaborated on the Hospicio report:

> Degenerative type, with observable physical stigmata in the formation of the face and skull, in the irregular placement of the ears, his teeth, etc. ... make us suspect a heavy heredity ... we find a source of weakness in the cerebral-spinal system which in such degenerates has great importance in awakening his delirium as well as masturbatory habits; he confesses with all candor that he frequently masturbates.[28]

They concluded that he was legally incompetent and that he suffered from "mania in a degenerate."[29]

Degeneration also helped doctors to explain the unexplainable. In August 1921, court medical examiners determined that a twenty-one-year-old woman, who was so severely disorientated that they could not communicate with her, had a "nervous temperament, with mild physically degenerative stigmata, that correspond to the psychic realm" and suffered from syphilis.[30] From an unnamed informant, they learned that she had an alcoholic father and a mother and two siblings with mental illness. Although the family background

> ... would suffice to explain her psychosis and determine its causes, keeping in mind the referred to stigmata, perhaps in addition to the hereditary etiological factor, we should also consider the fatal addition of syphilis.

In sum, her psychosis "certainly comes from far back, probably of congenital origin for reasons of the hereditary predisposition."[31]

Doctors believed that trauma or an upsetting situation could unveil a degenerative heredity. This was especially so for women, whose mental equilibrium was believed to be more easily disrupted by emotional challenges. Clara R., a seventeen-year-old domestic worker originally from Spain, was interned at the HNA by the federal police in September 1917. The hospital's communication to the court in the following month noted that "she is a sick person in a state of feeblemindedness, with light mania and puerilism at the root of which lies a surgery that she had two years ago."[32] The doctor recommended her quick release. In November, court doctors conducted an exam in which they established that her problems started after her operation, when she started to experience hallucinations, confusion, loss of memory, and odd conduct. The surgery had served to unveil a decayed family: "[h]er father abused alcohol, her mother is nervous, with an emotional and irritable character, and she has a married brother who is also violent in his reactions and friend to excesses."[33] They also sought and found other signs of her degeneration, including limited intelligence and various mild, but unspecified physical defects.[34]

"The insane woman is much more turbulent than her male counterpart"[35]

Psychiatrists saw evidence of female mental illness in behaviours and attitudes that deviated from a fairly narrow set of expectations about sexuality, reproduction, domesticity, and work. Any word or deed that transgressed the normative role of women could be brought to bear as evidence of mental disturbance. The healthy woman – whether a maid, a daughter, a wife, or a sister – should obey the male head of household or family. Women who accused a male head of household of sexual or physical abuse were therefore often viewed as troubled and troublesome women. Likewise women were expected to attend to domestic duties, abstain from cursing (a practice that was often used to prove a woman's mental imbalance). Mundane behaviours like attending parties, drinking, or dating "inappropriate" men were often mentioned as supporting evidence to confirm a mental imbalance. Yet even as hysteria and puerperal disorders disappeared from the medical lexicon, most doctors continued to look for somatic explanations for women's mental illnesses. Thus, while official hospital reports by the 1930s listed few women as suffering from these conditions, medical examiners continued to focus on women's reproductive organs, menses, and pregnancy to explain a wide variety of psychiatric disorders.[36]

Although much of psychiatric discourse revolved around sexual behaviour, the fundamental target of doctors was the family, an institution which psychiatrists felt duty-bound to defend. While doctors recognized that the male insane could unhinge a family, the threat posed by the female insane was more generalized. Discussion of the threat of the moral insane is instructive. A psychiatrist at the HNA defined "moral insanity:" "it is not simply a disturbance of character, but a true perversion of the instincts, a mental state in which the subject is incapable of acquiring moral sentiments."[37] While men who suffered these traits tended toward public deviance, women expressed it in the home.[38]

> Married, they disturb the order and seriousness of the home with their excessive purchases, with their life of intrigue, with

their lack of honor. Already bad wives, they are even worse mothers, repulsed by children and maternity.[39]

Doctors connected the moral to the physical, especially for women. Their interest, which often bordered on the obsessive, was itself, however, part of a broader effort by the medical profession to demonstrate the physical origins of all mental disorders.[40]

Despite the medical profession's interest in sexual matters, however, directors of the asylums were reticent to turn their institutions into houses of deposit for immoral women, for fear of the corrupting influence of such individuals on the debilitated minds of the majority of the asylum populations. In other words, while immorality could be a sign of madness, many doctors did not necessarily see their institutions as the appropriate place to confine "immoral" women (even if this was the desire of their families).[41]

When court doctors examined Máxima S. in 1907, they made the connection between the physical and the mental. Doctors noted that she had been so traumatized by the stillbirth of a child that she had left her husband and begun to work as a servant. Due probably to her "violent and easily irritated character" she stayed but briefly with a string of employers. Her physical examination revealed the existence of "hystero-genic zones, revealing disturbances common to hysteria."[42] As important as somatic explanations for mental illness were, social factors were equally important. Family or domestic conflict, especially when it involved women who challenged the authority of fathers or husbands, was often seen as evidence of immorality and mental imbalance. After Alberto requested that his neighbour Graciela E. be declared insane (and presumably confined), the police made a report to the judge: "Through our investigation we determined that Graciela E. lives an immoral and libertinous life and thus that she is mentally ill."[43] Although, there is no evidence from the documents that Graciela was institutionalized, the courts removed her daughter from her custody "having determined that she led an irregular life and was unbalanced."[44]

The medical focus on women's sexuality often amplified their precarious social position. The HNA's report to the judge about Rosa, a twenty-five-year-old married Uruguayan, described her as "unbalanced degenerate, psychotic, erotic, with pathological irresistible impulses, pathological liar, perverted, without ethics, cynical, without affect, feeling, and with a weak will because of her overwhelming expectations."[45] Although "tranquil, oriented, lucid and coherent," she suffered from a persecution delirium directed at her father, whom she accused of incestuous relations with both her and her sisters.

Her second hospitalization occurred in 1929, when she was eight months pregnant. While at the public Hospital Alvear, she had fought with nurses and spat on a doctor, whom she threatened. During her subsequent confinement in the HNA, she gave birth. Rosa's behaviour was described as "aggressive and perverse, with continued incidents with other patients." However, soon her behaviour improved. Rosa had become

> ... obedient, docile and helpful ... and no longer externalizes delirious ideas, nor psycho-sensorial traumas. In a correct manner, she rectifies her primitive delirious ideas in which she accuses her father of incest as well as her bad behavior, which she attributes to her prior state of madness and the abnormalities of conduct this time, for her nervous state brought on by pregnancy.[46]

Not only did the doctors not take seriously her accusations against her father, but they required that she "rectify" unpleasant notions relating to sexuality in order to gain her release. In other words, to prove that she was mentally balanced, she had to recant her accusation. Moreover, doctors felt that Rosa's willingness to work in the HNA and docility towards authority were also signs of recovery.

Carolina M. also accused her father of sexually assaulting her. Interned by the police in 1943, there was a delay of four years before her case was reviewed by medical examiners. Their report, of March 10, 1947, reveals how notions of domesticity related to psychiatric thought. Of her antecedents, the examiners noted that "her internment was due to multiple and repeated incidents of bad conduct, culminating in the assault on her father with a pair of scissors and the total abandonment of her chores."[47] As for her personal habits, "according to references she drank up to a litre of wine daily." Initially diagnosed as suffering from paranoid schizophrenia, she was treated with electroshock therapy. Carolina, doctors observed, "is at first sight tranquil, but psychically, she excites very easily." Although she "possessed good attention and memory, and she had quick association of ideas," she was also "reticent, distrustful, egocentric, proud, arrogant and willful." Without comment or question, the doctors duly noted that "she persists in her original accusation against her father who wants to rape her" and that he was "always a brute."[48] In addition, Carolina had the temerity not only to deny that she was ill, but even to request an audience with President Perón to protest her confinement. She also bristled under the doctors' questions. "In the midst of the interview she tells us '[d]on't pester me with your questions because I am not an imbecile.'"[49] As with other cases, resistant or defiant behaviour was taken as further evidence of continued mental imbalance.

In a familiar pattern, however doctors eventually reported that Carolina "recognizes that she had been 'ill with nerves' which reveals a certain consciousness of her formal mental state."[50] Although they concluded that she remained mentally incompetent to manage her own affairs, she could be released to the care of a responsible family member. Her father in May 1947 wrote to state that, as long as his daughter's cure was not more profound, he was not in a position to care for her adequately. Nevertheless, the next month, her father was named guardian, and according to documents of the Defensoría de Menores, he maintained contact with Carolina through fairly regular hospital visits. In October 1948, she was released, and the courts lifted civil interdiction in September 1952.

Doctors believed that both psychiatric and moral traits could be transmitted from parent to child, especially from mothers to daughters. When court doctors examined fifteen-year-old Antonia P. in 1921, they noted that according to the girl's foster family "the only hereditary antecedents that they can provide are that her mother was a prostitute."[51] After observing that Antonia possessed "facial asymmetry and that she had a weak and sickly appearance," the doctors recorded that, according to her family, Antonia had been healthy until her first menses when she "changed character, alternating between laughter and crying, singing and shouting, becomes aggressive and destroys everything in her reach."[52] Her supposed sexual delinquency was confirmed by the fact that she "talks about a boyfriend or lover to whom she has taken a fancy, although she does not know him well, as she has only seen him once from a distance." Antonia had "infantile reasoning, incoherent but revealing a persecutory and erotic base." Their final decision was that Antonia should remain at the HNA, as she suffered from "polymorphous delirium with tendencies towards dementia praecox in a degenerate." Antonia finally gained her release only to find herself returned to the HNA by her foster family. On the second examination, she was referred to as "a feebleminded woman who suffers acute episodes of mental disturbance that would probably evolve into dementia praecox." Her medical diagnosis, and particularly the pessimistic belief that her condition would only further deteriorate, was clearly linked not only to her "sexual" and moral behaviour but to that of her mother.

Yet in many cases doctors ignored the role that life situtations might play in the onset of mental diturbance. Instead they attributed many women's psychiatric disorders to conditions associated with childbirth, lactation, and menstruation.[53] Catalina M. was committed for a third time to the HNA in November 1916. The hospital communicated to the presiding judge that Catalina, a twenty-two-year-old Russian Jew suffered from "an episode of puerperal origin," in which she was "depressed, indifferent, confused, disoriented, and without attention or memory." When court doctors examined Catalina in April 1917, they reported that her life had been full of trauma, including the death of a recently born child and her abandonment by a bigamous husband. Her first symptoms of mental imbalance had presented themselves four months after her marriage, at which point the examiners referred to older medical reports from her first hospitalization; "sadness, silence, staring at the floor, neglect of personal hygiene and chores." At her second hospitalization, she was observed to have been prophesying future wars, mass killings, and the destruction of the universe. At her third stay at the HNA, the doctors noted that, at the time of her examination, she was "tranquil, correct, and attentive."[54]

While medical theory and social norms suggested a close intellectual connection between morality, women's bodies, and mental health, hospital administrations nonetheless often drew a clear distinction between the mentally ill and those who were merely 'immoral'. At the women's asylum, administrators demonstrated a profound anxiety about the hospital becoming a depository for "immoral women," and all of the Society's institutions reserved the right to refuse treatment to such women.[55] This may in part explain why, according to the hospital's official statistics, few known prostitutes entered the HNA.[56]

In one celebrated case, the HNA used concerns about a prospective patient's moral character to *deny* her admission. In 1939, the HNA's director wrote a letter to the *Señoras Inspectoras* of the Society in which he described a patient named Celia Esmeralda D. as a "congenitally amoral person," who acted out anti-social tendencies, publicly discussed with other patients her work as a prostitute, and had escaped several times. The director pleaded with the Society that they work with the courts and the police to prevent the admission of these "perverse women," for whom the HNA had neither separate nor secure facilities. The director also complained that, although the Ministry of Foreign Relations and Religion had authorized the hospital to refuse treatment to such individuals, the hospital lacked a sufficient number of staff to properly screen incoming patients.[57]

If sexuality was at the centre of psychiatric understanding of women, doctors had a much more limited approach to men's sexuality. When men's psychiatric disturbance was in any way connected to sexuality, it was usually based on an act, like masturbation, and not on an attitude. And although the Argentine medico-legal community had a clear fascination with male homosexuality, and believed it, along with lesbianism, to be a sign of mental imbalance, there is at present no evidence that this translated into coordinated efforts to contain such people.[58] It also seems likely that, as with the case of Celia Esmeralda, the asylums would have wished to exclude known homosexuals, in the interest of protecting the rest of the patients, whom they considered to be inherently suggestible.

"She notes that the *patrón* treated her violently": Domestic Servants

One of the most striking patterns that emerge from the insanity documents is the sizable number of female domestic servants (a term that encompasses a wide range of domestic duties) whose employers committed them to the HNA.[59] This is consistent with the inordinate proportion of domestic workers among the general female population and also reflects the occupational breakdown of the HNA's patient population.[60] In the first decade of the twentieth century, the overwhelming majority of female patients were employed in some form of domestic work; what percentage of them lived permanently with their employers, however, cannot be determined.[61] Even with the entrance of *porteña* women into certain white collar and clerical jobs during the next few decades, domestic service was still the predominant form of employment by the 1940s.[62]

Domestic labour (whether service or home industry) remained unregulated until the 1940s, and the use of child labour in private homes continued despite restrictions on underage work.[63] More than simply remaining unregulated, "[a] servant's work was regarded as a private affair between employer and employee, beyond the purview of the state."[64] At the same time there was probably a high level of conflict between employer and maid, as witnessed by the high ratio of maids in jail accused of theft in the homes where they worked.[65] Confinement of maids was bolstered by the tenets of *patria potestad*, a legal concept that gave the male head of household wide discretionary powers within the household.[66] Worse still, women's occupational opportunities were severely circumscribed during the first few decades of this century by various legal restrictions, and therefore many women may have been unable to find work other than as domestics.[67]

Although the circumstances varied, it is clear that employers enjoyed the status of relatives when it came to committing their charges. Subordinated by structures of gender, class, and nationality, the servants' power to control their destinies was even further compromised when employers tried to have them hospitalized. Maids' internment was often connected to behaviour that the head of the household deemed sexually dangerous, aberrant, or simply distasteful. Some of the cases illustrate the arbitrary power that employers exercised over these women. Just as in cases of family confinement, employers supplied a majority or all of the personal antecedents. Yet, while many employers used commitment as a way to either rid themselves of a troublesome servant, others acted in what they believed to be the best interest of their employee.[68]

The confinement of domestic servants raised thorny questions about familial authority. In 1918, Fernando M., a fifty-year-old illiterate Spanish labourer, residing in Córdoba province, dictated a letter to Judge Pedro

Meléndez in the capital. In the document, he expressed dismay and horror that his seventeen-year-old daughter Irene Carmen, who worked as a private maid, had been committed to the HNA. The young woman's employers had done the deed without his consent or knowledge and had thus betrayed the trust that he had given them to take care of his daughter. Aside from expressing anger at the daughter's employers, Fernando expressed relief that his daughter had written a letter to him to say that her physical and mental health had indeed improved. After seven months in the hospital, she was released.[69]

In April of 1916, the employers of Russian-born Mónica K. placed her in the custody of the police, who subsequently remanded her to the HNA. The following month, the court doctors examined her. Mónica's voice, albeit filtered through the doctors' report and the use of a translator, tells a tale that must have been familiar to many domestic servants.

> She attributes her internment to a quarrel that she had with former employers in Ramos Mejía [province of Buenos Aires], also of Russian nationality, who refused to pay her for her last year of work, for which she came to the capital very set back, entering into another home, where the employers also refused to pay her. As a result, her bad feelings grew, and she notes that the *patrón* treated her violently and upon her protesting, he called the police, who interned her in the Hospital. Thus she describes the cause of the development of all her woes.[70]

Examining doctors took this story as evidence of hallucination and paranoia and diagnosed her with acute mania, deeming her legally insane. Forensic doctors re-examined her in August 1916, and they confirmed that her mental state had deteriorated. The doctors noted that "[w]e can affirm that her illness has become more pronounced, presenting hallucinatory symptoms, not only visual, but also auditory, tactile and even genital. ... does not wish to eat because believes that the food has either been poisoned, or contains noxious substances."[71] Sometime after September 1916, an Officer for the Poor and Invalid became her permanent guardian.

Paulina C.'s employers interned her in the HNA in February 1933. By the end of that same month, the hospital had informed the court that Paulina's condition had improved enough that she could be released. The transcript of her interview with forensic psychiatrists suggests that Paulina's employers wasted no time in confining her and may have even used hospitalization to punish her. "[I]t seems that she was in love with an inappropriate person [*que no le corresponde*]."[72] "Her current illness began the morning of her internment in the Hospital, with pointless cries and laughter, incoherencies and puerility having afterwards a strong period of excitement, only to fall into a depression, in which she complained of headaches. She has had hysteri-form attacks."[73] At the time of her internment, she was described as "tranquil, asthenic [physically weak], her eyes swollen with tears, appearing coherent, but with evident emotional dullness." The inspectors noted that she "has appreciable degenerative physical stigmas," but did not specify the details. Noting that the subject was aware of her prior condition of melancholic depression and wished to leave the hospital to return to work with her old employers, they recommended her release, which occurred six weeks later. As with most of these cases, it also appears that the maid's employers provided the all-important family background. The fact that her romantic intentions may have been directed towards an individual not of her station in life, or perhaps the employers' son, is suggestive also of the ways in which maids could threaten the private domestic order.

"The family began to notice 'oddities' and changes of character": Women as Petitioners

While women's inferior legal status and the tradition of deposit placed them in a vulnerable position, they also possessed a degree of agency in confining husbands and fathers. Unlike the cases of women in which domestic conflict became a sign of mental imbalance, for men it was the abandonment or distortion of their roles as fathers and breadwinners that attracted psychiatric scrutiny. Women petitioners, then, had to appeal to normative ideas about both proper male and female behaviour; the men had failed to live up to their role as protector of the family while they themselves were acting as ideal mothers, protecting the home and children.[74] When women took such action, they were acting within their rights as laid out in Article 476 of the Argentine Civil Code of 1871.[75] Yet many women must have been aware of the legal and physical dangers associated with challenging their husbands in court. In the case of Juan P., the court doctors who visited the family's home found his wife's accusation of abuse groundless. The husband then turned around to complain that his wife was "paranoid," an accusation that court doctors found at least plausible.[76]

David G., a forty-six-year-old Russian-born carpenter, found himself in the Police Psychiatric Observation Unit in December of 1946 following complaints by his wife, Berta, that he posed a danger to her, their small children, and himself. With the signature of two doctors, David was committed to the Hospicio for the eighth time.[77] All of David G.'s hospitalizations seem to have resulted from complaints by his wife to the police about his drunken violent behaviour.[78] Of course, public authorities also stepped in to protect families. The police confined Alejo C., a tailor, in 1917 for waving a gun in public. Diagnosing him with megalomania, the examiners decided that he should remain at the Hospicio, largely because, during a prior release, he had posed "a true danger to his family whose members he threatened with death."[79]

In some cases, administrators and doctors found themselves caught up in complicated familial conflicts. In April 1947, the police confined Hussein A., a forty-seven-year-old Syrian labourer, after he threatened his wife and four children with a knife. After a period of observation at the Police Psychiatric Observation Unit, he was interned at the Hospicio. His June 1947 forensic examination noted that "his present illness began two years before his hospitalization, when the family began to notice 'oddities' and changes of character. Violent, he would brutally punish a son."[80] Hussein suffered delusions that his wife was cheating on him and often argued with her after episodes where he would abandon the home for up to twenty days. Suffering "delusional jealousy," doctors reported to the judge that he could not adapt to society and that his release would represent a danger to his family. Hussein's wife, Isabel, had provided the doctors with background information on her husband and was also attempting to have him declared officially insane and incompetent.

Meanwhile, a new character, the couple's adult daughter Isolina, appeared in the documents, claiming that her father was not abusive and that doctors had been unable to communicate with him because he did not speak Spanish. The daughter did not deny that her father had suffered some mental problems, but added that he had always been a hard worker who had fulfilled his "duties as head of household." Furthermore, her father's nervous condition at the time of his examination was a product of "finding himself deprived of his liberty." The daughter then suggested that marital conflict with his wife – the marriage had never been a happy one – might explain how her father ended up in a psychiatric hospital.[81] In requesting a new exam, the daughter offered to serve as translator. In March 1948, the court doctors ruled Hussein fit to leave the hospital, and a year later he requested that civil interdiction be lifted.

Women could also successfully petition for the confinement and loss of civil rights of husbands who acted irresponsibly with family money. In July of 1942, Julia S. initiated insanity proceedings against her husband, Gino I. When odd behaviour, including a pronounced loss of memory, made it impossible for him to continue his work at a North American branch bank, they gave him an early medical retirement. Soon thereafter the husband was interned in the Hospicio due to "danger to family and self." Julia noted that the family was having trouble gaining access to her husband's pension and requested a medical evaluation of her husband.[82] Financial issues also motivated Rosario L. to petition the courts to name her as guardian of her alcoholic husband Daniel P., who was already a patient at the Hospicio. According to depositions made in 1920, an acquaintance, familiar with Daniel's diminished mental state, had tricked him into signing a promissory note (*cobro ejecutivo*), for a significant sum of money. In and out of the Hospicio and the Colonia for several years, when at home, Daniel's behaviour had often been so dangerous that they had tied him to a bed.[83] The wife of Julio G., a former Hospicio patient, sought guardianship of him in 1951 in order to gain control of his retirement. In their report to the court, the forensic inspectors noted that Julio, who suffered from memory loss and irritability, brought on by progressive general paralysis, "most recently according to the wife, has been buying items which they already own or that they do not need." In this case, the court eventually granted guardianship to the wife.[84]

Life inside the Hospicio in the 1920s. Source: Archivo General de la Nación

"He rectifies his past": Leaving the Hospital

Just as reasons for confinement were highly variable, so too we find a wide range of motives and causes surrounding decisions to release patients. As with confinement, decisions about leaving could invite conflict within families and also between families and public authorities. To the extent that

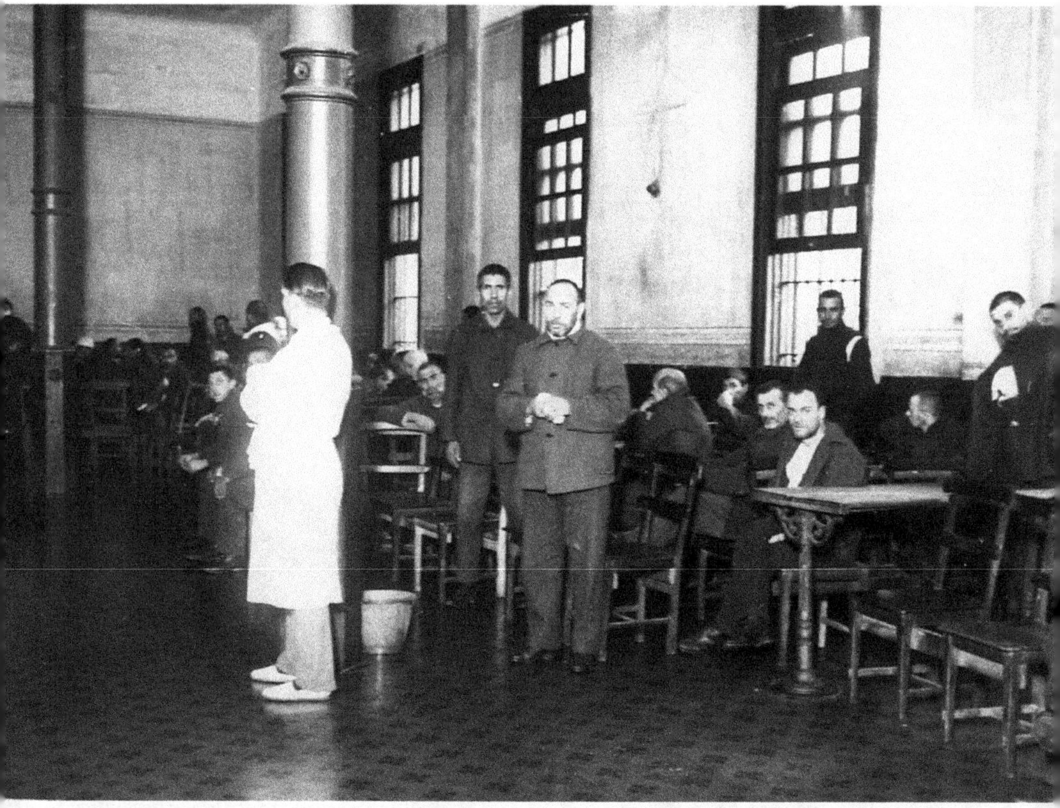

Life inside the Hospicio in the 1920s. Source: Archivo General de la Nación

patients had some agency to gain their release, it was generally premised on demonstrating awareness that they had been ill. It was also important that they had willingly conformed to the regimen of hospital life, for this was a sign that they were ready to return to the world of work and familial responsibility.[85]

While it was usually women who were obliged to recognize their sexual immorality (whether in acts or words), sometimes men also found themselves in this situation. In late 1921, the Hospicio communicated to the judge that they felt that Ricardo L. was ready to be released. Almost two more months elapsed before the medical examiners returned to re-examine the subject. They noted that Ricardo had come to recognize that masturbation and drink were driving him mad. "He rectifies his past and stands convinced that the weakness that has caused the onanism and alcoholism made him crazy and vows to abstain."[86]

Just as cooperation could lead to release, patients who manifested their disfavour with the process of psychiatric scrutiny and hospitalization did so at their own peril. Because medical examiners and hospital doctors expected their professional stature and legitimacy to be respected by their patients, complaints about any aspect of hospital life could be taken as signs of continued mental illness.[87]

The police sent Carlos B., a Russian-Polish-born merchant, to the Hospicio in late October 1918. In December, medical examiners determined that he suffered from *delirio de persecuciones* (persecutory delusions). A known alcoholic, he was obsessed with the notion of thieves robbing his business, and he claimed that for eight years no client had paid him. Yet many of his complaints about life in the hospital seem believable. "He says that he is bothered by the servants in the Hospicio who do not let him eat nor sleep, and who tease him. The doctors do not see him nor does he say that he needs them, since he believes that he is not sick. The food is bad, it tastes bad, [and] is dirty." The information was included in the report to further support the claims of his delirium. Two weeks later, however, the Hospicio reported that Carlos's condition had improved substantially and that he could be released.[88]

When medical examiners issued their report on Máxima S., who was diagnosed with hysteria, in June of 1907, they also noted her resistance to hospitalization. The doctors reported that she did not believe herself to be insane, "and by bringing her to [the HNA], the police have committed an arbitrary act because they have not produced a single piece of evidence that should motivate her sequestration."[89] Gilberto A.'s mother had him committed to the Hospicio in 1937. Doctors declared that he suffered from constitutional psychotic delirium, paranoia, and megalomania (*psicosis consitucional delirio sistematizado persecutorio y megalomaniaco*). Although Gilberto's file is brief, it includes a short note that he sent to the judge presiding of his case:

Finding myself interned in the Hospicio de las Mercedes, as a supposed lunatic, and fearing for my life given the circumstances that surround my seclusion, I ask, *por derecho propio* your honor for guarantees and security for my person.[90]

A later report by court doctors noted that Gilberto suffered from "perturbed judgment with delirious ideas of a persecutory character." Nevertheless, the case raises questions about the extent to which complaints imperilled one's chances of release and the degree to which doctors disregarded complaints about hospital life.[91]

Despite barriers to a timely release, psychiatric hospitalization was rarely permanent or even long-term. In reality, there was a fair amount of patient movement. In any given year, most of the hospitals' population was there for the first time in their life.[93] In 1920, for example, 75 per cent of the patients had been admitted for the first time.[92] And likewise, the overwhelming majority stayed in the hospital for less than a year. Furthermore, medical advances especially in the treatment of syphilis, as well as the practices of mental hygiene, also encouraged earlier releases. (The hospitals' statistics do not allow a precise calculation.)[94]

For many, the asylum was a place to come to die. Eva R.'s employer, a Señor Alfredo Pelosi, interned the French-born servant at the HNA in March 1941. The doctors learned from Pelosi that Eva had worked in his home as a *mucama* (maid) until her behaviour obliged him to intern her. The medical portion of the report noted that Eva would not speak, remained motionless for long periods of time, was unable to feed herself, and was soiling her clothes and bed. The diagnosis was progressive general paralysis, the terminal and often-fatal stage of syphilis. She passed away in March of 1943.[95] The admission of large numbers of nuns to the HNA – as many as twenty-four in 1939 – suggests that certain orders, including perhaps the Sisters of Charity, may have used the institution for the care of their most elderly members.[96] (See Appendix C. General Movement of Patients, Hospicio and HNA.)

Despite the increasing overcrowding, however, the likelihood that a patient would die while in the care of the hospitals actually declined during the first half of the century. At the Hospicio, 9.2 per cent of the patients died in 1893. The figure crept upwards towards 14 per cent by 1922, thereafter dropping steadily. By 1937, the mortality rate for all patients was at 7.6 per cent. Considering the frequent accusations of malfeasance and incompetence levelled at the HNA, it is noteworthy that their mortality rates were always much lower. In 1900, 6.3 per cent of all patients died while under the care of the hospital. By 1920, the figure had risen to 8.1 per cent, but thereafter dropped to 3.5 per cent in 1935 and an impressive 2.7 per cent in 1940. (See Appendix C. General Movement of Patients, Hospicio and HNA.)

Many patients left the two hospitals by being transferred to other hospitals. At the Hospicio, the percentage of the total patient population that was transferred to either the Colonia or Oliva grew from 10.77 per cent in 1910 to 15.69 per cent in 1925 to 14.92 per cent in 1935. The rate of transfer was even higher at the HNA, rising from 3.96 per cent in 1925 to 9.65 per cent in 1935 to 23.11 per cent in 1940. In all, between 1914 and 1928, 1,680 female patients from the HNA were transferred to the Oliva.[97] Figures for the number of transfers to the satellite facility at Lomas de Zamora were not given, perhaps because the two institutions were affiliates. (See Appendix C. General Movement of Patients, Hospicio and HNA.)

Both hospitals released a small percentage (anywhere from 3 to 6 per cent of the total population per year) of patients whose condition upon release was listed as "Not Improved." Most of these individuals were probably released at the request of their families, no doubt often against the medical advice of the hospital.[98] Family pressure to release patients to their care was a point of contention and annoyance for many Argentine psychiatrists. A prematurely released patient represented a potential threat to society, a legal liability to the profession and symbolized psychiatry's failure to win the confidence of the public. Ultimately, these cases reveal doctors' conflicts with society about who was qualified to diagnoses and care for the insane. (See Appendix C. General Movement of Patients, Hospicio and HNA.)

Families' influence only went so far, however, and doctors were more than willing to exert their de facto and de jure authority to thwart a petition. Ambivalence about releasing patients was in part a function of difficulty in determining objective criteria for what constituted a cure. Moreover, there were segments of the mentally disabled population for whom a cure was considered impossible. Finally, releasing patients raised questions of both doctors' legal liability and their resonsibility to protect fragile families.

Such a range of medical motives may have influenced the decision to delay the release of Rodolfo G. The police had confined the Russian-born labourer to the Hospicio in March 1932 for waving a pistol in the air and screaming. Medical examiners recommended that he remain at the Hospicio, where he had already been hospitalized once before in 1930. They took special note that his "father had died an alcoholic, and that he has an insane brother." Seven months later, his brother wrote from the provinces that he wished to take care of Rodolfo in his own home. Court examiners advised against this and eventually Rodolfo was transferred to the Colonia Nacional de Alienados. It was only six years later, in 1939, that doctors approved his release.[99]

The case of Julia B.'s mother, who spent several months trying to release her daughter from the HNA into her care, is both much more puzzling and tragic. The police had hospitalized Julia, after temporarily housing her in the Asilo San Miguel women's jail during the HNA's closure of 1933–34. In 1937, the mother, Clara, requested that the court reevaluate Julia's mental condition. Medical examiners promptly visited Julia at the HNA but concluded that she suffered from *dementia praecox* and was "not adaptable to society." A month later, in December 1937, Clara petitioned the court to gain guardianship and custody of her mentally disabled daughter. Never questioning the diagnosis, Clara stated that

> [m]y daughter suffers from Dementia Praecox, which means that it is a dementia that should present no danger to self or others; therefore I request a probationary release of my daughter, in order to bring her to Concordia, province of Entre Ríos. I believe the move will be of great benefit to her.[100]

In July 1939 the mother again requested that she be named guardian. Apparently neither the hospital nor the court deemed it wise to remand Julia to the care of her mother; Julia was transferred to Lomas de Zamora in 1940.[101]

Andrea P.'s husband requested her hospitalization in October 1930. Eight months later, medical examiners reported that Andrea suffered from "persecution delirium with interpretative and auditory hallucinations" and recommended that she be found insane and legally incompetent. A week prior to the inspection, Bonifacio A., Andrea's husband, petitioned the court to gain guardianship of his wife. In his letter to the judge, Bonifacio evoked images of matrimonial love and devotion to persuade.

> For fourteen years I have lived in marital union with said insane woman, until the moment that she became ill, for which I was obliged to hospitalize her.... The *insana* lacks relatives who can take care of her, and I have been the only person concerned about her welfare, since as I mentioned earlier, I have been married to her for fourteen years. Given the unfortunate state of her illness, I request that you name me as permanent guardian of the same, given that she lacks any material wealth and only the affection which I profess to her moves me to request this responsibility.[102]

Soon thereafter the court decreed Bonifacio as guardian, and within a month of his initial request, the husband was requesting that his wife be released into his care. Bonifacio noted that he had been informed by the hospital that his wife's condition had improved. Five days later, however, the medical examiners made a determination that Andrea "cannot leave [the hospital] as she poses a danger towards herself [and] others." Three years later, Bonifacio was again requesting that the court reevaluate his wife's condition. Andrea's file, as with so many, concludes without telling us the patient's final fate.

The courts also delayed the release of Mauricio S. to the care of a relative. In July 1924, the federal police communicated that Mauricio had been detained and, following an examination by two doctors, they sent him to the Hospicio. Two weeks later, the Hospicio reported that Mauricio suffered from "persecution delirium in a feebleminded person," but that he was now much improved. On July 25, 1924, Ana S. de R., a cousin of Mauricio, communicated to the judge that the subject's mental attack "is not of an alarming character, but rather that in childhood he suffered from typhoid which left him stupid."[103] Ana then assured the court that she would take good care of Mauricio. Despite the fact that the Hospicio had earlier reported that Mauricio's condition was improved, in August they reported to the court that, to date, the subject had experienced no improvement worthy of mention. Despite a failed escape in September of that year, by October the medical examiners finally deemed him fit to leave the hospital.

For reasons of professionalism and liability, the hospitals attempted, when possible, to release patients to responsible parties. This was a challenging endeavour, however since the families of patients, especially from the provinces, were often difficult to track down. The HNA's April 1920 report included the following note, "On the 21st the director's office requested from the Police of the Capital, due protection for a recently released patient during her return trip to Posadas, Misiones."[104] In some cases, the family had abandoned the patient requiring escort. In December 1916, the HNA made the following request:

> On the 29th a request was made to the Inspector General of the Technical Division of the Central Police Department to provide protection to the patient G.A. who is in condition to be released but whose family has abandoned her. The Hospital has decided to return her to place of origin, Estación Colman F-C-S.[105]

The release of non-resident foreign nationals could be even more challenging. In December 1924, forensic psychiatrists examined Henry R. to confirm the Hospicio's statement that he was fit to be released from their care. A forty-year-old engine man on a British ship, Henry had been arrested "for anomalies in his conduct in public ... he was screaming in the street ... and believed that 'they' wanted to kill him." The forensic psychiatrists changed his diagnosis from "acute alcoholism with ideas of persecution," to "persecution complex" and declared him "incapable of taking care of himself." Meanwhile, the Hospicio had recommended that Henry be returned to Britain. In January, the Ministry of Agriculture's General Office of Immigration advised the judge that the sailor's employers, the owners of his ship, had sent a certificate of safe passage.[106]

In April 1932, the police sent Benito, a thirty-year-old Italian worker, to its Police Psychiatric Observation Unit, from which he was remanded to the Hospicio. Diagnosed as suffering from systematized persecution delirium with hallucinations, "he is docile and obedient and his general state is satisfactory."[107] Meanwhile, Benito's parents in Italy were trying to repatriate their son through the good offices of a brother-in-law, Carlos C. In a letter to Carlos, Benito's parents swore that they would do anything to guarantee the safe return of their son. Sometime in 1932, Carlos communicated to the court that he had secured passage for Benito on an Italian-bound steamer. Carlos promised to take care of Benito from the moment he left the Hospicio until he boarded the boat. Gonzalo Bosch, the Hospicio's director noted that:

> He lacks insight. He does not believe himself to be insane and attributes his hospitalization to an error by the police and the doctors that examined him, which leads us to advise against his repatriation, unless someone takes charge of his care and vigilance during the voyage.[108]

We have no further news of Benito until 1936 when the Italian consulate in Buenos Aires communicated to the judge that Benito's family had requested that the Hospicio send him to their offices, noting that his condition had improved.[109]

Monitoring the release of patients became even more difficult as the hospitals grew increasingly overcrowded during the early 1930s. When presiding judge Jorge Figueroa Alcorta requested the release of Mariana R. "to the supervision of the Society of Beneficence or the Patronato de Liberados [presumably the judge was referring to the office charged with post-incarceration supervision for prisoners!]" the president of the Society responded that the HNA was unable to monitor released patients because of staff shortages.[110]

"With a Dedication That Only Paternal Love Is Capable of Giving": Insanity Proceedings without Institutionalization

A declaration of insanity by a court did not necessarily lead to commitment to a psychiatric facility. In certain cases, the declaration was intended as a way to protect the property and well-being of persons deemed mentally unfit to make decisions for self or family. Thus, insanity proceedings could be used by a wife to secure the pension of a senile husband or to guarantee the legal guardianship of a mentally retarded adult relative.

Aurelia P.'s parents began to notice disturbing behaviour in their thirty-year-old daughter in 1906. One day she came home, convinced that her students and fellow teachers were talking about her behind her back. According to the parents, she began to lock herself in her room, convinced that newspaper stories were about her. She went to church constantly and mixed food at meals (dessert into soup). After spending a year at the private Instituto Frenopático during 1907–08, her condition improved, but she remained prone to paranoia and continued to hide in her room, and refused to bathe. In August 1911, a year after the initial request, Aurelia's mother gained guardianship over her daughter.[111]

In April 1944, the siblings of Juana H., a thirty-eight-year-old mentally retarded woman, initiated insanity proceedings. They noted that their sister was "incapable of caring for herself."[112] In 1954, a father initiated guardianship proceedings to safeguard his mentally retarded son, Héctor M. In the initial proceedings, the father noted that the son was born retarded in 1928, posed no threat to himself or others, and that it was not necessary to hospitalize him. To have guardianship approved, the father needed to present declarations of his good character by neighbours. He also pointed out to the court that his son had no possessions. In June 1955, a forensic psychiatric report noted that Héctor was mentally retarded and that no treatment was possible. They saw no barriers to the subject remaining at home. In October 1958, members of the National Council of Minors visited Héctor's home to assess his care. They noted that Héctor shared a room with a brother but that they each had their own bed. Although the household enjoyed the benefit of a maid, the father, who had requested early retirement to care for the son, devoted himself full time to the care and comfort of Héctor. The son is reported to be "very well cared for, materially, spiritually and intellectually and with a dedication that only paternal love is capable of giving."[113]

It is impossible to determine whether overall home care was better or worse for the majority of mentally ill or retarded individuals. Families that bothered to gain custody were perhaps more likely to take an interest in their wards' welfare and to have the means to do so. Psychiatrists, however, generally frowned upon home care; their reasons may have been based on professional privilege but also fear of neglect or abuse of those not treated in hospitals.

Conclusions

The notion that the hospitals operated as agents of social control, and that medical ideas provided a blueprint for creating a hygienic and modern society, is increasingly untenable as we learn more about the lived experiences of patients, their families, and the doctors and staff of hospitals. While clearly the hospitals exerted a coercive influence over many individuals, the hospitals were also the site of a variety of conflicts that underscored psychiatry's tenuous relationship to civil society. Weak state support of the hospitals, in tandem with an overburdened legal system, produced hospitals that were profoundly influenced by social forces beyond the asylum walls.

Moreover, the experiences of people who were confined to the hospitals present us with a tangle of conflicts that involved families, neighbours, the police, judges, doctors, and the patients themselves. Patients resisted hospitalization in many cases and petitioned for their release. Families interested in confining or releasing relatives found themselves in conflict with the potential patients, but also sometimes with doctors and the police who suspected their motives. Whether motivated to find a safe place to put a dependent relative or to resolve a domestic conflict that had nothing to do with mental illness, families found in the hospitals a useful, if often unwitting, ally. Yet the same loose legal regimen that facilitated confinements, also undoubtedly encouraged authorities' skepticism. Finally, doctors and other public authorities acted out of a range of motives, of which the desire to help their patients cannot be discounted.

Although it is often difficult to determine what motivated individuals to see the hospitals in these ways, it is clear that these institutions were remarkably permeable and that psychiatric hospitals and the process of hospitalization need to be understood inside a broad social historical context. Hospitals, the doctors, and their medical ideas did not exist in a vacuum. Medical and lay ideas about mental health, the family, and gender were forever shaping one another. In the end, the hospitals served not only a medical function, but also a social one. It was the social definition, however, that was often so ambiguous. In sum, it is difficult to apply a single definition or description to institutions that could serve as a hospice, a jail, or an acute-care facility.

6

6: FROM PERÓN TO THE *PROCESO*: AUTHORITARIANISM, DEMOCRACY AND PSYCHIATRIC REFORM, 1943–83[1]

In the winter of 1946, a national deputy made a secret visit to the Hospicio to take pictures of the decrepit and overcrowded conditions in which patients were living. When news of the potentially embarrassing photographs reached the newly created Ministry of Public Health, a sympathetic psychiatrist working at the Hospicio suggested that Argentina's new president, Colonel Juan Domingo Perón, come to visit the asylum and offer a plan for its renovation. After all, Perón's government, barely in office for two months, could hardly be blamed for a situation that preceded his inauguration by several decades. Perón accepted the invitation, and his well-publicized visit on August 16, 1946 (seasons are reversed in the southern hemisphere) sparked a spate of renovations and institutional reforms that seemed to augur hope for the future.[2] The Peronist effort at renovation quickly fizzled, however, in the face of a myriad of economic, political, and institutional challenges and contradictions, which if anything grew even more pronounced during the ensuing decades.

From the military coup of 1943 to the end of the last dictatorship in 1983, the military's upper hierarchy repeatedly disrupted any semblance of formal democracy. With increasing political instability came bureaucratic chaos and indecision, programmatic disruption (as plans were made and then cancelled), and corruption. Most telling, there seemed to be an increased incidence of abandonment of the welfare of patients in the period before and after violent changes of government, an occurrence that became more common after 1955. As elsewhere in Argentine society, the political climate had an adverse effect on the daily operation of the hospitals, in terms of funding, staff retention, and long-range planning.[3]

In this context of marked military interference in the state, doctors made their peace with strongmen and dictators in order to try to transform public psychiatric care. Ironically, many of the military governments that followed after Perón's fall from power in 1955 were receptive to the ideas of progressive psychiatry. Against a backdrop of periodic swings between military and civilian regimes, a new generation of psychiatrists, influenced by psychoanalysis and the mental health movement, sought to transform the nation's psychiatric hospitals. They proposed that large asylums could be either transformed through the implementation of therapeutic communities, or even altogether replaced with day hospitals and community and general hospital clinics. It was hoped that by integrating psychiatry into the mainstream of medicine, services for patients and their relationship to doctors would improve. Such transformations might also help to eliminate the social isolation of hospital patients. Implicit in these projects was an expansion of the professional opportunities available to the growing numbers of mental health professionals. Between 1955 and 1970, sectors of Argentine psychiatry experienced a renaissance that promised to liberate patients and doctors from the confines of the asylum. Starting in 1970, however, military attitudes began to shift as the political climate grew more polarized. The military coup of March 1976 ushered in a period of unchecked repression and led to the evaporation of what had often been a tenuous alliance between progressive psychiatry and the state. Many psychiatrists and professionals in allied fields were targeted by the new military regime, which sought to eradicate all political and cultural challenges to "traditional" values and authority.

Although many psychiatrists, or their families, were targets of state repression, especially after 1976, psychiatry's public image was nonetheless ambiguous. In large part this was because, although many doctors, as well as other professionals, were targeted by the military, other psychiatrists participated in the repression. Equally disturbing were the ways that certain sectors of the profession updated the definition of social pathology to fit with the ideological needs of the military. The older dangerous categories of the immigrant as anarchist, prostitute, or public burden fell away and were replaced with new social dangers whose containment and "treatment" called for the expertise of psychiatrists: hippies, homosexuals, drug users, and members of left-wing organizations, whether guerrillas or publishers of pamphlets on Freud. The medicalization of these groups was all the more ominous considering the continued failure of the state to offer adequate legal oversight of the country's hospitals.

In part because of psychiatry's fractured image, post-dictatorship mental health professionals, and especially those who could be labelled as progressive, naturally began to re-envision the history of the profession. What began to emerge was a historical consciousness that looked for, and tried to explain, psychiatry's relationship to the authoritarian tradition.[4] Many of these same professionals helped to develop a uniquely Argentine perspective on mental health which blends psychoanalytic frameworks with a deep skepticism about biomedical approaches to understanding and treating mental illness. The biomedical framework is often associated with the allegiance of "traditional" psychiatrists to the Argentine military. More recently, it is also seen as a symbol and instrument of United States-led economic and ideological domination.[5]

The Perón Period

In June 1943 a clique of nationalist military officers, known as the GOU (Grupo de Oficiales Unidos, Group of United Officers), staged a coup and seized power. Inspired by Italian fascism and domestic nationalist ideologies, they began to modernize the Argentine state, in part through the creation of more specialized bureaucracies. The new regime saw its mission as one of purifying and modernizing the Argentine state by harmonizing tensions between labour and capital. Toward this end, many in the government, including future president Juan Perón, began to plan for the development of a coherent national health policy.[6]

Interest in reorganizing and modernizing Argentine health care had been growing throughout the 1930s and 1940s with politicians and social critics from across the political spectrum arguing for a national approach to health policy. It was impossible to ignore that Argentina's health system was inadequate, especially in the poorer provinces and in many rural areas.[7] The military's interest in these issues had also been growing following the introduction of universal male conscription. Medical examinations of prospective conscripts were revealing an appalling gap between rural and urban levels of health. In some provinces, rejection rates were often as high as 70 per cent.[8]

On October 21, 1943, following decree 12.311/43, the military government, of which Perón was secretary of labour, eliminated the ineffectual National Department of Hygiene and inaugurated the Dirección Nacional de Salud Pública y Asistencia Social (DNSPAS; National Directorate on Public Health and Social Assistance) within the Ministry of Interior. Under the new arrangement, the DNSPAS placed the Advisory Commission on Regional Hospitals and Asylums and the Society of Beneficence, along with other health entities under its authority. Thus ended the incongruous role of the Ministry of Foreign Relations and Religion in the oversight of national public health. Then, on August 16, 1944, Perón's Secretariat of Labour took over the DNSPAS, removing social welfare to his own office, and placed health into a newly created Dirección Nacional de Salud Pública (National Directorate of Public Health).[9] (The frequent changes of name and of lines of authority became increasingly commonplace from this point on.)

There appeared to be some initial decisiveness on the part of the National Directorate of Public Health to transform the delivery of mental health care. Under the leadership of Augusto Viera, it was granted 11 million pesos to oversee renovations in the existing institutions and support construction of small institutions in Rosario (400 beds), Corrientes (100 beds), Mendoza (100 beds), and Salta (50 beds).[10] The most ambitious single project was to be the wholesale remodelling of the Hospicio, where there were 3,500 patients but only room for 2,500.[11]

At the HNA, major remodelling and expansion permitted the hospital, which in the early 1940s had imposed a restrictive admissions policy, to start admitting new patients in July 1944. The government also approved a new admission policy, which stated that, if the prospective patient did not present an immediate danger to self or others, "the concerned party must obtain prior permission from the director of the institution, who will make a decision based on available space." Furthermore, the HNA would neither admit mentally retarded patients until the hospital had proper facilities for their care, nor allow the admission of patients from provinces that possessed a psychiatric hospital. Those entities that did send patients to the HNA would be required to provide medical certificates and a detailed case history. Likewise, the family or official that requested hospitalization could also request the patient's release without the approval of a judge or doctor. The hospital was also granted the right to commence judicial proceedings against anyone who had abandoned a patient.[12]

Meanwhile, Colonel Juan D. Perón was beginning his rise to political prominence through his control of the newly created Secretariat of Labour. Perón leveraged this influence over organized labour, and also social welfare under the help of his wife, to eclipse his fellow military officers. Popular support for Perón forced the military to allow free elections, which the colonel won easily in early 1946. Perón's government, which proved to be both populist and authoritarian, continued the process of state modernization. On May 23, 1946, following Decree 14,807, the Secretariat of Public Health was created, under the leadership of the renowned neurosurgeon Ramón Carrillo. By July 1949, the entity had been elevated to a ministry, the Ministry of Public Health.[13] With the establishment of a modern health bureaucracy, the government began to consolidate health institutions and began to dismantle the venerable Society of Beneficence. In September 1946, for the first time in its history, the federal government took over the Society of Beneficence and named Armando Méndez de San Martín as comptroller (*interventor*).[14] San Martín, who would later head the Fundación Eva Perón, a semi-official charitable organization, immediately improved the pay scale at former Society institutions and also eliminated patient uniforms and identification numbers. (Since the coup in 1943, the Society had begun to recognize that the modernization of health care would inevitably lead to the absorption of their institutions into the ever-growing formal state apparatus.) By September 1947, the Society had been dissolved, and all of its affiliated institutions had been distributed to the appropriate state agencies.[15]

It is telling of the GOU's ambitious reforms, however, that conditions were still quite dire at the nation's psychiatric facilities by the time that Perón came to office. Such was the state of affairs that nationwide, tens of thousands of patients lacked the appropriate legal or medical paperwork. And while patients suffered, thousands languished in prisons and on the streets for lack of adequate space in existing institutions.[16] Well-meaning families hesitated before committing relatives while administrators were forced to refuse new applications. There was also a massive backlog in

New and remodelled buildings at the Hospicio, ca. 1945–50. Source: Archivo General de la Nación.

releasing patients because of the lack of adequate post-hospital care and because the courts and hospitals lost or mismanaged paperwork.[17] Conditions in rural asylums were even more desperate.[18]

Perhaps reflecting the growing popular presence in the political arena (as well as the presence of Eva Perón as the semi-official intercessor of the people), patients and their families felt emboldened to complain directly to the president.[19] The relative of an HNA patient, Edmundo M., complained in a letter to the new president in October 1947:

> I found myself in the unfortunate position of having to intern a relative who was suffering from an altered mental state. From there began the dilemma, for despite the necessity of her hospitalization, we could not have her admitted as the establishment was above capacity. Thus it was necessary to get a *recommendation* [the implication here is that a bribe was required] in order to have her admitted.[20]

Once admitted, the relative began to lose weight. Edmundo quickly discovered that the ward where his relative was housed contained 750 patients, although it was designed for 250. The supplicant reminded the president of his recent and well-publicized visit to the Hospicio where similar conditions had been reported.

Judging at least from its public pronouncements, sectors of the new Peronist government were committed to deep and lasting reforms of Argentina's public institutions. While their accomplishments proved disappointing, there was nonetheless a profound change in the attitude of the state toward social welfare. Soon after his appointment to office, health minister Carrillo directed his attention to the asylums' repair as well as to updating thousands of patients' paperwork. This was an exceptional event: never before had a minister of state taken such an active and critical role in attempting to defend citizens' right to adequate health care. In a July 22, 1949, speech Carrillo noted that, upon assumption of the ministry, he had discovered that in national psychiatric facilities patients' legal paperwork was in total disarray:[21]

> In the Ministry of Public Health we have psychiatric establishments which house 15,000 patients, the majority of whom have been admitted without the authorization of a judge. In other words, we have a situation, in fact, at the margins of the Civil Code, since the code requires prior judicial authorization to intern a supposedly insane person. We have not been able to initiate all of the corresponding proceedings as there are an infinitely larger number of patients than available judges. In the past year, as I believe, the Official Curatory of the Insane, with great effort and few resources has been able to get 1,000 to 1,200 insanity judgments in a vain effort to correct a situation that has been neglected for years.[22]

According to Carrillo, at the root of these entanglements lay the antiquated and ineffectual Civil Code. This was the first time that a ministry of state had addressed the legal situation of psychiatric patients, and it was especially noteworthy that Carrillo offered a critique not only of the written law but of its application as well. Of particular concern for Carrillo was the requirement of prior judicial authorization, which resulted in large numbers of extra-legal hospitalizations because neither the courts nor the hospitals had sufficient personnel to keep up with paper work. Once confinement had taken place, it was easy for patients' cases to be forgotten by outside authorities.[23]

Carrillo proposed to resolve this situation through a reform of the Civil Code and the creation of a national health code partly in order to provide a more precise legal definition of insanity. His revised terminology read as follows: "The interdiction for mental illness only occurs when the person is above the age of 12 and cannot function normally in his personal life nor manage his personal or business affairs, because he suffers from such an affliction."[24] Carrillo astutely noted that, for judges, what was relevant was whether "the sick person can manage their affairs, conduct themselves normally and engage in relationships with others. It matters much less to them whether a person is manic, demented or imbecilic, or if he has lucid intervals at the moment of characterization."[25] Of great importance, therefore, was that the law should facilitate communication between doctors and judges by giving the presumed insane the right to speak before a judge during commitment proceedings:

> Under the actual system, the mentally ill person, represented totally by the guardian, cannot speak before the judge. As it is, if the ill person does not have a well-intentioned guardian who brings him or her before the judge, the latter will not have the opportunity to hear from the patient.[26]

Carrillo's modified Article 147 would have required the presence in court of the person in question and the person requesting the insanity proceedings. Likewise, Carrillo urged that Article 144, which governed who could initiate proceedings, needed to be restricted.[27] Despite some congressional efforts, no law was passed during the Perón years.[28]

Perhaps motivated by what he saw during his brief visit to the Hospicio in the winter of 1946, Perón immediately sanctioned the creation of a National Directorate for the Insane and Mental Hygiene within the nascent health ministry. The directorate was charged with renovating existing asylums, building new ones in underserved provinces, and regulating the admission and release of patients. Carrillo named Dr. Salomón Chichilnisky, the doctor who had suggested that the president visit the hospital, as its head. Although never a Peronist – he claims to have told this to the president during their first meeting – he was willing to work with a regime that could offer hope to Argentina's mentally disabled.[29]

In keeping with the long-standing desire to reduce the urban hospital populations, and with the cooperation of the Ministries of War and Public Works, Chichilnisky evacuated twelve hundred Hospicio patients in September of 1946 to the Open Door, Oliva, and Torres so that a wholesale renovation of the institution, which still had twenty-five hundred patients, could begin. Presumably many of those selected for transfer were youths, whose presence in the institutions was considered a problem of the first priority. Although the urban institutions were clearly overcrowded, transferring patients was problematic. Aside from the fact that it represented a continuation of earlier coercive practices, most rural institutions were as overcrowded as urban ones.[30] Nonetheless, renovations began in earnest the following month and several old buildings were torn down as new smaller specialized wards and clinics were built and the kitchen and sanitation works were modernized. Basic needs were also addressed, including the widespread shortage of suitable mattresses and clothing. The state also began to try to equalize the huge discrepancy between funding for urban and rural institutions.[31]

In many ways, the efforts at renovating the Hospicio mirrored the broader conflict between Argentina's traditional social order and what appeared at first glance to be the modernizing promise of the Peronist government. By his own account, Chichilnisky was rebuffed by Bosch when he announced to the director that as chief of the national directorate on the insane, he was ordering the demolition of the old asylum. He asked the director to relocate his spacious eight-room office from one of the old buildings within eight days. At the end of the allotted time, he returned to discover that Bosch had not moved. According to Chichilnisky, a tense exchange followed:

> "My distinguished professor, what about the move?" To this, [Bosch] replied angrily, repressing his nerves and puckering his lips. "Tell me Dr. Chichichilnisky [*sic*] (which in the Spanish of Argentina meant 'Shitty Russian [i.e., Jew]'), do you know who founded this hospital?"
>
> "Of course, it was Dr. Ventura Bosch."
>
> "Very well, Dr. Ventura Bosch was my grandfather!"
>
> "This I also knew (in truth it was his great uncle)."
>
> "So, to the grandson of the founder of this hospital, you, Chichichilnisky [*sic*], ask that I leave, or more accurately, that I evacuate my office?"
>
> In a dry manner, I responded. "It is not Chichilnisky who asks you to move. No! It is the future which asks that the past move on. But no matter, you have 72 hours to move your office out of this building. If you are still here when I return, I'll demolish it with you inside."[32]

Notwithstanding the conflict (and no doubt many others in the Hospicio were unhappy with the changes), Chichilnisky ordered the demolition of the director's office.

Considering the highly politicized nature of public posts in Argentina, it is hardly surprising that Perón eventually had the directors of both institutions removed. By May of 1947, Bosch had been obliged to abandon his position as director.[33] He held onto his position as dean of the school of psychiatry until December 12, 1952, when the Perón government removed him.[34] Bosch's replacement, Dr. Carlos Alberto Voss, served as interim director until April 1948, when the Secretariat of Public Health named him permanent director.[35] The director of the HNA, Luis Esteves Balado, met a similar fate during that same year and was replaced with Dr. Juan Carlos de Arizábalo.[36]

There were others ways in which reform of the hospitals seemed to herald a new approach to public administration and social welfare. Ministry of Public Health officials were interested in continuing the work of Bosch's mental hygiene clinic. However, the social workers who ran the Service of Social Visitors since 1942 did so on a volunteer basis. The new government reorganized the service under the direction of Delia María Lobo and elevated the largely female social workers' position to that of paid professionals.[37]

By early 1947, the HNA was also being targeted for major physical and administrative reforms. There, overcrowding had become so severe that the administration could not maintain order even to contain escapes and to regulate visitations. Of the 3,425 patients, about 10 per cent did not have proper beds.[38] The Technical Secretary of Hospitals reported that, despite repeated closures of the HNA, various renovation projects remained incomplete.[39] In early 1947, the new director recommended that San Martín, who was serving as the interventor of the Society of Beneficence, order the transfer of some patients to the Lomas facility to ease overcrowding at the HNA. In his communication, he also asked that San Martín advise on the proper "procedures for the release of those patients who are not dangerous and who only require outpatient attention."[40]

Chichilnisky's office also attempted to tackle the problem of the mentally disabled who had been confined in provincial prisons, jails, and rural hospitals. Spurred by the request of the governor of Corrientes, Chichilnisky visited that province's hospital for the insane. "It was a scene out of Dante, with the patients exposed to the elements and the agitated ones were chained to what was left of a wall." Upon his return to the capital, he commissioned Alfredo Sgrizzi to conduct a fact-finding mission throughout the country's jails, prisons, and hospitals. During the next several years, hundreds of mentally ill persons were transferred to national institutions.[41]

Perón's August 1946 visit to the Hospicio also sparked a flurry of broader national initiatives, though most centred on maintaining large institutions. Peronist deputy Humberto Messina presented an elaborate psychiatric reform bill to Congress in 1946, which included proposals for a network of hospitals. Messina suggested that reform would not only relieve patients from "idleness and inactivity" but might also "destroy once and for all the many prejudices, as old as they are recalcitrant, regarding both the asylum and the specialty of psychiatry. Those harboring such prejudices include members of professions close to psychiatry." Messina called for the creation of a National Neuropsychiatric Institute of the Federal Capital and the demolition of the old urban asylums. The new Institute would include a four-hundred-bed acute-care unit, external clinics, ambulatory treatment, and research centres. Following on several decades of similar proposals, Messina also called for the development of urban psychiatric clinics in general hospitals where he believed many patients would receive more appropriate care than in large custodial institutions.[42] Minister Carrillo likewise envisioned the development of a national network of psychiatric facilities that would include clinics, short- and long-term hospitals, hospitals for the so-called "criminally insane," and psychiatric clinics in general hospitals.[43]

Although the Peronist government's official rhetoric promised "social justice" to the people of Argentina, its psychiatric reform failed to either move psychiatric care beyond its dependence on large institutions or to develop a more flexible system. In many respects, the Perón government had an easier time attacking concrete issues, such as remodelling existing institutions and addressing the labour concerns of staff.[44] Indeed, the government was effective in creating more institutions outside of Gran Buenos Aires; new hospitals opened in Salta and Mendoza provinces. Yet there was also a marked interest on the part of Perón's government to construct large, even monumental, structures. In some cases, as in the construction of large new wards at the Hospico, this was done with a disregard of modern standards of care and contradicted the growing consensus among psychiatrists throughout the world who argued for smaller more specialized hospitals.[45] The proposal of Messina, for example, had advocated expanding the Open Door (province of Buenos Aires) hospital's capacity to six thousand and building a coed facility for three thousand just outside of Buenos Aires. (He suggested that Hospicio should be completely demolished and the state build a workers' housing complex in its place.) Ironically, the reconstruction and enlargement of existing hospitals, and the creation of new institutions in the province (the government's only successful initiative in this area) may have only served to invite a greater number of confinements.[46]

If the regime's ambitious building programs were misguided, the regime's overall approach to health administration was characterized by an *ad hoc* approach. Chichilnisky's National Directorate for the Insane and Mental Hygiene appears to have been literally created overnight. Furthermore, responsibilities were in a state of constant flux. In August 1954, the Office of Hospital Construction was moved from Public Health to the Ministry of Public Works. And in June 1954 Perón returned social welfare to the ministry, which was renamed the Ministerio de Asistencia Social y Salud Pública (Ministry of Social Welfare and Public Health).[47] Constant bureaucratic reorganizing, as well as frequent changing of names, became a trademark of the post-1943 period.

Equally problematic was the Peronist government's practice of dismissing competent professionals for political reasons. Although it was hardly a practice that they had invented, it seems to have become more widespread. Aside from hindering short-term reform effectiveness, it also set in motion a precedent that would last for forty years.[48] In some psychiatric institutions, including the former Colonia facility, new directors were named practically every year of the Perón government.[49]

Such instability undoubtedly contributed to the growing tendency of ambitious renovation projects to peter out before completion. Chichilnisky, for example, became disillusioned with the Peronist government's inability to follow through with funding and support for the renovations at the Hospicio, which eventually halted altogether. (The problem started during the GOU government when funds had been allocated for hospital renovations but had somehow become lost.) By the time that Perón was overthrown in 1955, renovations were unfinished.[50]

One of the principal impediments to deep structural reform was the Peronists' ambiguous attitude toward formal social welfare mechanisms. As historian Mariano Plotkin has suggested, "a rational structure for providing those services would have jeopardized Perón's ability to attract support from the unions."[51] Perón was probably more interested in projects and systems that would generate and solidify his political support, including building more hospitals and expanding their bed capacity. The latter was, for many of Perón's critics, an especially egregious error. By simply adding more beds, but often without developing appropriate medical services, the policy simply amplified overcrowding in all public hospitals.[52] Despite expansion in eligibility, the Peronist government also failed to significantly transform social insurance and welfare, which remained heavily dependent on specific unions.[53]

The attitude of many doctors no doubt also contributed to the slow pace of change. Most psychiatrists, for example, continued to adhere to an attitude that emphasized the social danger of the insane and the mentally retarded. Even Messina's call for modernizing the country's health system, for example, was based on now-familiar anxieties about the mentally ill, and especially those who evaded treatment. (He even continued to engage in the same kinds of statistical contortions about how many insane lived in Argentina: "like most civilized countries, have about 3 insane per 1,000 inhabitants.)"[54] Not only had anxiety about the non-institutionalized survived the transition to Peronism, but psychiatry remained fixated on the now largely imaginary problem of unregulated immigration.[55]

The survival of what we might call traditional psychiatric values helps to explain, perhaps, the failure to transform some portion of psychiatric care to an ambulatory or outpatient model. A 1955 report by Odair Pedroso, a consultant for the Oficina Sanitaria Panamericana determined that public mental health in Argentina continued to suffer from serious deficiencies and that the government was not allowing psychiatric practice to change in accordance with modern criteria.[56]

Strange Alliances: Reforms under Military and Civilian Governments

In mid-September 1955, a group of nationalist military officers forced Perón, who had been losing support from labour, the church, and the military, out of office. That faction quickly lost out to a hard-line anti-Peronist front led by General Pedro Aramburu, who upon assuming office promised to clean up Argentine public administration. Whilst purging Peronists from public office, the Aramburu government facilitated and supported a series of important mental health reform measures. The rancour that the coup itself produced between supporters and opponents of Peronist populism, as well as the immediate purging from government posts of Peronists, however, further destabilized Argentine public institutions and undermined long-range social policy planning, even as some areas of welfare and social insurance continued to expand.[57] The new political climate also inaugurated decades of internal strife within psychiatry and allied fields about how exactly to work with successive military governments.[58]

The new regime took the question of transforming psychiatric care seriously. Interest in this sector of health was no doubt partially a result of the fact that by the mid-1950s, Argentina had one of the largest public mental health systems in Latin America.

Number of Psychiatric Hospitals, 1957[59]

Argentina	25	Haiti	—
Bolivia	1	Honduras	—
Brazil	140	Mexico	6
Canada	74	Nicaragua	1
Colombia	16	Panama	1
Costa Rica	3	Paraguay	1
Cuba	1	Peru	6
Chile	3	Dominican Republic	3
Ecuador	2	Uruguay	2
El Salvador	1	Venezuela	16
United States	586		
Guatemala	1		

Emblematic of that commitment was the October 1956 order by Raúl Carrea, the Interventor of the Ministry of Public Health, to establish a psychiatric ward in a wing of the recently constructed Aráoz Alfaro Hospital in Lanús, Buenos Aires province. The hospital had been inaugurated in 1952 as Hospital Interzonal de Agudos "Evita," but was renamed after the 1955 coup.[60] Dr. Mauricio Goldenberg (1916–2006), who had trained in the Hospicio in the 1940s and had been connected to the mental hygiene movement, was named director of its Psychopathologic and Neurological Service. The initial program, which built upon two decades of similar efforts, was quite modest and included only fourteen beds, several doctors, and a small outpatient clinic, but by 1966 the Service had expanded to include a hundred part-time doctors, twenty psychologists, five social workers, three work therapists, several nurses, and thirty psychiatry residents. By then, almost 18 per cent of the hospital's patients were in Goldenberg's clinic.[61]

Goldenberg saw the location of psychiatric treatment in general hospitals as having a liberating effect on both patients and doctors. The clinic, which employed both the latest antipsychotics as well as psychotherapy, was intended to reduce the trauma and stigma associated with forced hospitalization as well as the likelihood of long-term confinement.[62] For doctors and medical students, who had traditionally received the bulk of their training in large asylums, the clinic offered a more humane setting in which to learn about the causes, evolution, and treatment of mental illness. They also had the opportunity to learn about mental illness within a broader view of human health. The Lanús clinic had a profound influence on a generation of young psychiatrists and medical students because it afforded them an opportunity to think more imaginatively about the causes and treatments of mental illness. For many doctors, as well as patients, the clinic also provided them with their first exposure to psychoanalysis. (The clinic therefore played a major role in the diffusion of psychoanalysis, not just into medical circles, but into the broader culture.)[63] The project also coincided with increasing numbers of women graduating from medical school, and it became an important professional experience for many of them.[64]

Goldenberg viewed Lanús as a model that could be replicated nationwide. In order to reduce the number of patients in closed facilities Argentina needed to increase the number of outpatient facilities, improve the training that all doctors received in psychiatry, and develop appropriately sized hospitals in all provinces. Encouraged by the early successes at Lanús, Goldenberg and his associates began a dialogue on national reform with the Aramburu government. The single most important development in that direction was the creation of the Instituto Nacional de Salud Mental (INSM; National Institute of Mental Health) in October 1957. The Institute was dedicated to "providing for the mentally ill the maximum opportunity for cure and re-adaptation into society, or when this is not medically possible, the best conditions for their rehabilitation and care."[65] This was to be accomplished through a coordinated effort at research, treatment, and prevention of mental illness through the development of integral assistance programs of primary care, recuperation, and re-adaptation, of which therapeutic communities would become central. Much of this was designed to lay the foundation for the dismantling of the large asylums.[66] At various points over the next few decades, the INSM also administered national psychiatric hospitals.[67]

Despite the frequent regime changes of the sixties and seventies, the INSM's institutional autonomy allowed it to maintain a fair degree of programmatic consistency. In the early 1960s, during the democratic interlude of presidents Arturo Frondizi (1958–1962), José Guido (1962–63), and Arturo Illía (1963–66), the INSM oversaw the development of several other psychiatric clinics in urban general hospitals.[68] Reforms were also underway in the large asylums. In May 1966, INSM director Alberto Bonhour, a well-regarded psychiatrist, inaugurated a day hospital within the Buenos Aires men's hospital. Its goal was to "[h]elp the sick, improve assistance, provide appropriate space to many mentally fragile persons without exposing them to the disadvantages inherent in hospitalization, where the patient loses his or her liberty."[69] Furthermore, the unit sought to reduce the high incidence of family abandonment so common among those hospitalized in regular psychiatric facilities.[70]

Despite these developments, political polarization and economic strife made it increasingly difficult to effect deeper changes within individual institutions. The Aramburu government's 1957 attempt to unite the men and women's hospitals of Buenos Aires into a single institution is a case in point. The government had proposed combining the two institutions (which sit across the street from each other), in order to end duplication of services and administration and to cut costs, but encountered massive resistance from professional and staff unions. The government quickly backed down.[71] During the next decade, stagnant wages, weak budgets, growing political polarization between pro- and anti-Peronists, and constant regime change also fostered new levels of corruption that often rendered the hospitals unmanageable by civilian and military governments alike.[72]

In 1958, the vice secretary of the Ministry of Social Welfare and Public Health, in blunt terms, noted:

> Unfortunately our psychiatric hospitals are places of chronification and not centers of therapeutic psychiatry. There are vast areas of the country where there is a total absence of psychiatric care and our psychiatry has not integrated itself as a specialty into general hospitals. To say that mental hygiene is in diapers is a euphemism to hide its complete nudity.[73]

Overcrowding in the traditional asylums had also returned to the horrific levels of the 1940s. In 1958, the men's and women's asylums in Buenos Aires had 2,000 beds each, but had patient populations of 3,475 and 3,800 respectively. According to a 1959 report by psychiatrist Sylvia Bermann, the Aramburu government had inherited an unmanageable situation from the Perón government. A shortage of private clinics, the total absence of psychiatric services in most provinces, the high costs of long-term care, and an incomplete social security network prevented hospitals from breaking out of a downward cycle of overcrowding and neglect of patients.[74]

In 1965, Gregorio Bermann, a prominent leftist psychiatrist (and Sylvia Bermann's father), issued a scathing indictment of the situation of psychiatric patients in Argentina. He noted that the hopes generated in 1957 by the creation of the INSM had largely gone unfulfilled due to "the lack of a radical reordering [of the health system], the lack of resources and political instability."[75] But Bermann was especially frustrated that most psychiatrists continued to see their primary mission as isolating the mentally ill from society.[76]

Return of the Military

In June 1966, General Juan Carlos Onganía overthrew the civilian government of Arturo Illía. Onganía sought to restore political order and modernize Argentina through military intervention of the bureaucracy, the repression of organized labour, and a crackdown on Peronists. In the field of mental health, however, his government took its cues from earlier reform-minded doctors and was willing to apply the resources of the military to the vexing and intractable problem of psychiatric care.[77] Military efficiency produced rather mixed results.

Concerned over the absence of clear legal norms for the hospitalization and release of psychiatric patients, Onganía named a commission to study the question. They suggested modifications to the Civil Code to give the police the right to quickly hospitalize "suspected lunatics," drug addicts (a social phenomenon of recent interest), and alcoholics for short periods of time. The changes, which quickly became law, were supposed to provide a degree of legal transparency to hospitalization. Unfortunately, the guidelines about informing the courts were unclear and enforcement was lax.[78] More troubling, the new law seemed to actually widen the range of people who could be subjected to forcible confinement, while not adequately addressing the long-standing legal ambiguities inherent in psychiatric hospitalization. The new law also placed limits on probationary releases, perhaps in order to reduce the influence of families on psychiatric and legal decisions of confinement.[79]

While the legal process for confinement changed, life in the hospitals remained similar to earlier eras. (For historians, it is difficult to make a more precise appraisal because the hospitals seem to have ceased publishing annual reports.) An independent report from August 1966 reiterated a list of problems that had been familiar to doctors since the early twentieth century. Ninety-five per cent of psychiatrists, and 97 per cent of psychiatric beds, were concentrated in only 15 per cent of the republic. As Gonzalo Bosch had argued in 1931, patients who were sent great distances to a hospital frequently lost touch with family and friends, thereby making social reintegration all the more difficult. While the hospitals suffered massive overcrowding, most of the country lacked any psychiatric services whatsoever. Most patients were suffering from unnecessarily prolonged stays because of the lack of medical attention. Poor diet, boredom, and filth, the inability to segregate patients along any diagnostic categories, and the lack of treatments for drug and alcohol abuse tended to delay recuperation rates. The report also noted that continued popular prejudice against psychiatric hospitals exposed recently released patients to intense social isolation and ostracism when they returned to their communities. Declining budgets and frequent and bitter conflicts between psychiatrists and staff, which was itself a product of increasing political polarization, impeded any kind of useful collaboration on treatments or research. The report even mentioned that this state of affairs had sullied the reputation of psychiatry "in a country that in theory has a good level of development."[80]

To tackle the lingering problem of the large asylums, the Onganía government took measures to decentralize mental health services and reduce the role of large asylums without directly confronting the vested interests, including both unions and doctors' organizations, within the hospitals.[81] Following guidelines already under formulation in the mid-1960s, the military interventor-director of the INSM, Colonel Julio Ricardo Estévez, who was a doctor, began a policy of reducing hospital populations by relocating so-called chronic patients from the decaying urban asylums to a variety of rural institutions. The project was intended to reorient urban institutions towards short-term care and to facilitate the development of therapeutic communities therein.[82] In August 1967, Estévez approved a plan to relocate several hundred patients from the Buenos Aires men's and women's hospitals, which had been renamed Borda and Moyano respectively, to vacant army barracks outside the agricultural city of Federal, in Entre Ríos province. Progressive psychiatrists' support of the project, and especially the involuntary transfer of patients, not only suggests that the situation in the hospitals was desperate, but also that the idea of moving patients had come to be seen as acceptable. The first patients arrived in March 1968. For many of them, the trip was the first time they had left the urban hospitals in years, or even decades.[83]

Facing a shortage of doctors and staff, the director of the Federal hospital, psychiatrist Raúl Camino, took a therapeutic community approach to all aspects of the hospital and trained local farmers to serve as staff. Therapy was conducted in daily assemblies where hospital governance, medication, and personal and interpersonal issues were discussed. Camino later commented that the therapeutic community, which was based on democratic principles and a rejection of social hierarchy, *was* the hospital.[84]

Simultaneously, the INSM began to support a range of community psychiatry programs within existing institutions.[85] In August 1967, the INSM named Peruvian-born Luis César Guedes Arroyo as interventor of the Dr. A.L. Roballos Psychiatric Hospital in Paraná, Entre Ríos province. The hospital had been founded in 1963 when a hundred female patients had been transferred there from a nearby asylum. Despite its recent creation, the Roballos had quickly declined and faced problems similar to older institutions. According to Guedes Arroyo's memoir, he transformed the culture of the institution, established a hospital-wide therapeutic community, eased restrictions on patients' movements, and placed limits on the use of electroshock and insulin shock treatments. He also attempted to restore the patients' case files, which by his account had been utterly neglected.[86] In a pattern that reformers found throughout Argentina, however, Guedes Arroyo faced tremendous pressure from the staff of the hospitals and also from the broader medical community in the province, which led to his resignation in September 1968.[87]

Similar efforts were also underway in Buenos Aires. In mid-1968, Dr. Wilbur Ricardo Grimson, a young psychiatrist, was given permission by the INSM to open the Centro Píloto Therapeutic Community at the National Hospital José Esteves. The institution, which had originally been the Lomas de Zamora satellite facility for the HNA, had been a co-educational provincial facility since the government of Perón.[88] The Centro Píloto, which opened in July 1969, worked with recently admitted patients in order to shorten their length of stay in the hospital. Eventually it also began to work with chronic patients (those whose recovery was deemed impossible or unlikely) throughout the hospital. Like Camino, Grimson and his team emphasized democratic process, dissolution of barriers between professionals – particularly psychiatrists and other mental health workers – as well as between professionals, staff, and patients. Therapy centred on group meetings and diverse therapeutic, recreational, and occupational activities and challenged modes of treatment that ignored the social aspects of mental illness and healing.[89]

Most of the major reform initiatives enjoyed either the support of, or direction from, the INSM, which, even during times of military rule, was often able to issue some very progressive directives. In June 1968, they banned uniforms in public hospitals. Reflecting the growing influence of psychoanalytical perspective at all levels of society, they emphasized that it was "important that patients who require re-personalization avoid uniformity in dress which results in depression and humiliation."[90] The Institute also issued a complete ban on the use of restraints, including straitjackets, and individual hospital interventors sought to better regulate the use of shock treatments.[91] Significantly, however, even with the backing of a military government, the INSM still faced considerable challenges when they attempted to target the "traditional" asylums. The unsuccessful effort to transform a ward of the Moyano hospital into a neighbourhood community mental health centre for the surrounding Barracas neighbourhood is a case in point.[92]

Municipal governments, with the support of the INSM, were also beginning to take an interest in mental health reform. Goldenberg, who was still active in public policy, oversaw the creation of the Buenos Aires Municipal Department of Mental Health in June 1967. Its goal was to create a network of municipal psychiatric and mental health services while also improving coordination with national and provincial authorities.[93] During the next several years, the Department opened several community mental health centres. Often affiliated with general hospitals, the centres integrated mental health programs into their communities' general health facilities to combat age-old popular prejudice against seeking psychiatric help. The centres also contributed to the continued popular interest in psychoanalysis. Further, the centres were to collect accurate statistical data (historically a rare commodity in Argentina) on the community that they were designed to serve. Eventually, each of the city's twenty-five hospitals was to contain a Psychopathology and Mental Health Service.[94]

While different levels of government were encouraging reform measures, patients and concerned citizens were offering up their own critique of mainstream psychiatry. Influenced by French and U.S. anti-psychiatry, as well as by a variety of leftist political positions, activist laypeople and patients challenged the established diagnostic and clinical practices, which they claimed had remained dominant within the large state-run hospitals. They also espoused a radical psychiatric nationalism and called for doctors and laymen to embrace Argentina's traditional healing practices and to view the situation of patients as emblematic of broader socio-political conditions.[95] Various community groups, motivated by a variety of social and political movements then current in Argentina, including leftist Peronism, began to volunteer in the traditional hospitals. Cultural activities began to emerge that involved collaboration between patients and what one activist referred to as the "externees." For some, like architect Alfredo Moffatt, psychiatric practice needed to fit better with the Argentine national character.

> In large part the Popular Community 'Carlos Gardel' was made possible by the prior existence of interned comrades. Thanks to the tremendous capacity for self therapy among our people and to the fact that within the hospital institutional 'therapy' (in other words, control) is reduced, these internees were able to create the nucleus of a community based in popular

communal traditions.... [T]hey were making the first steps in the work of creating a creole psychiatry – or popular, gaucho, peronist, whatever you may call it.[96]

Not surprisingly, they were also decidedly less optimistic about the success of the myriad projects that were arising out of a reformed psychiatry and the INSM. The most serious criticism, however, continued to be levelled at the oldest of the hospitals.[97]

Many doctors were also conscious of the limits of reform, the inherent contradiction of working on behalf of a military government, and the broader social implications of their work. Doctor Emiliano Galende provides a clear picture of the confusion of the era:

> When ten years after the creation of the INSM, in 1967, the latest dictator named Colonel Julio Ricardo Estévez as interventor of the INSM, it produced one of the most curious events of this history. In the name of the military dictatorship they launched a democratic reform of psychiatry. A strange front thus developed. Psychiatrists with fascist positions, specialists in therapeutic communities, dynamic psychiatrists with democratic reputations converged. And the Argentine Psychoanalytic Association gave its support while the Argentine Army handed over barracks to the INSM and provided transport to effect the redistribution of patients.[98]

While professionals of different political persuasions often put aside their differences, the polarization of the period nonetheless hindered collegiality in both the hospitals and academia. Moreover, in many ways, doctors' attitudes about the best treatment methods came to symbolize their political affiliations, notwithstanding the military's catholic approach to mental health care.[99]

Repression

While official and unofficial steps had been made towards the transformation of large state institutions, political violence and recurrent economic stagnation began to threaten existing reforms. Given the drift toward authoritarianism, the inherently democratic nature of many reforms, and especially therapeutic communities, made their existence especially precarious. In July 1970, a faction of the military overthrew Onganía, whom they considered ineffectual in maintaining political order. Of particular concern was the growth of left-wing guerrilla organizations. At the same time, the definition of political subversion was beginning to expand to cultural and professional practices previously ignored by adherents of national security doctrine. In such a climate, progressive psychiatrists, many of whom had become radicalized by Onganía's political authoritarianism, became targets.

In October 1970 General Roberto Levingston, who was finally named as Onganía's successor, ordered the military intervention of the INSM, which had been operating with a great deal of autonomy. He also ordered the complete repression of all therapeutic communities, which were viewed as hotbeds of radicalism and sexual licentiousness.[100] Ironically, just as progressive reformers had discovered that change came slowly within hospitals, so too did the new military government. In Lomas de Zamora, Grimson's announcement to the centre that he was being replaced was received with such a massive protest by the patients and staff that the hospital director quickly reversed the order. The status quo was sustained until late December when the hospital fired Lucila Edelman, chief of the centre's day hospital. This led to more confrontations between the patients and staff members against new INSM officials and the hospital administrators. Despite support from a wide array of newspapers, the centre was permanently closed in January 1971. Significantly, opposition within the hospital itself was critical to the destruction of the centre. Many staff and doctors were troubled by the centre's ample funding, its treatment of men and women together, and by the leftist affiliations of many of its staff.[101]

While many of the urban therapeutic communities quickly disappeared, the Federal community survived through the first half of the decade. Its distance from major urban centres afforded it protection from both government repression, and, perhaps more importantly, internal hospital politics. There was no established hierarchy of doctors and staff, and therefore no one for whom the innovations represented a threat. When the Levingston government ordered the closure of all therapeutic communities, Camino took advantage of his project's isolation to simply change the name to the more innocuous sounding "meetings." The project thus lasted until the March 1976 coup, when, after years of harassment and investigation by military personnel, he resigned.[102]

The repression that followed the fall of Onganía would prove to be but a prelude to a far worse situation. Unable to maintain political consensus, the new military government was forced to allow Perón to return from his Spanish exile in 1973. With his third wife, María Estela Martínez de Perón, as vice-presidential candidate, Perón won the presidency and held office for just over a year before dying. His wife then assumed the presidency in 1974, and the country quickly descended to new levels of political chaos and violence. This included the appearance of right-wing death squads that had the support of key players within the government and that claimed to be responding to the actions of the country's various guerrilla movements. In response to a perceived threat from the revolutionary leftist wing of the Peronist movement, as well as from a more generalized "moral decline," the military seized power in March 1976. The new government, which murdered up to thirty thousand people in the next six years, implemented the Proceso de Reorganización Nacional (Process for National Reorganization) to root out subversive activities, which included not only the by-now-decimated guerrilla movement, but also a wide variety of cultural and social movements.[103] As before, the new military government, whose leaders changed every few years, took over the administration of all public institutions, including hospitals, replacing civilian directors with military officers.[104]

A favoured target of the military was progressive or leftist professionals, including psychiatrists, psychologists, and other mental health workers, whose ideology, work, or Jewish ancestry supposedly challenged Argentina's traditional Catholic values.[105] The ruthlessness of the new regime (which was virulently anti-Semitic), became apparent when, in the first week of April 1976, the military passed a law intended to facilitate the removal of government employees from their posts for "presumed or potential ideological disturbance." By July 1977, virtually every psychiatric and general hospital and public health centre that offered alternatives to the traditional treatments had suffered serious loss of personnel. At the women's hospital (Moyano), two ward chiefs and eight professionals were fired, and eighty-five other professionals were prohibited from entering the hospital. At the men's hospital (Borda), "seven professionals were fired, including 4 chiefs with more than 18 years of experience. Next, they fired 20 nurses and administrative personnel. This occurred in a hospital were there are wards in which one nurse serves 400 patients."[106] There were also at least thirteen reported cases of psychiatrists who were "disappeared" (i.e., were murdered by the police or the military) while under military detention.[107] The military also quickly closed all of the mental health centres and outpatient psychiatric clinics, at least until new staff could be provided.

As reform-minded professionals lost whatever influence they may have had, old-guard staff and psychiatrists quickly began to return to power in the hospitals. Psychiatrist Sylvia Bermann, now in exile, observed that the situation had come full circle since the late 1950s:

> In mental care, dynamic techniques of patient care which gave priority to the study of the relationship between the patient and his family and society, emphasis on outpatient care, and rehabilitation of patients to the greatest possible extent have given way to 'custodial' techniques for patients which stress asylum care, make little effort toward rehabilitation, and consider their illness as basically a biological problem.[108]

Repression, as well as hostility in the workplace and shrinking state support of public health, led many progressive doctors to shift their activities away from the public sector towards the safer realm of the private psychoanalytic practice.[109]

The intense political polarization of the period leading up to the coup of 1976 had also encouraged a reformulation of the conservative social and political agenda of psychiatry. Some psychiatrists began to call for the application of their specialty to address current political threats, in a manner that echoed the earlier medicalization of the anarchist and immigrant threats.

The process was already underway following the coup of 1955, but by 1976, homosexuality, drug use, and membership in leftist groups, including guerrilla groups, were all being discussed as "evidence" of mental deviation. After 1976, the INSM's main publication argued that psychiatry needed to apply its expertise to confront these diffuse and insidious threats to the nation.[110]

Public confidence in the psychiatric profession was only further diminished by allegations that individual psychiatrists, as well as hospital administrators, had participated in the detention and torture of political prisoners. A post-dictatorship human rights report named Julio Ricardo Estévez, the former interventor of the INSM, for example, as the director of the detention and torture centre at Hospital Posadas.[111] Equally striking, the grassroots human rights organization Madres de la Plaza de Mayo (Mothers of the Plaza de Mayo) provided evidence in January 1984 that detained and disappeared persons may have been sent to the Borda hospital. Similar allegations emerged about the Torres hospital for the mentally retarded, though the director at the time vociferously denied it.[112]

Military defeat in the Falklands War of 1982, along with growing economic problems, forced the military to step down from power in 1983.[113] Since the return of democracy, psychiatrists and social critics have taken stock of the recent past. A study penned by eminent physicians and jurists two years after the fall of the military government observed that

> ... the authoritarianism in the last years has expressed itself in the following realities: the level of psychiatric attention has deteriorated to levels never before seen. The 35,000 beds in psychiatric hospitals represent an unjustifiable *cronicario* [a place where patients' conditions simply stagnate and deteriorate], a punishment whose collective horror is difficult to imagine and a flagrant violation of human rights. We did not reach these conditions merely because of budget restrictions, but rather because of the incapacity to generate and maintain a coherent program, by not listening to the demands and complaints of professionals, families, and patients, and because of the systematic destruction of advanced and alternative psychiatric practices. We should also

add to the list the deterioration and closing of psychopathological services and the ideological marginalization of professionals.[114]

The authors also argued that the national civil code's guarantees against arbitrary or inappropriate hospitalization were unenforceable and often ignored because of defects in the law's wording, its application by medical and judicial authorities, and because of the decrepit condition of the hospitals. Not surprisingly, when the military junta fell in 1983, upwards of 85 per cent of public psychiatric patients "[had been] there for years, in many cases until death, without anyone outside the hospital being charged to defend their rights."[115] This was true in cases in which hospitalization had been necessary and also when family or neighbours had conspired to deprive individuals of their liberty for personal gain. In many of the latter cases, patients wound up losing control over property. The authors concluded that many patients, lost to the outside world, simply became accustomed to hospital life and vanished behind asylum walls.[116]

> In the majority of the cases, the police acted in collaboration with family members, and they did not consider themselves responsible for the hospitalization. They therefore did not inform the judge of their actions. Nevertheless, in the hospital the person was considered as interned by the police, and was not allowed to leave until the hospital had received judicial authorization which never arrived since no judge had been apprised of the case.[117]

The authors concluded that Argentina's public psychiatric facilities, especially in terms of legal oversight of hospitalization, were decades behind countries of similar economic development. Similar attitudes were also evident in the popular press. An article that appeared in 1984 equated living conditions in public psychiatric hospitals and the continued use of electroconvulsive therapy with the torture inflicted on political prisoners by the former military government.[118] Hospital conditions in the post-dictatorship era were also affected by economic policies of both the military and democratic governments. What one Argentine researcher refers to as Argentina's "semi-welfare state," began to collapse in the 1980s. The trend only accelerated in the 1990s with adoption of structural reforms that slashed state subsidies in key areas such as health. A walk through any public hospital in Argentina today reveals their devastating impact.[119]

With the collapse of the public sector in the post-dictatorship period, the exercise of authority within hospitals became even more fragmented than in earlier periods. It became commonplace for authority to reside less in the hospital director than in the heads of individual wards. The result has been the emergence of a wide range of approaches, techniques, and attitudes within the same hospital. But although patient abuse existed, a far greater problem was that patients were often forgotten, left to wander the hospital grounds for long stretches of time. Like the character Rantés in the film *Man Facing Southeast*, there were even reported cases of individuals living on hospital grounds whose identity and provenance were unknown to administrators.[120]

In the period following the restoration of democracy, doctors also began to reformulate their historical memory of the profession. Enrique Pichón-Rivière, who became well known in the 1960s and 1970s for his communitarian approaches to mental health, offered a fascinating, if highly subjective, account of the 1928 murder of Doctor López Lecube, whose case introduced Chapter 3 of this book:

> The origin of the problem lay in the extreme authoritarianism with which López Lecube treated the patients, as if they were *peones* on his estancia. Many times, I wondered why such a similar incident had not occurred before. But the manner of the psychiatrist, who reflected the general behavior of the asylum doctors, had slowly produced in the patients the idea of a violent response. The patients formed a team to plan the attack. They had been meeting and organizing with the trappings of a plot. I uncovered the plot, unfortunately after the murder. They even chose the assassins by drawing lots.[121]

In reconstructing the history of the profession, a significant number of mental health professionals, also began to articulate an impassioned critique of biomedical interpretations of mental illness. To a certain extent, they see the biomedical framework as a residue of the conservative psychiatrists who had become dominant in the profession during the dictatorship but also as yet another example of the encroaching power of North American corporate and ideological aggression in Argentina.[122]

Conclusions

In post–World War II Argentina, significant national and local mental health reforms occurred despite the increasingly violent political situation. Critical to long-range policy change were institutions and individuals who were able to provide consistent policy planning and implementation in the face of often overwhelming political instability. The work of the INSM, for example, maintained surprising levels of program consistency. A factor common to the most successful reforms was that they *indirectly* attacked the hegemony of established interests inside the hospitals. Municipal outpatient clinics, for example, were designed to divert the movement of patients away from the large asylums. Likewise, therapeutic communities that operated in general hospitals or in other locations tended to fare better than those that were established inside existing institutions. In part this was because staff and professionals within psychiatric hospitals who opposed change were able to take advantage of the volatile political climate to successfully resist reforms.

The social and political context of these changes was also a critical factor. Worldwide, there was a push to reorient psychiatric practice away from the traditional asylums. Aramburu and Onganía saw the transformation of mental health care as part of a larger project to modernize the Argentine state. That some of the most effective reforms in these areas came under the auspices of military regimes can also be understood, in part, as a reflection of the relative strength and stability of the armed forces in a country where most public institutions were weak. Reformers everywhere faced daunting challenges in the post-war period, but in Argentina those challenges were aggravated by economic underdevelopment and political instability. Similarly, the continuous arrival of psychiatric patients from rural areas may have placed added pressure on community mental health clinics. Ultimately, however, it was the growing political strife of the period, culminating in full-blown state-sponsored terror after 1976, that undid the reformers' precarious balancing act.[123]

7

7: CONCLUSION: SOCIAL CONTROL IN A WEAK STATE

> [S]ome states have gained much more mastery than others in governing who may heal the sick and who may not; the duration, content, and quality of children's education; ... and countless other details of human action and relationship.[1]

From the late nineteenth century onwards, the Argentine state made significant strides in the development of its economic and social infrastructure. Its successful efforts in education, disease eradication, transportation, and attracting European immigration made Argentina the envy of elites elsewhere in Latin America. The state's ability to regulate civil society also grew exponentially, as seen in areas as diverse as prostitution regulation, penitentiary construction, the development of a national police force, and the imposition of military conscription, obligatory suffrage, and a national identification system. In sum, the state enacted policies that indeed penetrated civil society and shaped the behaviour of individuals and families. For some historians, these latter endeavours, and the ideology that supported them, reflect a particular form of Argentine authoritarianism, which has been heavily informed by medical and scientific notions of hygiene. Historian Donna Guy, for example, has argued persuasively with regard to the regulation of female prostitution that "there are tendencies within the Argentine democratic traditions that justify the systematic restriction of civil rights on the basis of gender, class, and health." She continues, reminding her readers that "the politics of moral reform in Argentina have failed to address authoritarian aspects of its agenda."[2] Historian Julia Rodriguez has added to this position by showing the importance of science and medicine in shaping these authoritarian practices.[3]

The precise relationship of these authoritarian traditions, with their varied and often horrific results, to the experiences of psychiatric patients is not so clear. Although from the perspective of proposals and publications, one would expect to find a well-regulated and tightly controlled system of psychiatric care, the final product has been more strongly characterized by a degree of chaos, neglect, and diffuse social control. In general terms, political and economic instability and social polarization have frequently interfered with state-building enterprises (which include both the creation of infrastructures and the elaboration of state authority into civil society). Moreover, the imprint of the state varies widely from one geographic area to another and certain social groups have not received the attention of the state (for good or ill) that reformers hoped. While psychiatric patients fit into this category, it would be a mistake to discount this population as anomalous. For certainly the historical record on state efforts in areas as diverse as labour legislation, social welfare, and even political repression would suggest similar patterns of bureaucratic disorder and programmatic inconsistency.[4]

Like their counterparts in late-nineteenth-century western Europe and North America, Argentine professionals tried to develop a strong and thorough psychiatric network as part of a broader project to create an orderly, rational, and modern society.[5] This effort involved identifying, diagnosing, and segregating those deemed sick, dangerous, or otherwise "defective."[6] Throughout the period under consideration, psychiatrists tried to convince society at large, state functionaries, and politicians how and why various psychiatric institutions and techniques could be used to enhance national welfare and strength. Moreover, psychiatrists sought to convince the broader population, as had been done with some success in the United States and elsewhere that certain segments of the population posed such a moral, biological, and physical danger that they should be confined.[7]

To better impose these normative behaviours on the populace, and also to improve national health, psychiatrists called for the creation of institutions to facilitate their penetration into civil society. First, and foremost, they asked for a vast array of hospitals that would treat distinct types of patients throughout the national territory. Similarly, they argued for the rationalization of care through the development of adequate legal norms for confinement and release of the mentally ill from hospitals. Such a system would protect patients from neglect, abuse, or abandonment and would shelter doctors from charges of abuse of power. Moreover, a proper legal system would help to buffer psychiatrists from untoward pressure from the families of patients who might attempt to gain their premature release. The state also needed to invest in providing better statistical data. Only when the exact number and location of mentally ill and retarded had been ascertained, they asserted, could a comprehensive and national program for their care and confinement be devised or implemented. At the same time, many psychiatrists argued that the state of Argentina's psychiatric health was seriously harmed by uncontrolled immigration. The presence of so many mentally ill immigrants was a burden on the ability of the hospitals to function properly, and those who remained unconfined represented a hidden threat to the nation's health and vitality.

These proposals reflected doctors' acute reading of developments in western Europe and North America. Particularly in the decades preceding World War I, it was common for social critics in Europe to compare the state of national health with that of potential military foes and use various medical standards to gauge military preparedness. Argentine psychiatrists, by contrast, looked to the states of Europe not in terms of potential military conflict, but rather to gauge the level of national civilization. As a country of mostly European descendants (or so popular myth held), Argentina should not only have had rates of insanity similar to certain European countries, but should also possess adequate means to control and care for the mentally ill. The great paradox, of course, was that these same Europeans that Argentines looked to were often full of their own anxieties about degeneration, racial poisons, increasing rates insanity, and society's general refusal to abide by the rationalizing efforts of psychiatry.[8]

Argentine psychiatrists' experiences inside a system which they viewed as defective produced paradoxical results for the profession. The relative lack of state support encouraged them to develop a rhetoric that emphasized the mentally ill's dangerousness to the Argentine nation. Psychiatrists, in essence, offered to protect national vitality through the confinement and cure of Argentina's "defective" citizens whose unknown number and location only heightened their threat.[9] Psychiatrists referenced the latest advances in eugenics, mental hygiene, and psychiatric practices in wealthier countries to bolster their claim that the large population of non-institutionalized insane not only burdened Argentina's national vigour, but diminished the country's international reputation. As early as the 1920s, these experiences also began to shape their consciousness of Argentina's true position in the world; the republic, they argued, had all of the problems of a modern nation, but few of the resources to combat them. While expressing frustration at this state of affairs, critics also complained about the behaviour and attitudes of the lay public towards psychiatric authority. Families, although increasingly willing to institutionalize relatives, maintained ambivalence about the usefulness and benefits of psychiatric institutions.

Many doctors also believed that the absence of legal protection of the mentally ill further weakened psychiatry's attempt to gain public trust and acceptance. With the state waiving its prerogative to regulate behaviour with regard to the confinement, treatment, and release of patients, the task fell to doctors and families to negotiate the rules of conduct. As parliamentary debates and professional journal articles indicate, doctors viewed this freedom with great ambivalence. The lack of firm guarantees and safeguards, as well as consistent and enforceable laws, exposed psychiatrists to the suspicion of the general public.

But the lack of what doctors considered adequate support may have also encouraged their professional creativity. Examples abound of doctors and staff (who get less credit than they deserved) engaging in innovative challenges to traditional psychiatry. Radio broadcasts by patients in the 1930s (and more recently as well), the creation of democratic therapeutic communities during the 1960s, and the recent broadbased challenges to the global hegemony of biomedical psychiatry all emerged at least in part as responses to a broken mental health care system.

What were the results of this situation for patients and their families? Because psychiatrists were less successful in expanding the scope and depth of their authority, fewer Argentines were formally labelled as mentally ill or retarded and confined, compared with the United States or western Europe, where insane asylums and institutions for the feebleminded proliferated and attained massive populations. And if psychiatrists' complaints are to be believed, Argentina's patients and their families enjoyed considerable success in challenging doctors' medical and legal authority. In some sense, the questioning of medical orthodoxy continues to be a vital part of Argentine popular culture to this day.

APPENDICES

APPENDICES

Note on Appendices: The data collected below comes from the annual reports of the Hospital Nacional de Alienadas and the Hospicio de las Mercedes. While most of the data is accurate, there are some areas where we must view the numbers with scepticism. First, while the hospitals recorded the provincial origins of patients, in many cases patients may have been listed as coming from Buenos Aires even though they had only recently arrived to the city from another province. Second, statistics concerning the percentage of alcoholics admitted to the Hospicio only indicates the official diagnosis of admitted patients. Finally, Appendix C provides data on the movement of patients in and out of the hospitals. In some years, the hospitals only listed the number of departing patients, and whether they were alive or deceased. In other years, they listed more precise information about the condition of released patients. It should be remembered, however, that the hospitals' designation of released patient as "cured," "improved," etc. were highly subjective categories that in some cases may reveal more about how the hospitals' administrators viewed their work than the actual condition of patients.

Appendix A

Hospicio de las Mercedes: Domestic Origin of Patients

Year	*Buenos Aires*	*Province of Buenos Aires*	*Interior*
1902	51.68%	19.74%	28.57%
1903	56.64%	9.44%	33.91%
1904	54.75%	19.34%	25.89%
1905	59.42%	16.80%	23.77%
1910	60.06%	15.32%	24.66%
1915	73.33%	15.30%	11.36%
1920	68.46%	20.45%	11.08%
1925	68.98%	22.34%	8.67%
1930	68.93%	22.51%	8.54%
1931	66.07%	23.26%	10.65%
1932	65.26%	25.71%	9.02%
1933	62.45%	27.82%	9.72%
1934	67.81%	23.63%	8.54%
1935	61.74%	26.72%	11.52%
1936	62.56%	24.78%	12.64%

Hospital Nacional de Alienadas: Domestic Origin of Patients

Year	*Buenos Aires*	*Province of Buenos Aires*	*Interior*
1900	67.57%	15.17%	17.25%
1903	60.52%	20.36%	19.10%
1905	58.76%	20.44%	20.78%
1910	54.45%	27.58%	17.95%
1915	66.10%	22.65%	11.23%
1920	61.20%	28.03%	10.75%
1925	64.34%	26.57%	9.07%
1933	63.29%	28.56%	8.14%
1934	67.56%	28.06%	4.36%
1935	74.81%	20.70%	4.47%
1936	75.40%	21.18%	3.40%
1937	71.12%	22.92%	5.94%
1939	71.78%	21.65%	6.56%
1940	71.01%	24.27%	4.70%
1941	71.79%	21.75%	6.44%
1942	71.56%	24.37%	4.06%
1943	68.35%	31.48%	0.16%

Appendix B
Hospicio de las Mercedes: Alcoholics Admitted 1901–39

Year	*Total Admitted*	*Alcoholics*	*% Alcoholic*
1901	853	495	57%
1902	784	421	53%
1903	905	384	43%
1904	977	583	39%
1905	1,220	531	43%
1906	1,158	471	40%
1907	1,289	549	42%
1908	1,177	505	42%
1909	1,384	600	43%
1910	1,253	568	45%
1911	1,348	552	40%
1912	1,465	573	38%
1913	1,598	625	39%
1914	1,535	476	31%
1915	1,549	567	36%
1916	1,592	562	35%
1917	1,502	510	33%
1918	1,546	514	33%
1919	1,501	529	35%
1920	1,633	479	29%

Year	*Total Admitted*	*Alcoholics*	*% Alcoholic*
1921	1,648	491	29%
1922	1,758	479	27%
1923	1,884	543	28%
1924	1,948	542	27%
1925	1,902	504	26%
1926	1,964	566	28%
1927	2,018	648	32%
1928	1,951	539	27%
1929	2,015	525	26%
1930	2,141	564	26%
1931	2,102	397	18%
1932	2,182	390	17%
1933	2,304	385	16%
1934	2,001	330	16%
1935	2,125	375	17%
1936	2,009	353	17%
1937	2,067	401	19%
1938	2,106	315	14%
1939	2,163	365	16%

Appendix C

Movement of Patients at the Hospital Nacional de Alienadas, 1890–1940

Year	*Admissions*	*Releases*	*Deaths*	*Patients at 31 December*
1890	270	261	63	556
1891	556	n/a	n/a	n/a
1892	n/a	n/a	n/a	
1893	324	212	76	625
1894	330	205	84	666
1895	502	341	85	742
1896	520	300	87	875
1897	449	244	90	990
1898	540	284	86	1,160
1899	566	344	95	1,287
1900	626	393	121	1,399
1901	657	418	140	1,488
1902	578	384	112	1,570
1903	717	484	168	1,635
1904	811	518	200	1,728
1905	861	542	190	1,857
1906	887	596	200	1,948
1907	923	691	233	1,947
1908	879	934	251	1,641
1909	1,011	702	209	1,741
1910	696	599	146	1,692
1911	848	483	245	1,812
1912	973	620	258	1,907
1913	911	711	282	1,825
1914	1,121	1,304	266	1,376

Year	*Admissions*	*Releases*	*Deaths*	*Patients at 31 December*
1915	1,068	717	224	1,503
1916	968	689	250	1,532
1917	1,030	676	227	1,659
1918	1,042	739	227	1,735
1919	1,105	813	268	1,759
1920	1,227	870	243	1,873
1921	1,142	815	241	1,959
1922	1,229	845	232	2,111
1923	1,340	1,617	221	1,613
1924	1,468	949	186	1,946
1925	1,366	1,063	269	1,980
1926	1,430	945	240	2,225
1927	1,479	1,053	275	2,376
1928	1,461	1,334	270	2,233
1929	1,594	1,042	289	2,496
1930	1,697	1,264	282	2,647
1931	1,713	1,515	216	2,629
1932	1,956	1,520	243	2,822
1933	1,970	1,457	281	3,054
1934	481	1,655	105	1,775
1935	826	620	93	1,888
1936	793	575	126	1,980
1937	1,278	912	133	2,213
1938	1,305	864	174	2,480
1939	1,173	983	121	2,549
1940	935	1,211	96	2,177

Movement of Patients at the Hospital Nacional de Alienadas, 1900–1943

YEAR	*1900*			*1910*		
		% of Depart.	*% of Total*		*% of Depart.*	*% of Total*
Number on January 1	1287			1741		
Admitted	626			696		
Assisted	1913			2437		
DEPARTED						
Cured	91	17.70%	4.76%	599	80.40%	24.58%
Improved	116	22.57%	6.06%	0	0.00%	0.00%
Not Improved	178	34.63%	9.30%	0	0.00%	0.00%
Transferred	0	0.00%	0.00%	0	0.00%	0.00%
Escaped	8	1.56%	0.42%	0	0.00%	0.00%
Not Insane	0	0.00%	0.00%	0	0.00%	0.00%
Dead	121	23.54%	6.33%	146	19.60%	5.99%
Total Departures	514			745		
Number on December 31	1399			1692		
Change in Population	112			–49		

YEAR	1925			1930		
		% of Depart.	*% of Total*		*% of Depart.*	*% of Total*
Number on January 1	1945			2496		
Admitted	1366			1697		
Assisted	3311			4193		
DEPARTED						
Cured	908	68.22%	27.42%	901	58.28%	21.49%
Improved	0	0.00%	0.00%	0	0.00%	0.00%
Not Improved	0	0.00%	0.00%	125	8.09%	2.98%
Transferred	131	9.84%	3.96%	206	13.32%	4.91%
Escaped	23	1.73%	0.69%	25	1.62%	0.60%
Not Insane	0	0.00%	0.00%	7	0.45%	0.17%
Dead	269	20.21%	8.12%	282	18.24%	6.73%
Total Departures	1331			1546		
Number on December 31	1980			2647		
Change in Population	35			151		

YEAR	1935			1940		
		% of Depart.	*% of Total*		*% of Depart.*	*% of Total*
Number on January 1	1775			2549		
Admitted	826			935		
Assisted	2601			3484		
DEPARTED						
Cured	358	51.00%	13.76%	21	1.61%	0.60%
Improved	0	0.00%	0.00%	369	28.23%	10.59%
Not Improved	0	0.00%	0.00%	3	0.23%	0.09%
Transferred	251	35.75%	9.65%	805	61.59%	23.11%
Escaped	0	0.00%	0.00%	13	0.99%	0.37%
Not Insane	0	0.00%	0.00%	0	0.00%	0.00%
Dead	93	13.25%	3.58%	96	7.35%	2.76%
Total Departures	702			1307		
Number on December 31	1899			2177		
Change in Population	124			–372		

YEAR	*1943*		
		% of Depart.	*% of Total*
Number on January 1	2379		
Admitted	613		
Assisted	2992		
DEPARTED			
Cured	0	0.00%	0.00%
Improved	278	38.40%	9.29%
Not Improved	1	0.14%	0.03%
Transferred	329	45.44%	11.00%
Escaped	13	1.80%	0.43%
Not Insane	1	0.14%	0.03%
Dead	102	14.09%	3.41%
Total Departures	724		
Number on December 31	2268		
Change in Population	–111		

Movement of Patients at the Hospicio de las Mercedes, 1893–1937

Year	*Admissions*	*Releases*	*Deaths*	*Patients at 31 December*
1893	495	405	121	791
1910	1253	877	396	1783
1912	1465	907	375	1919
1913	1598	1059	505	1953
1914	1535	1566	449	1473
1915	1549	1340	410	1272
1916	1592	1018	443	1403
1917	1502	934	515	1456
1918	1546	1123	544	1335
1919	1501	974	387	1475
1922	1758	1054	485	1976
1923	1884	1141	550	2169
1924	1948	1595	548	1974
1925	1902	1497	410	1969
1926	1964	1618	454	1861
1927	2018	1330	451	2098
1928	1951	1324	545	2180
1929	2015	1466	574	2155
1930	2141	1548	461	2287
1931	2102	1497	398	2494
1932	2182	2175	346	2155
1933	2304	2000	308	2151
1934	2001	1315	337	2500
1935	2125	1698	398	2529
1937	N/A	1515	362	2851

YEAR	1893			1910		
		% of Depart.	*% of Total*		*% of Depart.*	*% of Total*
Number on January 1	822			1803		
Admitted	495			1253		
Assisted	1317			3056		
DEPARTED						
Cured	144	27.38%	10.93%	180	14.14%	5.89%
Improved	164	31.18%	12.45%	285	22.39%	9.33%
Not Improved	27	5.13%	2.05%	63	4.95%	2.06%
Transferred	0	0.00%	0.00%	329	25.84%	10.77%
Escaped	70	13.31%	5.32%	15	1.18%	0.49%
Not Insane	0	0.00%	0.00%	5	0.39%	0.16%
Dead	121	23.00%	9.19%	396	31.11%	12.96%
Total Departures	526			1273		
Number on December 31	791			1783		
Change In Population	-31			-20		

YEAR	1915			1919		
		% of Depart.	*% of Total*		*% of Depart.*	*% of Total*
Number on January 1	1473			1335		
Admitted	1549			1501		
Assisted	3022			2836		
DEPARTED						
Cured	158	9.03%	5.23%	166	12.20%	5.85%
Improved	349	19.94%	11.55%	454	33.36%	16.01%
Not Improved	96	5.49%	3.18%	68	5.00%	2.40%
Transferred	719	41.09%	23.79%	254	18.66%	8.96%
Escaped	9	0.51%	0.30%	20	1.47%	0.71%
Not Insane	9	0.51%	0.30%	12	0.88%	0.42%
Dead	410	23.43%	13.57%	387	28.43%	13.65%
Total Departures	1750			1361		
Number on December 31	1272			1475		
Change In Population	-201			140		

YEAR	1922			1925		
		% of Depart.	*% of Total*		*% of Depart.*	*% of Total*
Number on January 1	1757			1974		
Admitted	1758			1902		
Assisted	3515			3876		
DEPARTED						
Cured	129	8.38%	3.67%	108	5.66%	2.79%
Improved	544	35.35%	15.48%	553	29.00%	14.27%
Not Improved	158	10.27%	4.50%	162	8.50%	4.18%
Transferred	167	10.85%	4.75%	608	31.88%	15.69%
Escaped	34	2.21%	0.97%	47	2.46%	1.21%
Not Insane	22	1.43%	0.63%	19	1.00%	0.49%
Dead	485	31.51%	13.80%	410	21.50%	10.58%
Total Departures	1539			1907		
Number on December 31	1976			1969		
Change In Population	219			-5		

YEAR	1930			1935		
		% of Depart.	*% of Total*		*% of Depart.*	*% of Total*
Number on January 1	2155			2500		
Admitted	2141			2125		
Assisted	4296			4625		
DEPARTED						
Cured	83	4.13%	1.93%	80	3.82%	1.73%
Improved	529	26.33%	12.31%	641	30.58%	13.86%
Not Improved	258	12.84%	6.01%	196	9.35%	4.24%
Transferred	628	31.26%	14.62%	690	32.92%	14.92%
Escaped	41	2.04%	0.95%	64	3.05%	1.38%
Not Insane	9	0.45%	0.21%	27	1.29%	0.58%
Dead	461	22.95%	10.73%	398	18.99%	8.61%
Total Departures	2009			2096		
Number on December 31	2287			2529		
Change In Population	132			29		

NOTES

NOTES

1: Introduction

1 Roberto Arlt, "Un cuidador de locos se ahorcó en el Hospicio de las Mercedes," *Aguafuertes porteñas* (Buenos Aires: Corregidor, 1995), 63–65. This story was originally published in the 1920s.

2 See also *La Raulito* (1975), which offers a similar critique of psychiatry. The film tells the story of a teenage girl who alternates between life on the streets, dressed as a man, and institutionalization. In part of the film she is confined to the Moyano asylum.

3 On the cultural history of psychoanalysis's diffusion and impact, see Mariano Ben Plotkin, *Freud in the Pampas: The Emergence and Development of a Psychoanalytic Culture in Argentina* (Stanford: Stanford University Press, 2001).

4 Particularly important works include: Wilbur R. Grimson, *Sociedad de locos: Experiencia y violencia en un hospital psiquiátrico* (Buenos Aires: Ediciones Nueva Visión, 1972); and Alfredo Moffatt, *Psicoterapia del oprimido: Ideología y técnica de la psiquiatría popular* (Buenos Aires: ECRO, 1974). For patient perspective on this question, see the extremely moving *Carta abierta a la sociedad: Un grito a través de los muros del hospicio* (Buenos Aires: Axis, 1974). Anarchists had made similar arguments in the early twentieth century. See Chapter 4.

5 Liliana Magrini and Mario Ganora, "Informe sobre violaciones graves de los derechos humanos" (Tratos y Penas Crueles Inhumanas y Degradantes) a preso y minusválidos psíquicos en los establecimientos psiquiátricos 'Colonia Nacional de Montes de Oca' y 'Hospital Neuropsiquiátrico Domingo Cabred.' Equipo Nizkor, <http:www.derechos.org/nizkor/arg/doc/psiquiatrico/>

6 Joel S. Migdal, *Strong Societies and Weak States: State-Society Relations and State Capabilities in the Third World* (Princeton: Princeton University Press, 1988), 22. See also Miguel Angel Centeno, *Blood and Debt: War and the Nation-State in Latin America* (University Park: Pennsylvania State University Press, 2003).

7 Hugo Vezzetti, *La locura en la Argentina* (Buenos Aires: Paidós, 1985); Donna J. Guy, *Sex and Danger in Buenos Aires: Prostitution, Family, and Nation in Argentina* (Lincoln: University of Nebraska Press, 1991); Julia Rodríguez, *Civilizing Argentina: Science, Medicine, and the Modern State* (Chapel Hill: University of North Carolina Press, 2005); Jorge Salessi, *Médicos, maleantes, y maricas: Higiene, criminología, y homosexualidad en la construcción de la nación argentina (Buenos Aires: 1871–1914)* (Rosario, Argentina: Beatriz Viterbo, 1995).

8 For a political and economic analysis of the economic decline that characterized Argentina, starting in 1929, see Carlos H. Waisman, *Reversal of Development in Argentina: Postwar Counterrevolutionary Policies and Their Structural Consequences* (Princeton: Princeton University Press, 1987).

9 Constance McGovern, "The Myths of Social Control and Custodial Oppression: Patterns in Psychiatric Medicine in Late Nineteenth-Century Institutions," *Journal of Social History* 20 (Fall 1986): 17.

10 Stanley Cohen and Andrew Scull, "Introduction: Social Control in History and Sociology," in Stanley Cohen and Andrew Scull, eds., *Social Control and the State: Historical and Comparative Essays* (Oxford: St. Martin's, 1983), 11. Similar cases of weak support for psychiatry include tsarist Russia.

11 Georges Clemenceau, *South America Today: A Study of Conditions, Social, Political and Commercial in Argentina, Uruguay and Brazil* (New York: G.P. Putnam, 1911), 123–32; Cesarina Lupati Guelfi, *Vida argentina (versión española)* (Barcelona: Casa Editorial Maucci, 1910); Jules Huret, *En Argentine: De Buenos-Aires au Gran Chaco* (Paris: Biblioteque-Charpentier, 1911), 100–107; Alberto Meyer Arana, *La caridad en Buenos Aires* (Buenos Aires, 1911); "Hommage au professeur Cabred," *L'hygiene mentale* 7:22 (July–August 1927): n.p.

12 Asunción Lavrín, *Women, Feminism, and Social Change in Argentina, Chile, and Uruguay, 1890–1940* (Lincoln: University of Nebraska Press, 1995), 83.

13 Arthur Kleinman and Alex Cohen, "Psychiatry's Global Challenge," *Scientific American* 276:3 (March 1997): 86–89; Shirley Christian, "In Argentina, Patients' Deaths Bring Focus on Health Care," *New York Times* (August 11, 1990): 5; "La nave de los locos," *Revista la Nación* (December 1, 1996): 84–92. The articles describe hospital conditions so horrific that, in one case, several dozen patients died of malnutrition.

14 For England, see Janet Saunders, "Quarantining the Weak-minded: Psychiatric Definitions of Degeneracy and the Late-Victorian Asylum," in *The Anatomy of Madness: Essays in the History of Psychiatry* – Vol. 3: *The Asylum and its Psychiatrists*, W.F. Bynum, Roy Porter, and Michael Shepherd, eds. (New York: Routledge, 1988), 291.

15 Jeffrey D. Needell, "Optimism and Melancholy: Elite Responses to the *fin de siècle bonarense*," *Journal of Latin American Studies* 32 (1999): 551–88.

16 On state support for psychiatric hospitals in Europe and North America, the literature is vast. See: Ian Dowbiggin, *Inheriting Madness: Professionalization and Psychiatric Knowledge in Nineteenth-Century France* (Los Angeles: University of California Press, 1991); Peter McCandless, "Build! Build!: The Controversy over the Care of the Chronically Insane in England, 1850–1870," *Bulletin of the History of Medicine* 53 (1979): 553–74; Roy Porter and David Wright, *The Confinement of the Insane: International Perspectives, 1800–1965* (Cambridge: Cambridge University Press, 2003); Gerald Grob, *Mental Illness and American Society, 1875–1940* (Princeton: Princeton University Press, 1983); James E. Moran, *Committed to the State Asylum: Insanity and Society in Nineteenth-Century Quebec and Ontario* (Montreal and Kingston: McGill-Queen's University Press, 2000); James W. Trent Jr., *Inventing the Feeble Mind: A History of Mental Retardation in the United States* (Berkeley: University of California Press, 1994); Elizabeth Lunbeck, *The Psychiatric Persuasion: Knowledge, Gender, and Power in Modern America* (Princeton: Princeton University Press, 1994).

17 On the relationship between experiences in hospitals and health policy, see Karen Mead, "Oligarchs, Doctors and Nuns: Public Health and Beneficence in Buenos Aires, 1880–1914" (Ph.D. diss., University of California, Santa Barbara, 1994), 172–242; and Ian Robert Dowbiggin, *Keeping America Sane: Psychiatry and Eugenics in the United States and Canada, 1880–1940* (Ithaca, NY: Cornell University Press, 1997).

18 Jonathan Sadowsky, *Imperial Bedlam: Institutions of Madness in Colonial Southwest Nigeria* (Los Angeles: University of California Press, 1999), 27.

19 For the United States, see Richard W. Fox, *'So far disordered in mind': Insanity in California, 1870–1930* (Los Angeles: University of California Press, 1978), 48.

20 For France, see Patricia E. Prestwich, "Family Strategies and Medical Power: 'Voluntary' Committal in a Parisian Asylum, 1876–1914," *Journal of Social History* (Summer 1994): 799–813.

21 See Kristin Ruggiero, "Wives on 'Deposit': Internment and the Preservation of Husband's Honor in Late Nineteenth-Century Buenos Aires," *Journal of Family History* 17:3 (1992): 253–70; Guy, *Sex and Danger in Buenos Aires*; Kristin Ruggiero, "Honor, Maternity, and the Disciplining of Women: Infanticide in Late Nineteenth Argentina," *Hispanic American Historical Review* 72:3 (1992): 353–73.

22 Lunbeck, *The Psychiatric Persuasion*, 4. Lunbeck has argued that ultimately the source of psychiatry's authority rests with the language that it has created to define and demarcate the deviant, aberrant, and deranged.

23 On the idea of medical pathways, see Olayiwoya A. Erinosho, "Pathways to Mental Health Delivery-Systems in Nigeria," *International Journal of Social Psychiatry* 23:1 (Spring 1997): 54–59.

24 Linda Gordon, "Feminism and Social Control: The Case of Child Abuse and Neglect," in Juliet Mitchell and Ann Oakley, eds., *What is Feminism?* (London: Basil Blackwell, 1986), 63–84; David Wright, "'Childlike in his Innocence': Lay Attitudes to 'Idiots' and 'Imbeciles' in Victorian England," in *From Idiocy to Mental Deficiency: Historical Perspectives on People with Learning Disabilities*, David Wright and Anne Digby, eds. (New York: Routledge, 1996), 118–33; and Prestwich, "Family Strategies and Medical Power," 803.

25 Sadowsky, *Imperial Bedlam*, 5.

26 Sadowsky, *Imperial Bedlam*, 5. Sadowsky also notes that "[t]he boundaries of incarcerable behavior were wider, though for people far from kin and community, even if these people were not violent."

27 For an insightful discussion of the failure of psychiatric diagnoses to achieve "stabilization" across cultures, see Andrew Lakoff, *Pharmaceutical Reason: Knowledge and Value in Global Psychiatry* (New York: Cambridge University Press, 2003): 3.

28 For an admission of the uncertainty of their work, see Nerio Rojas, "La alienación mental como causa de divorcio," *Revista de criminología, psiquiatría y medicina legal* 11 (1924): 129–38.

29 Allan V. Horwitz, *The Social Control of Mental Illness* (New York: Academic Press, 1982).

30 These cases come from the Archivo del Poder Judicial de la Nación [hereafter APJN].

31 For a discussion of the nomenclature used to describe patients, see Geoffrey Reaume, *Remembrance of Patients Past: Patient Life at the Toronto Hospital for the Insane, 1870–1940* (Oxford: Oxford University Press, 2000).

2: Foundations, Myths, and Institutions

1 José Ingenieros, *La locura en la Argentina* (Buenos Aires: 'Buenos Aires' Cooperativa Editorial Limitada, 1920), 33. Some authors cite an original publication date of 1919 for the book.

2 The hagiographic approach to the history of psychiatry is also seen in later works. See Osvaldo Loudet and Osvaldo Elías Loudet, *Historia de la psiquiatría argentina* (Buenos Aires: Troquel, 1971). For the similar case of Mexico, see María Cristina Sacristán, "Historiografía de la locura y de la psiquiatría en México. De la hagiografía a la historia posmoderna," *Frenia* 5:1 (2005): 9–33. Well into the 1960s, western European and North American scholarship on

psychiatry was decidedly Whiggish. But unlike Argentina, professional progress was less tightly linked to national progress. See Andrew Scull, "Psychiatry and its historians," *History of Psychiatry* 2 (1991): 239–50, and Roy Porter and Mark Micale, "Reflections on Psychiatry and Its Histories," in Mark Micale and Roy Porter, eds., *Discovering the History of Psychiatry* (New York: Oxford University Press, 1994), 6. Paul S. Holbo, "José Ingenieros, Argentine Intellectual Historian: *La evolución de las ideas argentinas*," *The Americas* 21:1 (July 1964): 23.

3 On the importance of scientific and medical institutions in forging national pride, see Rodriguez, *Civilizing Argentina*. Ingenieros' debt to Domingo Faustino Sarmiento's *Facundo: Civilization and Barbarism* and *Conflict and Harmony of the Races* and his pessimism about Argentina's Hispanic-African-Indian heritage is described in Diana Sorensen Goodrich, *Facundo and the Construction of Argentine Culture* (Austin: University of Texas Press, 1996), 113–16. On the similar role of the National Penitentiary, see Ricardo Salvatore, "Penitentiaries, Visions of Class, and Export Economies: Brazil and Argentina Compared," in Ricardo Salvatore and Carlos Aguirre, eds., *The Birth of the Penitentiary in Latin America: Essays on Criminology, Prison Reform, and Social Control, 1830–1940* (Austin: University of Texas Press, 1996), 214. Argentine elite were also interested in convincing Europe that Argentina was worthy of joining the ranks of "civilized" nations. See Ingrid E. Fey, "Peddling the Pampas: Argentina at the Paris Universal Exposition of 1889," in William H. Beezley and Linda A. Curcio-Nagy, eds., *Latin American Popular Culture: An Introduction* (Wilmington: SR Books, 2000), 61–85; and Alvaro Fernández-Bravo, "Ambivalent Argentina: Nationalism, Exoticism, and Latin Americanism at the 1889 Paris Universal Exposition," *Nepantla: Views from South* 2:1 (2001): 115–39. The first modern Mexican asylum, La Castañeda, was inaugurated with great fanfare in 1910, to commemorate the centennial. See María Cristina Sacristán, "Entre curar y contener: La psiquiatría mexicana ante el desamparo jurídico, 1870–1944," *Frenia* 2:2 (2002): 64.

4 Juan Carlos Stagnaro and José María Gonzáles Chaves, *Hospicio de las Mercedes: 130 años* (Buenos Aires: Editorial Polemos, 1993). This small publication reproduces twenty-five of the original laminations from a 1910 album. MREC, *Colonia Nacional de Alienados, Luján (Provincia de Buenos Aires)* (Buenos Aires: n.p., 1910), *Álbum histórico de la Sociedad de Beneficencia, 1823–1910* (Buenos Aires: n.d.), and *Origen y desenvolvimiento de la Sociedad de Beneficencia de la Capital, 1823–1912* (Buenos Aires: M. Rodríguez Giles, 1913). For a description of the neighbourhood where the hospitals were located, see Enrique Horacio Puccia, *Barracas: Su historia y sus tradiciones, 1536–1936* (Buenos Aires: n.p., 1975).

5 Georges Clemenceau, *South America Today: A Study of Conditions, Social, Political and Commercial in Argentina, Uruguay and Brazil* (New York: G.P. Putnam, 1911), 123–32. For similar assessments, see Cesarina Lupati Guelfi, *Vida argentina (versión española)* (Barcelona: Casa Editorial Maucci, 1910), 146–68; Huret, *En Argentine*, 100–107; Alberto Meyer Arana, *La caridad en Buenos Aires* (Buenos Aires, 1911); "Hommage au professeur Cabred," *L'hygiene mentale* 7:22 (July–August 1927): n.p.

6 Lupati Guelfi, *Vida argentina*, 148. Although she visited the men's asylum, she was denied access to the women's asylum.

7 Lupati Guelfi, *Vida argentina*, 145–48. According to one study, Buenos Aires was the healthiest city in the world in 1906. See "The Salubrity of Buenos Ayres," *Monthly Bulletin of the In-*

ternational Bureau of the American Republics 157: 23:4 (October 1906): 836–37. For a more critical view of health in Buenos Aires, and especially the response to a bubonic plague pandemic, see Myron Echenberg, *Plague Ports: The Global Urban Impact of Bubonic Plague, 1894–1901* (New York: New York University Press, 2007): 133–55.

8 Vezzetti, *Locura en la Argentina*, 14; Eduardo A. Balbo, "Argentinian Alienism from 1852–1918," *History of Psychiatry* 2:6, Part 2 (June 1991): 183. "The development of the hospices coincided with the *status nascendi* of the Argentinian State and with the positivist ideas of an entire generation of intellectuals who were to make social medicine an instrument of progress and ideals of that State. Ideologically, this was what united the interests of the medical profession to those of an important sector of the ruling elite...." On the thesis that public health was a key strategy of state building, see Agustina Prieto, "Rosario: epidemias, hygiene e higienistas en la segunda mitad del siglo XIX," in Mirta Zaida Lobato, ed., *Política, médicos y enfermedades: Lecturas de historia de la salud en la Argentina* (Buenos Aires: Editorial Biblos, 1996), 57. On the role of medicine and science in the state building project, see Rodriguez, *Civilizing Argentina*.

9 Adriana Álvarez, "Ramos Mejía: salud pública y multitud en la Argentina finisecular," in Lobato, *Política, médicos y enfermedades*, 82. According to the author, Ramos Mejía "sostenía que los predispuestos a la locura se contagian de los fanatismos dominantes en cada época, engrosando las filas de los sectores y determinando la aparición de esas locuras epidémicas de carácter religioso."

10 Andrea Orozco and Valeria Dávila, "Mujeres alienadas en la Argentina: Una loca historia," *Todo es historia* 324 (July 1994): 11; Ingenieros, *Locura en la Argentina*, 33–41, 79–80; George Reid Andrews, *The Afro-Argentines of Buenos Aires, 1800–1900* (Madison: University of Wisconsin Press, 1980). See: Humberto Roselli, "Aspectos medico-psiquiátricos de inquisición en Cartagena de Indias," *Acta psiquiátrica y psicológica de América Latina* 15:3 (September 1968): 252–61; Salomón Chichilnisky, "Historia de la psiquiatría argentina" (Buenos Aires: n.p., ca. 1967–1969); Samuel Gache, *El estado mental en la sociedad de Buenos Aires* (Buenos Aires: La Nación, 1881); and Cynthia Jeffress Little, "The Society of Beneficence in Buenos Aires, 1823–1900" (Ph.D. diss., Temple University, 1980), 225. See also: Peter McCandless, *Moonlight, Magnolias, and Madness: Insanity in South Carolina from the Colonial Period to the Progressive Era* (Chapel Hill: University of North Carolina Press, 1996), 15–39; and David J. Rothman, *The Discovery of the Asylum: Social Order and Disorder in the New Republic* (Boston: Little, Brown, 1971).

11 Ingenieros, *Locura en la Argentina*, 94.

12 Ingenieros, *Locura en la Argentina*, 45–47.

13 Ingenieros, *Locura en la Argentina*, 36. Colonial authorities took *hechiceria* quite seriously and punished practitioners with death, imprisonment, or exile. See Judith Faberman, "La fama de la hechicera: La buena reputación femenina en un proceso criminal del siglo XVIII," in Fernanda Gil Lozano, Valeria Silvina Pita, and María Gabriela Ini, eds., *Historia de las mujeres en la Argentina: Colonia y siglo XIX* (Buenos Aires: Taurus, 2000), 26–47. On the other hand, research on colonial Mexico has shown that the church, and specifically the Inquisition, made sincere efforts to distinguish between madness, witchcraft, and demonic possession. See María Cristina Sacristán, *Locura e inquisición en Nueva España, 1571–1760* (México: Fondo de Cultura Económica, 1992) and *Locura y disidencia en el México ilustrado, 1760–1810* (Zamora, México: El

Colegio de Michoacán; México: Instituto Mora, 1994).

14 Ingenieros, *Locura en la Argentina*, 36–39. According to the author, "it is noteworthy that this form of African superstition never translated into criminal acts against whites, as occurs in Brazil and Cuba to this day, where witch doctors come to demand the blood of white children to cure ailments." Ingenieros suggested that blacks and whites lived in close proximity in the city and that this had a salutary effect on the behaviour of Afro-Argentines. Ingenieros also recounted a story from his youth, when he accompanied the family's black servant, who herself was Europeanizing, to an Afro-Argentine ritual healing of a *negro loco*. The servant later reported that "they had brought the patient to the Convalescencia, as *El Tata* did not get better, adding disrespectfully that *bailes de santos* were 'black folk's things.' On the medicalization of African traditions elsewhere, see: Dain Borges, "'Puffy, Ugly, Slothful and Inert': Degeneration in Brazilian Social Thought, 1880–1940," *Journal of Latin American Studies* 25 (1993): 235–56; and Israel Castellanos, "Estudio antropológico de las asiladas en la Escuela Reformatoria de Aldecoa," *Revista de criminología, psiquiatría y medicina legal* 11:7–8 (January–April 1915): 212–21. Ingenieros was influenced by the medico-anthropological writings of Cubans Fernando Ortiz and Israel Castellanos and Brazilian Nina Rodrigues. For an astute analysis of the social and historical context of psychiatric diagnoses, see H.C. Erik Midelfort, *A History of Madness in Sixteenth-Century Germany* (Stanford: Stanford University Press, 1999).

15 Antonio Alberto Guerrino, *La psiquiatría argentina* (Buenos Aires: Editores Cuatro, 1982), 39–40. Ingenieros suggests the later date. The hospital was on the block encompassed by Méjico, Chile, Defensa and Balcarce streets.

16 Ingenieros, *Locura en la Argentina*, 57. The populace avoided treatment "por un vecino español que jamás había sangrado ni puesto sanguijuelas."

17 Ingenieros, *Locura en la Argentina*, 65.

18 Ingenieros, *Locura en la Argentina*, 74–75. See also Carlos María Birocco, "La primera Casa de Recogimiento de Huérfanas de Buenos Aires: El beatario de Pedro de Vera y Aragón (1692–1702)," in José Luis Moreno, ed., *La política social antes de la política social (Caridad, beneficencia y política social en Buenos Aires, siglos XVII a XX)* (Buenos Aires: Trama Editorial/Prometeo libros, 2000), 21–46. In 1745, Buenos Aires' first convent, the *Convento de Santa Catalina de Siena*, opened. On traditional Catholic attitudes towards poverty and its amelioration, see: A.J.R. Russell-Wood, *Fidalgos and Philanthropists: The Santa Casa da Misericórdia of Bahia, 1550–1755* (Los Angeles: University of California Press, 1968); and Silvia Marina Arrom, *Containing the Poor: The Mexico City Poor House, 1774–1871* (Durham, NC: Duke University Press, 2000).

19 Susan Socolow, *The Bureaucrats of Buenos Aires, 1769–1810* (Durham, NC: Duke University Press, 1987).

20 Little, "Society of Beneficence," 22–27; Orozco and Dávila, "Mujeres alienadas en la Argentina," 12.

21 Ingenieros, *Locura en la Argentina*, 79.

22 Orozco and Dávila, "Mujeres alienadas en la Argentina," 14–15; Little, "Society of Beneficence," 28; Susan Socolow, *The Merchants of Buenos Aires, 1778–1810* (Cambridge: Cambridge University Press, 1978), 95–97.

23 Ingenieros, *Locura en la Argentina*, 83–97, 130–33; Guerrino, *Psiquiatría argentina*, 23, 40. José Luis Moreno, "La Casa de Niños Expósitos de Buenos Aires, conflictos institucionales, condiciones de vida y mortalidad de los infantes, 1779–1823," in José Luis Moreno, ed., *La política social antes de*

la política social (Caridad, beneficencia y política social en Buenos Aires, siglos XVII a XX) (Buenos Aires: Trama Editorial/Prometeo libros, 2000), 91–128.

24 John Tate Lanning, *The Royal Protomedicato: The Regulation of the Medical Professions in the Spanish Empire* (Durham, NC: Duke University Press, 1985). Guerrino, *Psiquiatría argentina*, 23–26. See also Raúl F. Vaccarezza, *Vida de médicos ilustres* (Buenos Aires: Ediciones Troquel, 1980), 72.

25 Evidence from larger colonial cities suggests that Bourbon efforts to "modernize" attitudes toward poverty and illness often were met with stiff popular resistance. See Arrom, *Containing the Poor*, 1–11.

26 David Bushnell, *Reform and Reaction in the Platine Provinces, 1810–1852* (Gainesville: University of Florida Press, 1983), 125. According to Ingenieros, seizure of the order's possessions may have been a response to the alleged involvement of the order's Superior, Fray José de las Animas in the royalist plot of the Basque-born Martín de Alzaga. The two were executed by hanging, "a monopolist and a friar, a fitting symbol of the colonial regime." Ingenieros, *Locura en la Argentina*, 100–102.

27 Bushnell, *Reform and Reaction*, 126.

28 John Lynch, "From Independence to National Organization," in Leslie Bethell, ed., *Argentina since Independence* (New York: Cambridge University Press, 1993), 19–20; Jonathan Harris, "Bernardino Rivadavia: Benthamite 'Discipleship,'" *Latin American Research Review* 33:1 (1998): 129–49; Guillermo Gallardo, *La política religiosa de Rivadavia* (Buenos Aires: Ediciones Theoria, 1962).

29 Vaccarezza, *Vida de médicos*, 72–73. For a description of medical curriculum at the university, see Loudet and Loudet, *Historia de la psiquiatría argentina*, 14. On the history of early psychiatry training and research, see: Eduardo A. Balbo, trans., "Classic Text No. 6 – Dissertation on acute mania, Diego Alcorta." *History of Psychiatry* 2 (1991): 207; Loudet and Loudet, *Historia de la psiquiatría argentina*, 16–20; and *Temas en la historia de la psiquiatría argentina* 2 (Winter 1997): n.p. Diego Alcorta's thesis reflected heavy influence of French alienists Pinel and Esquirol. The young doctor argued for the recognition that mental functions were still but little understood and that a regimen of "moral therapy" that emphasized humane treatment would render the best results.

30 Guerrino, *Psiquiatría argentina*, 23–25.

31 Ingenieros, *Locura en la Argentina*, 103, 224. Calls for the wholesale confinement of the city's insane, which occurred in 1822, 1853, and 1881, all coincided with regime changes.

32 Austen Ivereigh, *Catholicism and Politics in Argentina, 1810–1960* (London: St. Martin's, 1995), 44.

33 Ingenieros, *Locura en la Argentina*, 103–4, 107–13. Guerrino, *Psiquiatría argentina*, 122; Ángel M. Gimenez, *Un debate histórico: La reforma eclesiástica de Rivadavia - la monja Vicenta Álvarez* (Buenos Aires: Imprenta Federación Gráfica Bonaerense, 1932).

34 John Lynch, *Argentine Dictator: Juan Manuel de Rosas, 1829–1852* (Oxford: Clarendon Press, 1981).

35 Ariel de la Fuente, *Children of Facundo: Caudillo and Gaucho Insurgency during the Argentine State-Formation Process (La Rioja, 1853–1870)* (Durham, NC: Duke University Press, 2000), 8.

36 Jorge Meyer, *Orden y virtud: El discurso republicano en el régimen rosista* (Quilmes: Universidad Nacional de Quilmes, 1995), 53. Meyer stresses that Rosas displayed a "classical republicanism" that stressed the importance of order to control the masses.

37 Ingenieros, *Locura en la Argentina*, 156. "Justo es consignar que la Restauración creó un ambiente desfavorable

para los estudios de patología mental, sospechosos de herejía."

38 Historian Ricardo Salvatore argues that "[t]he repression of anti-social behavior underscore[d] the importance of harmony and respectability to local communities" and that "shouting on the streets, for example, was considered an affront to public morality." Ricardo Salvatore, *Wandering Paysanos: State Order and Subaltern Experience in Buenos Aires during the Rosas Era* (Durham, NC: Duke University Press, 2003), 205; and Meyer, *Orden y virtud*, 53.

39 Ingenieros, *Locura en la Argentina*, 106. On the historiography of Rosas, see Edberto Oscar Acevedo, "Situación actual de la historia argentina," *Estudios americanos* 60:43 (May 1955): n.p. On the question of changes in the degree and nature of social control between the regime of Rivadavia and other Unitarios and that of Rosas, see: Richard W. Slatta and Karla Robinson, "Continuities in Crime and Punishment: Buenos Aires, 1820–50," in Lyman L. Johnson, ed., *The Problem of Order in Changing Societies: Essays on Crime and Policing in Argentina and Uruguay, 1750–1940* (Albuquerque: University of New Mexico Press, 1990), 19–45; and Ivereigh, *Catholicism and Politics in Argentina*, 46–47.

40 Ingenieros, *Locura en la Argentina*, 136. The author quotes J.M. Ramos Mejías' classic nineteenth-century text *Las neurosis de los hombres celebres*: "El terror en las clases superiores y ese brusco cambio de nivel que experimentaron las clases bajas, elevadas rápidamente por el sistema de Rosas a una altura y prepotencia inusitada, tuvieron también su parte en la patogenia de tales trastornos...." The idea that social mobility might contribute to mental illness among subordinate groups is not unique to Argentina. For the United States South, see John S. Hughes, "Labeling and Treating Black Mental Illness in Alabama, 1861–1910," *Journal of Southern History* 58 (1992): 435–60.

41 Vezzetti, *Locura en la Argentina*, 91–104. A lively debate also existed as to whether Rosas himself was mad.

42 Gache, *El estado mental*, 39–64; Ingenieros, *Locura en la Argentina*, 135, 146–52. Ingenieros perceived a tendency to label political opponents as mad. Rosas' ally in Mendoza province, Fraile Aldao, decreed in 1842 that all enemies of Rosas should be considered insane and treated accordingly. Political opponents during this period also labelled each other as homosexuals. See Salessi, *Médicos, maleantes, y maricas*, 61. See also Benigno Trigo, "Crossing the Boundaries of Madness: Criminology and Figurative Language in Argentina (1878–1920)," *Journal of Latin American Cultural Studies* 6:1 (1997): 13.

43 Ingenieros, *Locura en la Argentina*, 135. I have found no mention of this perception in the contemporary accounts from the Rosas period. Moreover, Little has suggested that the fact that women from pro-Rosas families were integral to the reconstitution of the Society of Beneficence suggests greater continuity across the regimes. See Little, "Society of Beneficence," 70.

44 As in any violent political transition, sectors of the Argentine elite sought to hide any personal or familial associations to the old regime. See Hilda Sábato, *The Many and the Few: Political Participation in Republican Buenos Aires* (Stanford: Stanford University Press, 2001), 23. On the asylums, see Eduardo A. Balbo, "El manicomio en el alienismo argentino," *Asclepio* 40:2 (1988): 153.

45 Many recent scholars have noted that, despite the rhetoric of the victorious anti-Rosistas, the new regime was in many respects as repressive as its predecessor. See Ricardo Salvatore, "Death and Democracy: Capital Punishment after the Fall of Rosas," Working Paper #43, Universidad Torcuato di Tella (August 1997): 1–29; and Mark D. Szuchman, *Order, Family, and Community*

in Buenos Aires, 1810–1860 (Stanford: Stanford University Press, 1988).

46 Balbo, "Argentinian Alienism," 186. Author quotes a newspaper article from 1855: "Today, corrupted individuals roam free in our society, when the experience of other countries has shown that it is a simple matter to purify them and restore them to their families and society so that they may be as useful as they are now pernicious." See also Gonzalo Bosch, "Resumen histórico de la psiquiatría," *La semana médica*, Tomo de Cincuentenario, fascículo II (1944): 601–5, as cited in Guerrino, *Psiquiatría argentina*, 43.

47 Ernest Allen Crider, "Modernization and Human Welfare: The Asistencia Pública and Buenos Aires, 1883–1910" (Ph.D. diss., Ohio State University, 1976), 91–92; Balbo, "Argentinian Alienism," 186.

48 Contrary to popular myth, many of the members of the Society of Beneficence came from "modest" economic backgrounds. Little, "Society of Beneficence," 76.

49 Orozco and Dávila note that the women's hospital was built out of a pre-existing structure. By contrast, the men's asylum was a completely new building. Orozco and Dávila, "Mujeres alienadas en la Argentina," 10.

50 Ingenieros, *Locura en la Argentina*, 198. As of December 1857, 120 of the 195 patients in the men's hospital were labelled as insane.

51 It was renamed *Hospicio de San Buenaventura* in 1873. Although Bosch came from a Unitarian family, he had served as Rosas' personal physician until he left for Paris in 1851. See: Meyer Arana, *La caridad*, 301; Loudet and Loudet, *Historia de la psiquiatría argentina*, 29–42; and Valeria Silvina Pita, "Damas, locas y médicos. La locura expropiada," in *Historia de las mujeres en la Argentina: Colonia y siglo XIX* (Buenos Aires: Tauras, 2000), 273.

52 At the invitation of the Society of Beneficence, the Italian Sisters of Charity – Hijas de María Señora del Huerto arrived in October 1860. Ivereigh, *Catholicism and Politics in Argentina*, 48.

53 Sub-directora Dr. María Catalina Gimeno, Hospital Braulio Moyano (formerly the HNA), conversation with author, Fall, 1997. Archivo Hermanas de Caridad-Hijas de María Señora del Huerto-Casa Provincial, "Hermanas del Huerto en América" (unpublished pamphlet); AHC-HNA, "Instituto Nacional de Salud Mental to La Reverenda Madre Superiora" (December 31, 1964); Mead, "Oligarchs, Doctors and Nuns, 186–92.

54 Loudet and Loudet, *Historia de la psiquiatría argentina*, 43–46; Little, "Society of Beneficence," 251; Mario Sbarbi, "Reseña histórica del Hospicio de las Mercedes," *Acta neuropsiquiátrica* 6 (1960): 420. Eguía was also credited with identifying the first case of yellow fever during the 1871 epidemic and with preventing the contagion from entering the asylum.

55 Pastor Servando Obligado, "La procesión de los locos" (1876) cited in Fernando Pagés-Larraya, unpublished paper, "Al Señor Director del Hospital Nacional 'José T. Borda,' Profesor Doctor Jorge Fernández Amallo" (December 1988), 18–19.

56 Vezzetti, *Locura en la Argentina*, 70–80. Moral therapy had first been discussed in Argentina in an 1827 medical thesis but was not published until decades after the fall of Rosas. See Diego Alcorta, "Disertación sobre la manía aguda," in *Temas en la historia de la psiquiatría argentina* 2 (Winter 1997): 41–47.

57 Little, "Society of Beneficence," 259–61. *Memoria del Hospicio de las Mercedes correspondiente al año 1893* (Buenos Aires: Tipografía del Hospicio de las Mercedes, 1900), 31.

58 Ingenieros, *Locura en la Argentina*, 189; Pita, "Damas, locas y médicos," 274.

59 *Hospicio de las Mercedes correspondiente al año 1893*, 4; Meyer Arana, *Caridad en Buenos Aires*, 336; Ingenieros, *Locura en la Argentina*,135–39. On the importance of inmate labour to the survival of institutions, but also on its abuse, see Michael D'Antonio, *The State Boys Rebellion: The Inspiring True Store of American Eugenics and the Men Who Overcame It* (New York: Simon and Schuster, 2004).

60 James Scobie, *Buenos Aires: Plaza to Suburb, 1870–1910* (New York: Oxford University Press, 1974), 56. Similar factors shaped the placement of asylums throughout Latin America. For Chile, see Pablo Camus Gayán, "Filantropía, medicina y locura: La Casa de Orates de Santiago, 1852–1894," *Historia* 27 (1993): 95.

61 Loudet and Loudet, *Historia de la psiquiatría argentina*, 44–45.

62 Roy Porter, *The Greatest Benefit of Mankind: A Medical History of Humanity* (New York: W.W. Norton, 1997), 502. Already by 1838, the French alienist Jean-Etienne Dominique Esquirol was arguing for the therapeutic benefits of isolation. See also: Pita, "Damas, locas y médicos," 274; and Little, "Society of Beneficence," 259. In 1881, Dr. Eguía wrote an essay where he argued that treatment for hysteria was most effective when the patient was removed from both the home environment and the tumult of urban life.

63 Guerrino, *Psiquiatría argentina*, 47–48. Quoted from Lucio Meléndez and Emilio Coni, "Estudio estadístico sobre la locura en Buenos Aires," *Revista médico-quirúrgica* 16 (1879). For a detailed description of the asylum from the 1880s, see Manuel T. Podesta, *Irresponsable* (Buenos Aires: Imprenta de la Tribunal, 1889), 69–73.

64 James R. Scobie, *Buenos Aires*, 6, 71.

65 Ingenieros, *Locura en la Argentina*, 194. Pita, "Damas, locas y médicos," 276. By 1900, there were 1,400 patients.

66 Little, "Society of Beneficence," 263; Pita, "Damas, locas y médicos," 286–87.

67 Pita, "Damas, locas y médicos," 260–61; Balbo, "Argentinian Alienism": 185.

68 In some cases, such as the city of Córdoba, local governments established a protocol for the transfer of the insane to the women's asylum in Buenos Aires. Conrado O. Ferrer, "La locura en Córdoba," *Boletín del Asilo de Alienados en Oliva* 7:26 (June–August 1939): 408.

69 Ameghino, "Meléndez," 528. In his 1881 essay, "Secuestración de alienados," Meléndez argued for the creation of a police observation unit to better screen prospective patients. On the legal culture of Buenos Aires, see: Szuchman, *Order, Family, and Community in Buenos Aires*, 27, 61–62; and Little, "Society of Beneficence," 235.

70 In explaining the hospitals' ever-unmanageable numbers, doctors could point to the first national census in 1869, which reported 2.3 *locos* (crazies) and *idiotas e imbéciles* (idiots and imbeciles) per thousand inhabitants. Eleven years later, a study projected a figure of 4.5 insane persons per thousand inhabitants for Buenos Aires. The authors observed that this was a full point higher than the highest known coefficient in northern Europe and England and suggested that the number of insane was growing faster than overall population growth. Ingenieros, *Locura en la Argentina*, 228–31. See also Gache, *El estado mental*, 80–104. Gache noted that for every 1 female patient there were 2.3 male patients and that there were more insane male immigrants than female. Gache also believed that most mental illness had an organic origin.

71 In Mexico, it was the majority *mestizo* population that raised the greatest concern among psychiatrists. In this case, unlike Argentina, the target of social pathology remained fairly constant. See Cristina Rivera-Garza, "Dangerous Minds: Changing Psychiatric Views of the Mentally Ill in Porfirian Mexico, 1876–1911," *Journal of the History of Medicine* 56 (January 2001): 38.

72 H.S. Ferns, Ezequiel Gallo, and Melville Watkins, "The Prairies and the Pampas: A Review Colloquium," *Business History Review* 67 (Summer 1993), 279–99; José C. Moya, *Cousins and Strangers: Spanish Immigrants in Buenos Aires, 1850–1930* (Los Angeles: University of California Press, 1997), 149. In 1887, of Buenos Aires 433,373 people, 53 per cent were foreign-born, in 1895, 52 per cent, in 1904, 45 per cent, in 1909, 46 per cent, in 1914, 51 per cent, and in 1936, 36 per cent. Sociedad de Beneficencia de la Capital l [hereafter SB], *Memoria del año 1902* (Buenos Aires: Imprenta y Encuadernación del Asilo de Huérfanos, 1903). In 1902, there were 541 white admissions, 31 described as *pardo* and 6 as *negro*. On the history of Afro-Argentines, see Andrews, *Afro-Argentines of Buenos Aires, 1800–1900*. Indigenous and mestizos are notably absent from scholarly discussions about race in twentieth-century Argentina. Eugenia Scarzanella's *Ni gringos ni indios: Inmigración, criminalidad y racismo en Argentina, 1890–1940* (Quilmes: Universidad Nacional de Quilmes, 1999) is an exception.

73 Gache, *El estado mental*, 71–76. Of the 294 patients admitted to the men's asylum in 1880, only 76 were born in Argentina. The ratio of foreign- to native-born was lower for the same year at the women's asylum, where of the 178 admitted, 97 were Argentine-born.

74 A major proponent of this thesis was Lucas Ayarragaray. Ayarragaray was born in Entre Ríos Province and received his medical degree in 1888. He served in Congress from 1891 through 1911, where he introduced legislation against alcohol and in favour of measures to increase the rate of naturalization of immigrants. He published books on anarchism (1904) and ethnicity (1911). See Rafael Huertas García-Alejo, "La aportación de la escuela argentina al concepto de criminal nato," *Ciencia, vida y espacio en Iberoamérica*, José Luís Peset, ed. (Madrid: Consejo Superior de Investigaciones Científicas, 1989), 111; and William Belmont Parker, *Argentines of Today* (Buenos Aires: The Hispanic Society of America, 1920). For a similar critique, see José T. Borda, "Inmigrantes enfermos," *El Diario* (January 12, 1906): n.p.

75 Eduardo A. Zimmermann, "Racial Ideas and Social Reform: Argentina, 1890–1916," *Hispanic American Historical Review* 72:1 (February 1992): 37.

76 Donald S. Castro, "Lunfardo, the Language of the Disenfranchised as a Source for Argentine Social History," *Proceedings of the Pacific Coast Council of Latin American Studies* 14:2 (Fall 1987): 109. Guy, *Sex and Danger in Buenos Aires*.

77 Vezzetti, *Locura en la Argentina*, 185–232; Eduardo A. Zimmermann, *Los liberales reformistas: La cuestión social en la Argentina, 1890–1916* (Buenos Aires: Editorial Sudamericana, 1994), 68; 105–17. See also: Ricardo D. Salvatore, "The Normalization of Economic Life: Representations of the Economy in Golden-Age Buenos Aires, 1890–1913," *Hispanic American Historical Review* 81:1 (February 2001): 1–44; Guy, *Sex and Danger in Buenos Aires*; and Salessi, *Médicos, maleantes, y maricas*.

78 Vezzetti, *Locura en la Argentina*, 185–91; Little, "Society of Beneficence," 242–43.

79 Gache, *El estado mental*, 87. "La influencia del alcohol sobre la locura es innegable; ella esta aceptada como

un axioma, y por los datos que hemos estudiado se ve que entre nosotros contribuye muy poderosamente al desarrollo de aquella anomalía." Between 1899 and 1913, 76 per cent of the confined alcoholics were immigrants. MREC, "Memoria del Hospicio de las Mercedes correspondiente al año 1913," *Memoria del Ministerio de Relaciones Exteriores y Culto correspondiente al años 1913–14* (Buenos Aires: 1914), 564. Alcohol was also a preoccupation of the police. See Sandra V. Gayol, "Ebrios y divertidos: la estrategia del alcohol en Buenos Aires, 1860–1900," *Siglo XIX, nueva época* 13 (January–June 1993): 55–80.

80 Héctor Recalde, *La salud de los trabajadores en Buenos Aires (1870–1910)* (Buenos Aires: Grupo Editor Universitario, n.d.), 255. Moises Malamud, *Domingo Cabred* (Buenos Aires: Buenos Aires: Ministerio de Cultura y Educación,1972), 84–88. The first ward for alcoholics was established at the Colonia Nacional de Alienados (1899). Cabred helped found the Argentine Anti-Alcoholism League in 1903, which eventually incorporated anti-alcohol education into the schools.

81 Domingo Cabred, *Informe sobre locura alcohólica* (Buenos Aires: Imprenta y Encuadernación del Hospicio de las Mercedes, 1903); Carlos Bernaldo de Quirós, "Consecuencias individuales, familiares y sociales del alcoholismo," *Archivos de psiquiatría y criminología* 2:2 (February 1903): 117.

82 Little, "Society of Beneficence," 244.

83 Gache, *El estado mental*, 85. Of the 3,266 individuals arrested for public drunkenness in 1878, only 399 were women. See also Domingo F. Sarmiento, "La embriaguez y la locura. Lectura en una reunión de médicos en su casa" (July 29, 1884) <http://www.argiropolis.com.ar/ameghino/documentos/locura.htm>, *Obras de D.F. Sarmiento* (1899). On the culture of drinking, see Gayol, "Ebrios y divertidos," 55–80.

84 Little, 242–43.

85 Beatriz C. Ruibal, "El control social y la policía de Buenos Aires, 1880–1920," *Boletín del Instituto de Historia Argentina y Americana 'Dr. E. Ravignani'* 3:2:1 (1990): 75–90; Julia Kirk Blackwelder, "Urbanization, Crime, and Policing: Buenos Aires, 1880–1914," in Johnson, *Problem of Order in Changing Societies*, 73–83.

86 Blackwelder, "Urbanization, Crime, and Policing," 76. "The highest arrest rates for order offenses occurred among the British..... The extremely high arrest rates among the British probably reflected the presence of British sailors on leave in the Argentine port city." For cases of sailors, see APJN, "Insania," "Iván G." Legajo 14235, Folio 91 (1911). See also: APJN, "Insania," "Henry R." Legajo 14675, Folio 303 (1924); and APJN, "Insania," "Andres H.," Legajo 20050, Folio 338, No. 1780 (1934).

87 Ruibal, "El control social," 75–90. On the marginalization of non-majority groups in psychiatric literature, see: Hughes, "Labeling and Treating Black Mental Illness in Alabama, 1861–1910," 435–60; Jan Goldstein, "The Wandering Jew and the Problem of Psychiatric Anti-Semitism in Fin-de-Siècle France," *Journal of Social History* 20 (1985); and Paul Jay Fink and Allan Tasman, eds., *Stigma and Mental Illness* (Washington, D.C.: American Psychiatric Press, 1992).

88 Ingenieros, *Locura en la Argentina*, 232–33. On the decline in the connection between madness and immigration in the United States prior to World War I, see Grob, *Mental Illness and American Society*, 170.

89 De la Fuente, *Children of Facundo*; Fernando López-Alves, *State Formation and Democracy in Latin America, 1810–1900* (Durham, NC: Duke University Press 2000); Centeno, *Blood and Debt*, 161; Gabriel L. Negretto and José Antonio Aguilar-Rivera, "Rethink-

ing the Legacy of the Liberal State in Latin America: The cases of Argentina (1853–1916) and Mexico (1857–1910)," *Journal of Latin American Studies* 32 (2000): 361–97.

90 On the control of prostitution, see Guy, *Sex and Danger in Buenos Aires*, 37–55. Although the rhetoric of reformers was often quite anti-clerical, the state took a complex view of the church. "Freedom of religion was advocated in order to break through the 'exclusivity' of Catholicism; while the Church was seen as the state's legitimating and moralizing agent." Ivereigh, *Catholicism and Politics in Argentina*, 53. See also Rodríguez, *Civilizing Argentina*, 256, who argues that scientific rhetoric was used to give legitimacy to the elite's political and social goals. Rodriguez, *Civilizing Argentina*, 256.

91 Juan Suriano, *La cuestión social en Argentina, 1870–1943* (Buenos Aires: Editorial La Colmena, 2000), 10–11. See also Prieto, "Rosario: Epidemias, hygiene e higienistas en la segunda mitad del siglo XIX," 57–71.

92 Julia Rodriguez raises the question of the extent to which Argentine reformers use of scientific and medical language was simply an excuse to maintain control over the populace. See Rodríguez, *Civilizing Argentina*, 247–57.

93 Ameghino, "Meléndez," 528; Gache, *El estado mental*, 68. On the history of ideas of heredity, see John C. Waller, "'The Illusion of an Explanation': The Concept of Hereditary Disease, 1770–1870," *Journal of the History of Medicine* 57 (October 2002): 410–48.

94 Rodriguez, *Civilizing Argentina*, 73; Vezzetti, *Locura en la Argentina*, 155–56. "En ese sentido, la teoría de la degeneración parecía ofrecer inicialmente la posibilidad de establecer signos físicos de la locura; con ello la psiquiatría buscaba un camino para reintegrarse a los métodos y criterios de la medicina científica, básicamente fundar una clasificación etiológica." For Brazil, see Dain Borges, "'Puffy, Ugly, Slothful and Inert': Degeneration in Brazilian Social Thought," *Journal of Latin American Studies* 25 (1993): 235–56. Vezzetti argues that many doctors viewed degeneration as the "price of civilization." Carlos Octavio Bunge, for example, argued that advances in medical science had diminished the role of natural selection in eliminating weak or "defective" individuals. Vezzetti, *Locura en la Argentina*,162.

95 Dowbiggin, *Inheriting Madness*, 1–2.

96 Rodriguez, *Civilizing Argentina*, 71–91; Kristin Ruggiero, *Modernity in the Flesh: Medicine, Law, and Society in Turn-of-the-Century Argentina* (Stanford: Stanford University Press, 2004),115–43. Mariano Ben Plotkin, "Freud, Politics, and the Porteños: The Reception of Psychoanalysis in Buenos Aires, 1910–1943," *Hispanic American Historical Review* 77:1 (February 1997): 49–50; Vezzetti, *Locura en la Argentina*, 143. Zimmerman, "Racial Ideas and Social Reform: Argentina 1890–1916," 23–46.

97 Eduardo O. Ciafardo and Daniel Espesir, "Patología de la acción política anarquista. Criminólogos, psiquiatras y conflicto social en Argentina, 1890–1910," *Siglo XIX, nueva época* 12 (July–December 1992): 33. During Congressional debates over the passage of the Social Defense Law of 1910, "Congress loudly applauded speakers who denounced foreign agitators as insane, vicious rabble." Vezzetti, *Locura en la Argentina*, 214–21. The psychiatric perspective on anarchism survived into the 1930s. See Arturo Ameghino, "La acción del estado en el mejoramiento de la raza," *Revista de criminología, psiquiatría y medicina legal* (January–February 1935): 131–52. See also Zimmermann, "Racial Ideas and Social Reform," 37, n. 42.

98 Vezzetti, *Locura en la Argentina*, 214–21.

99 Argentina. Congreso Nacional. *Diario de sesiones de la Cámara de Diputados* (September 12, 1894) (Buenos Aires: Imprenta y encuadernación del H. Cámara de Diputados, 1895), 754 (hereafter *Diputados*).

100 On the broader cultural transformations of the period, see: Jeane Delaney, "Making Sense of Modernity: Changing Attitudes toward the Immigrant and the Gaucho in Turn-of-the-Century Argentina," *Comparative Studies in Society and History* 38:3 (July 1996): 434–59; and Salvatore, "Normalization of Economic Life," 1–44.

101 With a trace of nostalgia, Ingenieros recounted that from the late colonial period through the beginning of the twentieth century, "many unbalanced and partially delirious persons lived on the streets of Buenos Aires, tolerated or celebrated by the locals." Ingenieros, *Locura en la Argentina*, 225. See also: Fernando Pagés-Larraya, "Spiritus merculialis - el 'loco lindo' en la antropología urbana," *Antropología psiquiátrica* 18:6 (1995); and Guerrino, *Psiquiatría argentina*, 129–32.

102 "Figuras que desaparecen: El marquesito," *Caras y Caretas* 3:111 (November 17, 1900): n.p.

103 Fabrio Carrezo, "Los atorrantes," *Caras y Caretas* 3:113 (December 1, 1900): n.p.

104 Carrezo, "El atorrantismo, la vagancia, la dejadez, el desabrimiento de la vida, el deseo de abandonarse y desaparecer, el suicidio moral, en resumidas cuentas, es una enfermedad social de Buenos Aires, digna de llamar la atención de nuestros higienistas, y este reportaje nuestro no es sino un pálido reflejo de los fenómenos que se observan en ese bajo fondo que pocos han estudiado, per que es digno de observación." See also "En el campamento de los bohemios," *Caras y Caretas* 3:113 (December 1, 1900): n.p. The author complained that gypsies embodied popular sympathy for the "right to laziness." For a similar transformation of attitudes in Mexico, see Cristina Rivera-Garza, "Dangerous Minds: Changing Psychiatric Views of the Mentally Ill in Porfirian Mexico, 1876–1911," *Journal of the History of Medicine* 56 (January 2001): 36–67.

105 Ingenieros, *Locura en la Argentina*, 224–25.

106 "Servicio de Observación de Alienados," *Archivos de psiquiatría y criminología* 9 (March–April 1910): 254–56. See also Ingenieros, *Locura en la Argentina*, 217. Before its relocation to the newly established national penitentiary in 1907, the Service examined 2,500 referrals, of whom 1,500 were remanded to institutions and 1,000 were released. On the connection between madness and other social ills in France, see Robert A. Nye, *Crime, Madness, and Politics in Modern France: The Medical Concept of National Decline* (Princeton: Princeton University Press, 1984), xi–xii.

107 Major reforms that involved law and medicine included the Central Commission of Immigration (1869, with subsequent reforms through the 1890s), the National Penitentiary (1878), National Department of Hygiene (1881), Public Assistance of the Capital (1883), which after 1890 became the General Directorate of Public Assistance and Sanitary Administration, *Dispensario de Salubridad* (for the registration of prostitutes).

108 Ciafardo and Espesir, "Patología de la acción política anarquista," 34–36.

109 Ruibal, "El control social," 196–97. On the role of psychiatrists in determining competence to stand trial, see Alberto Bonhour and Roberto Ciafardo, "Alienados delincuentes: Estadísticas según la forma clínica y el delito," *Revista de psiquiatría y criminología* 6 (1941): 193–200. For France, see Dowbiggin, *Inheriting Madness*, 136.

110 See Vezzetti, *Locura en la Argentina*, 127–71 and Rodríguez *Civilizing Argentina*; Ciafardo and Espesir,

"Patología de la acción política anarquista," 39. "The marriage of the alienist and the criminologist was perfect: in the theoretical universe that they had built together, the madman was a potential criminal, the criminal was a potential madman." Michel Foucault, "About the Concept of the 'Dangerous Individual' in Nineteenth-Century Legal Psychiatry," *International Journal of Law and Psychiatry* 1 (1978): 6.

111 Despite, the inauguration of a rural hospital in 1884 in the province of Buenos Aires, Hospital "Melchor Romero," the older urban asylums remained the primary destination for the mentally ill from all over the republic. Ironically, although Melchor Romero's rural location was celebrated as having a therapeutic benefit, it also made it difficult for much of the population to access and provincial authorities and private individuals continued to send prospective patients to the urban hospitals. Eduardo Balbo, "El Hospital Neuropsiquiátrico 'Melchor Romero' durante los años 1884–1918," in José Luís Peset, ed., *Ciencia, vida y espacio en Iberoamérica* (Madrid: Consejo Superior de Investigaciones Científicas, 1989), 53–75.

112 Ingenieros, *Locura en la Argentina*, "advertencia," n.p. Ramos Mejía's works included *La neurosis en los hombres celebres* (1878), *La locura en la historia* (1895), and *Las multitudes argentinas* (1899).

113 Ricardo González Leandri, "Médicos, damas y funcionarios: Acuerdos y tensiones en la creación de la Asistencia Pública de la Ciudad de Buenos Aires," in José Luís Peset, ed., *Ciencia, vida y espacio en Iberoamérica*, I (Madrid: Consejo Superior de Investigaciones Científicas, 1989), 85. See also: Crider, "Modernization and Human Welfare," 38–39; Mead, "Oligarchs, Doctors and Nuns," 42–52, 237; and Eduardo Ciafardo, "La práctica benéfica y el control de los sectores populares de la Ciudad de Buenos Aires, 1890–1910," *Revista de las Indias* 54:201 (1994): 383–405.

114 Mead, "Oligarchs, Doctors and Nuns," 239.

115 Ingenieros, *Locura en la Argentina*, 194; Loudet and Loudet, *Historia de la psiquiatría argentina*, 43–46; Crider, "Modernization and Human Welfare," 39–40; Mead, "Oligarchs, Doctors and Nuns," 179; Guy, *Sex and Danger in Buenos Aires*, 81–82.

116 Pita, "Damas, locas y médicos," 278–84.

117 Arturo Ameghino, "Lucio Meléndez, Conferencia inaugural de la Cátedra de Clínica Psiquiátrica," *Revista de criminología, psiquiatría y medicina legal* 18:107 (September–December 1931): 521–33.

118 Luis Meyer, "A cien años de la creación de la Cátedra en Enfermedades Mentales en Buenos Aires," *Acta psiquiátrica y psicológica de América Latina* 2:33 (June 1987): 169–70. See Ricardo González Leandri, "La profesión médica en Buenos Aires, 1852–1870," in Lobato, *Política, médicos y enfermedades*, 21–56. In 1875, Dr. Eduardo Wilde had founded a faculty of Legal Medicine and Toxicology at the UBA. Vezzetti, *Locura en la Argentina*, 140.

119 Loudet and Loudet, *Historia de la psiquiatría argentina*, 51–60; Crider, "Modernization and Human Welfare," 28, 34–35.

120 Sbarbi, "Reseña histórica del Hospicio de las Mercedes," 421. Luis Meyer, "Los comienzos del Hospicio de las Mercedes," *Acta psiquiátrica y psicológica de América Latina* 33 (1987): 338–39, claims that the name changed on August 23, 1873.

121 Meyer, "Los comienzos," 339. Some of his more ambitious projects, including a wholesale restructuring of the hospital (1879 proposal to the Municipal Government) and requests for the construction of a ward for the criminally insane, failed to attract support. Amegino,

"Meléndez," 526–28. *Hospicio de las Mercedes correspondiente al año 1893*, 4.

122 *Memoria del intendencia municipal* (Año 1903, Administración del Sr. Alberto Casares) (Buenos Aires: Imprenta y Litografía G. Kraft, 1904), 81; Crider, "Modernization and Human Welfare," 42–43, 61.

123 Balbo, "El Hospital Neuropsiquiátrico 'Melchor Romero'," 53–75.

124 *Memoria del Hospicio de las Mercedes correspondiente al año 1893.*

125 Loudet and Loudet, *Historia de la psiquiatría argentina*, 146.

126 Loudet and Loudet, *Historia de la psiquiatría argentina*, 194–95. On the issue of legal reform in western Europe and the United States, see: Peter McCandless, "Liberty and Lunacy: The Victorians and Wrongful Confinement," in Andrew Scull, ed., *Madhouses, Mad-doctors, and Madmen: The Social History of Psychiatry in the Victorian Era* (Philadelphia: University of Pennsylvania Press, 1981), 339–62; Fox, *'So far disordered in mind'*, 38; and Dowbiggin, *Inheriting Madness*, 93–115.

127 Loudet and Loudet, *Historia de la psiquiatría argentina*, 145–50; Little, "Society of Beneficence," 251–58; William Belmont Parker, *Argentines of Today* I & II (Buenos Aires: The Hispanic Society of America, 1920). Born in the Province of Buenos Aires in 1859, Piñero received his medical degree from the University of Buenos Aires in 1883. He was especially taken with the work of a Russian psychiatrist, Kovalesky, who was a proponent of work therapy and agricultural colonies.

128 Little, "Society of Beneficence," 251–55.

129 Loudet and Loudet, *Historia de la psiquiatría argentina*, 146; Little, "Society of Beneficence," 257.

130 Little, "Society of Beneficence," 261–66.

131 Loudet and Loudet, *Historia de la psiquiatría argentina*, 211.

132 *La Prensa* (August 1, 1898): n.p.

133 *Hospital Psiquiátrico Braulio A. Moyano: 140 aniversario, 1854–1994* (Buenos Aires: 1994).

134 SB, *Memoria del año 1902* (Buenos Aires: Imprenta y Encuadernación del Asilo de Huérfanos, 1903), 233.

135 Vezzetti, *Locura en la Argentina*, 79. Vezzetti's suggestion that such projects reflected elite desire to remove immigrants from urban areas lacks solid evidence, though it certainly reflects the attitudes of many native-born Argentines.

136 José Ingenieros, "Los asilos para alienados en la Argentina," *Revista de criminología, psiquiatría y medicina legal* 8 (1920): 145.

137 Mead, "Oligarchs, Doctors and Nuns," 190.

138 Mead, "Oligarchs, Doctors and Nuns," 196. In 1885, Dr. Cecilia Grierson established the first school of nursing. In 1892, it passed into the administration of Public Assistance. See Catalina H. Wainerman and Georgina Binstock, "La feminización de la enfermería argentina," in Martha Moscoso, ed., *Palabras del silencia: Las mujeres latinoamericanas y su historia* (1995), 259–83.

139 *Memoria del Hospicio de las Mercedes correspondiente al año 1893*, 49.

140 Loudet and Loudet, *Historia de la psiquiatría argentina*, 61–72; Malamud, *Domingo Cabred*, 27. On the first trip in 1889 he gathered information on rural asylums, and on the second in 1896 he visited medical schools.

141 *Memoria del Hospicio de las Mercedes correspondiente al año 1893*, 8–10.

142 *Memoria del Hospicio de las Mercedes correspondiente al año 1893*, 14.

143 *Memoria del Hospicio de las Mercedes correspondiente al año 1893*, "Proyecto de reglamentación del trabajo y peculio

de los alienados del Hospicio de las Mercedes."

144 See "Proyecto de reglamentación del trabajo y peculio de los alienados del Hospicio de las Mercedes."

145 *Memoria del Hospicio de las Mercedes correspondiente al año 1893*, 43. According to a municipal report from 1900, 220 patients still did not have beds. See Oscar Troncoso, *La modernización de Buenos Aires en 1900: Archivo del Intendente Municipal Adolfo J. Bullrich* (Buenos Aires: Archivo General de la Nación, 2004), 32.

146 Cabred's desire for well-trained nurses is reflected in the fact that he held award ceremonies for exemplary staff. See "En el Hospicio de las Mercedes – Distribución de premios á los enfermeros," *Caras y Caretas* 6:224 (January 17, 1903): n.p. "... la profesión de enfermero requiere condiciones poco comunes de vocación y de carácter, mayormente si se trata de la asistencia de dementes."

147 "Instrucciones para el Personal de Vijilancia-Disposiciones Generales," *Hospicio, 1893*, 53–69. For the United States, see John S. Hughes, "'Country Boys Make the Best Nurses': Nursing the Insane in Alabama, 1861–1910," *Journal of the History of Medicine and Allied Sciences* 49 (January 1994): 79–106.

148 "Instrucciones," in *Memoria del Hospicio de las Mercedes correspondiente al año 1893*, 61.

149 "Instrucciones," 59.

150 "Instrucciones," 31.

151 "Instrucciones," 31–35.

152 Domingo Cabred, "Discurso inaugural de la Colonia Nacional de Alienados," *Revista de Derecho, Historia, y Letras* 1:3 (1899): 610–11. See note 1. Proposals for a ward for the criminally insane had first been mentioned by Lucio Meléndez in the 1870s.

153 Helvio Fernández, "El servicio de alienados delincuente," *Archivos de psiquiatría y criminología* 8 (January–February 1909): 97–106.

154 Cabred, "Discurso inaugural." Cabred was particularly impressed by what he referred to as the "open door" colonies in Scotland: Argill, Five, Kinross, Inverness, Haddington, and Pert. Cabred also had visited the asylum at Gheel, Belgium.

155 Domingo Cabred, "Discurso inaugural," 610–22. Vezzetti, *Locura en la Argentina*, 195. Author notes that President Roca could not refuse the requests of only two people, Cabred and General Richieri. The latter, Vezzetti notes ironically, developed Argentina's military draft. See also Hugo Vezzetti, "Domingo Cabred y el asilo de puertas abiertas," *Revista Vertex* 2:3 (March–May 1994): 59–61.

156 Cabred, "Discurso inaugural," 617–18.

157 Cabred, "Discurso inaugural," 618.

158 Malamud, *Domingo Cabred*, 27–30.

159 Colonia Nacional de Alienados, *Memoria médico-administrativa correspondiente a los años 1908–1909* (Buenos Aires: Imprenta y Encuadernación del Hospicio de las Mercedes, 1910), v–vi. The Colony also had a special ward for alcoholics.

160 Lucía Lacoponi, "El Hospital Interzonal 'Colonia Dr. Domingo Cabred' y el método Open Door para asistencia y rehabilitación de pacientes psiquiátricos." *Centenario de la fundación: Hospital interzonal psiquiátrico 'Colonia Dr. Domingo Cabred'* (May 1999): 59–69. See also Nélida Agüeros and Yolanda Eraso, "Tratamiento en libertad a comienzos del siglo XX: Los asilos colonias de Puertas Abiertas en la Argentina" (unpublished paper, March 21, 1995).

161 Cabred, "Discurso inaugural," 620. Cabred was strongly influenced by the proposals of German psychiatrist Wilhelm Gresinger to develop urban clinics for acute psychiatric cases. Such hospitals would also serve to train medical students.

162 Malamud, *Domingo Cabred*, 33.

163 Domingo Cabred, *El Instituto Clínica de Psiquiatría de la Facultad de Medicina de Buenos Aires* (Buenos Aires: Wiebeck, Turtl & Co., 1919), n.p.

164 MREC, "Hospicio de las Mercedes: Memoria médico-administrativo correspondiente al año 1917," *Memorias del Ministerio de Relaciones Exteriores y Culto correspondiente al años 1917–1918* (1919), 981.

165 MREC, "Memoria del Hospicio de las Mercedes correspondiente al año 1910–1911," *Memorias del Ministerio de Relaciones Exteriores y Culto correspondiente al años 1910–11* (1912), 475.

166 For Bolivia, see Ann Zulawski, "Mental Illness and Democracy in Bolivia: The Manicomio Pacheco, 1935–1950," in Diego Armus, ed., *From Malaria to AIDS: Disease in the History of Modern Latin America* (Durham, NC: Duke University Press, 2003), 237–67. For Mexico, see the essays in *Secuencia, nueva época* 51 (September–December 2001) and María Cristina Sacristán, "La Granja de San Pedro del Monte para enfermos mentales: Los primeros años de una institución modelo, 1945–1948," *Ensayos sobre historia de la medicina* (Mexico: Instituto de Investigaciones Históricas, 2003): 101–21. For Peru, see Augusto Ruiz Zevallos, *Psiquiatras y locos: Entre la modernización contra los Andes y el Nuevo proyecto de modernidad. Perú: 1850–1930* (Lima: Instituto Pasado y Presente, 1994).

167 Dowbiggin, *Inheriting Madness*. The 1838 law was expanded in 1909.

168 Malamud, *Domingo Cabred*, 39–46. Malamud claims that Cabred decided to place the Commission in Foreign Relations to avoid "las presiones y a las influencias de tipo político tan comunes dentro de la jurisdicción del Ministerio del Interior." According to a conversation with workers at the Ministry of Foreign Relations in Buenos Aires, the records of the Commission were destroyed by Peronists in the late 1940s.

169 Domingo Cabred, "Asilo Colonia Regional de Retardos," *Archivos de psiquiatría y criminología* 7 (November–December 1908): 735.

170 *La Prensa* (November 24, 1905): n.p.; "El Hospicio de Alienadas.– La renuncia del doctor Piñero," *Caras y Caretas* 8:374 (December 2, 1905): n.p.

171 *La Nación* (November 10, 1905): 8. The fight between the Society and Piñero continued in the newspapers. See Archivo General de la Nación-Sociedad de la Beneficencia-Hospital Nacional de Alienados, (hereafter AGN-SB-HNA), Legajo 221, Expediente "Libro 1905–07," "Elementos de Juicio para comprobar las inexactitudes en que ha incurrido el Dr. A.F. Piñero en su artículo publicado por *La Nación* del 8 de abril 1906."

172 *Diputados* 1 (September 26, 1906), 1000–1018. On the Society's defence of sex-segregated health care, see González Leandri, "Médicos, damas y funcionarios," 87.

173 Zimmermann, *Los reformistas liberales*, 12–17. Reformers advocated an abandonment of pure laissez-faire but also eschewed state socialism. See also: David Rock, *State Building and Political Movements in Argentina, 1860–1916* (Stanford: Stanford University Press, 2002); and Hector Recalde, "Higiene pública y secularización," *Conflictos y procesos de la historia argentina contemporánea* (Buenos Aires: Centro Editor de América Latina, n.d.), vol. 30.

174 Carlos Andres Escudé, "Health in Buenos Aires in the Second Half of the Nineteenth Century," in D.C.M. Platt, ed., *Social Welfare, 1850–1950: Australia, Argentina and Canada Compared* (London: Macmillan, 1989), 69; Crider, 228–30.

175 Crider, "Modernization and Human Welfare," 180–95. On the Registro de Pobres and the idea of the deserving

poor, see Zimmermann, *Liberales reformistas*, 106–7; Vezzetti, *Locura en la Argentina*, 26.

176 Jonathan C. Brown, "The Bondage of Old Habits in Nineteenth-Century Argentina," *Latin American Research Review* 21:2 (1986): 3–31. Brown notes that Argentina's elite rejected the idea of its responsibility for social welfare. Crider, "Modernization and Human Welfare," 229–30. "Samuel P. Huntington noted that one essential characteristic of a modern state is that it is able to assert its authority throughout the social spectrum. The Asistencia Pública, as one of the primary institutions responsible for daily contact with much of the citizenry, could not 'penetrate' the conventillo population and other sectors of society sufficiently to support the conclusion that by 1910 Buenos Aires was as modernized as the elite believed it to be."

177 Karen Mead, "Beneficent Maternalism: Argentine Motherhood in Comparative Perspective, 1880–1920," *Journal of Women's History* 12:3 (Autumn 2000): 120.

3: The Era of Mental Hygiene

1 Archivo General de la Nación-Sociedad de la Beneficencia-Hospital Nacional de Alienadas, "1923–1947," Exp. 6323. "Señoras inspectoras del HNA desde la Presidenta del SdB" Feb. 7, 1925; Antonio Alberto Guerrino, *Psiquiatría argentina*, 46. Nogues, who was director from 1924 to 1934, spent most of his medical career at the HNA and also served as a medical examiner for the *Tribunales de Buenos Aires*. At the time of writing the letter, the HNA held 1980 patients but only had capacity for 1200.

2 "Sublevación de penados en el Hospicio de las Mercedes," *Caras y Caretas* (January 1928): n.p.; "La sublevación en el Hospicio de las Mercedes," *La nación* (January 4, 1928): n.p.

3 "Ya tenemos la nota trágica," *El Diario* (January 3, 1928): 3.

4 *La Nación* (February 8, 1928): 14. See also "Intensa tragedia en el Hospicio de las Mercedes," *Caras y caretas* 31:1533 (February 18, 1928): n.p.

5 "Lucio López Lecube, *médico del Hospicio de las Mercedes*, fallecido en Buenos Aires el 7 de febrero de 1928," *Revista argentina de neurología, psiquiatría y medicina legal* 2:7 (January–February 1928): 95. Fernandez had served as director of the Instituto de Criminología and supervisor of the Hospicio's *Lucio Meléndez Ward*. Guerrino, *Psiquiatría argentina*, 114.

6 "Lucio López Lecube," 95–96.

7 "En el Hospicio de las Mercedes," *La Nación* (February 9, 1928): n.p.

8 "La tragedia del Hospicio de las Mercedes," *El diario* (February 9, 1928): n.p.

9 Moya, *Cousins and Strangers*, 149.

10 There is also anecdotal evidence that patients were growing more militant in their demands for better treatment in public hospitals. See "Huelga de enfermos – una carta elocuente," *La Protesta* (December 30, 1919): n.p., which carries a letter from a patient of the Sanatorio Nacional Santa Maria F.C.C.N.A. (Córdoba). See also "La sublevación de los enfermos," *La Nación* (December 29, 1919): n.p. According to a later article, "En el Sanatorio de Tuberculosos de la Provincia de Córdoba," *La Protesta* (January 7, 1920): n.p., the director of the Hospicio, José T. Borda, was sent to act as *interventor* to restore order. The paper claimed that Borda withheld food and had a military unit hold patients incommunicado in an effort to restore order. They also reported that Borda accused the patients of being anarchists and threatened to expel them.

11 North American nineteenth-century reforms had created explicitly medical institutions, which over time, had deteriorated. See Ellen Dwyer, *Homes for the Mad: Life inside Two Nineteenth-Century Asylums* (New Brunswick, NJ: Rutgers University Press, 1983).

12 Vezzetti, *Locura en la Argentina*, 225. "Los locos internados son un emblema de los avances de la civilización occidental, y el precio obligado de la construcción de una nación moderna y una raza vigorosa." Vezzetti is referring here to Arturo Ameghino's 1923 "Datos para la profilaxis mental en la República Argentina."

13 Luis Alberto Romero, *A History of Argentina in the Twentieth Century* (University Park: Pennsylvania State University Press, 2002), 27–58.

14 "Hospicio Nacional de Alienadas – No hay legislación sobre esta materia," *La Unión* (July 24, 1918): n.p.; "En el hospital de Alienadas – Cargos contra la dirección," *La Razón* (23 July, 1918): n.p. In an echo of the accusations of Antonio Piñero, the HNA's former director, Pombo suggested that the Society may have played a hand in preventing the passage of a law governing psychiatric hospitals.

15 Juan José Soiza Reilly, "Muerte misteriosa de una señora," *La Revista Popular* (August 5, 1918): n.p. The Society had also recently raised the director's salary from 400 to 1,100 pesos. Soiza Reilly made the oft-repeated but false claim, however, that the HNA refused admission to non-Catholics. Soiza Reilly was active in the Unión Cívica Radical. See also his novel that deals with a fictional asylum modelled on the Hospicio, *La ciudad de los locos (Aventuras de Tartarín Moreira)* (Buenos Aires: Maucci Hermanos, n.d.).

16 Few psychiatrists who criticized the asylums would have mentioned this practice, as it was widespread and commonly accepted. Pombo, for instance, did not make mention of this in his statements.

17 Soiza Reilly, "Muerte misteriosa de una señora."

18 Soiza Reilly, "Muerte misteriosa de una señora."

19 "Hospicio Nacional de Alienadas - Cargos contra su dirección," *La Unión* (July 23, 1918): n.p. On his relationship to the Society, see Loudet and Loudet, *Historia de la psiquiatría argentina*, 157–61. The HNA charged Soiza Reilly with slander. See "Acusación por calumnia," *La Razón* (August 5, 1918): n.p. This article and numerous others are found in AGN-SB-HNA "HNA 1898–1947," Expediente 578. "Publicaciones con motivo denuncias de irregularidades en el H.N. de Alienadas."

20 "Los dramas secretos del Asilo de Alienadas-intervención de la justicia del crimen-la honrosa campaña de 'Revista Popular,'" *La Revista Popular* (August 19, 1918): n.p. The magazine also reported that the hospital was not open on Sundays, the one day that most workers could come to visit relatives. See also "¿Qué pasa en el Hospital Nacional de Alienadas?" *El monitor de la salud* 82 (n.d.); *La Nación* (September 6, 1918): n.p. In September of 1918, the Ministry of Foreign Relations and Religion approved a committee to investigate the Society's operation of the Hospital.

21 Paradoxically, the Radical period witnessed very little transformation of either the form of social assistance in Argentina, or the economic policies that supported them. See David Rock, *Politics in Argentina, 1890–1930: The Rise and Fall of Radicalism* (New York: Cambridge University Press, 1975).

22 Psychiatric hospitals are often targets for the political opposition. In the United States, levelling charges of malfeasance, corruption, and neglect against hospitals was commonplace. See: Fox, *'So far disordered in mind'*; McCandless, *Moonlight, Magnolias,*

and Madness; Andrew Scull, *Madhouse: A Tragic Tale of Megalomania and Modern Medicine* (New Haven, CT: Yale University Press, 2005); and Dwyer, *Homes for the Mad*.

23 Argentine Republic. Congreso Nacional. *Diputados* 6 (May 15, 1923), 208. Cited from a textual reproduction of the hospital's 1919 report.

24 *Diputados* 6 (May 15, 1923), 211. According to the HNA's annual report for 1921, the mortality rate for tuberculosis compared unfavourably with comparable European institutions from thirty years earlier.

25 *Diputados* 6 (March 7, 1923), 349. See also *La Prensa* (March 8, 15, 16, and 22, 1923).

26 AGN-SB-HNA 1898–1947, Legajo 205, Expediente 7593, SB, *Hospital Nacional de Alienadas: Antecedentes y medidas adoptadas para solucionar el hacinamiento de enfermas* (Buenos Aires: Talleres Gráficos del Asilo de Huérfanos, 1923). See also *La Nación* (March 15, 1923): n.p.

27 *Diputados* 6 (March 14, 1923), 453–55. The anticipated completion of wards for 600 women at the Oliva asylum, however, promised to end the latest crisis at the HNA.

28 *Diputados* 6 (March 14, 1923), 455–57.

29 *Diputados* 6 (March 14, 1923), 457–60.

30 *Diputados* 6 (March 7, 1923), 354. Richard J. Walter, *The Socialist Party of Argentina 1890–1930* (Austin: Institute of Latin American Studies, University of Texas at Austin, 1977), 181–204. On corruption and the sale of public offices, see Joel Horwitz, "Bosses and Clients: Municipal Employment in the Buenos Aires of the Radicals, 1916–30," *Journal of Latin American Studies* 3 (1999): 617–44. Horwitz notes that such practices were not the invention of the Radicals.

31 *Diputados* 6 (March 14, 1923), 470. The Socialist deputy concluded his remarks by admitting that "[w]e are in a moment of confusion and madness. Not all the insane are in the asylum, nor are all those in the asylum insane. I repeat: reason must illuminate Argentine politics." *Diputados* 6 (March 14, 1923), 483.

32 *Diputados* 6 (March 21, 1923), 744–53, 755–57. Rodeyro rejected Dickmann's charge that indigent patients were often clothed only for the benefit of visitors, noting that the insane often destroy their clothing and that it was difficult to keep them properly dressed.

33 *Diputados* 6 (March 21, 1923), 762.

34 *Diputados* 6 (March 21, 1923), 762.

35 Lucia Lacoponi, "Permisividad, abuso y desprotección," in *Centenario de la fundación: Hospital Interzonal Psiquiátrico 'Colonia Dr. Domingo Cabred'* (May 1999), 70–77. Raitzin was a protégé of Cabred. Guerrino, *Psiquiatría argentina*, 174.

36 "Normas aconsejadas para la dirección del Open Door de Luján," *La Nación* (July 15, 1924): n.p. The report argued that it was not feasible for the director of the Hospicio to exercise sufficient oversight over the distant rural asylum.

37 On the September 1930 coup, see Robert A. Potash, *The Army and Politics in Argentina, 1928–1945* (Stanford: Stanford University Press, 1969).

38 On the polarization of professional life in Argentina, see Plotkin, "Freud, Politics, and the *Porteños*," 45–74. The temporary director was Dr. Ricardo J. Valenzuela.

39 "Comprobaciones dolorosas," *La Nación* (August 20, 1931). "Pero hemos de llamar especialmente la atención acerca del delito que implica la reclusión de presuntos insanos en virtud de certificados provenientes de un simple empleado del Hospicio, sin título universitario habilitante, cuando el reglamento, proveyendo a las más elementales garantías, exige, en casos de esta naturaleza, el díctamen de dos médicos ajenos al establecimiento.

Como dice con razón el informe, esta anomalía resulta tanto más grave cuanto que afecta, no sólo a la salud, sino a la libertad de los individuos." Prior to the coup, media had reported on the deterioration of conditions. See also Adolfo Lanús, "Veintecuatro horas de libertad en el manicomio," *Caras y Caretas* 33:1647 (April 26, 1930): n.p.

40 "La investigación en el Hospicio de las Mercedes," *La Prensa* (August 20, 1931): 11. The investigation and intervention also extended to the Open Door colony. See "Fue intervenida la CNA – Inició sus funciones el interventor del Hospicio de las Mercedes," *La Nación* (December 3, 1930): 9.

41 Prior to his 1907 appointment as director of the HNA, the neurologist José Esteves (1863–1927) had helped to establish a neurology *consultorio* at the city's Children's Hospital. In keeping with the growing scientific approach to psychiatric care, he ordered the creation of a formal system of patient files, *historias clínicas*. In 1911, HNA director Esteves had written a memorandum to the Society of Beneficence in which he outlined a plan to convert the hospital into a hospital for the treatment of acute cases. See AGN-SB-HNA, Legajo 221, Expediente "Libro 1910–1911," Dr. Esteves, to Señoras Inspectoras (February 16, 1911). See also: Guerrino, *Psiquiatría argentina*, 46; and Loudet and Loudet, *Historia de la psiquiatría argentina*, 157–61. "Doctor José Antonio Esteves - Su jubilación," *La Nación* (May 15, 1924): n.p.

42 Simon Goodwin, *Comparative Mental Health Policy: From Institutional to Community Care* (London: Sage, 1997), 8. France had funded extramural care since 1851, while Griesinger developed the first psychopathic clinic in Germany at the end of the nineteenth century. For the United States, see Grob, *Mental Illness and American Society*, 150–57. The movement was not without its critics, many of whom pointed out that it was not really clear how medicine could prevent illnesses whose true etiology was still a mystery. For Spain, see Josep M. Comelles, "De médicos de locos a médicos de cuerdos. La transición del manicomio al gabinete en la psiquiatría de anteguerra (1890–1939)," *Asclepios* 1 (1992): 347–68. For France, Gregory M. Thomas, "Open Psychiatric Services in Interwar France," *History of Psychiatry* 15:2 (2004): 131–53.

43 Nancy Leys Stepan argues that "mental hygiene, though representing itself as a modern and innovative approach to insanity and crime, was, in the Latin American context, deeply tinged with hereditarianism, especially the extreme hereditarianism of the Italian criminologist Cesare Lombroso." Nancy Leys Stepan, *'The Hour of Eugenics': Race, Gender, and Nation in Latin America* (Ithaca, NY: Cornell University Press, 1991), 51. See also: Héctor Palma, *'Gobernar es seleccionar': Apuntes sobre la eugenesia* (Buenos Aires: Jorge Baudino Ediciones, 2002); and Vezzetti, *Locura en la Argentina*. On the relationship of psychoanalysis to mental hygiene, see Mariano Ben Plotkin, *Freud in the Pampas: The Emergence and Development of a Psychoanalytic Culture in Argentina* (Stanford: Stanford University Press, 2001), 17–22.

44 Vezzetti, *Locura en la Argentina*, 221–32.

45 Plotkin, *Freud in the Pampas*, 19. Mental hygiene became one of the important venues for the diffusion of a psychoanalytic culture in the succeeding decades.

46 Lanfranco Ciampi, "La asistencia de los enfermos mentales según los criterios reformadores modernos," *Revista de criminología, psiquiatría y medicina legal* 9:52 (July–August 1922): 393. Ciampi was born in Italy and soon after his arrival to Argentina had been named director of the *Instituto Psico-Pedagógico de Buenos Aires*.

47 Ciampi, "La asistencia de los enfermos mentales," 400.

48 Ciampi, "La asistencia de los enfermos mentales," 392.

49 On the growing fascination with statistics, see Fernando Gorriti, *Anamnesis general de 5,000 enfermos mentales clasificados* (Buenos Aires: Talleres Gráficos de la Penitenciaría Nacional, 1920). Gorriti (1876–1970) was director of the *Colonia Nacional de Alienados.* On the desire to dispel the myth that the incidence of mental illness was increasing, see Ciampi, "La asistencia de los enfermos mentales," 385–89.

50 To fund the project, Gorriti was optimistic that "no institution is better suited to execute the project than the National state, through its own institutions, without additional budgetary outlays." Fernando Gorriti, "Nueva extensión social en la asistencia hospitalaria de los enfermos mentales," *Revista de criminología, psiquiatría y medicina legal* 7 (1920): 615–17. The Ministry of Foreign Relations rejected a proposal by Gorriti, which he had made in the late 1920s. See Fernando Gorriti, "Higiene mental en la Argentina," *Revista argentina de neurología, psiquiatría y medicina legal* 2:8 (March–April 1928): 145.

51 Ciampi, "La asistencia de los enfermos mentales," 385–401. The author cited Tamburini, G.C. Ferrari, G. Antonini, *L'assistenza degli alienati in Italia e nelle altre nazioni*, Torino, Utet, 1918, who had recently rejected the idea of growing rates of insanity. Gorriti, "Nueva extensión social," 615–19. Gorriti (1876–1970) was serving as the director of the *Colonia Nacional de Alienados.*

52 Enrique Carpintero and Alejandro Vainer, *Las huellas de la memoria: Psicoanálisis y salud mental en la Argentina de los '60 y '70 (1957–1983), Tomo I (1957–1959)* (Buenos Aires: Topia Editorial, 2004), 64. In 1920, the Spanish Association of Mutual Aid had opened a *consultorio externo* for its members seeking psychiatric assistance.

53 MREC, "Memoria de la Sociedad de Beneficencia de la Capital," *Memoria del Ministerio de Relaciones Exteriores y Culto correspondiente al años 1924–25* (Buenos Aires: Imprenta de Cámara de Diputados, 1925), 707–8. It is possible that the external clinic did not open until 1926. See Director Nogués' request for a clinic from September, 1925, in AGN-SB-HNA, Legajo 203, Expediente 6097, Julio Nogues to Señoras Inspectoras (September 11, 1925). Nogués cited the establishment of similar clinics at the Salpêtrière and St. Anne hospitals in Paris. See also Gorriti, "Higiene mental en la Argentina," 145. In addition to his work at the HNA, the Obarrio ran the private "Clínica Obarrio," was *Jefe de Servicio de Neurología del Hospital de Niños*, and worked in several external pediatric neurology clinics.

54 SB, Annual Reports for years 1935, 1936, 1937, 1939, 1940, 1941, 1942. (See later citations in endnotes for individual reports.)

55 AGN-SB-HNA, Legajo 203, Expediente 5057, Dr. Luís Esteves Balado to Director Julio G. Nogués (September 1926).

56 On visitation at rural facilities, see also Conrado O. Ferrer, "Sobre las visitas a los alienados internados," *Boletín del Asilo de Alienados en Oliva* 6:19–20 (January–December 1938): 140–41.

57 AGN-SB-HNA, "SB-HNA," Legajo 203, Expediente 5057 (1924–26). Dr. Luís Esteves Balado to Director G. Nogués.

58 AGN-SB-HNA, Legajo 203, Expediente 5057 (1924–26). Dr. Luís Esteves Balado to Director Julio G. Nogués. "Hemos oido tantas reclamaciones en nuestro hospital, a miembros de las familias de las alienadas por que se las trasladaba a Lomas de Zamora, alegando los inconvenientes de las visita."

59 AGN-SB-HNA, "SB-HNA," Legajo 203, Expediente 5057 (1924–26). Dr. Luís Esteves Balado to Director Julio G.

Nogués. He also noted that Argentina's asylum population had more than quadrupled, from 2,505 in 1900 to 11,342 in 1925. Curiously, there is no mention of immigration in the memorandum. Esteves Balado was vice-president of the Liga Argentina de Higiene Mental from 1929 to 1947. Like most directors, he was a professor of psychiatry at the University of Buenos Aires. *Quien es quien en la Argentina: Biografías contemporáneas*, 5th ed. (Buenos Aires: Editorial Guillermo Kraft Limitada, 1950), 224; Guerrino, *Psiquiatría argentina*, 161–62.

60 AGN-SB-HNA, "El hacinamiento-1927," Legajo 204, Expediente 8888.

61 AGN-SB-HNA, "El hacinamiento-1927," Legajo 204, Expediente 8888.

62 Its goals were "the study and realization of the proper means that will favor the prevention of mental disturbance, to improve the conditions of treatment for psychopaths, to develop mental hygiene in individual, educational, professional and social arenas" and "to modernize assistance to the mentally ill in the widest way possible." Gorriti, "Higiene mental en la Argentina," 155.

63 *Diputados* 7 (July 1923), 551. "Con mucha frecuencia, hoy mismo, los señores médicos internos de este hospicio, reciben cartas de los deudos, en las que solicitan instrucciones con respecto a los enfermos egresados, cuando ya, en rigor, por el estado actual de cosas, con motivo de la salida de un asilado, se ha interrumpido toda relación oficial con el público."

64 MREC, *Hospicio de las Mercedes: Memoria médico-administrativa correspondiente al año 1927* (Buenos Aires: Imprenta y Encuadernación del Hospicio de las Mercedes, 1928), i–xi. His ambitious plans, however, produced few tangible results, and, by 1927, he was again requesting funds to hire more *asistentes* and to finish construction of a new pensioner unit. See also *Diputados* 7 (July 1923), 551–55. A collection of testing instruments can be found at the Museum on the grounds of the Hospital Borda (formerly the Hospicio). On industrial psychiatry in the United States and the efforts of the profession to expand its reach into society, see Lunbeck, *The Psychiatric Persuasion*.

65 Antonio Gentile, "La psiquiatría en Rosario," *Temas en la historia de la psiquiatría argentina* (Winter 1998) (entire issue).

66 Lanfranco Ciampi, "Un nuevo hospital psiquiátrico en la República Argentina," *Revista argentina de neurología, psiquiatría y medicina legal* 1:1 (January–February 1927): 481–89. The clinic was run by Dr. Antonio Martínez. It enjoyed the collaboration of Drs. Ciampi and Bosch. See also Gorriti "Higiene mental en la Argentina," 145.

67 Ciampi, "Un nuevo hospital psiquiátrico en la República Argentina," 486.

68 Ciampi, "Un nuevo hospital psiquiátrico en la República Argentina," 489. See also Ciampi, "La asistencia de los enfermos mentales," on the importance of rural asylums.

69 Lanfranco Ciampi, director, "Informaciones: Relación sobre el funcionamiento del Hospital de Alienados y sus dependencies durante el año 1928, elevada al señor Delegado Interventor de la Facultad de Ciencias Médicas, Dr. H. González," *Boletín del Instituto Psiquiátrico de la Facultad de Ciencias* (Rosario, Argentina: n.p., 1929): 50–60. The critical problem remained the absolute shortage of beds. Belgium, he observed, has 20,000 psychiatric beds in 50 different establishments. As director, Ciampi was finding himself forced to send prospective patients to "distant hospitals, outside of the province."

70 "La intervención en el Hospicio de las Mercedes," *La Prensa* (December 12, 1930): 13. Loudet and Loudet, *Historia de la psiquiatría argentina*, 87–89. During this same period, the President of the Society of Beneficence and the

Minister of Foreign Relations bore the same surname.

71 Exequias Bringas Núñez, "A propósito de la fundación de la Liga de Higiene Mental en Córdoba," *Boletín del Asilo de Alienados en Oliva* 10:42–3 (May–December 1942): 178–79. See: Gregorio Bermann, "Organización de la Asistencia Psiquiátrica e Higiene Mental en la República," *Revista argentina de neurología, psiquiatría y medicina legal* 4:24 (November–December 1930): 562; Plotkin, "Freud, Politics, and the *Porteños*," 50–51; and Sbarbi, "Reseña histórica del Hospicio de las Mercedes," 422.

72 Gonzalo Bosch, *El pavoroso aspecto de la locura en la República Argentina* (Buenos Aires: n.p., 1931), 21. *Quien es quien*, 105–6; Loudet and Loudet, *Historia de la psiquiatría argentina*, 87–89. Bosch was related to the first asylum director, Ventura Bosch.

73 "Inauguración de varios consultorios externos en el Hospicio de las Mercedes," *La Prensa* (September 27, 1931): n.p.

74 Gonzalo Bosch, "Asistencia de alienado," *Revista de la Asociación Médica Argentina* 57 (January–February 1943): 26.

75 On the role of female mental hygiene social workers in the United States, see Lunbeck, *The Psychiatric Persuasion*, 38–45.

76 Mario A. Sbarbi, "La Escuela de Visitadores y Visitadoras Sociales de Higiene Mental," *Index de neurología y psiquiatría* 1:1 (1939): 5–6.

77 "Se inauguró un nuevo servicio social de la Liga de Higiene Mental," *La Prensa* (September 23, 1938): 13. Later reforms were enacted in 1942. See Chichilnisky, "Historia de la psiquiatría argentina," 82.

78 Archivo del Hospital, "José T. Borda," "Historia clínica," 1938.

79 "Las visitadoras de higiene mental," *Caras y Caretas* 42:2109 (March 4, 1939): 26. Their work is a clear reflection of the growing number of women in the universities. See Mead, "Beneficent Maternalism": 136.

80 MREC, *Hospicio de las Mercedes: Memoria médico-administrativa correspondiente al año 1931* (Buenos Aires: Establecimiento Gráfico Tomás Palumbo, 1932), viii. "Conjuntamente con las prescripciones científicas, se ha considerado, así, el tratamiento moral del insano, asignándole tareas cuyo producto constituye innegables beneficios para el establecimientos, a la vez que un eficacísimo recurso terapéutico, y dotándolo de medios de entretenimiento y de solaz."

81 "Una emocionante transmisión radiotelefónica por los asilados del Hospicio de las Mercedes," *Caras y Caretas* 34:1715 (August 15, 1931): n.p. Since 1990, La Radio Colifata transmits every Saturday from within the Borda (formerly the Hospicio) Hospital.

82 *Hospicio de las Mercedes: Memoria médico-administrativa correspondiente al año 1931*, ix–xi. Bosch also reopened the Hospicio's nursing school in May 17, 1932, which continued to function until 1942, when it closed for unknown reasons. The first class consisted of 93 men and women. See: *Hospicio de las Mercedes: Memoria médico-administrativo correspondiente al año 1932* (Buenos Aires: Establecimiento Gráfico Tomás Palumbo 1933), vii; Guerrino, *Psiquiatría argentina*, 67; and Archivo de la Facultad de Medicina, Universidad de Buenos Aires, "Profesor Gonzalo Bosch," Letter to Décano Rafael Bullrich, May 12, 1932.

83 On the growing appeal of psychoanalysis by physicians at the asylums, see Plotkin (2000).

84 On the link between statistics and mental hygiene, see Rogelio de Lena, "Organización de la estadística en higiene mental," *Revista de psiquiatría y criminología* 7:39 (September–October 1942): 427–35. For a discussion of the

importance of statistical analysis in determining treatment effectiveness, see Joaquín J. Durquet and Eusebio Albinao, "Estudio estadístico de la parálisis general progresiva en el Hospital Melchor Romero," *Revista de criminología, psiquiatría y medicina legal* 11 (1924): n.p.

85 On the relationship of psychoanalysis to shock therapy, see Plotkin, *Freud in the Pampas*, 22–23, 102–4.

86 Niall McCrae, "'A Violent Thunderstorm': Cardiazol Treatment in British Mental Hospitals," *History of Psychiatry* 17:1 (2006): 69.

87 Enrique Roxo, "Régimen alimenticio en el tratamiento de las afecciones mentales," *Revista de psiquiatría y criminología* 3:13 (January–February 1938): 11–21.

88 The first patient treated with electroconvulsive therapy was a psychotic vagabond who had been detained by the police in Italy. Jonathan Sadowsky, "Beyond the Metaphor of the Pendulum: Electroconvulsive Therapy, Psychoanalysis, and the Styles of American Psychiatry," *Journal of the History of Medicine* 61 (January 2006): 1–25. On the quest for cures for mental illnesses, see Gerald N. Grob, "Psychiatry's Holy Grail: The Search for the Mechanisms of Mental Diseases," *Bulletin of the History of Medicine* 72 (1998): 189–219.

89 McCrae, "'A Violent Thunderstorm,'" 81.

90 Frances R. Frankenburg, M.D., "History of the Development of Antipsychotic Medication," *History of Psychiatry* 17:3 (September 1994): 531. An extreme case of medical experimentation on patients is discussed in Scull, *Madhouse*.

91 Joel T. Braslow, *Mental Ills and Bodily Cures: Psychiatric Treatment in the First Half of the Twentieth Century* (Berkeley: University of California Press, 1997). See also Joel T. Braslow, "Therapeutics and the History of Psychiatry," *Bulletin of the History of Medicine* 74 (2000): 794–802.

92 Ramón B. Silva and Héctor M. Piñero, "Lactoterapia en los estados de agitación," *Revista de criminología, psiquiatría y medicina legal* 19:109 (January–February 1932): 24–31.

93 Luís Esteves Balado, "Terapéutica por shocks en las enfermedades mentales," *Revista de criminología, psiquiatría y medicina legal* 19:110 (March–April 1932): 162–17.

94 César Castedo, "Electro-Shock en el Pabellón Charcot del Hospital Melchor Romero," *Revista de psiquiatría y criminología* 7:39 (September–October 1942): 419–24. In March, 1943, the Society of Beneficence approved the use of ECT at the HNA. SB, *Memoria correspondiente al año 1943* (Buenos Aires, 1944).

95 Gonzalo Bosch and Arturo Mó, "La malarioterapia en la parálisis general," *Revista de la Sociedad Argentina de Neurología y Psiquiatría* 1:6 (1925): 185–223; and "La importancia de la psicometría en psiquiatría. Contribución a su estudio," 1:6 (1925): 224–33.

96 Within two years of the introduction of cardiozol treatment, which had been developed in Central Europe, the HNA was using it. MREC, "Memorias de la Sociedad de Beneficencia," *Memoria del Ministerio de Relaciones Exteriores y Culto correspondiente al año 1937* (Buenos Aires, 1938), 371–73.

97 AGN-SB-HNA. Legajo 212, Expediente 6323 (May 14, 1943). "Servicio de shockterapia."

98 The procedures were also credited with aiding in the ever-evolving study of mental illness.

99 MREC, *Hospicio de las Mercedes: Memoria medico-administrativo correspondiente al año 1931* (Buenos Aires, 1932), x.

100 MREC, *Hospicio de las Mercedes: Memoria medico-administrativo correspondiente al año 1932* (Buenos Aires, 1933), v–vi.

101 Enrique Roxo, "Terapéutica moderna en enfermedades mentales," *Revista de criminología, psiquiatría y medicina legal* 19:114 (November–December 1932): 681. Roxo was professor of clinical psychiatry in Rio de Janeiro, Brazil.

102 Roxo, "Terapéutica moderna en enfermedades mentales," 688. For a similar critique about the usefulness of shock treatments for schizophrenia, see Osvaldo Loudet, Review of Julio Endara, "Tratamiento de la esquizofrenia," in Jornadas Neuropsiquiátricas Panamericanas (published in Lima 1939). *Revista de psiquiatría y criminología* 5 (1940): 149–50. Roxo's critique of European medical innovations is suggestive of Julia Rodriguez's well-argued thesis on the autonomy of Latin American science. See Julia Rodriguez, "South Atlantic Crossings: Fingerprints, Science, and the State in Turn-of-the-Century Argentina," *American Historical Review* 109:2 (2004): 387–416.

103 Esteves Balado, "Terapéutica por shocks en las enfermedades mentales," 170. Lobotomies were practised in Brazilian hospitals from 1936 until 1956. See André Luis Masiero, "A lobotomia e a leucotomía nos manicômios brasileiros," *História, ciencias, saúde-manguinhos* 10:2 (May–August 2003): 549–72. <http://www.scielo.br/scielo.php?script=sci_arttext&pid=S0104-59702003000200004&lng=pt&nrm=iso>.

104 MREC, *Hospicio de las Mercedes: Memoria medico-administrativo correspondiente al año 1936* (Buenos Aires, 1937), 19; MREC, *Hospicio de las Mercedes: Memoria medico-administrativo correspondiente al año 1937* (Buenos Aires, 1938), 16.

105 MREC, *Hospicio de las Mercedes: Memoria medico-administrativo correspondiente al año 1937* (Buenos Aires, 1938), 12.

106 APJN, "Insania," "Leopoldo M.," Legajo 22075 (1943). "En esa época, se lo sometió al tratamiento de elección, malarización, provocándosele once accesos palúdicos, seguido de intensos tratamientos con bismuto y arsenicales."

107 "Leopoldo M."

108 The report for the years 1929–30, for example, made the usual statement about overcrowding, yet also claimed that many patients were receiving advanced treatments. SB, *Memoria del año 1929–30* (Buenos Aires: Talleres de la Sociedad de Beneficencia de la Capital, 1931), 19–23.

109 McCrae, "'A Violent Thunderstorm,'" 67–90.

110 For Mexico, see María Cristina Sacristán, "Una valoración sobre el fracaso del Manicomio de La Castañeda como institución terapéutica, 1910–1944," *Secuencia, nueva época* 51 (September–December 2001): 91–120. For Bolivia, Zulawski, "Mental Illness and Democracy in Bolivia," 237–67.

111 "La hospitalización de alienados en el país constituye un serio problema de solución inmediato," *La Nación* (January 26, 1934): n.p. See also, "En muy malas condiciones se encuentran los asilos y hospitales públicos," *La Nación* (1938): n.p.

112 De Lena, "Organización de la estadística en higiene mental," 429.

113 Carlos Carreño and N. Alberto Yanzón R., *Hospitales: Unidades sanitaria* (Buenos Aires: El Ateneo, 1945). The Hospicio had 3,418 patients but only capacity for 2,250, while the Colonia had 3,514 patients but a capacity of 1,259. Torres' capacity of 1,050 was swamped with 1,550 patients. While the report did not list Oliva's official capacity, they reported a slight drop in the population from the 1934 figure to 3,399 patients.

114 AGN-SB-HNA, Legajo 205, Expediente 3595 (November 2, 1931) "HNA-Pide se gestione, que por dos agentes de investigaciones concurran a prestar servicios en el establecimiento los días

domingos de 13 a 16 horas." AGN-SB-HNA, Legajo 205, Expediente 3595 Adelia Maria Harilaos de Olmos to Prefecto General de Policía-Coronel Enrique Pilotto (November 9, 1931); Julio Nogues to Señoras Inspectoras (November 23, 1931); AGN-SB-HNA, Legajo 205, Expediente 3595 (January 25, 1934) and (October 31, 1934).

115 On the closing of Oliva, see AGN-SB-HNA, Legajo 199, "Traslado de enfermas, 1914–1933," Nicolas Lozano to Ministry of Foreign Relations and Religion (January 30, 1933). On the closure, see MREC, "Memorias de la Sociedad de Beneficencia de la Capital," *Memoria del Ministerio de Relaciones Exteriores y Culto correspondiente al año 1933* (Buenos Aires, 1934), 10, 406–12. "The anguishing situation that this hospital suffers, due to its excessive population, far from diminishing or staying the same, worsens with each passing day." On overcrowding, see also AGN-SB-HNA, Legajo 199, "Traslado de Enfermas, 1914–1933," December 26, 1932. Presidenta Harilaos de Olmos to Minister C. Saavedra Lamas. AGN-SB-HNA, Legajo 205, Expediente 7593. Minister of Foreign Relations and Religion to Señora Presidenta Doña Adelia Maria Harilaos de Olmos, (December 26, 1933). In 1894, the HNA had closed its doors to admissions. AGN-SB-HNA, Legajo 221, "Libro 1906–09," José A. Esteves to Señoras Inspectoras, (February 6, 1908). The new policy coincided with the resignation of Julio Nogués, who was replaced by Luis Esteves Balado.

116 AGN "SB-HNA, 1923–47," Expediente 6323, "Letter to Ministro de Obras Publicas – Dirección General de Arquitectura – August 7, 1931."

117 For pleas by families to admit sick relatives, see AGN-SB-HNA, "HNA 1931–1949," Expediente 2723 (1934), Letters May 1, 1934, and June 8, 1934.

118 *La Nación* (April 14, 1934). An insignificant number were placed in private hospitals.

119 "El grave problema que plantea el cierre del hospicio de alienadas," *La Nación* (February 1, 1934): n.p. "La policía, en efecto, recogió en la vía pública a una insana peligrosa y requieró del hospicio la admisión de la misma. Pero de allí contestaron que sólo por orden judicial podía recibirse. La jefatura recabó entonces la providencia del juez de feria y el doctor Orús habilitó horas y la extendió. Más, las autoridades del hospicio negaron a pesar de ello a recibir a la enferma."

120 AGN-SB-HNA, Legajo 204, Expediente 3602, Municipalidad de la Ciudad de Buenos Aires to the Minister of the Interior, Dr. Elpidio González (August 26, 1930).

121 MREC, "Memorias de la Sociedad de Beneficencia de la Capital," *Memoria del Ministerio de Relaciones Exteriores y Culto correspondiente al año 1934* (Buenos Aires, 1935), 447–48.

122 AGN-SB-HNA, "HNA 1923–47, Exp. 7501," SB, *Reglamento del Hospital Nacional de Alienadas* (Buenos Aires, 1935), 52.

123 MREC, "Memorias de la Sociedad de Beneficencia de la Capital," *Memoria del Ministerio de Relaciones Exteriores y Culto correspondiente al año 1935* (Buenos Aires, 1936), 13, 409.

124 MREC, "Memorias de la Sociedad de Beneficencia de la Capital," *Memoria del Ministerio de Relaciones Exteriores y Culto correspondiente al año 1937* (Buenos Aires, 1938), 20–23. AGN-SB-HNA, "SB-HNA 1898–1947," Expediente 7593, October–November, 1939.

125 "Diéronse normas para recibir enfermas en el Hospital de Alienadas," *La Nación* (July 18, 1940): n.p.

126 In October 1941, the director requested that the Ministry of Interior enforce Executive Order 67297 banning the practice of officials of the Province of Buenos Aires dumping patients across the border into the federal capital. SB, *Memoria del año 1941* (Buenos Aires, 1942), 399.

127 SB, *Memoria del año 1942* (Buenos Aires, 1943), 22. Executive Order No. 124, 443. For a description of the extent of overcrowding, see SB, *Memoria correspondiente al año 1941*, 20.

128 SB, *Memoria del año 1943* (Buenos Aires, 1944), 375. In 1943, there were 613 admissions sent by the Police, other institutes of the Society and also readmissions of women who were released on temporary leave. During this same period, there was some discussion about creating a social service at the HNA, presumably to help facilitate the release of patients back into the community. See AGN-SB-HNA, Legajo 211, Expediente 13,022 (January 10, 1941).

129 SB, *Memoria del año 1943* (Buenos Aires, 1944).

130 MREC, *Hospicio de las Mercedes: Memoria médico-administrativa correspondiente al año 1932* (Buenos Aires, 1933), x.

131 MREC, *Hospicio de las Mercedes: Memoria médico-administrativa correspondiente al año 1935* (Buenos Aires, 1937), i–xiii.

132 MREC, *Hospicio de las Mercedes: Memoria médico-administrativa correspondiente al año 1936* (Buenos Aires, 1938), xii.

133 *Diputados* (September 12, 1941), 365.

134 *Boletín del Asilo de Alienados en Oliva* 3:7 (March 1935): 1–10. Overcrowding had already become a problem at Oliva by at least 1925. See MREC, "Memorias de la Sociedad de Beneficencia," *Memoria del Ministerio de Relaciones Exteriores y Culto correspondiente al año 1926* (Buenos Aires: Imprenta de la H. Cámara de Diputados, 1927), 1216.

135 Emilio Vidal Abal, "El Asilo de Oliva al través de 25 años," *Boletín del Asilo de Alienados en Oliva*. 7:26 (June–August 1939): 246.

136 Manuel M. Cabeza, "Memoria del 'Asilo Colonia Regional Mixto de Alienados en Oliva (Prov. de Córdoba): Desde su fundación hasta el 31-XII-1941," *Boletín del Asilo de Alienados en Oliva* 10:42–43 (May–December 1942): 211–12. Oliva had also shut down on July 2, 1935.

137 *Diputados* 3 (August 11–September 7), 236–38. "Proyecto de ley, August 23, 1939," proposed increasing the funding to repair buildings, increase rations to patients and to acquire new equipment.

138 Jerónimo Sappia, "El problema asistencial de los alienados en la Provincia de Córdoba," *Boletín del Asilo de Alienados en Oliva* 10:42–43 (May–December 1942): 160.

139 Sappia, "El problema asistencial," 162.

140 Rodolfo Moyano and Manuel M. Cabeza, "Síntesis de las actividades desarrolladas durante el año 1940, en el 'Asilo Colonia Regional Mixto de Alienados' en Oliva (Prov. de Córdoba)," *Boletín del Asilo de Alienados en Oliva* 9:36 (March–April 1941): 56. On September 11, 1939, Oliva authorized the admission of ten emergency cases each month.

141 Conrado O. Ferrer, "A propósito de la clausura del Asilo de Oliva," *Boletín del Asilo de Alienados en Oliva* 8:30 (March–April 1940): 518–21. Ferrer attributed much of Cabred's success in constructing hospitals to his vast social and political contacts. For a detailed analysis of the budget of Oliva, see Emilio Vidal Abal, "Sobre presupuestos de establecimientos de alienados," *Boletín del Asilo de Alienados en Oliva* 9:36 (March–April 1941): 93–101.

142 During the hospital debates of 1923, conservative deputy Sanchez Sorondo made this assessment. *Diputados* (March 14, 1923), 460. For a record of the deputy's public statements regarding the corruption of the Radical years, see M.G. Sanchez Sorondo, *Historia de seis años* (Buenos Aires: Agencia General de Librería, 1923).

143 Ángel Mariano Gimenez, *Por la salud física y mental del pueblo*, Vol. 2 (Buenos Aires: Imprenta Federación Grafica Bonaerense, 1938), 56.

144 Gimenez, *Por la salud física y mental del pueblo*, 49.

145 Eduardo Crespo, *Nuevos ensayos políticos y administrativos* (Buenos Aires: Librería y Editorial 'La Facultad,' 1938). Crespo also noted that in Argentina only 10 per cent of all hospitalizations were in private institutions, whereas in the United States it was 30 per cent. See also Conservative deputy Sanchez Sorondo's discussion of overcrowding. *Diputados* (March 14, 1923), 460. "How strange that the sick do not have the beds that they need. The phenomenon finds its roots in the same cause: the disproportionate growth of this population [the insane]."

146 Arturo Ameghino, "Carácter y extensión de la locura en las diversas regiones de la República Argentina," *Revista argentina de neurología, psiquiatría y medicina legal* 1:1 (January–February 1927): 494. The same argument is found in Bermann, "Organización de la Asistencia Psiquiátrica e Higiene Mental en la República," 556–62.

147 The Ministry's regulations for transferring patients were both strict and clear. For each ten patients, there was to be one staff member, each patient was to be accompanied by the proper paper work, including an up-to-date photograph. Because of the long travel time, only patients deemed *tranquila* were to be transferred. AGN-SB-HNA, Legajo 199, "Traslado de enfermas, 1914–1933" (October 9, 1914).

148 AGN-SB-HNA, Legajo 199, "Traslado de enfermas, 1914–1933" (November 16, 1914). Once at Oliva, patients received new uniforms, and the HNA uniforms made the return trip with nurses and staff. Three more transfers were made on November 2, 9, and 16.

149 AGN-SB-HNA, Legajo 199, "Traslado de enfermas, 1914–1933" (October 5, 1932). Presidenta Ernestina de Paz Guerrero to Señoras Inspectoras.

150 AGN-SB-HNA, Legajo 199, "Traslado de enfermas, 1914–1933." An April 1915 memorandum ordered that no patients with family in the capital be sent to Oliva.

151 Manuel M. Cabeza, "Memoria del 'Asilo Colonia Regional Mixta de Alienados en Oliva' – Desde su fundación hasta el presente 1918–1941," *Boletín del Asilo de Alienados en Oliva* (January–April, 1942): 7–21. See also *Diputados* (May 15, 1923), 206.

152 Abal, "El Asilo de Oliva al través de 25 años": 243–50. AGN-SB-HNA, Legajo 199, "Traslado de enfermas, 1914–1933" (December 16 and 24, 1915).

153 AGN-SB-HNA, Legajo 199, "Traslado de enfermas, 1914–1933" (June 27, 1917). Dr. Esteves to Señoras Inspectoras; AGN-SB-HNA, Legajo 199, "Traslado de enfermas, 1914–1933" (November 19, 1917). In August 1919, internal documents indicate that the Ministry of Foreign Relations had promised Cabred a new ward at Oliva designed exclusively for HNA patients. AGN-SB-HNA, "Traslado de enfermas, 1914–1933," "Acta de Sociedad del día 22 de agosto de 1919." See also, *Diputados* 1 (May 15, 1923), 205–10. Deputy Leopoldo Bard quoted portions of the 1919 and 1921 annual reports of the HNA during the presentation of a bill to build a rural facility for the HNA. See also AGN-SB-HNA, Legajo 199, "Traslado de enfermas, 1914–1933" (n.d.). Presidenta Sofía A. de Bengolea. At some point in the intervening years, most likely in 1919–20, a new ward for 500 HNA patients had been opened at Oliva.

154 For communications with provinces, see AGN-SB-HNA, Legajo 223, "Libro March 15–December 16, 1915." Letter to Presidenta from Subsecretaría de Gobierno, Mendoza (August 11, 1915). On the problem of compliance, see AGN-SB-HNA, Legajo 199, "Traslado de enfermas, 1914–1933." Dr. Julio Nogués to Señoras Inspectoras. (August 3, 1926).

155 "Procedencia de los enfermos ingresados en el Hospicio de las Mercedes desde el año 1902 hasta 1936," in MREC, *Hospicio de las Mercedes: Memoria médico-administrativa correspondiente al año 1936* (Buenos Aires, 1937), 12–13.

156 SB, *Memoria del Hospital Nacional de Alienadas* (Buenos Aires, 1900), n.p.

157 SB, *Memoria del año 1920* (Buenos Aires, 1921), 427–38.

158 SB, *Memoria correspondiente al año 1940* (Buenos Aires, 1941), 385.

159 Ameghino, "Carácter y extension de la locura": 495.

160 Gimenez, *Por la salud física y mental del pueblo*, 51.

161 SB, *Memoria correspondiente al año 1942* (Buenos Aires, 1943), 15–17. For a detailed analysis of the last years of the Society, see Donna Guy, "La 'verdadera historia' de la Sociedad de Beneficencia," in José Luis Moreno, ed., *La política social antes de la política social* (2000): 321–41.

162 Bosch, *Pavoroso aspecto*, 33.

163 AGN-SB-HNA, Legajo 223, "Libro March 1915–December 1916," n.d.

164 *Diputados* (May 15, 1923), 205.

165 In 1943, around 15 per cent of the patients at the HNA were listed as having "imbecilidad," "idiotismo," or "debilidad mental." *Memorias correspondiente al año 1943* (Buenos Aires, 1944), 403. For the Hospicio, around 5 per cent of the patient population in any given year between 1926 and 1934 was listed as having these conditions. MREC, *Hospicio de las Mercedes: Memoria médico-administrativa correspondiente al año 1935* (Buenos Aires, 1936), 4–5. In historical terms, categories of mental retardation are extremely slippery.

166 MREC, *Hospicio de las Mercedes: Memoria médico-administrativo correspondiente al año 1937* (Buenos Aires, 1938), 34–37.

167 MREC. Comisión Asesora de Asilos y Hospitales Regionales, *Hospicio de las Mercedes: Memoria médico-administrativa correspondiente al año 1939* (Buenos Aires, 1940), 5–15.

168 See Ingenieros, *Locura en la Argentina*, 232–33. A similar critique of statistics on the criminality of immigrants had shown that, when age was taken into consideration, immigrants were not more prone to crime than the native-born. As with Ingenieros' calculations, the criminal study was ignored. Rodriguez, *Civilizing Argentina*, 63.

169 MREC, *Hospicio de las Mercedes: Memoria médico-administrativo correspondiente al año 1937* (Buenos Aires, 1938), 65.

170 For a similar downward shift in the percentage of alcoholic patients in Victorian England, see Peter McCandless, "'Curses of Civilization': Insanity and Drunkenness in Victorian Britain," *British Journal of Addictions* 79 (1984): 49–58. Between 1910 and 1930, Mexico experienced an *increasing* incidence of alcohol-related hospitalizations. See Cristina Rivera Garza, "Becoming Mad in Revolutionary Mexico: Mentally Ill Patients at the General Insane Asylum, Mexico, 1910–1930," in Porter and Wright, *Confinement of the Insane*, 266–67. Rivera Garza suggests that the change in Mexico had to do with growing attention on the part of doctors to this problem.

171 SB, *Memoria del año 1910* (Buenos Aires: 1911), n.p.

172 SB, *Memoria del año 1920* (Buenos Aires: 1921), n.p.

173 SB, *Memoria del año 1943* (Buenos Aires: 1944), 388. Diagnoses of schizophrenia are, like mental retardation, problematic. McCrae has observed that "in their rush for early treatment Meduna and others probably classified many affective states as manifestations of the alternating stupor and excitement of catatonic schizophrenia.... they unwittingly pushed a schizophrenic

salient into affective disorder." McCrae "'A Violent Thunderstorm,'" 85.

174 MREC, "Hospicio de las Mercedes: Memoria médico-administrativo correspondiente al año 1912–1913," *Memoria del Ministerio de Relaciones Exteriores y Culto correspondiente al años 1912–13* (Buenos Aires: 1915), 435; and "El pensionado en los asilos públicos," *El Diario* (June 13, 1905): n.p.

175 Several forces limited the impact of these efforts. The Santa Fé provincial asylum in Oliveros that opened in the late 1930s, for example, was funded largely from the earnings of the provincial lottery. *Diputados* (September 12, 1941), 365. For lottery funding at the HNA, see SB, *Memoria correspondiente al año 1942* (Buenos Aires: 1943), 23.

176 Mariano Ben Plotkin, "Politics of Consensus in Peronist Argentina (1943–1955)" (Ph.D. diss., University of California, Berkeley, 1992), 300.

177 See: SB, *Memorias del año 1903* (Buenos Aires: 1904); SB, *Memoria del año 1915* (Buenos Aires: 1916); and SB, *Memoria del año 1920* (Buenos Aires: 1921).

178 *Memoria del Hospicio de las Mercedes correspondiente al año 1893* (Buenos Aires: 1900),19.

179 MREC, "Hospicio de las Mercedes: Memoria médico-administrativa correspondiente al año 1917," *Memoria del Ministerio de Relaciones Exteriores y Culto correspondiente al años 1917–1918* (Buenos Aires: 1919), 980. For similar problems in the United States, see McCandless, *Moonlight, Magnolias, and Madness*.

180 See MREC, *Hospicio de las Mercedes* (1926): 5; (1927): 3.

181 MREC, *Hospicio de las Mercedes: Memoria médico-administrativa correspondiente al año 1925* (Buenos Aires: 1926), x. Scárano was hoping to erect a 450-bed pensioner unit.

182 Gimenez, *Por la salud física y mental del pueblo*, 50. "La situación se ha agravado en los últimos tiempos con la profunda crisis, la masa enorme de desocupados y la casi pauperización del proletariado argentino con salarios insuficientes y condiciones de vida precaria." For reports of conditions at other hospitals, see: "Salta la vista la necesidad de que se resuelve el problema hospitalario," *El Diario* (August 11, 1939): 12; "Deficientes en la hospitalización," *El Diario* (August 12, 1939): 4; and Roberto Arlt, "La cama del hospital se ha convertido hoy en articulo precioso," *El Mundo* (August 9, 1939): 16.

183 SB, *Reglamento del Hospital Nacional de Alienadas* (Buenos Aires, 1909), 18; MREC, *Documentación que pasó a poder de la Secretaría de Salud Pública de la Nación: Inventario, 1900–1929.* Expediente no. 43/910 (1910). "Manuel R. solicita que su hijo sea considerado en dicha categoría y se le exonera del pago de pensión en el Hospicio de las Mercedes" (1910) and Expediente 279/910 "Maria P d Y solicita que su hermano asilado en el Hospicio de las Mercedes sea asistido como pensionista sin cargo alguno" (1910) and Expediente No. 233/915 "Lina B de J solicita permanencia gratuita de su esposo en el Hospicio de las Mercedes." (1915); Expediente No. 303/914. "Ministerio de Guerra eleva nota de la Señora Urbana G de R solicitando pensión gratuita para su hijo internado en el Hospicio de las Mercedes." (1914). In some cases, the hospital had difficulty extracting payment from public authorities. See AGN-SB-HNA, Legajo 223, Libro 1917, Señoras Inspectoras to Señora Presidenta de la SB Maria Unzúa de Alvaer.

184 AGN-SB-HNA, Legajo 205, Expediente 2898 (1931–1941). "Concesión de rebajas del 50% a pensionistas de 3era y 4a categoría." There are several hundred letters from families requesting reductions in fees. Most mention the world depression. Families of the traditional

elite who had fallen on hard times were often given special consideration. See AG-SB-HNA, "SB, Hospital Nacional de Alienadas, 1931–1949," Expediente 2723, Año 1933.

185 AGN-SB-HNA, "SB, Hospital Nacional de Alienadas, 1931–1949," Expediente 2723, Año 1933.

186 Peter Lloyd-Sherlock, "Healthcare Financing, Reform and Equity in Argentina: Past and Present," in Peter Lloyd-Sherlock, ed., *Healthcare Reform and Poverty in Latin America* (London: Institute of Latin American Studies, 2000), 144–46.

187 María Fernanda Lorenzo, Ana Lía Rey, and Cecilia Tossounian, "Images of Virtuous Women: Morality, Gender and Power in Argentina between the World Wars," *Gender and History* 17:3 (2005): 567–92; Larry Sawyers, *The Other Argentina: The Interior and National Development* (Boulder, CO: Westview, 1996), 183–84.

188 *Memoria del Hospicio de las Mercedes correspondiente al año 1893* (Buenos Aires: 1900), 495, See also annual reports already cited from 1925, 1917–18, 1937. For the HNA, see (1910), 697 and (1943), 613.

189 John Fogarty, "Social Experiments in Regions of Recent Settlement: Australia, Argentina and Canada," in Platt, *Social Welfare, 1850–1950*, 190; Peter Alhadeff, "Social Welfare and the Slump: Argentina in the 1930s," in Platt, *Social Welfare, 1850–1950*, 172.

190 See *Hospicio* reports from 1893, 1913, and 1939. MREC, "Hospicio de las Mercedes: Memoria médico-administrativa, correspondiente al año 1917," *Memorias del Ministerio de Relaciones Exteriores y Culto correspondiente al años 1917–18* (Buenos Aires: 1919), 980. The director reported that "the medical treatment practiced in Las Mercedes inspires confidence in the general public."

191 MREC, "Hospicio de las Mercedes: Memoria correspondiente al años 1910–11," *Memoria del Ministerio de Relaciones Exteriores y Culto correspondiente al años 1910–11* (Buenos Aires: 1912), 469.

192 AGN-SB-HNA 1898–1947, Legajo 205, Expediente 7593, SB, *Hospital Nacional de Alienadas: Antecedentes y medidas adoptadas para solucionar el hacinamiento de enfermas* (Buenos Aires: Talleres Gráficos del Asilo de Huérfanos, 1923). See also *La Nación* (March 15, 1923): n.p.

193 MREC. Comisión Asesora de Asilos y Hospitales Regionales. *Hospicio de las Mercedes: Memoria médico-administrativa correspondiente al año 1939* (Buenos Aires: 1940), 7. A similar assessment was made in Ferrer, "La locura en Córdoba," 60.

194 For a long-range historical perspective on the ratio of immigrant to native-born in psychiatric hospitals, see Exequias Bringas Núñez, "Inmigración y locura (Algunos datos para la profilaxis de las enfermedades mentales en la República Argentina)," *Boletín del Asilo de Alienados en Oliva* 10:42–43 (May–December 1942): 168. Between 1914 and 1941, the Colonia Nacional de Alienados had cared for 8,360 foreigners and 7,371 Argentines and the Hospital Nacional de Alienadas between those same dates had cared for 18,856 foreigners and 16,609 natives. The Hospicio de las Mercedes, between 1883 and 1922, had cared for 45,084 foreigners and 14,613 Argentines. The foreign-born comprised 18 per cent of the national population; at a select number of psychiatric hospitals they constituted a full 38 per cent of the internees. The majority of the foreign-born patients ended up at the hospital within ten years of arriving in Argentina.

195 Anxiety about the Russian migratory wave came to a head during the general strike of 1919, when elite militancy against labour turned into a pogrom against *porteño* Jews. Victor A. Mirelman, *Jewish Buenos Aires, 1890–1930* (Detroit: Wayne State

University Press, 1990), 64. Horacio Beccar Varela argued "it is undeniable that the brain of those who were Nicholas' subjects can be considered sick. It is a type of collective insanity, which we should avoid." Another social critic wrote that Russia "is at present sick and most of those who emigrate from that country suffer from that sickness, thus spreading all over the world a perturbing current." There is no evidence of the kind of anti-Semitic writing by Argentine doctors that was found in France. See Goldstein, "The Wandering Jew and the Problem of Psychiatric Anti-Semitism in Fin-de-Siecle France," 521–52. On the impact of the First World War, see Mark S. Micale and Paul Lerner, *Traumatic Pasts: History, Psychiatry, and Trauma in the Modern Age, 1870–1930* (Cambridge: Cambridge University Press, 2001).

196 Stepan, *'Hour of Eugenics'*, 140. As historian Nancy Ley Stepan notes, "[t]he failure of many of the working-class immigrants to take up Argentinean nationality or to marry outside their own immigrant circles added to the sense among the elite that foreign 'cysts' were forming in their midst, fragmenting norms and values."

197 *Memoria del año 1900*, n.p.; *Memoria del año 1943 Hospicio*, 1893, 23; *Hospicio*, 1917, 979; Hospicio 1936, 10.

198 See SB, *Memoria del año 1905*, 126–28; and *Memoria del año 1943*, 382.

199 APJN "Insania," "Hussein A.," Legajo n.a., Entrada 23709, Folio 120 (1947).

200 APJN, "Insania," "Iván G," Legajo 14235, Folio 91 (1911). See also: APJN, "Insania," "Henry R." Legajo 14675, Folio 303 (1924); and APJN, "Insania," "Andres H.," Legajo 20050, Folio 338, No. 1780 (1934).

201 *Memoria correspondiente al año 1913–14*, 569–70. Studies from the Oliva argued that the rural asylums received in more meagre subsidies from the state.

202 AGN-SB-HNA, Legajo 221, Expediente "Libro 1910–11," Dr. José A. Esteves to Señoras Inspectoras, February 16, 1911. As an example of the ideal psychiatric hospital, Esteves cited the recently constructed 300-bed facility in Frankfurt am Main, Germany.

203 AGN-SB-HNA, Legajo 200, Expediente 711. Dr. José A. Esteves to Señoras Inspectoras, May 10, 1924; "Doctor José Antonio Esteves-su jubilación," *La Nación* (May 15, 1924): n.p.

204 *Hospicio de las Mercedes: Memoria médico-administrativa correspondiente al año 1925* (Buenos Aires: Imprenta y Encuadernación del Hospicio de las Mercedes, 1926), vi–vii.

205 "En el Hospicio de las Mercedes ocurrió un hecho grave," *La Nación* (April 30, 1926): n.p.; and "El loco por la pena es cuerdo," *El Diario* (April 30, 1926): n.p. The latter story suggested that the hospital seemed to follow the ancient dictum that "with punishment the insane shall become sane."

206 In a 1923, municipal hospitals Muñiz, Piñeros, and Tornú nurses and aides made $165 pesos and $130 per month respectively, and the hospitals provided uniforms. By contrast, HNA nurses and aides made $96 pesos and $87.50 pesos respectively, and the Society did not provide them with uniforms.

207 AGN-SB-HNA, Legajo 201, Expediente 8051, (December 30, 1923). Dr. Esteves to the Señoras Inspectoras. One possible explanation for the low pay was that HNA employees were under contract with the Society and therefore not privy to the kinds of largesse that were increasingly available to most government workers.

208 AGN-SB-HNA, Legajo 203, Expediente 8330. Julio Nogués, "Proyecto de preparación de celadoras y enfermeras" (Buenos Aires: Talleres de la Sociedad de Beneficencia, 1927). See also Mead, "Beneficent Maternalism," 136.

209 AGN-SB-HNA, Legajo 208, Expediente 8172 (April 12, 1935) "HNA-Reglamentación de la carrera hospitalaria en el establecimiento."

210 AGN-SB-HNA, Legajo 208, Expediente 8172, (April 12, 1935) "HNA-Reglamentación de la carrera hospitalaria en el establecimiento"; and Mead, "Oligarchs, Doctors and Nuns," 180–81.

211 SB, *Memoria correspondiente al año 1940*: 385. "La psiquiatría es una especialidad ingrata y por ello es que no se tiene en los Hospitales de la especialidad el número crecido de médicos que concurren a hacer práctica en otros Servicios Hospitalarios de otra índole."

212 "Hombres en un mundo de sombras," *¡Aquí Está!* 10:922 (March 19, 1945): 10–11.

213 Further study is needed on doctors' work in, and ownership of, private psychiatric clinics, which blossomed during the 1920s.

214 Ingenieros, *Locura en la Argentina*, 234–35. "According to these calculations the actual coefficient of insane in the Argentine Republic would be 1.85 per 1,000; that of retarded would be 1.3 per 1,000." These statistics place Argentina in a middle ranking among nations inhabited by the white races. Ingenieros also takes great pains to point to the problems of mental retardation in the mostly creole mountain regions, thereby taking a shot at anti-immigrant literature. On similar concerns in the United States, see Trent, *Inventing the Feeble Mind*, 131–83.

215 Ameghino, "Carácter y extensión de la locura": 494. The same argument is found in Bermann, "Organización de la Asistencia Psiquiátrica e Higiene Mental en la República," 556–62.

4: Ambiguous Spaces: Law, Medicine, Psychiatry, and the Hospitals, 1900–46

1 A version of this chapter originally appeared as "Law, Medicine, and Confinement to Public Psychiatric Hospitals in Twentieth Century Argentina," in Mariano Ben Plotkin, ed., *Argentina on the Couch: Psychiatry, State, and Society, 1880 to the Present* (Albuquerque: University of New Mexico Press, 2003).

2 Roy Porter, "Madness and its Institutions," in Andrew Weir, ed., *Medicine in Society: Historical Essays* (New York: Cambridge University Press, 1992), 277.

3 Ciafardo and Espesir, "Patología de la acción política anarquista," 39. See also Foucault, "About the Concept of the 'Dangerous Individual'," 6.

4 The Criminal Code did not mandate that the judge select a psychiatrist to perform the examination, but only a trained doctor. Beatriz Ruibal, "Medicina legal y derecho penal a fines del siglo XIX," in Lobato, *Política, medicos y enfermedades*, 196–97.

5 The medical literature on distinguishing the mentally ill from those feigning insanity is extensive. See: José Ingenieros, *Simulación de la locura* (Buenos Aires: Elmer Ediciones, 1956) (originally published in 1903); and José F. Capelli and Ramón B. Silva, "Simulación y disimulación," *Revista de psiquiatría y criminología* 3:16 (July–August 1938): 463–74. For an example from popular culture, see Antonio Monteavaro, "El loco lúcido," *Caras y Caretas* 16:787 (November 1, 1913): n.p. The story describes a journalist's visit to an asylum where he questions the director's wisdom in keeping a man who seems healthy confined. The doctor responds that "Fulano de Tal es un epiléptico de los más peligrosos, y especialmente de noche, su locura adquiere caracteres furiosos." The journalist decides not to

spend the night, but rather leaves. The author concluded that, while the patient seemed sane, he was not quite sure if the doctor was not a madman. "Me despedí del director, con un miedo terrible de que también él fuera un simulador."

6 José Ingenieros, "La alienación mental y los errores judiciales," *Archivos de psiquiatría y criminología* 6 (July–August 1907): 418–30.

7 Little, "Society of Beneficence," 231. See also Osvaldo Barrenche, *Dentro de la ley, todo: Crime and the administration of justice in Buenos Aires, 1785–1853* (Lincoln: University of Nebraska Press, 2006).

8 *Código civil de la República Argentina y legislación complementaria*, "Título X, De los dementes e inhabilitados, artículos. 140-152bis" (Buenos Aires: Abeledo-Perrot, 1976), 42–44.

9 "Servicio de Observación de Alienados," *Archivos de psiquiatría y criminología* 9 (March–April 1910): 254–56.

10 *Código civil*, 42. "Se declaran dementes los individuos de uno y otro sexo que se hallen en estado habitual de manía, demencia o imbecilidad, aunque tengan intervalos lúcidos, o la manía sea parcial."

11 *Código civil*, 42, Article 144: "Los que pueden pedir la declaración de demencia son: 1. El esposo o esposa no divorciados; 2. Los parientes del demente; 3. El Ministro de Menores; 4. El respectivo cónsul, si el demente fuese extranjero; 5. Cualquiera persona del pueblo, cuando el demente sea furioso, o incomode a sus vecinos."

12 *Código civil*, 43, Articles 147–52.

13 *Código civil*, Article 484, 103. "Titulo XIII, De la curatela, Capitulo I, Curatela a los incapaces mayores de edad" reads "El demente no será privado de su libertad personal sino en los casos en que sea de temer que, usando ella, se dañe a sí mismo o dañe a otros. No podrá tampoco ser trasladado a una casa de dementes sin autorización judicial."

14 The available evidence suggests that most of the people who were confined to the hospitals did not receive any judicial review. One possibility is that where there was a question about the disposition of property, the courts were more likely to intervene.

15 For the problem of delays and other pitfalls in the United States, see McCandless, *Moonlight, Magnolias, and Madness*, 264. "Until the early 1900s, the rules required that the regents personally examine the patients prior to dismissal. But the regents normally met only once a month, and sometimes they did not examine all or any of the patients the physicians recommended for discharge. Months might pass between the physicians' recommendation and the actual time of release."

16 APJN, "Insania," "María," Legajo 14592, No. 4689, Folio 564 (1921).

17 APJN, "Insania," "Josefina D.," Legajo 19981, No. 20,373, Folio 44 (1937).

18 APJN, "Insania," "Silvia O.," Legajo 19981, No. 20,621 (1937).

19 APJN, "Insania," "Carolina M.," Legajo 38678 (1943).

20 APJN, "Insania," "José P.," Legajo 10248, Folio 183 (1925).

21 APJN, "Insania," "Iván G.," Legajo 14235, Folio 91 (1911).

22 APJN, "Insania," "Samuel J.," Legajo 20008 (1934).

23 APJN, "Insania," "Carlos Luis B.," Legajo 19978 (1932). Hospicio de las Mercedes to Judge Francisco Quesada, October 21, 1932. "Como hasta la fecha no se ha tenido conocimiento de resolución alguna en favor de la libertad de B. y persistiendo su mejoría, reitero a V.S., el pedido que hacía en la citada nota."

24 APJN, "Insania," "Paulina C.," Legajo 19999 (1933).

25 APJN, "Insania," "Jaime M.," Legajo 20023, No. 13914, Folio 25 (1931). This subject was confined at the Hospicio's

rural facility in the Province of Buenos Aires. In order to be inspected by court doctors, he had to be transferred to the Hospicio.

26 APJN, "Insania," "Francisco N.," Legajo 22117, Folio 189 (1946).

27 See Little, "Society of Beneficence," 234. In October 1888, for example, the director of the Hospital Nacional de Alienadas reported that "husbands sometimes institutionalized their wives as a means to punish them or to wrest their inheritance." On depositing practices, see Ruggiero, "Wives on 'Deposit'" 253–70. Although Argentine women did enjoy greater control over assets than women elsewhere on the continent, husbands still exercised a great deal of control. See Dora Barrancos, "Problematic Modernity: Gender, Sexuality, and Reproduction in Twentieth-Century Argentina," *Journal of Women's History* 18:2 (2006): 123–50; and Donna J. Guy, "Lower-class Families, Women, and the Law in Nineteenth-Century Argentina," *Journal of Family History* (Fall 1985): 318–31. The civil code reforms of 1926 expanded women's rights regarding property. See Lavrín, *Women, Feminism, and Social Change*, 210.

28 For more recent studies on patients' loss of property, see Eduardo José Cárdenas, "Para internar a un enfermo mental hace la falta la intervención de un juez," *El Observador* (May 4, 1984): 33.

29 Roberto Ciafardo, *Psicopatología forense* (Buenos Aires: 'El Ateneo,' 1972), 351.

30 APJN, "Insania," "Santiago D.," Legajo 14259, Folio 145, Entrado 973 (1912). The three conditions for release are as follows: the illness disappears, subject is sufficiently improved so as to not pose a danger to self or others, and "Cuando lo solicitaren las autoridades que ordenaron su resolución o las personas que la pidieron voluntariamente."

31 Eduardo José Cárdenas, Ricardo Grimson, and José Atilio Álvarez, *El juicio de insania y la internación psiquiátrica* (Buenos Aires: Astrea, 1985), 46–47.

32 Edwin M. Borchard, *Library of Congress Guide to the Law and Legal Literature of Argentina, Brazil and Chile* (Washington, D.C.: Government Printing Office, 1917), 95. Antonio Montarcé Lastra, *La incapacidad civil de los alienados* (Buenos Aires: Librería y Editorial 'La Facultad,' 1928), xv. Author notes that there was some regional variation. For example, in the city of Buenos Aires, the judge did not see the patient, whereas in the Province of Buenos Aires the patient was present for his insanity proceeding. This may explain, in part, the practice of *bonaerense* [province of Buenos Aires] public officials and private citizens dumping the insane into the city of Buenos Aires.

33 Ingenieros, "La alienación mental y los errores judiciales," 418–30.

34 Ramón Carrillo, *Clasificación sanitaria de los enfermos mentales: Relaciones entre código civil y sanitario* (Buenos Aires: Talleres Gráficos del Ministerio de Salud Pública de la Nación, 1950), 61.

35 APJN, "Insania," "Celia B.," Legajo 55176 (1949).

36 Little, "Society of Beneficence," 235.

37 APJN, "Insania," "Graciana E.," Legajo 22116 (1946).

38 In August 1920, for example, the HNA sent 52 official reports on the mental status of patients to the courts and an additional 246 letters to the relatives of patients. In that same month, the HNA received 103 new patients. At a minimum 51 of these women did not have their cases communicated by the hospital to the presiding judge. In September 1920, there were 122 admissions but only 44 communications to the courts. AGN-SB-HNA, Legajo 223, Libro 1917; AGN-SB-HNA, Legajo 200, Expediente 1934 (February 1920). See also AGN-SB-HNA, Legajo 200, Expediente 2784 and 2659; and AGN-SB-HNA, Legajo 223, Libro 1917.

39 "Comprobaciones dolorosas," *La Nación* (August 20, 1931): n.p.

40 Ingenieros, "La alienación mental y los errores judiciales," 414.

41 When charges of abuse are levelled against staff in institutions, staff can often evade sanction. See Reaume, *Remembrance of Patients Past*, 80.

42 At the HNA, see AGN-SB-HNA, Legajo 203, Expediente 7933, "HNA-Comunica Suicidas." See the case of Ana T de R (1926–27). See also AGN-SB-HNA, Legajo 203, Expediente 7933, "HNA-Comunica Suicidas." Dr. Julio Nogués to Señora Inspectora de Turno (March 29, 1932). Case of Rosa P. and Felisa A de M. The nurses named in the case were Filomena Taboada Fernandez and Maria Gamalta Gil.

43 AGN-SB-HNA, Legajo 267, Expediente 6260 (September 1933). "HNA-Comunica hechos occurridos con motivo [del] fallecimiento de Sñra Angela López de Defina." It was her son, who had come to retrieve her body, who noticed that she was still breathing. Despite efforts to revive Angela, she died a few hours later. An official inquiry by the hospital determined that the on-duty doctor was at fault for not making independent confirmation of the patient's demise.

44 "Un proceso celebre. La muerte de Tallarico. Nuevas investigaciones de la justicia," *La Nación* (November 20, 1902): 6; "Tallarico-las informaciones de 'La Nación' – Completamente confirmadas," *La Nación* (November 23, 1902): 8; "En busca de los restos de Tallarico," *Caras y Caretas* 5:219 (December 13, 1902): n.p.; Argentina. Congreso Nacional. *Diputados* 2 (1902) (Buenos Aires: Imprenta y Encuadernación de la H. Cámara de Diputados, 1930), 15–54. The Federal Police took great umbrage at the initial presumption of their guilt.

45 "El caso Tallarico," *Solidaridad: Periódico obrero* (Rosario de Santa Fe) (November 22, 1902): 3.

46 It is likely that he claimed medical confidentiality. See: "El lamentable suceso en que perdieron la vida tres alienados," *La Prensa* (August 10, 1939), 20; and "Un imprudente descuido de enfermeros causó la muerte de 3 alienados," *La Prensa* (August 9, 1939): n.p. The article went on to complain that the police were withholding information. See also "No se justifica la reserva policial sobre la muerte de tres alienados," *El Diario* (August 10, 1939), 11. Archive of Hospital José T. Borda, "Admission Book: 1939." By pure chance, I found the only existing Admission Book in the former Hospicio. A cross was listed by the patients' names and the dates of their admission and death.

47 Ferrer, "Sobre las visitas a los alienados internados," 142.

48 SB, *Reglamento del Hospital Nacional de Alienadas* (Buenos Aires, 1909), 42. Friends, legal guardians, and relatives could visit from 8 to 11 a.m. on Mondays and Thursdays, except for holidays.

49 AGN-SB-HNA, "HNA 1923–47," Expediente 7501. SB, *Relgamento del Hospital Nacional de Alienadas* (Buenos Aires, 1935), 52. The new rules allowed for Saturday visits.

50 See the file of Tomás Manuel C. (December 1949) in the Archive of Hospital José T. Borda. Doctors decided that he should not see a letter from his brother, who was informing him of his continued stay in the hospital.

51 See the interview with psychiatrist Fernando Pagés Larraya in Renato D. Alarcón, ed., *Identidad de la psiquiatría latinoamericana: Voces y exploraciones en torno a una ciencia solidaria* (Mexico: Siglo Veintiuno, 1990), 477. Pagés Larraya recalls seeing patients riding in the last car of the train, sometimes in manacles or tied to their seats.

52 AGN-SB-HNA, Legajo 223, "Libro March 1915–December 1916," n.d. Similar policies existed for the transfer

of patients to the Torres asylum for the mentally retarded.

53 AGN-SB-HNA, Legajo 205, Expediente 7593, Letter to Presidenta de la Sociedad de Beneficiencia from Asesoria de Menores de la Capital, April 14, 1934.

54 AGN-SB-HNA, Legajo 199, "Traslado de enfermas, 1914–1933" (October 9, 1914). AGN-SB-HNA, Legajo 199, "Traslado de enfermas, 1914–1933" (November 16, 1914). Once at Oliva, patients received new uniforms and the HNA ones made the return trip with nurses and staff.

55 AGN-SB-HNA, Legajo 199, "Traslado de enfermas, 1914–1933" (April 1915).

56 AGN-SB-HNA, Legajo 199, "Traslado de enfermas, 1914–1933" (April 1915).

57 AGN-SB-HNA, Legajo 199, "Traslado de enfermas, 1914–1933" (April 28, 1915).

58 AGN-SB-HNA, Legajo 199, "Traslado de enfermas, 1914–1933" (April 10, 1915). Advisory Commission to Presidenta Elena Napp de Green.

59 For several other examples of communications between the CAHAR and the Society regarding the release of transferees from the HNA to Oliva, see AGN-SB-HNA, "Libro March 1915–December 1916" (March 4, 1915).

60 Máximo Agustín Cubas, "Los certificados médicos de alienación mental," *Boletín del Asilo de Alienados en Oliva* 3:7 (March 1935): 35–45. Such accusations were levelled against Hospicio director Alfredo Scárano after he was fired in 1930. See "Comprobaciones dolorosas," *La Nación* (August 20, 1931).

61 Cubas, "Los certificados médicos," 37–38. Cubas cited a recent case in which a patient arrived with physical wounds that the medical certificates did not mention.

62 Cubas, "Los certificados médicos," 38.

63 Cubas, "Los certificados médicos," 39–40. As was common in the psychiatric literature of the period, Cubas expressed concern that countries at the "vanguard of humanity" had passed adequate legislation protecting their insane. Thus, the task of creating better laws was necessarily connected to Argentina's international reputation as a civilized country.

64 Cubas, "Los certificados médicos," 35. Cubas alludes to a recent case at the HNA where doctors were charged with kidnapping. Unfortunately, the author does not provide precise details.

65 Ferrer, "Sobre las visitas a los alienados internados," 142.

66 The issue of professional protection survived at least until the 1960s, and probably later. See Bruno A.L. Fantoni, "Internación de enfermos mentales – Responsibilidad de los directores," *Gaceta del Instituto Nacional de Salud Mental* 1:1 (September 1963): n.p.

67 Loudet and Loudet, *Historia de la psiquiatría argentina*, 194–95.

68 On the issue of legal reform in Western Europe and the United States, see: McCandless, "Liberty and Lunacy," 339–62; Fox, *'So far disordered in mind'*, 38; and Dowbiggin, *Inheriting Madness*, 93–115.

69 Loudet and Loudet, *Historia de la psiquiatría argentina*, 178–85.

70 *Diputados* 1, 26th sesión ordinaria (September 14, 1894), 781–86.

71 *Diputados* 1 (September 26, 1906), 1011. "y como el loco sólo puede ser trasladado a un hospital especial por orden del juez ... es evidente que los locos en cuya internación no se han llenado estas tramitaciones previas han sido ilegalmente internados."

72 *Diputados* 1 (September 14, 1894), 788.

73 *Diputados* 1 (September 14, 1894), 788.

74 *Diputados* 1 (September 12, 1894), 752. Cantón observed that "la inmensa mayoría de los dementes pueden ser secuestrados sin llenar requisito alguno,

sin certificado médico, a pedido de cualquier persona interesada, con el único encargo por parte del director del manicomio de dar cuenta al gobernador de la localidad."

75 By 1918, the women's hospital had a patient capacity of 800 but cared for over 1,600 souls. See "Hospicio Nacional de Alienadas - Cargos contra su dirección," *La unión* (July 23, 1918). For the 1920s, see *Diputados* 6 (March 7, 1923), 349.

76 Leopoldo Bard, "Proyecto de ley sobre legislación para los establecimientos destinados a alienados," *Revista de criminología, psiquiatría y medicina legal* 9:52 (July–August 1922): 452–74.

77 *Diputados* 6 (September 29, 1926), 432. Fonrouge's figures probably included patients at the Colonia Nacional de Alienados.

78 APJN, "Insania," Legajo 19551, Folio 66. See also "Un millonario secuestrado en un sanatorio," *Crítica* (April 22, 1928).

79 *Diputados* 6 (September 29, 1926), 418.

80 Adolfo M. Sierra, "Entorno de tres proyectos legislativos sobre alienados," *La Nación* (December 29, 1926): n.p. Sierra also used the argument of medical confidentiality to oppose a proposal that doctors be obliged to report all drug addicts to the police.

81 Adolfo M. Sierra, "Problemas médicos actuales sobre tratamiento, profilaxis y eugénesis mentales," *Revista argentina de neurología, psiquiatría y medicina legal* 4:19 (January–February 1930): 34.

82 Sierra, "Problemas médicos actuales sobre tratamiento, profilaxis y eugénesis mentales," 34.

83 Rodriguez, *Civilizing Argentina*, 208. See also Rafael Huertas García-Alejo, *El delincuente y su patología: Medicina, crimen y sociedad en el positivismo argentino* (Seville, Spain: Consejo Superior de Investigaciones Cientificas, 1991).

84 Rodriguez, *Civilizing Argentina*, 203–6. Lucas Ayarragaray and José Ingenieros had both proposed a variety of measures to incorporate social defence into Argentina's legal codes and hoped to thereby "rationalize" the legal system.

85 Ruibal, "Medicina legal y derecho penal a fines del siglo XIX," 198. See also Michel Foucault, "About the Concept of the 'Dangerous Individual' in 19th Century Legal Psychiatry," *International Journal of Law and Psychiatry* 1 (1978):1-18. Foucault argues that the subject of control is now viewed not so much by what he or she has done as by who they are.

86 Vezzetti argues that its resurgence in the 1920s was a product of a growing pessimism about the prospects of psychiatry to reform deviant individuals. Vezzetti, *Locura en la Argentina*, 142.

87 Rodriguez, *Civilizing Argentina*, 47, 88–91.

88 Ciafardo and Espesir, "Patología de la acción política anarquista," 23–40. For the anarchist response to psychiatry, see Álvaro Girón, "Los anarquistas españoles y la criminología de Cesare Lombroso," *Frenia* 2:2 (2002): 81–108.

89 "La tragedia del Hospicio de las Mercedes," *Caras y Caretas* 28:1416 (November 21, 1926): n.p.

90 "Esteban Lucich, o 'El anarquista suicidado por la sociedad,'" *Espejos y miradas* 1:1 (December 1988): 7; and "Un insano que cometió anteriormente otros dos crimenes, dió muerte de un balazo a un médico del Hospicio de las Mercedes," *La Prensa* (October 2, 1932): 14. Although I have found no concrete evidence that the Hospicio was used to confine anarchists, future research is needed to explore this question. I am indebted to Ray Craib for sharing a suggestive case from Chile concerning the confinement of an anarchist to the Santiago asylum in the 1920s.

91 Alberto Bonhour, *Delirantes homicidas: Atentados contra la vida de médicos argentinos* (Buenos Aires: Tésis de Profesorado, University of Buenos Aires, 1941), 2.

92 José M.L. Vega, "Alienación y delito," *Revista de policía y criminalística* 9:42–45 (January–December 1946): 48–52.

93 APJN, "Insania," "Pedro O.," Legajo 7335, Folio 7, No. 2445 (1917).

94 APJN, "Insania," "Catalina F.," Legajo 12607 (1914).

95 APJN, "Insania," "Samuel J.," Legajo 20008 (1934). On public nudity, see "No están todos los que son.... Una hora en el Hospicio de las Mercedes," *Caras y caretas* 26:1300 (September 1, 1923): n.p. See photograph and caption, "'Oh padre Adán ... esta es la mía!' Y este hombre que quiso, como el primer hombre, andar desnudo, es sujetado y cubierto por sus guardianes."

96 APJN, "Insania," "Gustavo N.," Legajo n.a. (1916).

97 APJN, "Insania," "Rodolfo G.," Legajo 19515, Entrada 8933 (1932).

98 "La cárcel de Tucumán," *Caras y Caretas* 15:721 (July 27, 1912). One picture of a prisoner reads: "Alfredo Fontes, or Tomas de Santos, author of a triple homicide, with a bomb, in the *quebrada* de Lules, who is insane."

99 *Diputados* 2 (1902), 15.

100 Vezzetti was the first scholar to articulate the relationship between the appeal of social defence and Argentina's low rates of confinement. Vezzetti, *Locura en la Argentina*, 221–31. On the United Status, see Trent, *Inventing the Feeble Mind*, 185. By the 1920s, 42 of the 48 states in the United States had at least one institution for the "feebleminded," and some had two or three. The state of New York alone had six such institutions.

101 Vega, "Alienación y Delito," 48–52. The following is a list of diagnoses and the crimes that were most highly correlated to them: Progressive General Paralysis – robo pueril; epilepsy – *homicidio, feroz e insantanea*, depressive mania – erotism and rape; melancholy and alcoholism – suicide; hypochondria – murder attempts, especially against doctors. On the supposed connection between criminal behaviour and epilepsy, see Javier Brandam, "Responsibilidad de los epilépticos," *Revista de criminología, psiquiatría y medicina legal* 2:7–8 (January–April 1915): 3–41.

102 José Belbey, "La delincuencia de los débiles mentales," *Revista de psiquiatría y criminología* 2 (November–December 1937): 713–24.

103 Belbey, "La delincuencia de los débiles mentales," 717.

104 Belbey, "La delincuencia de los débiles mentales," 722–23. Reflecting a trend in Latin American psychiatry, Belbey demonstrated equal interest in hereditary explanations and environmental factors. After all, if the feebleminded were excessively influenced by their surroundings, then it followed that in addition to constructing institutions for this class of patients, and also passage of legislation for the institutionalization of persons in a state of "pre-criminal dangerousness," it was necessary to improve the social conditions in which poor Argentines lived and worked. On the debate between acquired and inherited traits in Argentina, as well as Mexico and Brazil, see Stepan, '*The Hour of Eugenics*.'

105 See also Moyano and Cabeza, "Síntesis de las actividades desarrolladas durante el año 1940, en el 'Asilo Colonia Regional Mixto de Alienados' en Oliva (Prov. de Córdoba)," 66–67.

106 Bosch, *Pavoroso aspecto*, 7–9. Bosch considered the calculations made by Lucio Meléndez and Emilio Coni in their 1880 survey of insanity.

107 Bosch, *Pavoroso aspecto*, 9.

108 Bosch, *Pavoroso aspecto*, 10.

109 Nerio Rojas, *Medicina legal* (Buenos Aires: Editorial 'El Ateneo' 1959), 464. In the 1936 edition of his book, Rojas calculated the total lunatic population at 20,000.

110 Juan José Soiza Reilly, "Cuarenta mil locos en libertad: Una visita al Hospicio de las Mercedes," *Caras y Caretas* 37:1863 [or 1864?] (June 16 or June 23, 1934).

111 Soiza Reilly, "Cuarenta mil locos," n.p.

112 Soiza Reilly, "Cuarenta mil locos," n.p. "Cuarenta mil locos sin hospitalización; cuarenta mil locos sueltos que andan en el país sin asistencia y sin encierro, son cuarenta mil bombas de dinamita en manos de otros tantos niños inocentes."

113 Arturo Ameghino, "Higiene mental – la acción del estado en el mejoramiento de la raza," *Revista de criminología, psiquiatría y medicina legal* 22:127 (January–February 1935): 139. On Ameghino's work, see: Guerrino, *Psiquiatría argentina*, 84–85; and Loudet and Loudet, *Historia de la psiquiatría argentina*, 79–86.

114 Ameghino, "Higiene mental," 147. One piece of evidence that he used was the claim that crime dropped in Argentina during World War I when immigration rates had dropped.

115 See also a study from 1942 that used as a base the calculation of the number of insane in the French department of Seine to argue that for 1932 there should have been at least 9,563 admissions to Buenos Aires' two hospitals. Instead, there were only 4,122. De Lena, "Organización de la estadística en higiene mental," 427–29.

116 Ameghino, "Higiene mental," 145–46. Ameghino also blamed the problem on the lack of coordination between the Sociedad de Beneficencia, the Comisión Asesora de Asilos y Hospitales Regionales, and the Liga Argentina de Higiene Mental.

117 Ameghino, "Higiene mental," 147.

118 Ameghino, "Higiene mental," 40–44. Ameghino's argument that mental hygiene advocates were overly concerned with the mentally ill's rights contravenes Stepan's social control interpretation of mental hygiene. See Stepan, *'Hour of Eugenics,'* 142.

119 *Diputados* 4 (September 12, 1941), 364.

120 *Diputados* 4 (September 12, 1941), 363–65. Particularly influential in connecting war trauma to increased rates of madness was Arturo Ameghino's *El incremento de la locura en la República Argentina despues de la guerra* (1923).

121 In 1900, there had been a proposal in Congress to amend the criminal code to allow continued monitoring of mentally ill convicts whose sentence had been served. See "Los alienados delincuentes y la defensa social: Sentencia del Dr. Tomas de Veiga (de Buenos Aires)," *Archivos de psiquiatría, criminología y ciencias afines* 8 (November–December 1909): 671–79.

122 See: *Diputados* 6 (September 30, 1926), 617–21; and Luis Jiménez de Asúa, "Ley de vagos y maleantes: Un ensayo legislativo sobre peligrosidad sin delito," *Revista de criminología, psiquiatría y medicina legal* 20:120 (November–December 1933): 610–11.

123 *Diputados* 6 (September 30, 1926), 617–21. Sussini criticized the legal reform proposals of Bard and Piñero for being overly concerned with the rights of patients, and not of the broader social defence. He also paid special attention to the supposed threat of the feebleminded. On the expansion of categories of mental illness in France, see Dowbiggin, *Inheriting Madness*, 125–37.

124 De Asúa, "Ley de vagos y maleantes;" 615. "El mejor modo de acabar con esas ficciones antilegales, es abordar de frente y con valentía el problema del estado peligroso sin delito, como se hace en España con la ley de vagos y maleantes. Toda Sociedad, tiene dere-

cho a defenderse de los sujetos temibles, aún antes de que delincan. Encargando esta tarea a los funcionarios judiciales, quedaré mejor garantida la libertad humana, que con el sistema de antes, liberalílismo en las leyes y anticonstitucional y arbitrario en las practicas policíacas y gubernativas." Another law of interest to Argentine doctors was the social defence law of Belgium. See Luis Vervaeck, "La ley de defensa social del 9 de Abril de 1930, encarada desde el punto de vista pisquiátrica," *Revista de criminología, psiquiatría y medicina legal* 20:116 (March–April 1933): 97–116.

125 Bard, "Proyecto de ley sobre legislación para los establecimientos destinados a alienados," 472.

126 Vega, "Alienación y délito," 50. "Por regla general, las internaciones en sanatorios o manicomios, de alienados no delincuentes, es lograda por sus parientes quienes, en este caso, son dueños de retirarlo en todo momento, en contra de la opinión de los medicos y aún cuando se repute peligroso al enfermo. Es muy humano que los parientes se dejen guiar por sus impulsos afectivos, sin parar mientras en que reintegran al hogar y al seno de la sociedad a un individuo que es un peligro latente."

127 Vega, "Alienación y délito," 51.

128 In 1936, the government of President Justo enacted a law that created a national Registry of the Disabled, which was charged to take charge of disabled persons' welfare. "Registro de incapaces," *Psiquiatría y criminología* 1:4 (July–August 1936): 345–49.

129 Rodriguez *Civilizing Argentina*, 242. The first step towards national identification cards was the 1911 military service and voter registration law, which stipulated the issuance of identity cards to all male citizens. See Jonathan D. Ablard "Military Conscription in Argentina," presented at the Latin American Studies Program, Cornell University (September 13, 2005).

130 Rogelio de Lena, "Organización de la estadística en higiene mental," *Revista de psiquiatría y criminología* 7:39 (September–October 1942): 427–36.

131 See Carlos Lambruschini, "Ficha psiquiátrica, psicotécnica y antropológico-criminal del inmigrante," *Revista argentina de neurología y psiquiatría* 3:3–4 (December 1938): 329–36. On the growth of anti-immigrant rhetoric, see David Rock, *Authoritarian Argentina: The Nationalist Movement, Its History and Its Impact* (Berkeley: University of California Press, 1993), 103.

132 Raul Ocampo Oromi, "Inspección sanitaria neuropsiquiátrica en los puertos," *Boletín del Asilo de Alienados en Oliva* 10:42–43 (May–December 1942): 174.

133 Ocampo Oromi, "Inspección sanitaria," 176.

134 Ocampo Oromi, "Inspección sanitaria," 176.

135 Bringas Núñez, "Inmigración y locura," 170.

136 Bringas Núñez, "Inmigración y locura," 170. See also deputy Carlos Pita's 1941 proposal to fund psychiatric hospital construction. Like Bringas Núñez, Pita cited a number of studies which linked mental disorder to the traumas of war. Most important for both was Ameghino's *El Incremento de la locura en la República Argentina despues de la Guerra* (1923). *Disputados* 4 (September 12, 1941): 363–65. Pita also cited the statistics from Bosch's 1931 book.

137 Nerio Rojas, *Medicina legal* (7th ed.) (Buenos Aires: Editorial 'El Ateneo,' 1959), 465–66.

138 Rojas *Medicina legal*, 466.

139 The extent to which psychiatric patients have been neglected and forgotten is well documented in Sadowsky, *Imperial Bedlam*, 27. "The colonial lunatic asylums of Nigeria were simply not benign enough to be insidious. Nor would a view of colonial asylums as 'panoptic' really be apt. More to the point is how little these institutions saw, or cared to."

140 Michel Foucault, *Discipline and Punish: The Birth of the Prison* (New York: Pantheon, 1977). See "Panopticism."

141 Plotkin, "Politics of Consensus in Peronist Argentina (1943–1955)," 284.

142 See Chapter 3. For a critique of the influence of private hospitals, see "La hospitalización privada de alienados," *La Nación* (February 10, 1934): n.p. For a more recent analysis, see Cárdenas, "Para internar a un enfermo mental hace la falta la intervención de un juez," 33. Of the failure to pass reform, Cárdenas, who is a family judge, observes: "None managed to pass into law, thanks to the resistance of economic interests of the private clinics, *obras sociales*, and the resistance to change among certain sectors."

143 Sacristán, "Entre curar y contener": 69–70.

144 U.S. Department of Commerce, *Patients in Hospitals for Mental Disease, 1933* (Washington, D.C.: United States Government Printing Office, 1934), 17.

145 See Trent, *Inventing the Feeble Mind.*

146 See the highly polemical, Alfredo Moffatt, *Socioterapia para sectores marginados: Terapia comunitaria para grupos de riesgo* (Buenos Aires: Lumen Humanitas, 1997). See also Christián Courtis, "La locura no da derechos," *Desbordar* 3:41–43 (October 1991): 42. Courtis notes that there is little legal literature on cases of judicial neglect or medical abuse. Likewise, medical malpractice has only recently entered into Argentine jurisprudence. Luís Frontera, "La dictadura del Valium," *Caras y Caretas* 2212:85 (July 1984): 32; Hugo Vezzetti, "Secuestrados en los manicomios," *Página12* (March 5, 1998).; Grimson, *Sociedad de locos.*

5: Pathways to the Asylum, 1900–1946

1 McGovern, "Myths of Social Control and Custodial Oppression" 17. See also Gordon, "Feminism and Social Control" 76. Gordon looks at how women shaped and defined the uses of social control agencies, in her case, child welfare, to further personal interests related to the safety of both themselves and their children. Gordon argues that the historiographic trend which highlights social control tends to view "the flow of initiative going in only one direction: from top to bottom, from professionals to clients, from elite to subordinate." See also her later book, *Heroes of Their Own Lives: The Politics and History of Family Violence, Boston, 1880–1960* (New York: Viking, 1988).

2 For the United States, see Fox, *'So far disordered in mind'*, 98–99. Guy, "Lower-Class Families, Women and the Law in Nineteenth-Century Argentina," 318–31.

3 Prestwich, "Family Strategies and Medical Power": 799. See also Horwitz, *Social Control of Mental Illness*, 57.

4 Lakoff, *Pharmaceutical Reason*, 3. Lakoff observes that even today, "psychiatry is a field that has not achieved ... stabilization."

5 Sadowsky, *Imperial Bedlam*, 58. Sadowsky notes that those without kin or community were more likely to be interned in colonial Nigeria.

6 Mead, "Beneficent Maternalism": 133–34; and Karen Mead, "Gendering the Obstacles to Progress in Positivist Argentina, 1880–1920," *Hispanic American Historical Review* 77:4 (1997): 645–75.

7 Fermín Rodríguez, "Influencia del estado civil sobre el suicidio," *Archivos de psiquiatría, criminología y ciencias afines* (1905): 389.

8 Argentina. Congreso Nacional. *Diputados* (1927): 618.

9 Argentina. *Tercer Censo Nacional. Tomo IV Población* (Buenos Aires: Talleres Gráficos de L.J. Rosso y Cia, 1915). See also: Juan Vucetich, "Diez años de suicidios en Buenos Aires: Síntesis estadísticas," *Archivos de psiquiatría, criminología y ciencias afines* (1903): 537–41; Hector Piñero, "El suicidio en la Ciudad de Buenos Aires," *Revista de psiquiatría y criminología* (May–June 1939): 393–404; and Roberto Ciafardo and Juan Carlos Vizcarra, "Etiopatogenía y profilaxis del suicidio," *Sociedad Argentina de Criminología* 9:49 (September–October 1944): 345–66.

10 Pedro I. Oro Raffinetti, "Locura comunicada familiar" (Medical thesis, Buenos Aires: La Semana Médica Imprenta de Obras de E. Spinelli, 1909), 80. For a later study of the same issue, see Hector M. Piñero, "Consideraciones sobre 'Psicosis comunicada familiar,'" *Boletín del Asilo de Alienados en Oliva* 12 (1936): 95–100.

11 Domingo Cabred, "Asilo Colonia Regional de Retardos," *Archivos de psiquiatría, criminología y ciencias afines* 7 (November–December 1908): 735. For a more benign view of the mentally retarded, see A. Alberto Palcos, "Educación de los Anormales," *Revista de criminología, psiquiatría y medicina legal* 11:9 (May–June 1915): 331. "Los idiotas son seres innocuos para la sociedad: no trabajan para la misma; pero tampoco la dañan."

12 See also Nerio A. Rojas, "Homicidio cometido por dos alienados," *Revista de criminología, psiquiatría y medicina legal* 1:4 (July–August 1914): 391.

13 "Anormales," *Caras y Caretas* 28:1373 (January 24, 1925). The story ends on a pessimistic note: "Acaso si no para aprender mucho, en la escuela se olvidan de su miseria mientras juegan y rien, ignorantes de la tragedia que llevan consigo, para toda la vida...." See also Arlt, "Un cuidador de locos se ahorco en el Hospicio de las Mercedes," 63–65.

14 "Dierónse normas para recibir enfermas en el Hospital de Alienadas," *La Nación* (July 18, 1940): n.p.

15 AGN-SB-HNA, Legajo 200, Expediente 2784. September 1920 monthly report listed three patients withdrawn by relatives "a su insistente pedido y contra la opinión médica."

16 MREC, *Memorias correspondiente al año 1913–14* (Buenos Aires: Talleres Gráficos de Selin Suarez, 1915), 505–6.

17 Arturo Ameghino, "Locura familiar homócrona en tres hermanos," *Revista de criminología, psiquiatría y medicina legal* 12 (1925): 3–8. Medical belief in the pathology of certain families was probably bolstered by the popular media's fascination with murder-suicides that occurred within the home. "Gente que no quiere vivir," *El Diario* (May 5, 1926): n.p. *El Diario* also occasionally published a small column entitled "Tentativas de suicidio." See August 9 and 25; September 4, 5, 17, and 18, 1905; January 7 and 8, 1906. "Los suicidios originales: Uno que se mata para 'salir' en 'Caras y Caretas,'" *Caras y Caretas* 5:215 (November 8, 1902): n.p., featured a story about a man who had had himself photographed with a revolver at his head; he then shot himself. They noted that the victim, "era francés de nacionalidad y suicida por vocación." There were also romanticized stories about the tragedy of suicide, "En Mar del Plata: Dos jovenes suicidas" and "Uxoricidio y sucidio en Mercedes," *Caras y Caretas* 6:224 (January 17, 1903): n.p. "Drama conyugal," *Caras y Caretas* 30:1633 (January 18, 1930): n.p. *Caras y Caretas* 33:1643 (March 29, 1930): n.p. "Varias" (Husband Cristóbal Baigorria murdered his wife, Adela Romero de B. and then killed himself.) *Caras y Caretas* 33:1645 (April 12, 1930): n.p.; "La obra de un neurasténico," *Caras y Caretas* 16:795 (November 22, 1913): n.p.

18 Prestwich, "Family Strategies and Medical Power," 803. In Paris in the

nineteenth century, "families had their own definitions of the asylum and of medical treatment, definitions that did not always accord with the hopes or interests of the psychiatric profession." See Porter, "Madness and its Institutions," 277.

19 On the importance of the visual assessment of psychiatric patients, see Emilio Catalán, *La fisonomía en los alienados* (Buenos Aires: Talleres Gráficos de la Penitenciaría Nacional, 1924).

20 In the popular press, acts of criminal violence were often discussed in terms of the degeneration of both culprit and victim. "Un loco asesino," *Caras y Caretas* 4:119 (January 12, 1901): n.p. and "Horrible tragedia en un hogar," *Caras y Caretas* 23:1147 (September 25, 1920): n.p. "Solamente un desequilibrado mental puede haber sido el autor de este terrible drama, del que fueron víctimas tres personas, dos de ellas pobres seres a los que el estigma de males incurables hacíanlos impotentes para la lucha diaria."

21 D. Rosenhahn, "On Being Sane in Insane Places," *Science* 179 (1973): 250–58. Erving Goffman, *Asylums: Essays on the Social Situation of Mental Patients and Other Inmates* (New York: Anchor Books, 1961). Magazine articles from the 1920s to the 1940s show patients in tattered clothing, dirty and dishevelled. See: "No están todos los que son ... Una hora en el Hospicio de las Mercedes," *Caras y Caretas* 26:1300 (September 1, 1923): n.p.; and Soiza Reilly, "Cuarenta mil locos en libertad": n.p. Patients wore uniforms, with serial numbers on the shirt, until 1946. See also Plotkin, "Freud, Politics, and the *Porteños*," 49–50.

22 APJN, "Insania," "Iván G." Legajo 14235, Folio 91 (1911). "A simple vista, se le observan algunos signos degenerativos, es de cabeza chica, tiene asimetria craneo...." See also APJN, "Insania," "Enrique M.," Legajo 12409, Folio 59 (1908), which simply noted that the subject "[p]resenta estigmas faciales degenerativas."

23 APJN, "Insania," "Pedro O.," Legajo 7335, Folio 7, No. 2445. Doctors then proceeded to provide a list of physical attributes commonly ascribed to degenerates and deemed the patient incompetent with sub-acute alcoholism, melancholic depression, and mental confusion.

24 APJN, "Insania," Legajo 14592, No. 4689, Folio 564 (1921).

25 APJN, "Insania," "Graciela E.," Legajo 8313, No. 9966, Folio 160 (1922). "... sufrió las impertinencias de la mencionada mujer que busca por todos los medios hacer me aparecer ante el vecindario como dejenerado, culpándome de delitos fantasticos."

26 APJN, "Insania," "Lorenzo A.," Legajo 12735 (1916).

27 APJN, "Insania," "Lorenzo A.," Legajo 12735 (1916). This case finds a striking parallel in Horacio Quiroga's "The Decapitated Chicken," first published in 1917. In the story, the parents of four severely mentally retarded sons bitterly accuse one another of being the cause of their "defective" progeny. The husband points out that the wife has a defective lung. The wife retorts that the husband's father died mad. Quiroga's chilling tale demonstrates how everyday people may have internalized the rhetoric of degeneration theory and also the pervasiveness of its influence. Horacio Quiroga, *Cuentos de amor, de locura y de muerte* (Buenos Aires: Losada, 1994). On string of suicides in Quiroga's family, that ended with him, see Horacio Sanguinetti, "Los suicidas del '30," *Todo es historia* 254:22 (August 1988): 26–35.

28 On men and sexuality, see Salessi, *Médicos, maleantes, y maricas*.

29 APJN, "Insania," "Ricardo L.," Legajo 14581, Folio 306, No. 8773 (1921).

30 APJN, "Insania," "María José E.," Legajo 8309 (1921).

31 Her final diagnosis was "polymorphous delirium of a psycho-neurotic degenerate evolving towards hebephrenic dementia praecox."

32 APJN, "Insania," "Clara R." (Legajo, or dossier number, is not listed for this case.) (1917):

33 APJN, "Insania," "Clara R."

34 APJN, "Insania," "Clara R." They concluded that "Being a physical and psychiatric degenerate, she presented after her operation a series of alterations that can be attributed as much to the chloroform as to the operation itself, which has caused the disturbance that she suffers. But for the moment we consider her merely a feebleminded person and she can be returned home without danger to self or others."

35 AGN-SB-HNA, Legajo 221, Expediente "Libro 1910–11," Dr. José A. Esteves to Señoras Inspectoras, February 16, 1911. In his plea for more dormitories for patients, the director of the HNA in 1911 reminded the *Señoras Inspectoras* that "the insane woman is much more turbulent than her male counterpart, and this explains the need for more bedrooms."

36 See Nancy Theriot, "Diagnosing Unnatural Motherhood: Nineteenth-Century Physicians and 'Puerperal Insanity,'" in Judith Walzer Leavitt, ed., *Women and Health in America: Historical Readings* (Madison: University of Wisconsin Press, 1999), 405–22; Lunbeck, *The Psychiatric Persuasion*; Nancy Tomes, "Feminist Histories of Psychiatry," in Mark S. Micale and Roy Porter, eds., *Discovering the History of Psychiatry* (New York: Oxford University Press, 1994), 348–83. See also Peter McCandless, "A Female Malady? Women at the South Carolina Lunatic Asylum, 1828–1915," *Journal of the History of Medicine and Allied Sciences* 54:4 (October 1999): 543–71.

37 Italo D. Chiama, "Locura moral" (Tesis presentado para optar al título de Doctor en Medicina-UNBA, 1911) (Buenos Aires: Talleres Gráficos M. Rodríguez Giles, 1911), 45. "... es, no un simple trastorno del carácter, sino una verdadera perversión de los instintos, un estado mental en el cual el sujeto es incapaz de adquirir sentimientos morales."

38 Chiama, "Locura moral," 55. By the 1930s, the term was losing favour in medical circles to the term *perversion instinctiva*. See José F. Capelli, "Perversidad y locura moral," *Revista de psiquiatría y criminología* 4:23 (September–October 1939): 613–18.

39 Chiama, "Locura moral," 51–52.

40 On hysteria, see Julia Rodriguez, "The Argentine Hysteric: A Turn-of-the-Century Psychiatric Type," in Plotkin, *Argentina on the Couch*, 25–47.

41 On the decline of gendered diagnoses, see MREC, "Memorias de la Sociedad de Beneficencia de la Capital," *Memoria del Ministerio de Relaciones Exteriores y Culto correspondiente al año 1935* (Buenos Aires: 1936), 420, which lists one person suffering from *locura histerica* and none from *Psicosis de la puerperalidad*.

42 APJN, "Insania," "Máxima S.," Legajo 12368, Entrada 42, Folio 9 (1907).

43 APJN, "Insania," "Graciela E.," Legajo 8313, No. 9988, Folio 160 (1922).

44 Although she was confined to a private hospital, see APJN, "Insania," "Celia B.," Legajo 551 (?)76 (1949). Since age 17, the subject had disobeyed parents, and among other behaviours was going to dances with lower-class people.

45 APJN, "Insania," "Rosa A." Legajo 304 (1929).

46 APJN, "Insania," "Rosa A." Legajo 304 (1929).

47 APJN, "Insania," "Carolina M.," Legajo 38678 (1943). "De los antecedentes que nosotros hemos logrado recoger merece destacarse que su internación se debe multiples y reiteradas inconductas que acusaba, culminando con la agresión a su padre con una tijera y el abandono total de sus tareas."

48 APJN, "Insania," "Carolina M.," Legajo 38678 (1943). "Insiste en sus primeras acusaciones contra su padre que la quiere violar. 'Siempre fue un bruto' nos afirma."

49 APJN, "Insania," "Carolina M.," Legajo 38678 (1943)

50 APJN, "Insania," "Carolina M.," Legajo 38678 (1943).

51 APJN, "Insania," "Antonia P.," Legajo 14581, Folio 228 (1921). "... la madre era prostituta, único dato que poseen como antecedente hereditario." Kristin Ruggiero, "Sexual Abberation, Degeneration, and Psychiatry in Late-Nineteenth Century Buenos Aires," and Rodríguez, "Argentine Hysteric," 25–84.

52 On notions of the relationship between menstruation and insanity, see Janet Oppenheim, *'Shattered Nerves': Doctors, Patients, and Depression in Victorian England* (New York: Oxford University Press, 1991), 188–89.

53 For another case of puerperal insanity where profanity was an issue, see APJN, "Insania," "Maria Paz M.," Legajo 20025, (1933). The patient was sent to the HNA from her home town of Puerto Madryn. Theriot, "Diagnosing Unnatural Motherhood," 405–21. Theriot sees puerperal insanity on the decline in the United States by around 1910 because of changes in the social position of women in society and advances in psychiatry.

54 APJN, "Insania," "Catalina M.," Legajo 12735 (1916).

55 Guy, *Sex and Danger in Buenos Aires*, 85. Socialist deputy Angel Gimenez drew suggestive inferences about the survival of traditions of depositing women well into the twentieth century. See Gimenez, *Un debate histórico.*

56 SB, *Memoria del año 1905* (Buenos Aires: 1906), 126–28. According to the hospital's official statistics, few prostitutes entered the HNA. Of the 861 admissions in 1905, only 6 were listed as prostitutes.

57 See AGN-SB-HNA, Legajo 205, Expediente 7593. Dr. Luis Esteves Balado to Señoras Inspectoras del HNA (October 4, 1939).

58 On psychiatrists' obsession with homosexuality, see Jorge Salessi, "The Argentine Dissemination of Homosexuality, 1890–1914," *Journal of the History of Sexuality* 4:3 (1994): 337–69.

59 MREC, "Memorias de la Sociedad de Beneficencia,"*Memoria del Ministerio de Relaciones Exteriores y Culto correspondiente al año 1939* (Buenos Aires: 1940), 410. At the beginning of 1939 there 24 patients whose listed profession was *religiosa.* Starting in the 1920s, other common professions included school teacher, waitress, and cigarette seller.

60 Of the 1,287 admissions in 1941, 1,014 worked in some form of domestic service. SB, *Memoria del año 1941* (Buenos Aires: 1942), 406.

61 SB, *Memoria del Hospital Nacional de Alienadas, 1900* (Buenos Aires: Imprenta, Litografía y Encuadernación, 1901), n.p. SB, *Memoria del año 1905* (Buenos Aires: 1906), 126–28. The report for 1905 listed 535 domestic workers, 41 servants, and 24 cooks among the HNA's 861 admissions.

62 SB, *Memoria del año 1943* (Buenos Aires: 1944), 381. Of the 613 admissions for 1943, 549 were listed as *quehaceres domesticos.*

63 Lavrín, *Women, Feminism, and Social Change*, 83. On the vulnerability of servants in Buenos Aires, see Ruggiero, *Modernity in the Flesh.* See also "Servicio doméstico en Buenos Aires," *Caras y Caretas* 15:715 (June 15, 1912): n.p. Charitable organizations, including the Society of Beneficence often released orphan teenage girls to serve in households.

64 Lavrín, *Women, Feminism, and Social Change*, 72.

65 Blackwelder, "Urbanization, Crime, and Policing," 70.

66 Guy, "Lower-Class Families, Women, and the Law in Nineteenth-Century Argentina," 321–22. For a discussion of the erosion of legal patriarchy, see Donna J. Guy, "Parents before the Tribunals: The Legal Construction of Patriarchy in Argentina," in Elizabeth Dore and Maxine Molyneux, eds., *Hidden Histories of Gender and the State in Latin America* (Durham, NC: Duke University Press, 2000), 172–93.

67 Donna Guy, "White Slavery, Public Health, and the Socialist Position on Legalized Prostitution in Argentina, 1913–1936," *Latin American Research Review* 23:3 (1988): 60. As part of a campaign to control female prostitution, women's access to work in restaurants and other public places was severely restricted.

68 For other cases of domestic servants, the employer's decision to seek confinement seems to have been motivated by profound psychic and physical illness, including late stages of progressive general paralysis. See: APJN, "Insania," "Isabel R.," Legajo 8308 (1921); and APJN, "Insania," "Eva R.," Legajo 19491, No. 22070 (1941).

69 APJN, "Insania," "Irene Carmen M.," Legajo 12854 (1918).

70 APJN, "Insania," "Mónica K.," Legajo 7324 (1916).

71 APJN, "Insania," "Mónica K.," Legajo 7324 (1916). "... podemos afirmar que su enfermedad ha vuelto a acentuarse, presentando sintomas alucinatorios, tanto de la vista, como del oido, del tacto, como tambien genitales ... es logorreica, no quiere comer muchas veces porque cree que la comida le echan veneno o sustancias nocivas."

72 APJN, "Insania," "Paulina C.," Legajo 19999 (1933). It is not clear if this means that the subject was in love with a person of a higher social status, the son of her employers or simply with someone who did not reciprocate.

73 APJN, "Insania," "Paulina C.," Legajo 19999 (1933), "Su actual enfermedad se inicia en la mañana de su ingreso al Hospital, con llantas y risas inmotivadas, incoherencias y puerilidades teniendo despues un fuerte periodo de excitación, para caer despues en un estado depresivo, quejándose de cefaleas. Ha tenido ataques histeriformes."

74 On the history of domestic violence in the United States, see Gordon, *Heroes of Their Own Lives.*

75 Angela C. de T. referred to said article when she successfully petitioned for custody of her insane husband's 400 peso pension, APJN, "Insania," "Diego T.," Legajo 20097 (1933).

76 APJN, "Insania," "Juan P.," Legajo 14521 (1919). The wife claimed that the husband was slowly poisoning her and their children.

77 APJN, "Insania," "David G.," Legajo 22117, Folio 162 (1946).

78 APJN, "Insania," "David G.," Legajo 22117, Folio 162 (1946).

79 APJN, "Insania," "Alejo C.," Legajo 7339, No. 1295 (1917)

80 APJN, "Insania," "Hussein A.," Legajo n.a., Entrada 23709, Folio 120.

81 APJN, "Insania," "Hussein A.," Legajo n.a., Entrada 23709, Folio 120.

82 APJN, "Insania," "Gino I.," Legajo 19491, no. 23736 (1942). In September, inspectors found that Gino was "confused, disoriented in space and time; does not recognize anyone and excites easily. Silence, it seems that the patient wishes to answer us, but cannot do it." In May 1942, Gino died of heart failure.

83 APJN, "Insania," "Daniel P.," Legajo 14555, No. 9786, Folio 177 (1920).

84 APJN, "Insania," "Julio G.," Legajo 46092 (1951).

85 APJN, "Insania," Legajo 304 (1929). Subject is described as "obediente, docil y ayuda"; and "Insania," Legajo 19981 (1937). Doctors of the court noted that she was helpful with chores on her ward. See also McCandless, "A Female Malady?", 568. McCandless finds that

at the South Carolina Lunatic Asylum, "the physicians also viewed domestic work as both therapeutic and as a sign of recovery in women."

86 APJN, "Insania," "Ricardo L.," Legajo 14581, Folio 306, No. 8773 (1921). "Rectifica su pasado y es un convencido de que el debilitamiento que ha ocasionado el onanismo y abuso alcohólico lo ha vuelto loco y protesta de abstenerse."

87 On the credibility of patients, see Geoffrey Reaume, "Accounts of Abuse of Patients at the Toronto Hospital for the Insane, 1883–1937," *Canadian Bulletin of Medical History/Bulletin canadien d'histoire de la médicine* 14:1 (1997): 65–106.

88 APJN, "Insania," "Carlos B.," Legajo 14496 (1918).

89 APJN, "Insania," "Máxima S.," Legajo 12368, Entrada 42, Folio 9 (1907).

90 APJN, "Insania," "Gilberto A.," Legajo 23460 (1937).

91 See also APJN, "Insania," "Graciana C.," Legajo 53587 (1946). When Graciana C.'s sister decided to have her declared judicially incompetent, the court doctors encountered a feisty 90-year-old woman who mocked their medical authority. The doctors reported that, at their first meeting, they asked Graciana why she woke up so late; "she responded quickly and with a puerile laugh: 'because I want to.'" The doctors then relayed a series of interactions where Graciana mocked the tests that they were giving her.

92 Hospicio de las Mercedes, *Memoria médico-administrativa correpondiente al año 1920* (Buenos Aires: Imprenta y Encuadración de las Mercedes, 1923), 5.

93 See Chapter 3.

94 On escapes, see *Censo general de población, edificación, comercio e industrias de la Ciudad de Buenos Aires* (Buenos Aires: Compañía Sud-Americana de Billetes de Banco, 1910), 274. Between 1900 and 1909, for example, of 7,951 admissions, there were 236 escapes from the HNA. During the same years, of 10,619 admissions to the Hospicio, there were 216 escapes.

95 APJN, "Insania," "Eva R.," Legajo 19491, No. 22070 (1941).

96 MREC, "Memorias de la Sociedad de Beneficencia," *Memoria del Ministerio de Relaciones Exteriores y Culto correspondiente al año 1939* (Buenos Aires: 1940), 410.

97 AGN-SB-HNA, Legajo 221, "Libro 1905–07," and AGN-SB-HNA, Legajo 221, "Libro 1910–11." At least one patient gave birth every month at the HNA. In some cases, the newborns were quickly transferred to the Society's *Casa de Expósitos* [orphanage]; in the event that no suitable relative could be located, it is likely that the children remained at the Casa until they reached their majority. In a few cases, children with developmental or psychiatric problems who reached their majority as wards of the Society were directly transferred to the HNA. On children and public charity, see Fabio Adalberto González, "Niñez y beneficencia: Un acercamiento a los discursos y las estrategias disciplinarias en torno a los niños abandonados en Buenos Aires de principios del siglo XX (1900–1930)," in José Luis Moreno, ed., *La política social antes de la política social (Caridad, beneficencia y política social en Buenos Aires, siglos XVII a XX)* (Buenos Aires: Trama Editorial, 2000).

98 For cases where families removed a relative with relative ease, see APJN, "Insania," "Teresa R.," Legajo 20032 (1934) (#76); "Felix C.," Legajo 7337, Entrada 22348, Folio 15 (1917).

99 APJN, "Insania," "Rodolfo B.," Legajo 19515 (1932).

100 APJN, "Insania," "Julia B.," Legajo 19981, No. 15267, Folio 196 (1934).

101 Hospital "Braulio Moyano," Office of Statistics. Patient file.

102 APJN, "Insania," "Ana P.," Legajo 2005 (1930).

103 APJN, "Insania" "Mauricio S.," Legajo 14671, Entrada 4763.

104 AGN-SB-HNA, Legajo 200, Expediente 1934 "Abril 1920." A similar request was made on the 29th to return a patient to the province of Misiones.

105 AGN-SB-HNA, Legajo 223, Libro 1917 "December 1916."

106 APJN, "Insania," "Henry R." Legajo 14675, Folio 303 (1924).

107 APJN, "Insania," Benito R., (1932) Legajo 19733, Folio 12, Entrada 9331.

108 APJN, "Insania," Benito R., (1932) Legajo 19733, Folio 12, Entrada 9331.

109 APJN, "Insania," Benito R., (1932) Legajo 19733, Folio 12, Entrada 9331.

110 AGN-SB-HNA, Legajo 206, Expediente 3759 (December 17, 1931) and (January 8, 1932).

111 APJN, "Insania," "Aurelia P.," Legajo 12438 (1910). That the mother received guardianship may in part been due to the fact that the court doctors found no evidence of degenerative heredity in either parent.

112 APJN, "Insania," "Juana H.," Legajo 20056, Folio 109, Entrada 1722 (1944), Case #20. Juana passed away before the legal proceedings were terminated.

113 APJN, "Insania," "Hector M.," Legajo 58555 (1954).

6: From Perón to the Proceso: Authoritarianism, Democracy and Psychiatric Reform, 1943–83

1 A version of this chapter appeared as "Authoritarianism, Democracy and Psychiatric Reform in Argentina, 1943–83," *History of Psychiatry* 14:3 (2003): 361–76.

2 Chichilnisky, "Historia de la psiquiatría argentina," 78–80.

3 In 1949, the Hospicio de las Mercedes was renamed National Neuro-psychiatric Hospital for Men, and in 1967, it became the "José T. Borda" National Hospital. The National Hospital for the Female Insane was renamed the National Neuro-psychiatric Hospital for Women in the late 1940s and was subsequently renamed the "Braulio Moyano" National Hospital. Both institutions reverted to the municipality of Buenos Aires in the 1990s. Hugo Marietán, *Boletín Borda* 44:5 (1996): 1–4.

4 Vezzetti, *Locura en la Argentina.* Vezzetti's work is a brilliant analysis of the origins of psychiatry in Argentina, but it can also be read as a meditation on this problem.

5 Lakoff, *Pharmaceutical Reason.* Lakoff's work provides a fascinating study of contemporary attitudes towards mental health in Argentina and complements the works of Plotkin and Visacovsky.

6 On the coup, see Potash, *The Army and Politics in Argentina.*

7 Socialist deputy Angel Gimenez called for the creation of a National Department of Social Welfare in 1933. Giménez, *Por la salud física y mental del pueblo*, 50. For similar proposals from conservatives, see Crespo, *Nuevos ensayos politicos y administrativos*, 113–24.

8 Ablard, "Military Conscription in Argentina."

9 Plotkin, "Politics of Consensus in Peronist Argentina (1943–1955)," 290.

10 "Efectuaráse un vasto plan de construcción para enfermos mentales," *La Prensa* (July 7, 1944): n.p. and "Asistencia de los enfermos mentales," *La Prensa* (July 8, 1944): n.p.

11 "Hombres en un mundo de sombras," *¡Aquí Está!* 10:922 (March 19, 1945): 10–11.

12 *Recopilación de leyes, reglamentaciones, decretos y resoluciones de enero 1944–junio 1946*. II. Estadísticas de Salud (Buenos Aires, 1947), 145–46. "a) Cuando la peligrosidad de la enferma o su necesidad urgente de tratamiento medico asi lo requiere. Estos estados serán valorados por la Dirección del establecimiento. B)Cuando no se trate de casos de peligrosidad o urgencia de tratamiento médico, deberá solicitarse previamente a la Dirección del establecimiento el ingreso de la enferma, al que se hará lugar de acuerdo a la existencia de camas." "Ha sido levantada la clausura del Hospital Nacional de Alienadas," *La Prensa* (July 22, 1944): n.p.

13 Plotkin, "Politics of Consensus in Peronist Argentina (1943–1955)," 290, 300–301. Argentine Republic. Poder Ejecutivo Nacional, Ministerio de Asistencia Social y Salud Pública, *Política sanitaria y social* (Buenos Aires: 1966), 5. On Carrillo and public health reform, see Rodolfo F. Alzugaray, "Ramón Carrillo o la salud pública," *Todo es historia* 117 (February 1977): 7–27.

14 Nicholas Fraser and Marysa Navarro, *Eva Perón* (New York: Norton, 1980), 114–15.

15 Guy, "La 'verdadera historia' de la Sociedad de Beneficencia," 321–41.

16 Carrillo suggested that only a third of the nation's 60,000 mentally ill were in hospitals. Those not hospitalized: "wander about ... they are the 'externals' whom we trip over as we walk down the street." Carrillo. *Clasificación sanitaria*, 128–29. Carrillo, *Clasificación sanitaria*, 11–43; 244–50. See also his speech, "El viejo Hospicio de las Mercedes frente al nuevo Hospital Nacional de Neuropsiquiatría" (July 22, 1949).

17 Archivo General de la Nación-Sociedad de Beneficencia-Hospital Nacional de Alienadas (AGN-SB-HNA) Legajo 205, Expediente 7593. Dr. Armando Méndez San Martín, Interventor to Señor Jefe de Policía Federal, November 4, 1947; Legajo 215, Expediente 28,027.

18 Argentine Republic. Congreso Nacional *Diario de sesiones de la Cámara de Diputados, año 1946* v (Buenos Aires: Imprenta del Congreso de la Nación, 1947), 61 (August 21, 1946).

19 APJN, "Insania," "Carolina M.," Legajo 38678 (1943). See Eduardo Elena, "What the People Want: State Planning and Political Participation in Peronist Argentina, 1946–1955," *Journal of Latin American Studies* 37 (2005): 81–108.

20 AGN-SB-HNA, Edmundo M. to President Perón, October 31, 1947; Legajo 216, Expediente 7593 (1948–51), Dr. Juan Carlos de Arizábalo to Interventor, Armando Méndez San Martín (no date).

21 Carrillo, *Clasificación sanitaria*, 11. "La situación jurídica de 'nuestros' enfermos mentales, los que tenemos internados oficialmente en los establecimientos del Ministerio, fué uno de los primeros problemas que me enfrenté como Ministro."

22 Carrillo, *Clasificación sanitaria*, 43.

23 Carrillo, *Clasificación sanitaria*, 42–43. "Es decir, se ha planteado una situación de hecho, al margen del Código Civil, pues éste exige la declaración judicial previa a la internación del llamado demente."

24 Carrillo, *Clasificación sanitaria*, 49–50. "La interdiccion por enfermedad mental solo procede cuando la persona es mayor de 12 años y no puede actuar normalmente en la vida de relación ni conducirse a si mismo ni manejar sus negocios por padecer una afeccion de aquella indole."

25 Carrillo, *Clasificación sanitaria*, 50. This idea was already put forth in Alberto Molinas, "Restricción de la capacidad en las personas faltas de normal sanidad mental. Diverso fundamentos," *Revista de ciencias jurídicas y sociales* (Universidad del Litoral) 10:45–46 (3a época) (1945): 141.

26 Carrillo, *Clasificación sanitaria*, 61.

27 Carrillo, *Clasificación sanitaria*, 57–64. Carrillo also argued for the development of partial interdiction for persons who could exercise some civil rights. A restriction of who could commit finally occurred during the dictatorship of Onganía, who also expanded police powers with regard to hospitalization.

28 *Diputados* 1 (June 27, 1946), 121. Nerio Rojas' law came before Congress in 1943, 1946, and 1961, but never passed. Rojas resubmitted his bill in 1961. See *Diputados* 1 (May 16, 1961), 137–40.

29 Chichilnisky was born to a Russian-Jewish family that had immigrated to Entre Ríos province when he was two or three years old. Correspondence with his children, January 2006.

30 *Diputados* 5 (August 21, 1946), 61. A similar process was underway by the early 1940s in Mexico, though it met with better success as it involved what became a massive project of building rural institutions. See Sacristán, "La Granja de San Pedro del Monte," 101–21.

31 "Transforman el Hospicio de las Mercedes: Realizanse mejoramientos y nuevos pabellones," *La Razón* (September 10, 1947): n.p.; and "En el Hospicio de las Mercedes hacen obras importantes," *La Nación* (September 11, 1947): n.p. Chichilnisky, "Historia de la psiquiatría argentina," 82–93. Change at the HNA may have moved more slowly, given the administrative transition that was underway.

32 Chichilnisky, "Historia de la psiquiatría argentina," 80. Chichilnisky also confronted bureaucratic obstacles. He relates that an engineer, whom he describes as a "pundororoso funcionario publico," refused to authorize the demolition of a public building without the proper permits, etc.

33 At that time he was also co-director of the private clinic Sanatorio Flores.

34 Loudet and Loudet, *Historia de la psiquiatría argentina*, 89.

35 "Designóse Director del Hospicio de las Mercedes," *La Prensa* (April 3, 1948): 12.

36 By 1947, Esteves Balado was director of the private Instituto Frenopático in Buenos Aires.

37 Chichilnisky, "Historia de la psiquiatría argentina," 77–82. The following women were listed as social workers: *Señoritas* Blanca Guzmán, Nicolasa de Genaro, Guillermina Lavigne, Valentina Marquiani, and *Señora* Carmen H.P. de Güeri. From this point forward, women's presence in psychiatry and allied fields began to expand significantly. Future research is needed to explain what impact this shift had on both the profession and on the lives of patients.

38 AGN-SB-HNA, Legajo 205, Expediente 7593. Dr. Armando Méndez San Martín, Interventor to Señor Jefe de Policía Federal (November 4, 1947).

39 AGN-SB-HNA, Legajo 215, Expediente 28,027. Carlos Julio de More, Secretaría Tecnico de Hospitales to Señor Interventor (November 27, 1947).

40 AGN-SB-HNA, Legajo 216, Expediente 7593 (1948–51), Dr. Juan Carlos de Arizábalo to Interventor, Armando Mendez San Martín (no date). The letter makes reference to a reorganization plan of February 10, 1947.

41 Chichilnisky, "Historia de la psiquiatría argentina," 83.

42 *Diputados* 5 (August 21, 1946), 122–29. See also: "Asistencia de los alienados," *La Prensa* (August 21, 1946): 11; and AGN-SB-HNA, Legajo 215, Expediente 28,027. Carlos Julio de More, Secretaría Tecnico de Hospitales to Señor Interventor, November 27, 1947.

43 Carrillo, *Clasificación sanitaria*, 156–65.

44 *Diputados* 5 (September 20, 1946), 61. Proposal to Investigate labour practices at the Oliva asylum.

45 For a fascinating account of one of the less-well-known experiments, see John

C. Burnham, "A Clinical Alternative to the Public Health Approach to Mental Illness: A Forgotten Social Experiment," *Perspectives in Biology and Medicine* 49:2 (Spring 2006): 220–37.

46 "Transforman el Hospicio de las Mercedes: Realizanse mejoramientos y nuevos pabellones," *La Razón* (September 10, 1947): n.p.; "En el Hospicio de las Mercedes hacen obras importantes," *La Nación* (September 11, 1947): n.p.; *Diputados* (August 21, 1946), 122. Even Messina suggested expanding the Open Door [province of Buenos Aires] hospital's capacity to 6,000, and building a coed facility for 3,000 outside of Buenos Aires. Reflecting the populist politics of the period, Messina proposed the development of a workers' housing complex on the grounds of the old asylums. New hospitals were constructed in Salta and Guayamallen. Chichilnisky, "Historia de la psiquiatría argentina," 117.

47 Argentine Republic, Poder Ejecutivo Nacional, Ministerio de Asistencia Social y Salud Pública, *Política sanitaria y social*, 5.

48 "Designóse Director del Hospicio de las Mercedes": 12; Plotkin, "Freud, Politics, and the Porteños," 45–74.

49 *Hospital Interzonal Psiquiátrico 'Colonia Dr. Domingo Cabred': Centenario de la fundación* (Open Door-Luján, Provincia de Buenos Aires, 1999). Between 1947 and 1955, the Open Door had eight directors, or director-interventors. During this time it became an independent hospital.

50 Chichilnisky, "Historia de la psiquiatría argentina," 84–87. There were also widespread conflicts between different ministries, including between the Ministry of Public Works and Public Health. In fact, it is commonly believed that many of the unfinished structures on the grounds of the Borda to this day were first started under Perón! In his unpublished memoir, Chichilnisky noted that "only God knows when these projects will be started up again and finally finished."

51 Plotkin, "Politics of Consensus in Peronist Argentina (1943–1955)," 294. The failure to pass legal reforms may have been the result of pressure from private clinics who benefited from unclear codes governing confinement.

52 Ramacciotti, Karina Inés. "Las voces que cuestionaron la política sanitaria del peronismo *(1946–1949)*," in Daniel Lvovich and Juan Suriano, eds., *La políticas sociales en perspectiva histórica: Argentina, 1870–1952* (Buenos Aires: Prometeo Libros, 2006), 174–75.

53 Lloyd-Sherlock, "Healthcare Financing, Reform and Equity in Argentina," 146–48.

54 *Diputados* (August 21, 1946), 124.

55 Hector M. Piñero, "Función del médico psiquiatra en la selección del potencial humano," *Neuropsiquiatria* 2:4 (December 1951): 263–72. Piñero, who had been director of the Moyano, called for a *libreta sanitaria* for all immigrants, a medical and psychiatric inspection of all immigrants and their families who may follow, as well as a national registry of all psychiatric patients for the purpose of monitoring recent immigrants.

56 Enrique Carpintero and Alejandro Vainer, *Las huellas de la memoria: Psicoanalisis y salud mental en la Argentina de los '60 y '70 (1957–1983)*, Tomo I (Buenos Aires: Topia, 2004), 64–66. The number of total hospital beds jumped from 63,000 in 1946 to 108,000 in 1955.

57 Lloyd-Sherlock, "Healthcare Financing, Reform and Equity in Argentina," 148–54.

58 On the politicization of government posts in this period, see: Mónica Esti Rein, *Politics and Education in Argentina, 1946–1962* (Armonk, NY: M.E. Sharpe, 1998); and Celia Szusterman, *Frondizi and the Politics of Developmentalism in Argentina, 1955–62* (Pittsburgh: University of Pittsburgh Press, 1993).

59 Organization of American States, *America en Cifras, 1960* (Washington, D.C.: Organization of American States, 1961), 7.

60 Hugo Vezzetti, "Los origenes del movimiento de la salud mental en la Argentina," *Documental* 1:1 (1997): n.p. Since 1950, a small psychiatric clinic had operated out of the Rawson Hospital. Plotkin, *Freud in the Pampas*, 137. For a detailed analysis of the founding of the clinic at Lanús, see Sergio Visacovsky, *El Lanús: Memoria y política en la construcción de una tradición psiquiátrica argentina* (Buenos Aires: Alianza Editorial, 2002): 96–103.

61 Mauricio Goldenberg and Carlos E. Sluzki, "Setting Up a Psychiatric Service in a General Hospital," *Mental Hygiene* 55:1 (January 1971): 85–89.

62 Mauricio Goldenberg, "Estado actual de la asistencia psiquiátrica en el país," *Acta neuropsiquiátrica* 4 (1958): 401–10; Hugo Vezzetti, "Las ciencias sociales y el campo de la salud mental en la década del sesenta," *Punto de Vista* 54 (April 1996): 30–31.

63 Plotkin, *Freud in the Pampas* provides a fascinating analysis of this subject.

64 Goldenberg and Sluzki, 88–89; Mauricio Goldenberg et al., "Historia y estructura actual del Servicio de Psicopatología y Neurología del Policlínico 'Profesor Dr. Gregorio Aráoz Alfaro,'" *La semana médica* 63:4015 tomo 118, no. 1 (January 4, 1966): 1–3. Lía Ricón, "Un plan de otra gente y para otra época," *Clarín* (August 13, 1992): n.p.; W. Ricardo Grimson, "Hospital Lanús: La primera alternativa al manicomio," *Clarín* (August 13, 1992): n.p.; Wilbur Ricardo Grimson, "El cumpleaños del maestro Goldenberg," *Clarín* (September 5, 1996): 21; Inés Vidal and Edgardo Gili, " Memoria de la influencia de Lanús en el sistema de atención en salud mental en la Capital Federal, o cuando los porteños se pusieron la camiseta de Lanús" (Trabajos pre-publicados) *Primeras jornadas - Encuentro del Servicio de Psicopatología del Policlinico Lanús* (Buenos Aires, 1982). Plotkin, *Freud in the Pampas*, 135–39.

65 *Boletín nacional de salud mental* 1:1 (June 1959): 2; Guerrino, *Psiquiatría argentina*, 64. The INSM took over the responsibilities previously held by the Director de Establecimientos Neuropsiquiatricos and the Director de Higiene Mental. See Carpintero and Vainer, *Las huellas de la memoria*, 68–69.

66 INSM goals fit squarely into global post-war mental health policies. See Goodwin, *Comparative Mental Health Policy*. "In a therapeutic community all facets of the institution, including the relationships between patients and staff and among patients themselves, became therapeutic tools." Plotkin, *Freud in the Pampas*, 140–41.

67 There was concern on the part of many psychiatrists, however, that the composition of the INSM's advisory council was placed solely in the hands of the military government. See Patricia Weissmann, *Cuarenta y cinco años de psiquiatría argentina desde las páginas de Acta* (La Plata: Universidad de Mar de Plata, 1999), 17–18.

68 Roberto Kertesz, Edgardo P. Gili, Ronaldo Ucha Udabe, and Mauricio Knobel, "El equipo psiquiátrico en los hospitales generales en Argentina," *La prensa médica* 55:43–44 (1968): 2093–2099. In 1960, psychiatric clinics were established in the municipal Hospital Piñero (1960) and in Hospital Rawson (1962). Clinics also began to open in private hospitals, including the Hospital Italiano.

69 Alberto Bonhour, "El Hospital de Día: Una realidad," *Revista latino americana de salud mental* 10 (November 1966): 236–37.

70 Bonhour, "El Hospital de Día," 238.

71 "Los hospitales para alienados - Ha creado un agudo problema la unión de los mismos," *La Nación* (July 13, 1957): n.p.

72 "Manifestación de enfermeras ante la CGT – Pertenencen al personal del Instituto Neuropsiquiátrico de Mujeres," *La Nación* (May 13, 1964): n.p.; "El pleito en un organismo asistencial – Declaraciones del interventor en el Hospital de Neuropsiquiatría," *La Nación* (April 22, 1964): n.p. The hospital interventor complained of the need to put an end to "indiscipline, failure to work scheduled hours, and even crimes against the interest of patients." On the constant reorganization of public health, see República Argentina, Poder Ejecutivo Nacional, Ministerio de Asistencia Social y Salud Pública, *Política sanitaria y social.* On budget problems, see "Cuesta más un preso que un alienado," *La Razón* (April 24, 1963): 7.

73 Weissmann, *Cuarenta y cinco años de psiquiatría*, 19.

74 Sylvia Bermann, "Análisis de algunos datos de estadística psiquiátrica," *Acta neuropsiquiátrica* 5 (1959): 150–60. Bermann (1957), 152. "A high percentage of the patients ... must move to locations where psychiatric help is available, thereby contributing to their concentration.... All of this in turn leads to overcrowding and concentration of the nation's mentally ill in a few insane asylums."

75 Gregorio Bermann, *La salud mental y la asistencia psiquiátrica en la Argentina* (Buenos Aires: Paidós, 1965), 113.

76 Bermann, *Salud mental*, 110–13.

77 "La agonía de los hospitales argentinos," *Primera Plana* 202 (November 8, 1966): 45–51. Overcrowding was so severe that patients went months without seeing a doctor. See also the photographs in Sara Facio, Alicia D'Amico, and Julio Cortázar, *Humanario* (Buenos Aires: La Azotea, 1976).

78 Eduardo José Cárdenas, Ricardo Grimson, and José Atilio Álvarez, *El juicio de insania y la internación psiquiátrica* (Buenos Aires: Astrea, 1985), 46–47.

79 Roberto Ciafardo, *Psicopatología forense* (Buenos Aires: Librería 'El Ateneo' Editoria, 1972), 318–65. Even critics of the law argued for the necessity of curtailing the power of families in cases of psychiatric hospitalization.

80 Luis César Guedes Arroyo, *El tratamiento moral: Experiencia Roballos - Comunidad terapéutica* (Buenos Aires: Vinciguerra, 2005), 41–45. The INSM report was "Panorama psiquiátrico argentine en agosto de 1966."

81 The INSM was very optimistic about these projects. The newly appointed director of the Borda proclaimed "without doubt, we shall create a model hospital for Argentine and Latin American psychiatry." "Instituto Nacional de Salud Mental," *Acta psiquiátrica y psicológica de América Latina* 15:1 (March 1969): 15–17. Yet according to Guedes Arroyo, his suggestion to streamline the administration of the Borda and Moyano, which came out of an ISNM-sponsored research project, was met with such strong resistance that the idea was dropped. See Guedes Arroyo (2005), 46–47. During this period, the INSM removed the Sisters of Charity from their work in the Moyano (women) Hospital. See Chapter 2.

82 "Instituto Nacional de Salud Mental (Argentina): Habilitación de pabellones psiquiatricos en Punilla, Córdoba," *Acta psiquiátrica y psicológica de América Latina* 14:2 (1968): 75–79. Interest in therapeutic communities had been growing in Argentina since the World Health Organization's 1953 directive that advocated their creation. Dina Barrionuevo, Silvia García, and Alicia Silva, "Hospital T. de Alvear: Residencia de trabajo social en salud mental - Trabajo Final" (unpublished paper) (May 1998). By 1968, Mexico had managed to close its major asylum, La Castañeda, and had transferred all of its patients to a network of rural hospitals. See Sacristán, "La Granja de San Pedro del Monte," 120–21.

83 "Los hospitales neuropsiquiátricos de la capital serán despoblados, llevándose a los enfermos a ex cuarteles," *La Nación* (n.d.): n.p.

84 Raúl Antonio Camino, "Historia de las instituciones en salud mental: Colonia de rehabilitación de la Ciudad Federal de la Provincia de Entre Ríos, Argentina," *Revista argentina de clínica psicológica* 2 (1993): 211.

85 The INSM also began to develop therapeutic workshops at the major hospitals. See Secretary of Health, Municipality of Buenos Aires. *Talleres protegidos de rehabilitación psiquiátrica* (March 1994). The INSM issued decrees that severely restricted religious orders' activities within hospitals.

86 Guedes Arroyo, *Tratamiento moral*, 51–56. The author mentions a memoir by the hospital's *administradora*, Raquel Follonier de Basso. See also *Acta psiquiátrica y psicológica de América Latina* 15:3 (September 1968): 177.

87 During this time, mental health centres were also established in Viale, Gualeguaychú, and Victoria. After his resignation, he helped to found the *Comisión Teológica Interconfesional Asesora del INSM*. Guedes Arroyo, *Tratamiento moral*, 209, 225–72.

88 Grimson was also in charge of the INSM's Department of Community Psychiatry. "Instituto Nacional de Salud Mental," *Acta psiquiátrica y psicológica de América Latina* 14 (1968): 289.

89 Grimson, *Sociedad de locos*, 256–70.

90 Decree Num. 3549 (Buenos Aires, June 24, 1968), in *Acta psiquiátrica y psicológica de América Latina* 15:3 (September 1968): 173.

91 See "Chalecos," *El Diario* (Paraná) (June 29, 1968): n.p., as cited in Guedes Arroyo *Tratamiento moral*, 101.

92 Guedes Arroyo (2005), 322–36. The project was called Proyecto Piloto de Sectorización Moyano-Ameghino.

93 Mauricio Goldenberg, "El Departamento de Salud Mental de la Ciudad de Buenos Aires," in Organización Panamericana de la Salud (*Grupo de trabajo sobre la administración de Servicios Psiquiátricos y de Salud Mental*, 1970). Municipalidad de la Ciudad de Buenos Aires, "Plan de salud mental," July 1969.

94 Municipalidad (1969), section 1.4. Pedro Herscovici, "La salud mental necesita algo más que la asistencia clásica," *El observador* (May 25, 1984): 31. "La psiquiatría comunitaria en un centro de salud mental," *Acta psiquiátrica y psicológica de América Latina* 17:6 (December 1971): 313–19; Carpintero and Vainer, *Las huellas de la memoria*, 104–6. Within the ranks of the profession, some criticized Goldenberg for working with the Onganía government. For his part, he seems to have attempted to maintain a proper distance from the regime.

95 Debates even included discussion of how psychiatry fit into broader geopolitical concerns; Goldenberg, for example, was harshly criticized for applying for a grant from the U.S. Ford Foundation.

96 Moffatt, *Socioterapia para sectores marginados*, 176. The book was originally published in 1974.

97 Dr. Alejandro Tarnopolsky drew my attention to the wide array of experiences and projects during this period. For the experiences in the Melchor Romero asylum, see *Carta abierta a la sociedad* (Buenos Aires: Axis, 1974). See also reports on conditions at the La Plata hospital in *La gaceta* (April and May, 1972) (La Plata): n.p. On anti-psychiatry movements in western Europe and the United States, see Mark S. Micale and Roy Porter, *Discovering the History of Psychiatry* (New York: Oxford University Press, 1994), especially the essays in "Critics of Psychiatry."

98 Emiliano Galende, "Modernidad y modelos de asistencia en salud mental en Argentina," in *Segundas jornadas de atención primaria de la salud* (April 3–May 7, 1988): 444. In the field of

mental health, the Federacion Argentina de Psiquiatras, created in 1959 as an alternative body, was emblematic of the leftist orientation of many doctors.

99 Guillermo Vidal, "Mauricio Goldenberg," *Acta psiquiátrica y psicológica de América Latina* 17:6 (December 1971): 422. Goldenberg, for example, was denied an important academic position in 1966 because of resistance from powerful conservative psychiatrists.

100 "Fue intervenido el Instituto de Salud Mental," *La Nación* (October 22, 1970): n.p.; Plotkin, *Freud in the Pampas*, 139–41. "Aclara los origines del conflicto el interventor del Hospital José Esteves," *Clarín* (January 12, 1972); "Disolvióse el Instituto de Salud Mental," *La Nación* (February 10, 1972): n.p.

101 Grimson, *Sociedad de locos*, 255–70. See also: "La Bola de Nieve," *Analisis* (January 19, 1971): n.p.; Ronald Hansen, "Imaginative treatment of mental disease under fire," *Buenos Aires Herald* (January 11, 1971): n.p.; and "La gran ilusión," *Primera plana* (January 5, 1971): n.p. Goodwin's analysis of western Europe and North America would suggest that such resistance is not unique to Argentina. Goodwin, 29–50.

102 Raúl A. Camino, conversation with author, June 1999, Buenos Aires, Argentina. María Luisa Gonnet, "Una experiencia de aquí y antes: Colonia de Rehabilitación de la Ciudad Federal de la Provincia, Entre Ríos (1967–76), *Riachuelo* (n.d.). Miguel Orellana, "Encuentros: Dialogando con el Dr. Raúl Camino," *ARJE* (n.d.): 20–26.

103 *Nunca más: Informe de la Comisión Nacional sobre la Desaparición de Personas* (Buenos Aires: EUDEBA, 1987).

104 "El Instituto Nacional de Salud Mental," *La Nación* (April 24, 1976): n.p.

105 Nancy Caro Hollander, "Psychoanalysis and State Terror in Argentina," *American Journal of Psychoanalysis* 52:3 (1992): 273–89; Nancy Caro Hollander, ""Psychoanalysis confronts the politics of Repression: The Case of Argentina," *Social Science and Medicine* 28:7 (1989): 751–58; Plotkin, *Freud in the Pampas*, 216–30. For a right-wing critique of progressive psychiatry, see Roberto J. Brie, "Psicología y marxismo," *Verbo: Formación para la acción* 165 (1976): 11–19.

106 Sub-Comisión de Salud Mental: Casa Argentina en México, "¿Salud mental en la Argentina de hoy?" *Cuadernos americanos* 36:204 (September–October 1977): 36–46.

107 Sub-Comisión, 42–43. Many of those targeted were members the leftist Federación Argentina de Psiquiatras, though political moderates such as Goldenberg were also forced into exile.

108 Sylvia Bermann and José Carlos Escudero, "Health in Argentina under the Military Junta," *International Journal of Health Services* 8:3 (1978): 535.

109 Hollander, "Psychoanalysis and State Terror in Argentina," 284; Plotkin, *Freud in the Pampas*, 216–27.

110 Weissmann, *Cuarenta y cinco años de psiquiatría*, 30–45.

111 *Nunca Más*, 148–51.

112 "Visita al Hospital Borda de Psiquiatría," *La Prensa* (January 4, 1984): 6. Interviews with staff suggested that between 1976 and 1978, at least 302 unidentified persons were admitted to the hospital, including its criminal unit. Their fate remains unknown. See also Horacio Riquelme U., *Entre la obediencia y la oposicion: Los medicos y al ética profesional bajo la dictadura militar* (Caracas: Editorial Nueva Sociedad, 1995). On the denial of the charges, see Florencio E. Sánchez, *El desnudo de la inocencia: la verdad sobre la Colonia Montes de Oca* (Buenos Aires: Editorial Galerna, 1992). I am indebted to Nancy Scheper-Hughes, who has done a tremendous amount of research on this institution

and shared some of her findings with me. Nancy Scheper-Hughes, "Parts Unknown: Undercover Ethnography of the Organs-Trafficking Underworld, " *Ethnography* 5:1 (2004): 29–73.

113 In September 1983, the interim government passed Law 22,914, which regulated hospitalization. José María Martínez Ferretti, "Aportes para la legislación sobre internación de enfermos mentales," *Psiquiatría forense sexología praxis-9* 5:3:1 (July 1998): n.p. See also "Se propician consultorios ambulantes para atender la salud mental en crisis," *La Razón* (April 25, 1981): n.p.

114 Cárdenas, Grimson, and Álvarez, *Juicio de insania*, 64–65; Guedes Arroyo, *Tratamiento moral* also confirms the authoritarian tradition within psychiatry.

115 The authors were not suggesting that military rule necessarily was to blame. Future research may demonstrate a correlation between regime type and adherence to these legal procedures.

116 Cárdenas, Grimson, and Álvarez, *Juicio de insania*, 111. See also Cárdenas, "Para internar a un enfermo mental hace la falta la intervención de un juez," 33.

117 Cárdenas, Grimson, and Álvarez, *Juicio de insania*, 46–47.

118 Frontera, "La dictadura del Valium," 32. The article suggests that, during the military government, many psychiatrists came to believe that the mentally ill were impervious to pain or hunger. See also "Salud mental en Argentina: Creación democrática o locura fascista," *Caras y Caretas* 2201: 85 (August 1983): 61–62.

119 José Carlos Escudero, "The Health Crisis in Argentina," *International Journal of Health Services* 33:1 (2003): 129–36. The themes of this essay echo those found in Escudero's 1978 analysis of mental health under the dictatorship. See Bermann and Escudero, "Health in Argentina under the Military Junta," 535.

120 Isabel Ares, "Recorrido por el Borda," *Gaceta psicológica* (1985): 9; Claudia Olrog, "Antropología del Hospicio," *Programa de Investigaciones sobre Epidemiologia Psiquiatrica: Documenta Laboris* 4:59 (March 1984). Norberto Baruch Bertochi, "Pabellón de Adolescentes: Matadero-Borda," *Cerdos y Peces* (April 1984): 17–18. See also Liliana Magrini and Mario Ganora, "Informe sobre violaciones graves de los derechos humanos (Tratos y Penas Crueles Inhumanas y Degradantes) a preso y minusválidos psíquicos en los establecimientos psiquiátricos 'Colonia Nacional de Montes de Oca' y Hospital Neuropsiquiatrico Domingo Cabred." Equipo Nizkor, <http//:www.derechos.or/nizkor/arg/doc/psiquiatrico/>

121 Vicente Zito Lema, *Conversaciones con Enrique Pichon-Riviere sobre el arte y la locura* (Buenos Aires: Ediciones Cinco, 1997), 84. On the abuse of psychiatric patients, see Reaume, *Remembrance of Patients Past.*

122 Lakoff, *Pharmaceutical Reason.*

123 Not only have patients and doctors suffered, but so too have the archives that might reveal more details of the story. The INSM archives have virtually disappeared, and the major hospitals have few extant records. Future research will require systematic oral histories and careful review of periodical and journal literature from the period. It is beyond the scope of this book to examine the legacy of state terror, including economic restructuring, on the current operation of mental health services in Argentina.

7: Conclusion: Social Control in a Weak State

1 Migdal, *Strong Societies and Weak States*, 18.

2 Guy, *Sex and Danger in Buenos Aires*, 208.

3 Rodriguez, *Civilizing Argentina*, 247–57.

4 During the Proceso, the Argentine military government proved to have one of the most decentralized and least bureaucratized repressive apparatuses of the entire continent. See Anthony W. Pereira, *Political (In)justice: Authoritarianism and the Rule of Law in Brazil, Chile, and Argentina* (Pittsburgh: Pittsburgh University Press, 2005). On the problem of enforcement of labour legislation and social welfare in Argentina, see Lavrín, *Women, Feminism, and Social Change*, 83; Joel Horowitz, *Argentine Unions, the State and the Rise of Perón, 1930–1945* (Institute of International Studies, University of California, Berkeley, 1990), 35; Mariano Plotkin, *Mañana es San Perón: Propaganda, rituales políticos y educación en el régimen peronista (1946–1955)* (Buenos Aires: Ariel Historia Argentina, 1993), 216–18. Crider, "Modernization and Human Welfare," 229–30.

5 For the United States, see Robert H. Wiebe, *The Search for Order, 1877–1920* (Westport, CT: Greenwood, 1980).

6 James C. Scott, *Seeing Like a State: How Certain Schemes to Improve the Human Condition Have Failed* (New Haven, CT: Yale University Press, 1998), 78.

7 Fox, *'So far disordered in mind'*, 32. "The California State Board of Charities and Corrections itself asserted in 1916 that 'a nation-wide awakening to the menace of the feebleminded' was 'one of the most noteworthy movements of public thought.'"

8 See: Dowbiggin, *Inheriting Madness*; and Nye, *Crime, Madness, and Politics in Modern France*, 330–39. On the politics of health statistics, see Richard Soloway, "Counting the Degenerates: The Statistics of Race Deterioration in Edwardian England," *Journal of Contemporary History* 17:1 (January 1982): 137–64. Daniel Pick, *Faces of Degeneration: A European Disorder, c. 1848–c. 1918* (New York: Cambridge University Press, 1989); Prestwich, "Family Strategies and Medical Power": 799–815.

9 Vezzetti, *Locura en la Argentina*; Salessi, "Argentine Dissemination of Homosexuality, 1890–1914," 337–68; Salessi, *Médicos, maleantes, y maricas*.

BIBLIOGRAPHY

BIBLIOGRAPHY

Primary Sources

Archives

Archivo General de la Nación-Sociedad de la Beneficencia-Hospital Nacional de Alienadas.
Archivo del Poder Judicial de la Nación.
Archivo de las Hermanas de la Caridad, Hijas de la Sna. María (Buenos Aires).
Archivo del Hospital Psiquiátrico "Braulio A. Moyano."
Archivo del Hospital Psiquiátrico "José T. Borda."
Archivo de la Municipalidad de Buenos Aires.
Archivo de la Facultad de Medicina de la Universidad de Buenos Aires.

Official Publications

Actas del Consejo Municipal de la Ciudad de Buenos Aires.

Anuario Estadístico de la Ciudad de Buenos Aires.

Argentine Republic. Congreso Nacional. *Diario de sesiones de la Cámara de Diputados* (1893–73).

Argentine Republic. Poder Ejecutivo Nacional. Ministerio de Asistencia Social y Salud Pública, *Política sanitaria y social (October 12, 1963–December 31, 1965).* Buenos Aires, 1966.

Argentine Republic. Poder Ejecutivo Nacional, *Reforma del régimen técnico-administrativo de los organismos asistenciales y sanitarios del Ministerio de Asistencia Social y Salud Pública.* Buenos Aires: n.p., 1965.

Argentine Republic. *Tercer censo nacional. Tomo IV población* (Buenos Aires: Talleres Graficos de L.J. Rosso y Cia, 1915).

Censo general de población, edificación, comercio e industrias de la Ciudad de Buenos Aires (Buenos Aires: Compañía Sud-Americana de Billetes de Banco, 1910).

Colonia Nacional de Alienados: Memoria médico-administrativo correspondiente a los años 1908–10.

Ley y decretos relacionados con la creación de la Comisión Asesora de Asilos y Hospitales Regionales. Imprenta del Asilo de Torres, 1923.

Memoria del intendencia municipal (Año 1903, Administración del Sr. Alberto Casares). (Buenos Aires: Imprenta y Litografía G. Kraft, 1904).

Memoria de la Comisión Asesora de Asilos y Hospitales Regionales.

Ministerio de Relaciones Exteriores y Culto, *Colonia Nacional de Alienados, Luján (Provincia de Buenos Aires)* (Buenos Aires: n.p., 1910).

Ministerio de Relaciones Exteriores y Culto, *Documentación que pasó a poder de la Secretaría de Salud Pública de la Nación: Inventario, 1900–1929.*
Ministerio de Relaciones Exteriores y Culto. "Memoria de la Comisión Asesora de Hospitales y Asilos Regionales. Asilo Colonia Regional Mixto de Alienados, Oliva," *Memoria del Ministerio de Relaciones Exteriores y Culto correspondiente al años 1926–1927* (Buenos Aires, 1928).
Municipalidad de la Ciudad de Buenos Aires, "Plan de Salud Mental" (July 1, 1969).
Recopilación de leyes, reglamentaciones, decretos y resoluciones de enero 1944–junio 1946. II. Estadisticas de Salud (Buenos Aires, 1947).
Referencias estadísticas sobre la asistencia y funcionamiento de los hospitales, asilos, escuelas y sociedades de caridad sostenidos o subvencionados por el Tesoro Nacional (Buenos Aires: Talleres Gráficos de Selín Suárez, 1915).
Secretaria de Estado de Cultura y Educación. *Planeamiento y desarrollo de la acción de gobierno.* Buenos Aires: Centro Nacional de Documentación e Información Educativa, 1968.
Secretaria de Salud. Municipalidad de Buenos Aires. *Talleres protegidos de rehabilitación psiquiátrica* (March 1994).

Medical Journals

Acta psiquiátrica y psicológica de América Latina.
Archivos de salud pública.
Archivos de la secretaría de salud pública.
Archivos de psiquiatría, criminología y ciencias afines (1903–10).
Boletín del asilo de alienados en Oliva (1932–42).
Boletín del Departamento Provincial de Higiene (Córdoba).
Boletín del Instituto Psiquiátrico de la Facultad de Ciencias (Rosario, Argentina).
Boletín nacional de salud mental (1959–60).
Psiquiatría social.
Revista argentina de neurología, psiquiatría y medicina legal (1927–30).
Revista argentina de neurología y psiquiatría (1938–39).
Revista de criminología, psiquiatría y medicina legal (1914–34).
Revista latinoamericana de salud mental.
Revista de psiquiatría y criminología (1914–34).

Popular Periodicals

Análisis.
¡Aquí Está!
Buenos Aires Herald.
Caras y Caretas.
Clarín.
El Diario.
International Journal of Health Services.
La Gaceta.
L'hygiene mental.
La Nación.
New York Times.
Página12.
La Prensa.
La Protesta.
La Unión.
La Razón.
La Revista Popular.
Solidaridad: Periódico obrero.
Somos.

Hospital Reports: Hospital Nacional de Alienadas (in chronological order)

Sociedad de Beneficencia de la Capital. *Memoria del Hospital Nacional de Alienadas* (Buenos Aires: Imprenta, Litografia y Encuadernación de J. Peuser, 1901).

Sociedad de Beneficencia de la Capital. *Memoria del año 1902* (Buenos Aires: Imprenta y Encuadernación del Asilo de Huérfanos, 1903).

Sociedad de Beneficencia de la Capital. *Memoria del año 1903* (Buenos Aires: Imprenta, Litografia y Encuadernación de J. Peuser, 1904).

Sociedad de Beneficencia de la Capital. *Memoria del año 1905* (Buenos Aires: Imprenta, Litografia y Encuadernación de G. Kraft, 1906).

Sociedad de Beneficencia de la Capital. *Memoria del año 1910* (Buenos Aires: 'La Semana Médica' Imprenta de Obras de E. Spinelli, 1911).

Ministerio de Relaciones Exteriores y Culto. "Memorias de la Sociedad de Beneficencia," *Memoria del Ministerio de Relaciones Exteriores y Culto correspondiente al años 1913–1914* (Buenos Aires: Talleres Gráficos de Selín Suarez, 1915).

Ministerio de Relaciones Exteriores y Culto. "Memorias de la Sociedad de Beneficencia," *Memoria del Ministerio de Relaciones Exteriores y Culto correspondiente al años 1916–1917* (Buenos Aires: Talleres Gráficos de Selín Suarez, 1918).

Sociedad de Beneficencia de la Capital. *Memoria del año 1915* (Buenos Aires: Talleres del Asilo de Huérfanos, 1916).

Ministerio de Relaciones Exteriores y Culto. "Memorias de la Sociedad de Beneficencia," *Memoria del Ministerio de Relaciones Exteriores y Culto correspondiente al años 1917–1918* (Buenos Aires: Talleres Gráficos de Selín Suarez, 1919).

Ministerio de Relaciones Exteriores y Culto. "Memorias de la Sociedad de Beneficencia," *Memoria del Ministerio de Relaciones Exteriores y Culto correspondiente al años 1918–1919* (Buenos Aires: Talleres Gráficos de Selín Suarez, 1920).

Ministerio de Relaciones Exteriores y Culto. "Memorias de la Sociedad de Beneficencia," *Memoria del Ministerio de Relaciones Exteriores y Culto correspondiente al años 1919–1920* (Buenos Aires: Talleres Gráficos de Selín Suarez, 1922).

Sociedad de Beneficencia de la Capital. *Memoria del año 1920* (Buenos Aires: Talleres Gráficos del Asilo de Huérfanos, 1921).

Ministerio de Relaciones Exteriores y Culto. "Memorias de la Sociedad de Beneficencia," *Memoria del Ministerio de Relaciones Exteriores y Culto correspondiente al años 1923–24* (Buenos Aires, 1925).

Ministerio de Relaciones Exteriores y Culto. "Memorias de la Sociedad de Beneficencia," *Memoria del Ministerio de Relaciones Exteriores y Culto correspondiente al años 1924–25* (Buenos Aires: Imprenta de la Cámara de Diputados, 1925).

Sociedad de Beneficencia de la Capital. *Memoria del año 1925* (Buenos Aires: Talleres de la Sociedad de Beneficencia de la Capital, 1926).

Ministerio de Relaciones Exteriores y Culto. "Memorias de la Sociedad de Beneficencia," *Memoria del Ministerio de Relaciones Exteriores y Culto correspondiente al año 1926* (Buenos Aires: Imprenta de las Honorables Cámaras de Diputados, 1927).

Sociedad de Beneficencia de la Capital. *Memoria del año 1929–30* (Buenos Aires: Talleres de la Sociedad de Beneficencia de la Capital, 1931).

Ministerio de Relaciones Exteriores y Culto. "Memorias de la Sociedad de Beneficencia correspondiente al año 1933," *Memoria del Ministerio de Relaciones Exteriores y Culto correspondiente al año 1933* (Buenos Aires, 1934).

Ministerio de Relaciones Exteriores y Culto. "Memorias de la Sociedad de Beneficencia correspondiente al año 1934," *Memoria del Ministerio de Relaciones Exteriores y Culto correspondiente al año 1934* (Buenos Aires, 1935).

Ministerio de Relaciones Exteriores y Culto. "Memorias de la Sociedad de Beneficencia," *Memoria del Ministerio de Relaciones Exteriores y Culto correspondiente al año 1935* (Buenos Aires, 1936).
Ministerio de Relaciones Exteriores y Culto. "Memorias de la Sociedad de Beneficencia," *Memoria del Ministerio de Relaciones Exteriores y Culto correspondiente al año 1936* (Buenos Aires, 1937).
Ministerio de Relaciones Exteriores y Culto. "Memorias de la Sociedad de Beneficencia," *Memoria del Ministerio de Relaciones Exteriores y Culto correspondiente al año 1937* (Buenos Aires, 1938).
Ministerio de Relaciones Exteriores y Culto. "Memorias de la Sociedad de Beneficencia," *Memoria del Ministerio de Relaciones Exteriores y Culto correspondiente al año 1939* (Buenos Aires, 1940).
Sociedad de la Beneficencia de la Capital, *Memoria del año 1940* (Buenos Aires: Imprenta de la Escuela de Artes y Oficios del Hogar de Huérfanos, 1941).
Sociedad de la Beneficencia de la Capital, *Memoria del año 1941* (Buenos Aires: Imprenta de la Escuela de Artes y Oficios del Hogar de Huérfanos, 1942).
Sociedad de la Beneficencia de la Capital, *Memoria del año 1942* (Buenos Aires: Imprenta de la Escuela de Artes y Oficios del Hogar de Huérfanos, 1943).
Sociedad de la Beneficencia de la Capital, *Memoria del año 1943* (Buenos Aires: Imprenta de la Escuela de Artes y Oficios del Hogar de Huérfanos, 1944).

Hospital Reports: Hospicio de las Mercedes (in chronological order)

Memoria del Hospicio de las Mercedes correspondiente al año 1893 (Buenos Aires: Tipografía del Hospicio de las Mercedes, 1900).
Ministerio de Relaciones Exteriores y Culto. *Hospicio de las Mercedes: Memoria medico-administrativo correspondiente al año 1903* (Buenos Aires: Imprenta del Hospicio de las Mercedes, 1904).
Ministerio de Relaciones Exteriores y Culto. "Hospicio de las Mercedes: Memoria medico-administrativa, correspondiente al años 1908–1910," *Memoria del Ministerio de Relaciones Exteriores y Culto correspondiente al años 1910–1911* (Buenos Aires, 1912).
Ministerio de Relaciones Exteriores y Culto. "Hospicio de las Mercedes: Memoria medico-administrativa, correspondiente al años 1912–1913," *Memoria del Ministerio de Relaciones Exteriores y Culto correspondiente al años 1912–1913* (Buenos Aires, 1914).
Ministerio de Relaciones Exteriores y Culto. "Hospicio de las Mercedes: Memoria medico-administrativa, correspondiente al año 1914," *Memoria del Ministerio de Relaciones Exteriores y Culto correspondiente al años 1913–1914* (Buenos Aires, 1915): 562–75.
Ministerio de Relaciones Exteriores y Culto. "Hospicio de las Mercedes: Memoria medico-administrativa, correspondiente al año 1916," *Memoria del Ministerio de Relaciones Exteriores y Culto correspondiente al años 1916–1917* (Buenos Aires, 1917): 551–67.
Ministerio de Relaciones Exteriores y Culto. "Hospicio de las Mercedes: Memoria medico-administrativa, correspondiente al año 1917," *Memoria del Ministerio de Relaciones Exteriores y Culto correspondiente al años 1917–1918* (Buenos Aires, 1919): 977–93.

Ministerio de Relaciones Exteriores y Culto. "Hospicio de las Mercedes: Memoria medico-administrativa, correspondiente al año 1918," *Memoria del Ministerio de Relaciones Exteriores y Culto correspondiente al años 1918–1919* (Buenos Aires, 1920): 539–49.

Ministerio de Relaciones Exteriores y Culto. *Hospicio de las Mercedes: Memoria medico-administrativo correspondiente al año 1919* (Buenos Aires: Imprenta y Encuadernación del Hospicio de las Mercedes, 1922).

Ministerio de Relaciones Exteriores y Culto. *Hospicio de las Mercedes: Memoria medico-administrativo correspondiente al año 1920* (Buenos Aires: Imprenta y Encuadernación del Hospicio de las Mercedes, 1923).

Ministerio de Relaciones Exteriores y Culto. *Hospicio de las Mercedes: Memoria medico-administrativo correspondiente al año 1925* (Buenos Aires: Imprenta del Hospicio de las Mercedes, 1926).

Ministerio de Relaciones Exteriores y Culto. *Hospicio de las Mercedes: Memoria medico-administrativo correspondiente al año 1927* (Buenos Aires: Imprenta del Hospicio de las Mercedes, 1928).

Ministerio de Relaciones Exteriores y Culto. *Hospicio de las Mercedes: Memoria medico-administrativa correspondiente al año 1931* (Buenos Aires: Establecimiento Gráfico Tomás Palumbo, 1932).

Ministerio de Relaciones Exteriores y Culto. *Hospicio de las Mercedes: Memoria medico-administrativa correspondiente al año 1932* (Buenos Aires: Establecimiento Gráfico Tomás Palumbo, 1933).

Ministerio de Relaciones Exteriores y Culto. *Hospicio de las Mercedes: Memoria medico-administrativo correspondiente al año 1935* (Buenos Aires: Talleres Gráficos 'Tomás Palumbo,' 1937).

Ministerio de Relaciones Exteriores y Culto. *Hospicio de las Mercedes: Memoria medico-administrativo correspondiente al año 1936* (Buenos Aires: Talleres Gráficos 'Tomás Palumbo,' 1938).

Ministerio de Relaciones Exteriores y Culto. *Hospicio de las Mercedes: Memoria medico-administrativo correspondiente al año 1937* (Buenos Aires: Talleres Gráficos 'Tomás Palumbo,' 1938).

Ministerio de Relaciones Exteriores y Culto. Comisión Asesora de Asilos y Hospitales Regionales. *Hospicio de las Mercedes: Memoria medico-administrativo correspondiente al año 1939* (Buenos Aires: Talleres Gráficos 'Gadola,' 1940).

Argentina Medical Literature: Articles and Books

Alba Carreras, J., and N. Acuña. "Curanderismo y locura: El caso de la 'Hermana María,'" Archivos de psiquiatría, criminología y ciencias afines (1903): 649–53.

Ameghino, Arturo. "Higiene mental – la acción del estado en el mejoramiento de la raza," *Revista de criminología, psiquiatría y medicina legal* 22:127 (January–February 1935).

———. "Lucio Meléndez, Conferencia inaugural de la cátedra de clínica psiquiátrica," *Revista de criminología, psiquiatría y medicina legal* 18:107 (September–December 1931): 521–33.

———. "Carácter y extensión de la locura en las diversas regiones de la República Argentina," *Revista argentina de neurología, psiquiatría y medicina legal* 1:1 (January–February 1927): 493–504.

———. "Locura familiar homócrona en tres hermanos," *Revista de criminología, psiquiatría y medicina legal* 12 (1925): 3–8.

———, Niceforo Castellano, and Ramón M. Arana. "La responsabilidad de los degenerados hereditarios," *Revista argentina de neurología, psiquiatría y medicina legal* 1:3 (May–June 1927): 343–53.

Austi, Elio García. "Concepto actual de la enfermedad mental," *Revista de psiquiatría y criminología* 3:13 (January–February 1938): 21–44.

Bard, Leopoldo. "Proyecto de ley sobre legislación para los establecimientos destinados a alienados," *Revista de criminología, psiquiatría y medicina legal* 4:52 (July–August 1922): 452–74.

Belbey, José. "La delincuencia de los débiles mentales," *Revista de psiquiatría y criminología* 2:12 (November–December 1937): 713–24.

Bermann, Gregorio. *La salud mental y la asistencia psiquiátrica en la Argentina.* Buenos Aires: Editorial Paidós, 1965.

———. "Organización de la asistencia psiquiátrica e higiene mental en la República," *Revista argentina de neurología, psiquiatría y medicina legal* 4:24 (November–December 1930): 556–62.

Bermann, Sylvia. "Análisis de algunos datos de estadística psiquiátrica," *Acta neuropsiquiátrica* 5 (1959): 150–60.

Bermann, Sylvia, and José Carlos Escudero. "Health in Argentina under the Military Junta," *International Journal of Health Services* 8:3 (1978): 531–40.

Bonhour, Alberto. "El hospital de día," *Revista latinoamericana de salud mental* 10 (November 1966): 235–40.

———. "Delirantes homicidas: Atentados contra la vida de médicos argentinos," Thesis, University of Buenos Aires, School of Medicine, 1941.

———, and Juan Martín E. González. "Capacidad civil de un presunto 'retardo mental,'" *Revista de psiquiatría y criminología* 2:9 (May–June 1937): 295–304.

Borda, José. T. "Ensayo de clasificación de las enfermedades mentales," *Revista de criminología, psiquiatría y medicina legal* 4:53 (September–October 1922): 513–21.

Bosch, Gonzalo. "La modernización del Hospicio de las Mercedes," *Boletín del Hospicio de las Mercedes* 1:1 (1938).

———. *El pavoroso aspecto de la locura en la República Argentina.* Buenos Aires: n.p. 1931.

———, and Arturo Mó. "La malarioterapia en la parálisis general," *Revista de la Sociedad Argentina de Neurología y Psiquiatría* 1:6 (1925): 185–223 and "La importancia de la psicometría en psiquiatría. Contribución a su estudio." 1:6 (1925): 224–33.

Brandam, Javier. "Responsabilidad de los epilépticos," *Revista de criminología, psiquiatría y medicina legal* 2:7–8 (January–April 1915): 3–41.

Bringas Núñez, Exequias. "Inmigración y locura (Algunos datos para la profilaxis de las enfermedades mentales en la República Argentina)," *Boletín del Asilo de Alienados en Oliva* 10:42–43 (May–December 1942): 167–73.

———. "A propósito de la fundación de la Liga de Higiene Mental en Córdoba," *Boletín del Asilo de Alienados en Oliva* 10:42–43 (May–December 1942): 177–80.

Cabeza, Manuel. "Memoria del Asilo Colonia Regional Mixta de Alienados en Oliva desde su fundación hasta el presente, 1918–1941," *Boletín del Asilo de Alienados en Oliva* 10:40–41 (March–April 1942): 3–76.

———. "Memoria del Asilo C.R.M. de Alienados en Oliva desde su fundación hasta el 31 XII 1941 (continuación)," *Boletín del Asilo de Alienados en Oliva* 10:40–41 (March–April 1942): 3–76.

Cabral, César Augusto. "Terapéutica de la psicosis en comunidad hospitalaria," *Acta psiquiátrica y psicológica de América Látina* 22 (1976): 71–75.

Cabred, Domingo. "Antecedentes de la fundación del Asilo-Colonia de Luján," *Revista de criminología, psiquiatría y medicina legal* 7 (1920): 357–62.

———. El Instituto Clínica de Psiquiatría de la Facultad de Medicina de Buenos Aires (Buenos Aires: Wiebeck, Turtl & Company, 1919), n.p.
———. *Discursos sobre asilos y hospitales regionales.* Edición personal, 1918.
———. "Asilo Colonia Regional de Retardados," *Archivos de psiquiatría, criminología y ciencias afines* 7 (1908): 733–35.
———. "Discurso inaugural de la Colonia Nacional de Alienados," *Revista de derecho, historia, y latras* 1:3 (1899): 610–22.
Camino, Raúl Antonio. "Historia de las instituciones en salud mental: Colonia de rehabilitación de la Ciudad Federal de la Provincia de Entre Ríos, Argentina," *Revista argentina de clínica psicológica* 2:2 (1993): 207–12.
Capelli, José F. "Perversidad y locura mental," *Revista de psiquiatría y criminología* 4:23 (September–October 1939): 613–18.
———. Ramón B. Silva, "Simulación y disimulación," *Revista de psiquiatría y criminología* 3:16 (July–August 1938): 463–74.
Cárdenas, Eduardo José, Ricardo Grimson, and José Atilio Álvarez. *El juicio de insania y la internación psiquiátrica.* Buenos Aires: Astrea, 1985.
Carreño, Carlos, and N. Alberto Yanzón R. *Hospitales: Unidades sanitaria.* Buenos Aires: El Ateneo, 1945.
Carrillo, Ramón. *Clasificación sanitaria de los enfermos mentales: Relaciones entre código civil y sanitario.* Buenos Aires: Talleres gráficos del Ministerio de Salud Pública de la Nación, 1950.
Castedo, César. "Electro-shock en el Pabellón Charcot del Hospital Melchor Romero," *Revista de psiquiatría y criminología* 7:39 (September–October 1942): 419–24.
Castellanos, Israel. "Estudio antropológico de las asiladas en la Escuela Reformatoria de Aldecoa," *Revista de criminología, psiquiatría y medicina legal* 11:7–8 (January–April 1915): 212–21.
Catalán, Emilio. *La fisonomía en los alienados* (Buenos Aires: Talleres Gráficos de la Penitenciaría Nacional, 1924).
Chiama, Italo D. "Locura moral" (Tesis presentado para optar al título de Doctor en Medicina-UNBA, 1911). Buenos Aires: Talleres Gráficos M. Rodriguez Giles, 1911. Roberto Ciafardo, *Psicopatología forense* (Buenos Aires: 'El Ateneo,' 1972).
Ciafardo, Roberto, and Juan Carlos Vizcarra."Etiopatogenía y Profilaxis del Suicidio," *Sociedad Argentina de Criminología* 9:49 (September–October 1944): 345–66.
Ciampi, Lanfranco. "La asistencia de los enfermos mentales según los criterios reformadores modernos," *Revista de criminología, psiquiatría y medicina legal* 9:52 (July–August 1922): 385–401.
———. "Un nuevo hospital psiquiátrico en la República Argentina," *Revista argentina de neurología, psiquiatría y medicina legal* 1:4 (July–August 1927): 481–89.
Crespo, Eduardo. *Nuevos ensayos políticos y administrativos.* Buenos Aires: Libreria y Editorial "La Facultad," 1938.
Cubas, Máximo Agustín. "Los certificados médicos de alienación mental," *Boletín del Asilo de Alienados en Oliva* 3:7 (March 1935): 35–45.
De Lena, Rogelio. "Higiene mental y medidas legislativas," *Revista de psiquiatría y criminología* 10:54 (September–October 1945): 369–82.
———. "Organización de la estadística en higiene mental," *Revista de psiquiatría y criminología* 7:39 (September–October 1942): 427–36.
de Quirós, Carlos B. "Consecuencias individuales, familiares y sociales del alcoholismo," *Archivos de psiquiatría y criminología* 2:2 (February 1903): 108–17.
De Veyga, Francisco. "Estadísticas de la 'Sala de Observación de alienados,'" *Archivos de psiquiatría, criminología y ciencias afines* (1903): 42–45.
Durquet, Joaquín J., and Eusebio Albino. "Estudio estadístico de la parálisis general progresiva en el Hospital Melchor Romero," *Revista de criminología, psiquiatría y medicina legal* 11 (1924): 37–51.

"El conflicto del Hospital Esteves," *Boletín de la Asociación Psiquiátrica de América Látina* 3:13–14 (November 1970–March 1971): n.p.

Esteves Balado, Luís. "Terapéutica por shocks en las enfermedades mentales," *Revista de criminología, psiquiatría y medicina legal* 19:110 (March–April 1932): 162–74.

Fantoni, Bruno A.L. "Internación de enfermos mentales – responsabilidad de los directores," *Gaceta del Instituto Nacional de Salud Mental* 1:1 (September 1963): n.p.

Fernández, Helvio. "El servicio de alienados delincuentes," *Archivos de psiquiatría, criminología y ciencias afines* 8 (1909): n.p.

Fernández Amallo, Jorge, and María E. Balsells de Ragazzo. "Bases para un plan nacional de salud mental," *Neuropsiquiatría y salud mental* 12:3 (September–December 1981): 20–28.

Ferrer, Conrado. "Asistencia de los alienados en el Asilo de Oliva," *Boletín del Asilo de Alienados en Oliva* 5:17 (September 1937): 248–54.

———. "Sobre las visitas a los alienados internados," *Boletín del Asilo de Alienados en Oliva* 6:19–22 (January–December 1938): 140–46.

———. "Proyecto de asistencia familiar en el Asilo Colonia de Oliva," *Boletín del Asilo de Alienados en Oliva* 6:19–22 (January–December 1938): 36–42.

———. "La locura en Córdoba," *Boletín del Asilo de Alienados en Oliva* 8:29 (1940): 55–65.

———. "A propósito de la clausura del Asilo de Oliva," *Boletín del Asilo de Alienados en Oliva* 8:29 (1940): 518–22.

Fontanorossa, Hector O., and Nestor Stingo. "Normatización de un servicio de emergencia psiquiátrica," *Neuropsiquiatría y salud mental* 12:3 (September–December 1981): 29–41.

Foradori, I.A. *La psicología en la República Argentina*. Buenos Aires: n.p., 1935.

Fragueyro, Martín. *Capacidad jurídica de los alienados ante la justicia civil. Escrito presentado en la causa seguida por d. Tristan Garcilas, denunciando la insanidad mental de su madre política Doña Petrona Lencina de Lencina*. Buenos Aires: Imprenta Roma de J. Carbone, 1889.

Goldenberg, Mauricio. "El departmento de Salud Mental de la Ciudad de Buenos Aires." In *Organización Panamericana de la Salud* (Grupo de trabajo sobre la administración de Servicios Psiquiátricos y de Salud Mental) (1970).

———, Valentin Barenblit, Octavio Fernandez Moujan, Vicente A. Galli, Hernán Kesselman, Anatolio Müller, Aurora Perez, Lia Gladys Ricón, Carlos E. Sluzki, Gerardo Stein. "La psiquiatría en el hospital general: Historia y estructura actual del Servicio de Psicopatología y Neurología del Policlínico 'Profesor Dr. Gregorio Aráoz Alfaro,'" *Semana médica* 73:4015:118:1 (January 4, 1966): 1–20.

———. "Estado actual de la asistencia psiquiátrica en el país," *Acta neuropsiquiátrica* 4 (1958): 401–10.

———, and Carlos E. Sluzki. "Setting Up a Psychiatric Service in a General Hospital," *Mental Hygiene* 55:1 (January 1971): 85–90.

Gorriti, Fernando. "Higiene mental en la Argentina," *Revista argentina de neurología, psiquiatría y medicina legal* 2:8 (March–April 1928): 145–55.

———. "Nueva extensión social en la asistencia hospitalaria de los enfermos mentales," *Revista de criminología, psiquiatría y medicina legal* 7 (1920): 615–19.

———. *Anamnesis general de 5,000 enfermos mentales clasificados* (Buenos Aires: Talleres Gráficos de la Penitenciaría Nacional, 1920).

Grimson, Ricardo. "La comunidad terapéutica y el hospital psiquiátrico," *Revista argentina de psicología* 1:3 (March 1970): 41–49.

Hernández Ramírez, Rafael. "El trabajo en los alienados desde el punto de vista económica-social," *Boletín del Asilo de Alienados en Oliva* 3:8 (June 1935): 129–37.

Ingenieros, José. "El primer hospital de Buenos Aires y sus primeros locos," *Semana médica* (1920): 376–82.
———. "Los asilos para alienados en la Argentina," *Revista de criminología, psiquiatría y medicina legal* 7 (1920): 129–56.
———. "La alienación mental y los errores judiciales," *Archivos de psiquiatría y criminología* 6 (July–August 1907): 418–30.
———. *Simulación de la locura* (Buenos Aires: Elmer Ediciones, 1956) (originally published in 1903).
———. *Rehabilitación de alienados.* Buenos Aires: Editor Etchepareborda, 1904.
———. "La alienación mental y los errores judiciales," *Revista frenopática española* 6 (1908): 174–85.
"Instituto Nacional de Salud Mental (Argentina): Habilitación de pabellones psiquiátricos en Punilla, Córdoba," *Acta psiquiátrica y psicológica de américa latina* 14:2 (1968): 75–79.
"Instituto Nacional de Salud Mental," *Acta psiquiátrica y psicológica de américa latina* 14 (1968): 289.
Jimenez Asúa, Luís. "Ley de vagos y maleantes. Un ensayo legislativo sobre peligrosidad sin delito," *Revista de criminología, psiquiatría y medicina legal* 20:120 (November–December 1933): 567–615.
"Juicio de insania-apercibimiento de un asesor," *Revista de criminología, psiquiatría y medicina legal* 1:4 (July–August 1914): 458–61.
Kertesz, Roberto, Edgardo P. Gili, Ronaldo Ucha Udabe, and Mauricio Knobel. "El equipo psiquiátrico en los hospitales generales en Argentina," *La prensa médica argentina* 55:43–44 (1968): 2093–2099.
Lafora, Gonzalo. "Sobre la educación de los niños deficientes mentales," *Revista de criminología, psiquiatría y medicina legal* 14 (1927): 554–62.
Lambruschini, Carlos. "Ficha psiquiátrica, psicotécnica y antropológico-criminal del inmigrante," *Revista argentina de neurología y psiquiatría* 3:3–4 (December 1938): 329–36.
"Los alienados delincuentes y la defensa social: Sentencia del Dr. Tomas de Veiga (de Buenos Aires)," *Archivos de psiquiatría, criminología y ciencias afines* 8 (November–December 1909): 671–79.
Loudet, Osvaldo. "Los prejuicios en psiquiatría: Algunas reflexiones sobre la locura," *Revista de psiquiatría y criminología* 14:72 (July–September 1949): 177–93.
———. "Sobre el tratamiento de los llamados delincuentes alienados y alienados delincuentes," *Revista de criminología, psiquiatría y medicina legal* 20:118 (July–August 1933): 419–24.
———. "La locura evitable," *Revista de criminología, psiquiatría y medicina legal* 21:124 (July–August 1934): 484–86.
———. Review of Julio Endara, "Tratamiento de la esquizofrenia" (Jornadas Neuropsiquiátricas Panamericanas). Lima. 1939. *Revista de psiquiatría y criminología* 5 (1940): 149–50.
Lucero, Amador. "Melancolía e incapacidad civil," *Archivos de psiquiatría, criminología y ciencias afines* 9 (March–April 1910): 180–83.
Lucio Meléndez, and Emilio Coni. "Estudio estadístico sobre la locura en Buenos Aires," *Revista médico-quirúrgica* 16 (1879).
Montarcé Lastra, Antonio. *La incapacidad civil de los alienados.* Buenos Aires: Librería y Editorial 'La Facultad,' 1928.
Morixe, Francisco, and Augusto Bunge. "Incapacidad civil por alienación mental," *Revista de psiquiatría, criminología y medicina legal* 2:10 (July–August 1915): 392–419.

Moyano, Rodolfo, and Manuel M. Cabeza. "Síntesis de las actividades desarrolladas durante el año 1940, en el Asilo Colonia Regional Mixto de Alienados en Oliva (Prov. de Córdoba)," *Boletín del Asilo de Alienados en Oliva* 9:36 (March–April 1941): 53–92.

Ocampo Oromi, Raúl. "Inspección sanitaria neuropsiquiátrica en los puertos," *Boletín del Asilo de Alienados en Oliva* 10:42–43 (May–December 1942): 174–76.

Oro Raffinetti, Pedro I. "Locura comunicada familiar," (Thesis) Buenos Aires: La Semana Médica Imprenta de Obras de E. Spinelli, 1909.

Palcos, A. Alberto. "Educación de los anormales," *Revista de criminología, psiquiatría y medicina legal* 2:9 (May–June 1915): 328–40.

Piñero, Hector M. "El suicidio en la ciudad de Buenos Aires," *Revista de psiquiatría y criminología* 4:21 (May–June 1939): 393–404.

———. "Consideraciones sobre 'psicosis comunicada familiar,'" *Boletín del Asilo de Alienados en Oliva* 4:12 (June 1936): 95–100.

Quirós, C.D. "Consecuencias individuales, familiares y sociales del alcoholismo," *Archivos de psiquiatría, criminología y ciencias afines* 2:2 (February 1903): 108–17.

"Registro de incapaces," *Revista de psiquiatría y criminología* 1:4 (July–August 1936): 345–49.

Rodríguez, Fermín. "Estudios sobre el suicidio en Buenos Aires – influencia de la edad y sexo," *Archivos de psiquiatría, criminología y ciencias afines* 3 (January–February 1904): 1–21.

———. "Influencias del estado civil sobre el suicidio en Buenos Aires," *Archivos de psiquiatría, criminología y ciencias afines* 4 (1905): 385–404.

———. "Influencia del alcoholismo sobre el suicidio en Buenos Aires," *Archivos de psiquiatría, criminología y ciencias afines* 4 (1905): 531–47.

Rojas, Nerio. *Medicina legal* (Séptima edición). Buenos Aires: Editorial 'El Ateneo,' 1959.

———. "Capacidad de los débiles de espíritu," *Revista de criminología, psiquiatría y medicina legal* 14 (1927): 322–35.

———. "Definición medico-legal del alienado," *Revista de criminología, psiquiatría y medicina legal* 14 (1927): 545–53.

———. "Homicidio cometido por dos alienados," *Revista de criminología, psiquiatría y medicina legal* 1:4 (July–August 1914): 385–93.

———. "La alienación mental como causa de divorcio," *Revista de criminología, psiquiatría y medicina legal* 11 (1924): 129–38.

———. "La encrucijada actual de la psiquiatría," *Revista de criminología, psiquiatría y medicina legal* 19:113 (September–October 1932): 562–71.

———. "Limites entre el delincuente 'nato' y el 'loco,'" *Revista de psiquiatría y criminología* 2:9 (May–June 1937): 263–74.

Roxo, Enrique. "Terapeútica moderna en enfermedades mentales," *Revista de criminología, psiquiatría y medicina legal* 19:114 (November–December 1932): 681–98.

———. "Régimen alimenticio en el tratamiento de afecciones mentales," *Revista de psiquiatría y criminología* 3:13 (January–February 1938): 11–20.

Saforcada, Enrique. "Aspectos generales de planeamiento y asistencia en salud mental," *Acta psiquiátrica y psicológica de américa latina* 22 (1976): 195–204.

Sappia, Jerónimo. "El problema asistencial de los alienados en la Provincia de Córdoba," *Boletín del Asilo de Alienados en Oliva* 10:42–43 (May–December 1942): 160–66.

Sarmiento, Domingo F. "La embriaguez y la locura. Lectura en una reunión de médicos en su casa" (Julio 29, 1884); <http://www.argiropolis.com.ar/ameghino/documentos/locura.htm>), as cited in *Obras de D.F. Sarmiento* (1899).

Sbarbi, M.A. "La escuela de visitadores y visitadoras de higiene mental," *Index de neurología y psiquiatría* 1 (1938): 5–6.

———. "Reseña historica del Hospicio de las Mercedes," *Acta neuropsiquiátrica Argentina* 6 (1960): 420–23.

"Servicio de Observación de Alienados," *Archivo de criminología, psiquiatría y ciencias afines* 9 (March–April 1910): 254–56.

Sierra, Adolfo M. "Problemas médicos actuales sobre tratamiento, profilaxis y eugénesis mentales," *Revista de neurología, psiquiatría y medicina legal* 4:19 (January–February 1930): 1–39.

Silva, Ramón B., and Hector M. Piñero. "Lactoterapia en los estados de agitación," *Revista de psiquiatría, criminología y medicina legal* 19:109 (January–February 1932): 24–31.

Vega, José M.L. "Alienación y delito," *Revista de policía y criminalística* 9:42–45 (January–December 1946): 48–52.

Vervaeck, Luís. "La ley de defensa social del 9 de abril de 1930, encarada desde el punto de vista psiquiátrico," *Revista de criminología, psiquiatría y medicina legal* 20:116 (March–April 1933): 97–116.

Vidal, Guillermo. "Mauricio Goldenberg," *Acta psiquiátrica y psicológica de américa latina* 17:6 (December 1971): 422.

———, and Hugo M. Dopaso. "Proposiciones para una mejor asistencia psiquiátrica nacional," *Acta psiquiátrica y psicológica argentina* 2:8 (1962): 215–16.

———, and Jorge Fukelman. "El psiquiatra en la sala de clínica médica," *Acta psiquiátrica y psicológica argentina* 8:322 (1962): n.p.

Vidal Abal, Emilio. "Algo sobre presupuestos para establecimientos de asistencia de enfermos mentales," *Boletín del Asilo de Alienados en Oliva* 9:36 (March–April 1941): 93–101.

———. "Algunas cifras de la estadística del Asilo de Oliva: Consideraciones resultadas de la observación durante 25 años," *Boletín del Asilo de Alienados en Oliva* 7:26 (June–August 1939): 264–83.

———. "Conceptos básicos para la selección del personal," *Boletín del Asilo de Alienados en Oliva* 4:12 (June 1936): 124–33.

———. "Consideraciones sobre profilaxis mental a propósito del tema praxiterapia," *Boletín del Asilo de Alienados en Oliva* 5:16 (June 1937): 119–30.

———. "El Asilo de Oliva al traves de 25 años," *Boletín del Asilo de Alienados en Oliva* 7:26 (June–August 1939): 243–63.

———. "Sintesis de las actividades desarrolladas durante el año 1934, en el orden técnico y administrativo, en el Asilo Colonia Regional Mixto de Alienados en Oliva," *Boletín del Asilo de Alienados en Oliva* 3:7 (March 1935): 5–26.

———. "Sintesis de las actividades desarrolladas en el Asilo de Oliva durante el año 1938," *Boletín del Asilo de Alienados en Oliva* 23 (1939): 5–16.

———. "Sintesis de las actividades desarrolladas en el Asilo de Oliva durante el año 1939," *Boletín del Asilo de Alienados en Oliva* 8:29 (1940): 5–16.

———. "Sobre asistencia del alienado," *Boletín del Asilo de Alienados en Oliva* 3:8 (June 1935): 89–105.

Vucetich, Juan. "Diez años de suicidios en Buenos Aires," *Archivos de psiquiatría, criminología y ciencias afines* (1903): 537–41.

Other Primary Sources

Álbum histórico de la Sociedad de Beneficencia, 1823–1910 (Buenos Aires: n.p., n.d.).
Borchard, Edwin M. *Library of Congress Guide to the Law and Legal Literature of Argentina, Brazil and Chile.* Washington: Government Printing Office, 1917.
Carta abierta a la sociedad: Un grito a través de los muros del hospicio. Buenos Aires: Axis, 1974.
Chichilnisky, Salomón. "Historia de la psiquiatría argentina." Buenos Aires: n.p., 1967–69.
Clemenceau, Georges. *South America Today: A Study of Conditions, Social, Political and Comercial in Argentina, Uruguay and Brazil.* New York: Putnam, 1911.
Código civil de la República Argentina y legislación complementaria. Buenos Aires: Abeledo-Perrot, 1976.
Courtis, Christián. "La locura no da derechos," *Desbordar: Taller de periodismo-frente Artistas del Borda* 3:41–43 (October 1991): 42.
Desbordar: Taller de periodismo-frente Artistas del Borda 1 (November 1990).
Gache, Samuel. *El estado mental en la sociedad de Buenos Aires.* Buenos Aires: La Nación, 1881.
Gimenez, Ángel M. *Por la salud física y mental del pueblo.* Buenos Aires: Sociedad Luz, 1932.
———. *Un debate histórico: La reforma eclesiástica de Rivadavia - la monja Vicenta Álvarez* (Buenos Aires: Imprenta Federación Gráfica Bonaerense, 1932).
Grimson, W.R., ed. *Nuevas perspectivas en salud mental. Instituciones y problemas.* Buenos Aires: Ediciones Nueva Visión, 1973.
Grimson, Wilbur R. *Sociedad de locos: Experiencia y violencia en un hospital psiquiátrico* (Buenos Aires: Ediciones Nueva Visión, 1972).
Herscovici, Pedro. "La salud mental necesita algo más que la asistencia clásica," *El observador* (May 25, 1984): 31.
Lupati Guelfi, Cesarina. *Vida argentina.* Barcelona: Casa Editorial Maucci, 1910.
"Melchor Romero (II) la rebelión de los locos," *Ciencia nueva* no. 19 n.d.
Meyer Arana, Alberto. *La caridad en Buenos Aires.* Buenos Aires: n.p., 1911.
Moffatt, Alfredo. *Psicoterapia del oprimido: Ideología y técnica de la psiquiatría popular.* Buenos Aires: ECRO, 1974.
Organization of American States, *America en Cifras, 1960.* Washington, D.C.: Organization of American States, 1961.
———. *America en Cifras, 1974.* Washington, D.C.: Organization of American States, 1975.
Origen y desenvolvimiento de la Sociedad de Beneficencia de la Capital, 1823–1912 (Buenos Aires: M. Rodríguez Giles, 1913).
Parker, William Belmont. *Argentines of Today.* Buenos Aires: The Hispanic Society of America, 1920.
Podestá, Manuel T. *Irresponable.* Buenos Aires: Imprenta de la Tribunal, 1889.
"The Salubrity of Buenos Ayres," *Monthly Bulletin of the International Bureau of the American Republics* 157: 23:4 (October 1906): 836–37.
Sociedad de Beneficencia, *Hospital Nacional de Alienadas: Antecedentes y medidas adoptadas para solucionar el hacinamiento de enfermas* (Buenos Aires: Talleres Gráficos del Asilo de Huérfanos, 1923).
———. *Reglamento del Hospital Nacional de Alienadas* (Buenos Aires, 1909).
Soiza Reilly, Juan José. *Los mejores reportajes de Juan José Soiza Reilly.* Buenos Aires: Editorial Bayardo, 1921.
———. *La escuela de los pillos.* Buenos Aires: Vicente Matera, 1920.
———. *La ciudad de los locos (aventuras de Tartarín Moreira).* Barcelona: Casa Editorial Maucci, 1914.

Subcomisión de Salud Mental, Casa Argentina en México. "¿Salud mental en la Argentina de hoy?" *Cuadernos americanos* 36:214:5 (September–October 1977): 36-46.
U.S. Department of Comerse, *Patients in Hospitals for Mental Disease, 1933*. Washington, D.C.: United States Government Printing Office, 1935.
Zito Lema, Vicente. *Conversaciones con Enrique Pichón-Riviere sobre el arte y la locura.* Buenos Aires: Ediciones Cinco, 1997.
———. "El hospicio: Testimonios y lenguaje de los oprimidos," *Crisis* 11 (March 1974): 3–25.

Secondary Sources

Ablard, Jonathan D. "Law, Medicine and Confinement to Psychiatric Hospitals in Twentieth Century Argentina," in Mariano Ben Plotkin, ed., 87–112. *Argentina on the Couch: Psychiatry, State, and Society, 1880 to the Present.* Albuquerque: University of New Mexico Press, 2003.
———. "The Limits of Psychiatric Reform in Argentina, 1890–1945," in Roy Porter and David Wright, eds., 226–47. *The Confinement of the Insane: International Perspectives, 1800–1965.* Cambridge: Cambridge University Press, 2003.
———. "Authoritarianism, Democracy and Psychiatric Reform in Argentina, 1943–83," *History of Psychiatry* 14:3 (2003): 361–76.
———. "¿Dónde está el delirio? La autoridad psiquiátrica y el estado argentino en perspectiva histórica," in Maria Silvia Di Liscia and Ernesto Bohoslavsky, eds., 199–216. *Instituciones y formas de control social en América Latina, 1840–1940: Una revisión.* Buenos Aires: Prometeo Libros, 2005.
———. "Military Conscription in Argentina" Presented to the Latin American Studies Program, Cornell University (September 13, 2005).
Agüeros, Nélida, and Yolanda Eraso. "Tratamiento en libertad a comienzos del siglo XX: Los asilos colonias de Puertas Abiertas en la Argentina," (unpublished paper, March 21, 1995).
Alarcón, Renato D. *Identidad de la psiquiatría latinoamericana: Voces y exploraciones en torno a una ciencia solidaria.* México: Siglo Veintiuno Editores, 1990.
Alhadeff, Peter. "Social Welfare and the Slump: Argentina in the 1930s," in D.C.M. Platt, ed., 169–78. *Social Welfare, 1850–1950: Australia, Argentina and Canada Compared* London: Macmillan Press, 1989.
Álvarez, Adriana. "Ramos Mejía: Salud pública y multitud en la Argentina finisecular," in Mirta Zaida Lobato, ed., 57–92. *Política, médicos y enfermedades: Lecturas de historia de la salud en la Argentina* Buenos Aires: Editorial Biblos, 1996.
Alzugaray, Rodolfo F. "Ramón Carrillo o la salud pública," *Todo es Historia* 117 (February 1977): 7–27.
Andrews, George Reid. *The Afro-Argentines of Buenos Aires, 1800–1900.* Madison: University of Wisconsin Press, 1980.
Argandoña, Mario and Ari Kiev. *Mental Health in the Developing World: A Case Study in Latin America.* New York: The Free Press, 1972.
Balbo, Eduardo A. "El Hospital Neuropsiquiátrico 'Melchor Romero' durante los años 1884–1918," in José Luís Peset, ed., 53–75. *Ciencia, vida y espacio en Ibero-América.* Madrid: Consejo Superior de Investigaciones Científicas, 1989.
———. "El Manicomio en el alienismo argentino," *Asclepio* 40:2 (1988): 51–62.
———. "Argentinian alienism from 1852–1918," *History of Psychiatry* 2:6, Part 2 (June 1991): 181–92.
Barrancos, Dora. "Problematic Modernity: Gender, Sexuality, and Reproduction in Twentieth-century Argentina," *Journal of Women's History* 18:2 (2006): 123–50.

Barrenche, Osvaldo. *Crime and the Administration of Justice in Buenos Aires, 1785–1853.* Lincoln: University of Nebraska Press, 2006.

Bassa, Daniela. "Insania y justicia en el territorio nacional de la Pampa argentina," *Frenia* 3:1 (2003): 31–66.

Belmartino, Susana, and Carlos Bloch. *El sector salud en Argentina: Actores, conflictos de intereses y modelos organizativos, 1960–1985.* Buenos Aires: Representación OPS/OMS Argentina, 1994.

Birocco, Carlos María. "La primera Casa de Recogimiento de Huérfanas de Buenos Aires: El beaterio de Pedro de Vera y Aragón (1692–1702)," in José Luís Moreno, ed., 21–46. *La política social antes de la política social (Caridad, beneficencia y política social en Buenos Aires, siglos XVII a XX).* Buenos Aires: Trama Editorial/Prometeo Libros, 2000.

Blackwelder, Julia Kirk. "Urbanization, Crime, and Policing: Buenos Aires, 1880–1914," in Lyman L. Johnson, ed., 65–88. *The Problem of Order in Changing Societies: Essays on Crime and Policing in Argentina and Uruguay, 1750–1940.* Albuquerque: University of New Mexico Press, 1990.

Blum, Alan F. "The Sociology of Mental Illness," in J. Douglas, ed., 31-60. *Deviance and Respectability.* New York: Basic Books, 1970.

Borges, Dain. "'Puffy, Ugly, Slothful and Inert': Degeneration in Brazilian Social Thought," *Journal of Latin American Studies* 25 (1993): 235–56.

Braslow, Joel. *Mental Illness and Bodily Cures: Psychiatric Treatment in the First Half of the Twentieth Century.* Berkeley: University of California Press, 1997.

———. "Therapeutics and the History of Psychiatry," *Bulletin for the History of Medicine* 74 (2000): 794–802.

Brown, Jonathan C. "The Bondage of Old Habits in Nineteenth-Century Argentina," *Latin American Research Review* 21:2 (1986): 3–31.

Burnham, John C. "A Clinical Alternative to the Public Health Approach to Mental Illness: A forgotten social experiment," *Perspectives in Biology and Medicine* 49:2 (Spring 2006): 220–37.

Bushnell, David. *Reform and Reaction in the Platine Provinces, 1810–1852.* Gainesville: University of Florida Press, 1983.

Camus Gayán, Pablo. "Filantropía, medicina y locura: La Casa de Orates de Santiago, 1852–1894," 27 *Historia* (1993): 89–140.

Carpintero, Enrique, and Alejandro Vainer. *Las huellas de la memoria: Psicoanálisis y salud mental en la Argentina de los '60 y '70 (1957–1983): Tomo I (1957–1959).* Buenos Aires: Topia Editorial, 2004.

Castro, Donald S. "Lunfardo, the Language of the Disenfranchised as a Source of Argentine Social History," *Proceedings of the Pacific Coast Council of Latin American Studies* 14:2 (Fall 1987): 105–16.

Centeno, Miguel Angel. *Blood and Debt: War and the Nation-State in Latin America.* University Park: Pennsylvania State University Press, 2002.

Ciafardo, Eduardo O. "Las damas de beneficencia y la participación social de la mujer en la Ciudad de Buenos Aires, 1880–1930," *Anuario del IEHS* (1990): 161–70.

———, and Daniel Espesir. "Patología de la acción política anarquista. Criminólogos, psiquiatras y conflicto social en Argentina, 1890–1910," *Siglo XIX, nueva época* 12 (July–December 1992): 23–40.

Cohen, Stanley, and Andrew Scull. "Introduction: Social Control in History and Sociology," in Stanley Cohen and Andrew Scull, eds. *Social Control and the State: Historical and Comparative Essays.* Oxford: St. Martin's, 1990.

Conklin, Margaret, and Daphne Davidson. "The I.M.F. and Economic and Social Human Rights: A Case Study of Argentina, 1958–1985," *Human Rights Quarterly* 8:2 (1986): 227–69.

Comelles, Josep M. "De médicos de locos a médicos de cuerdos. La transición del manicomio al gabinete en la psiquiatría de anteguerra (1890–1939)," *Asclepios* 1 (1992): 347–68.
Crider, Ernest Allen. "Modernization and Human Welfare: The *Asistencia Pública* and Buenos Aires, 1883–1910." Ph.D. diss., Ohio State University, 1976.
D'Antonio, Michael. *The State Boys Rebellion: The Inspiring True Store of American Eugenics and the Men Who Overcame It.* New York: Simon and Schuster, 2004.
De la Fuente, Ariel. *Children of Facundo: Caudillo and Gaucho Insurgency during the Argentine State-Formation Process (La Rioja, 1853–1870).* Durham, NC: Duke University Press, 2000.
Delaney, Jeane. "Making Sense of Modernity: Changing Attitudes toward the Immigrant and the Gaucho in Turn-of-the-Century Argentina," *Comparative Studies in Society and History* 38:3 (July 1996): 434–59.
Di Liscia, María Herminia B., and José Maristany. *Mujeres y estado en la Argentina: Educación, salud y beneficiencia.* Buenos Aires: Editorial Biblos, 1997.
Dowbiggin, Ian Robert. *Keeping America Sane: Psychiatry and Eugenics in the United States and Canada, 1880–1940.* Ithaca, NY: Cornell University Press, 1997.
———. *Inheriting Madness: Professionalization and Psychiatric Knowledge in Nineteenth Century France.* Los Angeles: University of California Press, 1991.
———. "French Psychiatric Attitudes towards the Dangers Posed by the Insane, ca. 1870," in Steven Spitzer and Andrew T. Scull, eds. *Research in Law, Deviance and Social Control* 9. Greenwich, CT: JAI Press, 1988.
Dwyer, Ellen. *Homes for the Mad: Life inside Two Nineteenth-Century Asylums.* New Brunswick, NJ: Rutgers University Press, 1983.
Echenberg, Myron. *Plague Ports: The Global Urban Impact of Bubonic Plague, 1894–1901.* New York: New York University Press, 2007.
Elena, Eduardo. "What the People Want: State Planning and Political Participation in Peronist Argentina, 1946–1955," *Journal of Latin American Studies* 37 (2005): 81–108.
Escudero, José Carlos. "The Health Crisis in Argentina," *International Journal of Health Services* 33:1 (2003): 129–36.
Faberman, Judith. "La fama de la hechicera: La buena reputación femenina en un proceso criminal del siglo XVIII," in Fernanda Gil Lozano, Valeria Silvina Pita, and María Gabriela Ini, eds., 26–47. *Historia de las mujeres en la Argentina: Colonia y siglo XIX.* Buenos Aires: Taurus, 2000.
Facio, Sara, Alicia D'Amico, and Julio Cortázar. *Humanario.* Buenos Aires: La Azotea, 1976.
Fernández-Bravo, Álvaro. "Ambivalent Argentina: Nationalism, Exoticism, and Latin Americanism at the 1889 Paris Universal Exposition," *Nepantla: Views from South* 2:1 (2001): 115–39.
Ferns, H.S., Ezequiel Gallo, and Melville Watkins. "The Prairies and the Pampas: A Review Colloquium," *Business History Review* 67 (Summer 1993): 279–99.
Fey, Ingrid E. "Peddling the Pampas: Argentina at the Paris Universal Exposition of 1889," in William H. Beezley and Linda A. Curcio-Nagy, eds., 61–85. *Latin American Popular Culture: An Introduction.* Wilmington: SR Books, 2000.
Fijman, Jacobo. *Obra Poética.* Buenos Aires: La Torre Abolida, 1983.
Fink, Paul Jay, and Allan Tasman, eds. *Stigma and Mental Illness.* Washington: American Psychiatric Press, 1992.
Fogarty, John. "Social Experiments in Regions of Recent Settlement: Australia, Argentina and Canada," in D.C.M. Platt, ed., 179–99. *Social Welfare, 1850–1950: Australia, Argentina and Canada Compared.* London: Macmillan, 1989.
Foucault, Michel. *Discipline and Punish: The Birth of the Prison.* New York: Pantheon, 1977.

———. *Madness and Civilization: A History of Insanity in the Age of Reason.* New York: Vintage, 1988.
———. "About the Concept of the 'Dangerous Individual' in 19th Century Legal Psychiatry," *International Journal of Law and Psychiatry* 1 (1978): 1–18.
Fox, Richard W. *'So far disordered in mind:' Insanity in California, 1870–1930.* Los Angeles: University of California Press, 1978.
Frankenburg, Frances R., M.D. "History of the Development of Antipsychotic Medication," *History of Psychiatry* 17:3 (September 1994): 531–39.
Fraser, Nicholas, and Marysa Navarro. *Eva Perón.* New York: Norton, 1980.
Galende, Emiliano. "Modernidad y modelos de asistencia en salud mental en Argentina," in *Segundas jornadas de atención primaria de la salud* (April 3–May 7, 1988).
Gallardo, Guillermo. *La política religiosa de Rivadavia.* Buenos Aires: Ediciones Theoria, 1962.
Gayol, Sandra V. "Ebrios y divertidos: La estrategia del alcohol en Buenos Aires, 1860–1900," *Siglo XIX, nueva época* 13 (January–June 1993): 55–80.
Gentile, Antonio. "La psiquiatría en Rosario," *Temas en la historia de la psiquiatría argentina* (Winter 1998).
Gervasio Paz, Juan, and Emiliano Galende. *Psiquiatría y sociedad.* Buenos Aires: Granica, 1975.
Girón, Álvaro. "Los anarquistas españoles y la criminología de Cesare Lombroso," *Frenia* 2:2 (2002): 81–108.
Goffman, Erving. *Asylums: Essays on the Social Situation of Mental Patients and Other Inmates.* New York: Anchor, 1961.
Goldstein, Jan. "The Wandering Jew and the Problem of Psychiatric Anti-semitism in Fin-de-Siecle France," *Journal of Contemporary History* 20 (1985): 521–52.
Goldwert, Marvin. *Democracy, Militarism, and Nationalism in Argentina, 1930–1966: An Interpretation.* Austin: University of Texas Press, 1972.
Gonnet, María Luisa. "Una experiencia de aquí y antes: Colonia de Rehabilitación de Federal, Entre Ríos (1967–76)," *Riachuelo.* Buenos Aires: n.d., n.p.
González Leandri, Ricardo. "La profesión médica en Buenos Aires, 1852–1870," in Mirta Zaida Lobato, ed., 21–56. *Política, médicos y enfermedades: Lecturas de historia de la salud en la Argentina.* Buenos Aires: Editorial Biblos, 1996.
———. "Medicos, damas y funcionarios: Acuerdos y tensiones en la creación de la Asistencia Pública de la Ciudad de Buenos Aires," in José Luís Peset, ed., 77–93. *Ciencia, vida y espacio en Ibero-América.* Madrid: Consejo Superior de Investigaciones Científicas, 1989.
Goodwin, Simon. *Comparative Mental Health Policy: From Institutional to Community Care.* London: Sage, 1997.
Gordon, Linda. "Feminism and Social Control: The Case of Child Abuse and Neglect," in Juliet Mitchell and Ann Oakley, eds., 63–84. *What is Feminism?* London: Basil Blackwell, 1986.
Grob, Gerald. *Mental Illness and American Society, 1875–1940.* Princeton: Princeton University Press, 1983.
———. "Mad, Homeless, and Unwanted – A History of the Care of the Chronically Mentally Ill in America," *Psychiatric Clinics of North America* 17:3 (September 1994): 541–58.
———. "Psychiatry's Holy Grail: The Search for the Mechanisms of Mental Diseases," *Bulletin for the History of Medicine* 72 (1998): 189–219.
Gualdo, Jorge N., and Alberto S.J. de Paula. *Temperley: Su historia, su gente.* Buenos Aires: Editorial Pleamar, 1988.
Guedes Arroyo, Luis César. *El tratamiento moral: Experiencia Roballos – comunidad terapéutica.* Buenos Aires: Vinciguerra, 2005.

Guerrino, Antonio Alberto. *La psiquiatría argentina.* Buenos Aires: Editores Cuatro, 1982.
Guy, Donna. *Sex and Danger in Buenos Aires: Prostitution, Family, and Nation in Argentina.* Lincoln: University of Nebraska Press, 1991.
———. "La 'verdadera historia' de la Sociedad de Beneficencia," in José Luís Moreno, ed., 321–41. *La política social antes de la política social (Caridad, beneficencia y política social en Buenos Aires, siglos XVII a XX).* Buenos Aires: Trama editorial/ Prometeo libros, 2000.
———. "Parents before the Tribunals: The Legal Construction of Patriarchy in Argentina," in Elizabeth Dore and Maxine Molyneux, eds., 172–93. *Hidden Histories of Gender and the State in Latin America.* Durham, NC: Duke University Press, 2000.
———. "White Slavery, Public Health, and the Socialist Position on Legalized Prostitution in Argentina, 1913–1936," *Latin American Research Review* 23:3 (1988): 60–80.
———. "Lower-Class Families, Women, and the Law in Nineteenth-Century Argentina," *Journal of Family History* 10:3 (Fall 1985): 318–31.
Harris, Jonathan. "Bernardino Rivadavia: Benthamite 'Discipleship,'" *Latin American Research Review* 33:1 (1998): 129–49.
Holbo, Paul S. "José Ingenieros, Argentine Intellectual Historian: *La evolución de las ideas argentinas,*" *The Americas* 21:1 (July 1964): 20–35.
Hollander, Nancy Caro. "Psychoanalysis and State Terror in Argentina," *American Journal of Psychoanalysis* 52:1 (1992): 273–89.
———. "Psychoanalysis Confronts the Politics of Repression: The Case of Argentina," *Social Science and Medicine* 28:7 (1989): 751–58.
Horowitz, Joel. "Bosses and Clients: Municipal Employment in the Buenos Aires of the Radicals, 1916–30," *Journal of Latin American Studies* 3 (1999): 617–44.
———. *Argentine Unions, the State and the Rise of Perón, 1930–1945.* Berkeley: Institute of International Studies, 1990.
Hospital Interzonal Psiquiátrico 'Colonia Dr. Domingo Cabred': Centenario de la fundación. Open Door-Luján, Provincia de Buenos Aires, n.p., 1999.
Hospital Psiquiátrico Braulio A. Moyano: 140 aniversario, 1854–1994. Buenos Aires: n.p., 1994.
Huertas García-Alejo, Rafael. "La aportación de la escuela argentina al concepto de criminal nato," in José Luís Peset, ed., 95–113. *Ciencia, vida y espacio en Ibero-América* (Madrid: Consejo Superior de Investigaciones Científicas, 1989).
———. *El delincuente y su patología. Medicina, crimen y sociedad en el positivismo argentino* (Seville, Spain: Consejo Superior de Investigaciones Cientificas, 1991).
Iacoponi, Lucia. "Permisividad, abuso y desprotección," in *Centenario de la fundación: Hospital Interzonal Psiquiátrico 'Colonia Dr. Domingo Cabred'* (May 1999): 70–77.
———. "El Hospital Interzonal Colonia Dr. D. Cabred y el metódo Open Door," in *Centenario de la Fundación: Hospital Interzonal Psiquiátrico 'Colonia Dr. Domingo Cabred'* (May 1999): 59–69.
Ingenieros, José. *La locura en la Argentina.* Buenos Aires: Cooperativa Editorial Limitada, 1920.
"Investigación especial: En estos lugares vive el horror," *Gente* (November 18, 1982): n.p.
Ivereigh, Austen. *Catholicism and Politics in Argentina, 1810–1960.* London: St. Martin's, 1995.
Katz, Jorge M. *El sector salud en la República Argentina: Su estructura y comportamiento.* Mexico: Fondo de Cultura Económica, 1993.
Knecher, Lidia, and Marta Panaia, eds. *La mitad del país: La mujer en la sociedad argentina.* Buenos Aires: Centro Editor de América Látina, 1994.
Knobel, Mauricio. "The Rights of the Mentally Ill: Towards a Review of the Concept of Psychiatry and the Psychiatrist," *Mental Health Sociology* 1 (1974): 228–45.

Kushner, Howard I. "Suicide, Gender and the Fear of Modernity in Nineteenth-century Medical and Social Thought," *Journal of Social History* 26:3 (Spring 1993): 450–70.

Lakoff, Andrew. *Pharmaceutical Reason: Knowledge and Value in Global Psychiatry*. New York: Cambridge University Press, 2005.

Lanning, John Tate. *The Royal Protomedicato: The Regulation of the Medical Professions in the Spanish Empire*. Durham, NC: Duke University Press, 1985.

Lavrín, Asunción. *Women, Feminism, and Social Change in Argentina, Chile, and Uruguay, 1890–1940*. Lincoln: University of Nebraska Press, 1995.

Lewis, Paul. *The Crisis of Argentine Capitalism*. Chapel Hill: University of North Carolina Press, 1990.

Lloyd-Sherlock, Peter. "Healthcare Financing, Reform and Equity in Argentina: Past and Present," in Peter Lloyd-Sherlock, ed., 143–62. *Healthcare Reform and Poverty in Latin America*. London: Institute of Latin American Studies, 2000.

Lomax, Elizabeth. "Infantile Syphilis as an Example of Nineteenth Century Belief in the Inheritance of Acquired Characteristics," *Journal of the History of Medicine* (January 1979): 23–39.

López-Alves, Fernando. *State Formation and Democracy in Latin America, 1810–1900*. Durham, NC: Duke University Press 2000.

Lorenzo, María Fernanda, Ana Lía Rey, and Cecilia Tossounian. "Images of Virtuous Women: Morality, Gender and Power in Argentina between the World Wars," *Gender and History* 17:3 (2005): 567–92.

Loudet, Osvaldo, and Osvaldo Elías Loudet. *Historia de la psiquiatría argentina*. Buenos Aires: Troquel, 1971.

Lunbeck, Elizabeth. *The Psychiatric Persuasion: Knowledge, Gender, and Power in Modern America*. Princeton: Princeton University Press, 1994.

Lynch, John. "From Independence to National Organization," in Leslie Bethell, ed., 1–46. *Argentina since Independence*. New York: Cambridge University Press, 1993.

———. *Argentine Dictator: Juan Manuel de Rosas, 1829–1852* (Oxford: Clarendon Press, 1981)

Magrini, Liliana, and Mario Ganora. "Informe sobre violaciones graves de los derechos humanos (Tratos y Penas Crueles Inhumanas y Degradantes) a preso y minusválidos psíquicos en los establecimientos psiquiátricos 'Colonia Nacional de Montes de Oca' y Hospital Neuropsiquiatrico Domingo Cabred." Equipo Nizkor, <http: www.derechos.or/nizkor/arg/doc/psiquiatrico/>.

Malamud, Moises. *Domingo Cabred*. Buenos Aires: Ministerio de Cultura y Educación, 1972.

Manzur, Jorge. *Crónica de amor, de locura y de muerte*. Buenos Aires: Editorial Sudamericana, 1986.

Marietán, Hugo. *Boletín Borda* 44:5 (1996): n.p.

Martínez Ferretti, José María. "Aportes para la legislación sobre internación de enfermos mentales," *Psiquiatría forense sexología praxis* 5 (3) 1 (July 1998): n.p.

Masiero, André Luis. "A lobotomia e a leucotomía nos manicômios brasileiros," *História, ciencias, saúde-manguinhos* 10:2 (May–August 2003): 549–72. <http://www.scielo.br/scielo>.

McCandless, Peter. *Moonlight, Magnolias, and Madness: Insanity in South Carolina from the Colonial Period to the Progressive Era*. Chapel Hill: University of North Carolina Press, 1999.

———. "Build! Build! The Controversy over the Care of the Chronically Insane in England, 1855–1870," *Bulletin for the History of Medicine* 53 (1979): 553–74.

———. "'A Female Malady?' Women at the South Carolina Lunatic Asylum, 1828–1915," *Journal of the History of Medicine and Allied Sciences* 54:4 (October 1999): 543–71.

———. "'Curses of Civilization': Insanity and Drunkenness in Victorian Britain," *British Journal of Addictions* 79 (1984): 49–58.
———. "Liberty and Lunacy: The Victorians and Wrongful Confinement," in Andrew Scull, ed., 339–62. *Madhouses, Mad-Doctors, and Madmen: The Social History of Psychiatry in the Victorian Era.* Philadelphia: University of Pennsylvania Press, 1981.
McGovern, Constance. "The Myths of Social Control and Custodial Oppression: Patterns of Psychiatric Medicine in Late Nineteenth-century Institutions," *Journal of Social History* 20 (Fall 1986): 3–23.
Mead, Karen. "Beneficent Maternalism: Argentine Motherhood in Comparative Perspective, 1880–1920," *Journal of Women's History* 12:3 (2000): 120–45.
———. "Gendering the Obstacles to Progress in Positivist Argentina, 1880–1920," *Hispanic American Historical Review* 77:4 (1997): 645–75.
———. "Oligarchs, Doctors and Nuns: Public Health and Beneficence in Buenos Aires, 1880–1914." Ph.D. diss., University of California, Santa Barbara, 1994.
Meyer, Jorge. *Orden y virtud: El discurso republicano en el régimen rosista.* Quilmes: Universidad Nacional de Quilmes, 1995.
Meyer, Luís. "Los comienzos del Hospicio de las Mercedes," *Acta psiquiátrica y psicológica de América Latina* 33 (1987): 338–39.
Micale, Mark S., and Paul Lerner, eds. *Traumatic Pasts: History, Psychiatry, and Trauma in the Modern Age, 1870–1930.* Cambridge: Cambridge University Press, 2001.
Midelfort, H.C. Erik. *A History of Madness in Sixteenth-Century Germany.* Stanford: Stanford University Press, 1999.
Migdal, Joel. *Strong Societies and Weak States: State-Society Relations and State Capabilities in the Third World.* Princeton: Princeton University Press, 1988.
Mirelman, Victor A. *Jewish Buenos Aires, 1890–1930.* Detroit: Wayne State University Press, 1990.
Moran, James E. *Committed to the State Asylum: Insanity and Society in Nineteenth-Century Quebec and Ontario.* Montreal and Kingston: McGill-Queen's University Press, 2000.
Moreno, José Luis. "La Casa de Niños Expósitos de Buenos Aires, conflictos institucionales, condiciones de vida y mortalidad de los infantes, 1779–1823," in José Luis Moreno, ed., 91–128. *La política social antes de la política social (Caridad, beneficencia y política social en Buenos Aires, siglos XVII a XX).* Buenos Aires: Trama Editorial/ Prometeo libros, 2000.
Moya, José. *Cousins and Strangers: Spanish Immigrants in Buenos Aires, 1850–1930.* Los Angeles: University of California Press, 1998.
Muzilli, Carolina. *El trabajo femenino.* Buenos Aires: L.J. Rosso, 1916.
Needell, Jeffrey D. "Optimism and Melancholy: Elite Responses to the *fin-de-siècle bonarense,*" *Journal of Latin American Studies* 32 (1999): 551–88.
Negretto, Gabriel L., and José Antonio Aguilar-Rivera. "Rethinking the Legacy of the Liberal State in Latin America: The cases of Argentina (1853–1916) and Mexico (1857–1910)," *Journal of Latin American Studies* 32 (2000): 361–97.
Nunca Más: Informe de la Comisión Nacional sobre la Desaparición de Personas (Buenos Aires: EUDEBA, 1987).
Nye, Robert. *Crime, Madness, and Politics in Modern France: The Medical Concept of National Decline.* Princeton: Princeton University Press, 1984.
Odem, Mary E. *Delinquent Daughters: Protecting and Policing Adolescent Female Sexuality in the United States, 1885–1920.* Chapel Hill: University of North Carolina Press, 1995.
Olrog, Claudia. "Antropología del hospicio," *Programa de investigaciones sobre epidemiología psiquiátrica.* Buenos Aires: CONICET, 1984.

Oppenheim, Janet. *"Shattered Nerves": Doctors, Patients, and Depression in Victorian England*. New York: Oxford University Press, 1991.

Orellana, Miguel. "Encuentros: Dialogando con el Dr. Raúl Camino," *ARJE* (Buenos Aires, n.d): 20–26.

Orozco, Andrea, and Valeria Dávila. "Mujeres alienadas en la Argentina: Una loca historia," *Todo es historia* 324 (Julio 1994): 8–19.

Pagés-Larraya, Fernando. "Spiritus merculialis-el 'loco lindo' en la antropología urbana," *Antropología psiquiátrica* 18:6 (1995): n.p.

Palma, Héctor. *'Gobernar es seleccionar:' Apuntes sobre la eugenesia* Buenos Aires: Jorge Baudino Ediciones, 2002.

Pereira, Anthony W. *Political (In)justices: Authoritarianism and the Rule of Law in Brazil, Chile, and Argentina*. Pittsburgh: University of Pittsburgh Press, 2005.

Pick, Daniel. *Faces of Degeneration: A European Disorder, c.1848–1918*. New York: Cambridge University Press, 1989.

Pita, Valeria Silvina. "Damas, locas y médicos. La locura expropiada," in Fernanda Gil Lozano, Valeria Silvina Pita, and María Gabriela Ini, eds., 273–93. *Historia de las mujeres en la Argentina: Colonia y siglo XIX*. Buenos Aires: Tauras, 2000.

Plotkin, Mariano Ben. *Freud in the Pampas: The Emergence and Development of a Psychoanalytic Culture in Argentina*. Stanford: Stanford University Press, 2001.

———. "Freud, Politics, and the Porteños: The Reception of Psychoanalysis in Buenos Aires, 1910–1943," *Hispanic American Historical Review* 77:1 (1997): 45–74.

———. *Manaña es San Perón: A Cultural History of Perón's Argentina*. Wilmington: S.R. Books, 2003.

———. "Politics of Consensus in Peronist Argentina (1943–1955)," Ph.D. diss. University of California, Berkeley, 1992.

Porter, Roy. "Madness and its institutions," in Andrew Wear, ed., 277–301. *Medicine in Society: Historical Essays*. Cambridge: Cambridge University Press, 1992.

———. *The Greatest Benefit to Mankind: A Medical History of Humanity*. New York: W.W. Norton, 1997.

———, and Mark Micale. "Reflections on Psychiatry and Its Histories," in Mark Micale and Roy Porter, eds., 3–38. *Discovering the History of Psychiatry*. New York: Oxford University Press, 1994.

Potash, Robert A. *The Army and Politics in Argentina, 1928–1945*. Stanford: Stanford University Press, 1969.

Prestwich, Patricia. "Family Strategies and Medical Power: 'Voluntary' Committal in a Parisian Asylum, 1876–1914," *Journal of Social History* (Summer 1994): 799–815.

Prieto, Agustina. "Rosario: Epidemias, hygiene e higienistas en la segunda mitad del siglo XIX," in Mirta Zaida Lobato, ed., 57–71. *Política, médicos y enfermedades: Lecturas de historia de la salud en la Argentina*. Buenos Aires: Editorial Biblos, 1996.

Puccia, Enrique Horacio. *Barracas: Su historia y sus tradiciones, 1536–1936*. Buenos Aires: n.p., 1975.

Quien es quien en la Argentina: Biografías contemporáneas 5th ed. Buenos Aires: Editorial Guillermo Kraft Limitada, n.d.

Quiroga, Horacio. *Cuentos de amor, de locura y de muerte*. Buenos Aires: Losada, 1997.

Ramacciotti, Karina Inés. "Las voces que cuestionaron la política sanitaria del peronismo *(1946–1949)*," in Daniel Lvovich and Juan Suriano, eds., 169–96. *La políticas sociales en perspectiva histórica: Argentina, 1870–1952*. Buenos Aires: Prometeo Libros, 2006.

Reaume, Geoffrey. *Remembrance of Patients Past: Patient Life at the Toronto Hospital for the Insane, 1870–1940*. Oxford: Oxford University Press, 2000.

———. "Accounts of Abuse of Patients at the Toronto Hospital for the Insane, 1883–1937," *Canadian Bulletin of Medical History/Bulletin canadien d'histoire de la médicine* 14:1 (1997): 65–106.
Recalde, Héctor. *La salud de los trabajadores en Buenos Aires (1870–1910).* Buenos Aires: Grupo Editor Universitario, n.d.
Rein, Mónica Esti. *Politics and Education in Argentina, 1946–1962.* Armonk, NY: M.E. Sharpe, 1998.
Riquelme U., Horacio. *Entre la obediencia y la oposicion: Los medicos y al ética profesional bajo la dictadura militar.* Caracas: Editorial Nueva Sociedad, 1995.
Rivera-Garza, Cristina. "Becoming Mad in Revolutionary Mexico: Mentally Ill Patients at the General Insane Asylum, Mexico, 1910–1930," in Roy Porter and David Wright, eds., 248–72. *The Confinement of the Insane: International Perspectives, 1800–1965.* Cambridge: Cambridge University Press, 2003.
———. "'Dangerous Minds': Changing Psychiatric Views of the Mentally Ill in Porfirian Mexico, 1876–1911," *Journal of the History of Medicine and Allied Sciences* 6 (2001): 36–67.
———. "'She neither Respected nor Obeyed Anyone': Inmates and Psychiatrists Debate Gender and Class at the General Insane Asylum La Castañeda, Mexico, 1910–1930," *Hispanic American Historical Review* 81:3–4 (2001): 653–88.
Rock, David. *Authoritarian Argentina: The Nationalist Movement, its History and its Impact.* Los Angeles: University of California Press, 1993.
———. *Argentina, 1516–1987: From Spanish Colonization to Alfonsín.* Berkeley: University of California Press, 1987.
———. *Politics in Argentina, 1890–1930: The Rise and Fall of Radicalism.* New York: Cambridge University Press, 1975.
Rodriguez, Julia. *Civilizing Argentina: Science, Medicine, and the Modern State.* Chapel Hill: University of North Carolina Press, 2005.
———. "South Atlantic Crossings: Fingerprints, Science, and the State in Turn-of-the-Century Argentina," *American Historical Review* 109:2 (2004): 387–416.
———. "The Argentine Hysteric: A Turn-of-the-Century Psychiatric Type," in Mariano Plotkin, ed., 25–47. *Argentina on the Couch: Psychiatry, State, and Society, 1880 to the Present.* Albuquerque: University of New Mexico Press, 2003.
Romero, Luis Alberto. *A History of Argentina in the Twentieth Century.* University Park, PA: Penn State University Press, 2002.
Roselli, Humberto. "Aspectos medico-psiquiátricos de inquisición en Cartagena de Indias," *Acta psiquiátrica y psicológica de américa latina* 15:3 (September 1968): 252–61.
Rosenhahn, D. "On Being Sane in Insane Places," *Science* 179 (1973): 250–58.
Rothman, David J. *Conscience and Convenience: The Asylum and its Alternatives in Progressive America.* Boston: Little, Brown and Co., 1980.
Ruggiero, Kristin. *Modernity in the Flesh: Medicine, Law, and Society in Turn-of-the-Century Argentina.* Stanford: Stanford University Press, 2004.
———. "Sexual Aberration, Degeneration, and Psychiatry in Late-Nineteenth-Century Buenos Aires," in Mariano Plotkin, ed., 49–84. *Argentina on the Couch: Psychiatry, State, and Society, 1880 to the Present.* Albuquerque: University of New Mexico Press, 2003.
———. "Honor, Maternity, and the Disciplining of Women: Infanticide in Late Nineteenth-century Buenos Aires," *Hispanic American Historical Review* 72:3 (1992): 353–73.
———. "Wives on 'Deposit:' Internment and the Preservation of Husband's Honor in Late Nineteenth-century Buenos Aires," *Journal of Family History* 17:3 (1992): 253–70.

Ruibal, Beatriz. "Medicina legal y derecho penal a fines del siglo XIX," in Mirta Zaida Lobato, ed., 193–207. *Política, médicos y enfermedades: Lecturas de historia de la salud en la Argentina*. Buenos Aires: Editorial Biblos, 1996.

Ruiz Cevallos, Augusto. *Psiquiatras y locos: Entre la modernización contra Los Andes y el nuevo proyecto de modernidad. Perú: 1850–1930*. Lima: Instituto Pasado y Presente, 1994.

Russell-Wood, A.J.R. *Fidalgos and Philanthropists: The Santa Casa da Misericódia of Bahia, 1550–1755*. Los Angeles: University of California Press, 1968.

Sábato, Hilda. *The Many and the Few: Political Participation in Republican Buenos Aires*. Stanford: Stanford University Press, 2001.

Sacristán, María Cristina. "Historiografía de la locura y de la psiquiatría en México. De la hagiografía a la historia posmoderna," *Frenia* 5:1 (2005): 9–33.

———. "Entre curar y contener: La psiquiatría mexicana ante el desamparo jurídico, 1870–1944," *Frenia* 2:2 (2002): 61–80.

———. "Una valoración sobre el fracaso del Manicomio de La Castañeda como institución terapéutica, 1910–1944," *Secuencia, nueva época* 51 (September–December 2001): 91–120.

———. "La Granja de San Pedro del Monte para enfermos mentales: Los primeros años de una institución modelo, 1945–1948," 101–21. *Ensayos sobre historia de la medicina*. Mexico: Universidad Michoacana de San Nicolás de Hidalgo, 2003.

———. *Locura e inquisición en Nueva España, 1571–1760*. México: Fondo de Cultura Económica, 1992.

———. *Locura y disidencia en el México ilustrado, 1760–1810*. Zamora, México: El Colegio de Michoacán; México: Instituto Mora, 1994.

Sadowsky, Jonathan. *Imperial Bedlam: Insitutions of Madness in Colonial Southwest Nigeria*. Los Angeles: University of California Press, 1999.

———. "Beyond the Metaphor of the Pendulum: Electroconvulsive Therapy, Psychoanalysis, and the Styles of American Psychiatry," *Journal of the History of Medicine* 61 (January 2006): 1–25.

Salvatore, Ricardo D. *Wandering Paysanos: State Order and Subaltern Experience in Buenos Aires during the Rosas Era*. Durham, NC: Duke University Press, 2003.

———. "The Normalization of Economic Life: Representations of the Economy in Golden-Age Buenos Aires, 1890–1913," *Hispanic American Historical Review* 81:1 (February 2001): 1–44.

———. "Death and Democracy: Capital Punishment after the Fall of Rosas," *Working Papers/Documentos de Trabajo* 43 (August 1997): 1–29.

———. "Penitentiaries, Visions of Class, Export Economies: Brazil and Argentina Compared," in Ricardo Salvatore and Carlos Aguirre, eds., 194–223. *The Birth of the Penitentiary in Latin America: Essays on Criminology, Prison Reform, and Social Control, 1830–1940*. Austin: University of Texas Press, 1996.

———. "Criminology, Prison Reform, and the Buenos Aires Working Class," *Journal of Interdisciplinary History* 23:2 (Autumn 1992): 279–99.

Sánchez, Florencio. *El desnudo de la inocencia: La verdad sobre la Colonia Montes de Oca*. Buenos Aires: Editorial Galerna, 1999.

Sánchez Sorondo, M.G. *Historia de seis años*. Buenos Aires: Agencia General de Librería, 1923.

Saunders, Janet. "Quarantining the Weak-minded: Psychiatric Definitions of Degeneracy and the Late-Victorian Asylum," in W.F. Bynum, Roy Porter, and Michael Shepherd, eds., 273–96. *The Anatomy of Madness: Essays in the History of Psychiatry* – Vol. 3: *The Asylum and its Psychiatrists*. New York: Routledge, 1988.

Sawyers, Larry. *The Other Argentina: The Interior and National Development*. Boulder, CO: Westview, 1996.

Scarzanella, Eugenia. *Ni gringos ni indios: Inmigración, criminalidad y racismo en Argentina, 1890–1940.* Quilmas, Argentina: Universidad Nacional de Quilmes, 1999.
Scheper-Hughes, Nancy. "Parts unknown: Undercover ethnography of the organs-trafficking underworld, " Ethnography 5:1 (2004): 29–73.
Scobie, James R. *Buenos Aires: Plaza to Suburb, 1870–1910.* New York: Oxford University Press, 1974.
Scott, James C. *Seeing Like a State: How Certain Schemes to Improve the Human Condition Have Failed.* New Haven, CT: Yale University Press, 1998.
Scull, Andrew. *Madhouse: A Tragic Tale of Megalomania and Modern Science.* New Haven, CT: Yale University Press, 2005.
———. "Psychiatry and its Historians," *History of Psychiatry* 2 (1991): 239–50.
———, ed. *Madhouses, Mad-Doctors, and Madmen: The Social History of Psychiatry in the Victorian Era.* Philadelphia: University of Pennsylvania Press, 1981.
Segundas jornadas de atención primaria de la salud. Buenos Aires: n.p., 1988.
Slatta, Richard W., and Karla Robinson, "Continuities in Crime and Punishment: Buenos Aires, 1820–50," in Lyman L. Johnson, ed., 19–45. *The Problem of Order in Changing Societies: Essays on Crime and Policing in Argentina and Uruguay, 1750–1940.* Albuquerque: University of New Mexico Press, 1990.
Smith, William C. *Authoritarianism and the Crisis of the Argentine Political Economy.* Stanford: Stanford University Press, 1989.
Socolow, Susan. *The Bureaucrats of Buenos Aires, 1769–1810.* Durham, NC: Duke University Press, 1987.
———. *The Merchants of Buenos Aires, 1778–1810.* Cambridge: Cambridge University Press, 1978.
Solberg, Carl. *Immigration and Nationalism: Argentina and Chile, 1890–1914.* Austin: University of Texas Press, 1970.
Soloway, Richard. "Counting the Degenerates: The Statistics of Race Deterioration in Edwardian England," *Journal of Contemporary History* 17:1 (January 1982): 137–64.
Sorensen, Diana Goodrich. *Facundo and the Construction of Argentine Culture.* Austin: University of Texas Press, 1996.
Stagnaro, Juan Carlos, and José María Gonzales Chaves. *Hospicio de las Mercedes: 130 años.* Buenos Aires: Editorial Polemos, 1993.
Stepan, Nancy Leys. *'The Hour of Eugenics': Race, Gender and Nation in Latin America.* Ithaca: Cornell University Press, 1991.
Szusterman, Celia. *Frondizi and the Politics of Developmentalism in Argentina, 1955–62.* Pittsburgh: University of Pittsburgh Press, 1993.
Terry, Jennifer. "Theorizing Deviant Historiography," *Difference* 3 (1991): 55–74.
Theriot, Nancy. "Diagnosing Unnatural Motherhood: Nineteenth-Century Physicians and "Puerperal Insanity," in Judith Walzer Leavitt, ed., 405–24. *Women and Health in America: Historical Readings.* Madison: University of Wisconsin Press, 1999.
Thomas, Gregory M. "Open Psychiatric Services in Interwar France," *History of Psychiatry* 15:2 (2004): 131–53.
Tobias, José W. *Los problemas de la Administración Sanitaria y Asistencia Pública de la Capital Federal, como fueron encarados en el periodo, 1938–1940.* Buenos Aires: Artes gráficas Concordia, 1942.
Torrey, E. Fuller. *Out of the Shadows: Confronting America's Mental Illness Crisis.* New York: John Wiley, 1997.
Trent, James W. *Inventing the Feeble Mind: A History of Mental Retardation in the United States.* Los Angeles: University of California Press, 1994.

Trigo, Benigno. "Crossing the Boundaries of Madness: Criminology and Figurative Language in Argentina (1878–1920)," *Journal of Latin American Cultural Studies* 6:1 (1997): 7–20.

Troncoso, Oscar. *La modernización de Buenos Aires en 1900: Archivo del Intendente Municipal Adolfo J. Bullrich.* Buenos Aires: Archivo General de la Nación, 2004.

Ugalde, Antonio, and Rodolfo R. Vega. "Review Essay: State Terrorism, Torture, and Health in the Southern Cone," *Social Science and Medicine* 28:7 (1989): 759–67.

Vaccarezza, Raúl F. *Vida de médicos ilustres.* Buenos Aires: Ediciones Troquel, 1980. Vezzetti, Hugo. *La locura en la Argentina.* Buenos Aires: Paidós, 1985.

———."Domingo Cabred y el Asilo de Puertas Abiertas," *Revista Vertex* 2:3 (1991).

———. "Las ciencias sociales y el campo de la salud mental en la década del sesenta," *Punto de Vista* 54 (April 1996): 29–33.

———. "Los origenes del movimiento de la salud mental en la Argentina," *Documental* 1:1 (1997): n.p.

Vidal, Inés, and Edgardo Gili. "Memoria de la influencia de Lanús en el sistema de atención en salud mental en la Capital Federal, o cuando los porteños se pusieron la camiseta de Lanús," (Trabajos pre-publicados) *Primeras jornadas - Encuentro del Servicio de Psicopatología del Policlínico Lanas.* Buenos Aires: n.p., 1982.

Visacovsky, Sergio. *El Lanús: Memoria y política en la construcción de una tradición psiquiátrica argentina.* Buenos Aires: Alianza Editorial, 2002.

Wainerman, Catalina H., and Georgina Binstock. "La feminización de la enfermería argentina," in Martha Moscoso, ed., 259–83. *Palabras del silencia: Las mujeres latinoamericanas y su historia.* Quito: UNICEF, 1995.

Waisman, Carlos. *Reversal of Development in Argentina: Postwar Counterrevolutionary Policies and Their Structural Consequences.* Princeton: Princeton University Press, 1987.

Waller, John C. "'The Illusion of an Explanation': The Concept of Hereditary Disease, 1770–1870," *Journal of the History of Medicine* 57 (October 2002): 410–48.

Walter, Richard J. *The Socialist Party of Argentina, 1890–1930.* Austin: Institute of Latin American Studies at the University of Texas at Austin, 1977.

———. *Politics and Urban Growth in Buenos Aires, 1910–1942.* New York: Cambridge University Press, 1993.

Weissmann, Patricia. *Cuarenta y cinco años de psiquiatría argentina desde las páginas de Acta.* La Plata: Universidad de Mar de Plata, 1999.

Wright, David. "'Childlike in his Innocence': Lay Attitudes to 'Idiots' and 'Imbeciles' in Victorian England," in David Wright and Anne Digby, eds., 118–33. *From Idiocy to Mental Deficiency: Historical Perspectives on People with Learning Disabilities.* New York: Routledge, 1996.

Zimmermann, Eduardo A. *Los liberales reformistas: La cuestión social en la Argentina, 1890–1916.* Buenos Aires: Editorial Sudamericana, 1994.

———. "Racial Ideas and Social Reform: Argentina 1880–1916," *Hispanic American Historical Review* 72:1 (1992): 23–46.

Zulawski, Anne. "Mental Illness and Democracy in Bolivia: The Manicomio Pacheco," in Diego Armus, ed., 237–67. *From Malaria to AIDS: Disease in the History of Modern Latin America.* Durham, NC: Duke University Press, 2003.

INDEX

INDEX

d

e

f

g

h

i

j

l

m

Printed in the USA
CPSIA information can be obtained
at www.ICGtesting.com
LVHW021406071223
765823LV00005B/306

9 781552 382332